Latent Variable Models

An Introduction to Factor, Path, and Structural Equation Analysis

Fourth Edition

Latent Variable Models

An Introduction to Factor, Path, and Structural Equation Analysis

Fourth Edition

John C. Loehlin

2004

LAWRENCE ERLBAUM ASSOCIATES, PUBLISHERS

Mahwah, New Jersey   London

Camera ready copy for this book was provided by the author.

Lawrence Erlbaum Associates, Inc., Publishers
10 Industrial Avenue
Mahwah, New Jersey 07430

Cover design by Sean Trane Sciarrone

Library of Congress Cataloging-in-Publication Data

Loehlin, John C.
Latent variable models : an introduction to factor, path, and structural equation analysis / John C. Loehlin.—4th ed.
p.   cm.
Includes bibliographical references and index.
ISBN 0-8058-4909-2 (cloth : alk. paper)
ISBN 0-8058-4910-6 (pbk. : alk. paper)
1. Latent variables. 2. Latent structure analysis. 3. Factor analysis.
4. Path analysis. I. Title.
QA278.6.L64   2004
519.5'35—dc22   2003063116
                                                          CIP

Books published by Lawrence Erlbaum Associates are printed on acid-
free paper, and their bindings are chosen for strength and durability.

Printed in the United States of America
10 9 8 7 6 5 4 3 2 1

Contents

Preface

This book is intended as an introduction to an exciting growth area in social science methodology--the use of multiple-latent-variable models. Psychologists and other social scientists have long been familiar with one subvariety of such modeling, factor analysis--more properly, exploratory factor analysis. In recent decades, confirmatory factor analysis, path analysis, and structural equation modeling have come out of specialized niches and are making their bid to become basic tools in the research repertoire of the social scientist, particularly the one who is forced to deal with complex real-life phenomena in the round: the sociologist, the political scientist, the social, educational, clinical, industrial, personality or developmental psychologist, the marketing researcher, and the like.

All these methods are at heart one, as I have tried to emphasize in the chapters to follow. I have used earlier versions of this book in teaching graduate students from psychology and related disciplines, and have found the particular approach used--via path diagrams--to be effective in helping not-too-mathematical students grasp underlying relationships, as opposed to merely going through the motions of running computer programs. In some sections of the book a certain amount of elementary matrix algebra is employed; an appendix on the topic is provided for those who may need help here.

In the interests of accessibility, I have tried to maintain a relatively informal style, and to keep the main text fairly uncluttered with references. The notes at the end of each chapter are intended to provide the serious student with a path into the technical literature, as well as to draw his or her attention to some issues beyond the scope of the basic treatment.

The book is not closely tied to a particular computer program or package, although there is some special attention paid to LISREL, EQS, AMOS, and Mx. I assume that most users will have access to a latent-variable model-fitting program on the order of LISREL, EQS, CALIS, AMOS, Mplus, Mx, RAMONA, or SEPATH, and an exploratory factor analysis package such as those in SPSS or SAS. In some places, a matrix manipulation facility such as that in MINITAB, SAS, or SPSS would be helpful. I have provided some introductory material but have not tried to tell students all they need to know to run actual programs--such information is often local, ephemeral, or both. The instructor should expect to provide some handouts and perhaps a bit of hands-on assistance in getting students started. The reader going it on his or her own will require access to current manuals for the computer programs to be used.

Finally, it gives me great pleasure to acknowledge the help and encouragement that others have provided. Perhaps first credit should go to the students who endured early versions of the manuscript and cheerfully pointed out various errors and obscurities. These brave pioneers included Mike Bailey, Cheryl Beauvais, Alan Bergman, Beth Geer, Steve Gregorich, Priscilla Griffith, Jean Hart, Pam Henderson, Wes Hoover, Vivian Jenkins, Tock Lim, Scott Liu, Jacqueline Lovette, Frank Mulhern, Steve Predmore, Naftali Raz, and Lori Roggman. Among other colleagues who have been kind enough to read and comment on various parts of the manuscript are Carole Holahan, Phil Gough, Maria Pennock-Roman, Peter Bentler, and several anonymous reviewers. I am especially grateful to Jack McArdle for extensive comments on the manuscript as a whole, and to Jack Cohen for his persuasive voice with the publishers. Of course, these persons should not be blamed for any defects that may remain. For one thing, I didn't always take everybody's advice.

I am grateful to the University of Chicago Press, to *Multivariate Behavioral Research,* and to the Hafner Publishing Co. for permission to reprint or adapt published materials, and to the many previous researchers and writers cited in the book--or, for that matter, not cited--whose contributions have defined this rapidly developing and exciting field.

Finally, I owe a special debt to the members of my family: Jennifer and James, who worked their term papers in around my sessions at the Macintosh, and Marj, who provided unfailing support throughout.

J. C. L.

Note to the second edition: Much of the first edition is still here, but a certain amount of new material has been added, some exercises changed, and one topic (multidimensional scaling) dropped to make room. Also, I've tried to make the book more helpful to those who are using programs other than LISREL. I still appreciate the contributions of the people I thanked before. In addition, I am grateful to Peter Bentler, Robert Cudeck, and Jeff Tanaka for their helpful comments on draft material for the present edition, and to the American Mathematical Society for permission to adapt the table in Appendix H.

Note to the third edition: It is still the case that more remains than has been changed. What's gone: IPSOL, BMDP, EzPATH, and a few other items supplanted by the march of events in our field. What's new: more SEM programs, more fit indices, many new references, connections to the Internet, more on means, more on power, and, maybe as important as anything, emphasis on the RMSEA and its use in rejecting null hypotheses of poor fit.

I remain grateful to all those I thanked in the first and second editions, and have a good many names to add--people who gave me advice or encouragement, sent me reprints or preprints or programs, spotted errors, answered queries. These helpful persons include: Jim Arbuckle, Kenneth Bollen, Michael Browne, David Burns, Hsin-Yi Chen, Mike Coovert, Stan Gaines, Steve Gregorich, Greg Hancock, David Kaplan, Timothy Keith, Robert MacCallum, Herbert Marsh, Tor Neilands, Frank Norman, Eddie Oczkowski, Ed Rigdon, Doris Rubio, Bill Shipley, Jim Steiger, Bob Thorndike, and Niels Waller. And if I've left anybody out---well, them, too.

Note to the fourth edition: The basic approach of the fourth edition remains the same as that of previous editions, and, mostly, so do the contents of the book, with some mild reorganization. Chapters 3 and 4 are now divided slightly differently, so that Chapter 3 covers single-group, single-occasion models, and Chapter 4 deals just with models involving multiple groups or multiple occasions. Chapters 5 and 6, exploratory factor analysis, have also been rearranged, so that Chapter 5 covers a few basic factor extraction and rotation methods, for the benefit of instructors who prefer a briefer brush with EFA, and Chapter 6 treats more advanced matters. Chapter 7 has become less of a grab bag of specialized topics, with some of these (e.g., models with means, nonlinear models, and higher-order factors) being promoted to appropriate earlier chapters, and others (e.g., phantom variables) moving to an appendix. The detailed description of most goodness-of-fit indices is now in an appendix for reference rather than encumbering the main text. A few items, such as the centroid method and multivariate path models, have disappeared from the book altogether, and a few items have been added, such as sections on missing data, nonnormality, mediation, factorial invariance, and automating the construction of path diagrams. To save students labor in typing, a CD is supplied containing the various correlation and covariance matrices used in the exercises (details are given at the end of Chapter 2). A few new easy exercises have been added in the early chapters, and a number of the existing exercises have moved or changed in conformity with the text shifts. Overall, there has been a substantial expansion and updating of the reference list and the end-of-chapter notes.

I continue to be grateful to the people mentioned previously, as well as to several additional anonymous referees, and to the folks at Erlbaum: Debra Riegert has been very helpful as editor, Art Lizza continues as an invaluable resource on the production side, and of course Larry Erlbaum beams benevolently upon us all.

If you happen to notice any errors that have slipped by, I would be grateful if you would call them to my attention: loehlin@psy.utexas.edu. Enjoy the book.

Chapter One:
Path Models in Factor, Path, and Structural Equation Analysis

Scientists dealing with behavior, especially those who observe it occurring in its natural settings, rarely have the luxury of the simple bivariate experiment, in which a single independent variable is manipulated and the consequences observed for a single dependent variable. Even those scientists who think they do are often mistaken: The variables they directly manipulate and observe are typically not the ones of real theoretical interest but are merely some convenient variables acting as proxies or indexes for them. A full experimental analysis would again turn out to be multivariate, with a number of alternative experimental manipulations on the one side, and a number of alternative response measures on the other.

Over many years, numerous statistical techniques have been developed for dealing with situations in which multiple variables, some unobserved, are involved. Such techniques often involve large amounts of computation. Until the advent of powerful digital computers and associated software, the use of these methods tended to be restricted to the dedicated few. But in the last few decades it has been feasible for any interested behavioral scientist to take a multivariate approach to his or her data. Many have done so. The explosive growth in the use of computer software packages such as SPSS and SAS is one evidence of this.

The common features of the methods discussed in this book are that (a) multiple variables--three or more--are involved, and that (b) one or more of these variables is unobserved, or *latent*. Neither of these criteria provides a decisive boundary. Bivariate methods may often be regarded as special cases of multivariate methods. Some of the methods we discuss can be--and often are--applied in situations where all the variables are in fact observed. Nevertheless, the main focus of our interest is on what we call, following Bentler (1980), *latent variable analysis*, a term encompassing such specific methods as factor analysis, path analysis, and structural equation modeling (SEM), all of which share these defining features.

Path Diagrams

An easy and convenient representation of the relationships among a number of variables is the *path diagram.* In such a diagram we use capital letters, A, B, X, Y, and so on, to represent variables. The connections among variables are represented in path diagrams by two kinds of arrows: a straight, one-headed arrow represents a causal relationship between two variables, and a curved two-headed arrow represents a simple correlation between them.

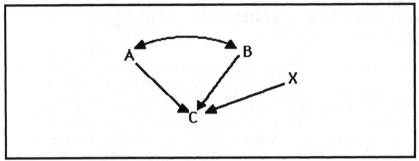

Fig. 1.1 Example of a simple path diagram.

Figure 1.1 shows an example of a path diagram. Variables A, B, and X all are assumed to have causal effects on variable C. Variables A and B are assumed to be correlated with each other. Variable X is assumed to affect C but to be uncorrelated with either A or B. Variable C might (for example) represent young children's intelligence. Variables A and B could represent father's and mother's intelligence, assumed to have a causal influence on their child's intelligence. (The diagram is silent as to whether this influence is environmental, genetic, or both.) The curved arrow between A and B allows for the likely possibility that father's and mother's intelligence will be correlated. Arrow X represents the fact that there are other variables, independent of mother's and father's intelligence, that can affect a child's intelligence.

Figure 1.2 shows another example of a path diagram. T is assumed to affect both A and B, and each of the latter variables is also affected by an additional variable; these are labeled U and V, respectively. This path diagram could represent the reliability of a test, as described in classical psychometric test theory. A and B would stand (say) for scores on two alternate forms of a test. T would represent the unobserved true score on the trait being measured, which is assumed to affect the observed scores on both forms of the test. U and V would represent factors specific to each form of the test or to the occasions on which it was administered, which would affect any given performance but be unrelated to the true trait. (In classical psychometric test theory, the variance in A and B resulting from the influence of T would be called *true score variance,*

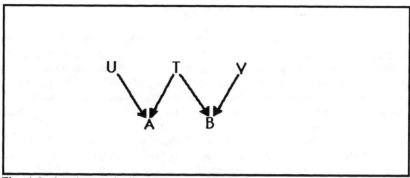

Fig. 1.2 Another path diagram: test reliability.

and that caused by U or V would be called *error variance*. The proportion of the variance of A or B due to T would be called the *reliability* of the test.)

    Figure 1.3 shows a path representation of events over time. In this case, the capital letters A and B are used to designate two variables, with subscripts to identify the occasions on which they are measured: Both A and B are measured at time 1, A is measured again at time 2, and B at time 3. In this case, the diagram indicates that both A_1 and B_1 are assumed to affect A_2, but that the effect of A_1 on B at time 3 is wholly via A_2--there is no direct arrow drawn leading from A_1 to B_3. It is assumed that A_1 and B_1 are correlated, and that A_2 and B_3 are subject to additional influences independent of A and B, here represented by short, unlabeled arrows. These additional influences could have been labeled, say, X and Y, but are often left unlabeled in path diagrams, as here, to indicate that they refer to other, unspecified influences on the variable to which they point. Such arrows are called *residual arrows* to indicate that they represent causes residual to those explicitly identified in the diagram.

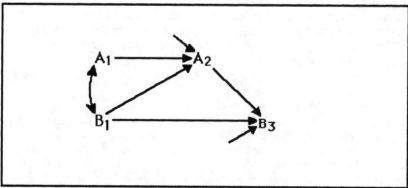

Fig. 1.3 A path diagram involving events over time.

The meaning of "cause" in a path diagram

Straight arrows in path diagrams are said to represent *causal relationships*--but in what sense of the sometimes slippery word "cause"? In fact, we do not need to adopt any strict or narrow definition of cause in this book, because path diagrams can be--and are--used to represent causes of various kinds, as the examples we have considered suggest. The essential feature for the use of a causal arrow in a path diagram is the assumption that a change in the variable at the tail of the arrow will result in a change in the variable at the head of the arrow, all else being equal (i.e., with all other variables in the diagram held constant). Note the one-way nature of this process--imposing a change on the variable at the head of the arrow does *not* bring about a change in the tail variable. A variety of common uses of the word "cause" can be expressed in these terms, and hence can legitimately be represented by a causal arrow in a path diagram.

Completeness of a path diagram

Variables in a path diagram may be grouped in two classes: those that do not receive causal inputs from any other variable in the path diagram, and those that receive one or more such causal inputs. Variables in the first of these two classes are referred to as *exogenous, independent,* or *source variables.* Variables in the second class are called *endogenous, dependent,* or *downstream variables. Exogenous variables* (Greek: "of external origin") are so called because their causal sources lie external to the path diagram; they are causally *independent* with respect to other variables in the diagram--straight arrows may lead away from them but never toward them. These variables represent causal *sources* in the diagram. Examples of such source variables in Fig. 1.3 are A_1, B_1, and the two unlabeled residual variables. *Endogenous variables* ("of internal origin") have at least some causal sources that lie within the path diagram; these variables are causally *dependent* on other variables-- one or more straight arrows lead into them. Such variables lie causally *downstream* from source variables. Examples of downstream variables in Fig. 1.3 are A_2 and B_3. In Fig. 1.2, U, T, and V are source variables, and A and B are downstream variables. Look back at Fig. 1.1. Which are the source and downstream variables in this path diagram? (I hope you identified A, B, and X as source variables, and C as downstream.)

In a proper and complete path diagram, all the source variables are interconnected by curved arrows, to indicate that they may be intercorrelated-- unless it is explicitly assumed that their correlation is zero, in which case the curved arrow is omitted. Thus the absence of a curved arrow between two source variables in a path diagram, as between X and A in Fig. 1.1, or T and U in Fig. 1.2, is not an expression of ignorance but an explicit statement about assumptions underlying the diagram.

Downstream variables, on the other hand, are never connected by curved arrows in path diagrams. (Actually, some authors use downstream curved arrows as a shorthand to indicate correlations among downstream variables caused by other variables than those included in the diagram: We use correlations between residual arrows for this purpose, which is consistent with our convention because the latter are source variables.) Residual arrows point at downstream variables, never at source variables. Completeness of a path diagram requires that a residual arrow be attached to every downstream variable unless it is explicitly assumed that all the causes of variation of that variable are included among the variables upstream from it in the diagram. (This convention is also not universally adhered to: Occasionally, path diagrams are published with the notation "residual arrows omitted." This is an unfortunate practice because it leads to ambiguity in interpreting the diagram: Does the author intend that all the variation in a downstream variable is accounted for within the diagram, or not?)

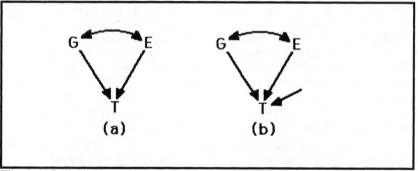

Fig. 1.4 Path diagrams illustrating the implication of an omitted residual arrow.

Figure 1.4 shows an example in which the presence or absence of a residual arrow makes a difference. The source variables G and E refer to the genetic and environmental influences on a trait T. The downstream variable T in Fig. 1.4(a) has no residual arrow. That represents the assumption that the variation of T is completely explained by the genetic and environmental influences upon it. This is a theoretical assumption that one might sometimes wish to make. Fig. 1.4(b), however, represents the assumption that genetic and environmental influences are not sufficient to explain the variation of T--some additional factor or factors, perhaps measurement error or gene-environment interaction--may need to be taken into account in explaining T. Obviously, the assumptions in Figures 1.4(a) and 1.4(b) are quite different, and one would not want it assumed that (a) was the case when in fact (b) was intended.

Finally, all significant direct causal connections between source and downstream variables, or between one downstream variable and another, should be included as straight arrows in the diagram. Omission of an arrow between A_1 and B_3 in Fig. 1.3 is a positive statement: that A_1 is assumed to affect B_3 only by way of A_2.

The notion of completeness in path diagrams should not be taken to mean that the ideal path diagram is one containing as many variables as possible connected by as many arrows as possible. Exactly the opposite is true. The smallest number of variables connected by the smallest number of arrows that can do the job is the path diagram to be sought for, because it represents the most parsimonious explanation of the phenomenon under consideration. Big, messy path diagrams are likely to give trouble in many ways. Nevertheless, often the simplest explanation of an interesting behavioral or biological phenomenon does involve causal relationships among a number of variables, not all observable. A path diagram provides a way of representing in a clear and straightforward fashion what is assumed to be going on in such a case.

Notice that most path diagrams could in principle be extended indefinitely back past their source variables: These could be taken as downstream variables in an extended path diagram, and the correlations among them explained by the linkages among their own causes. Thus, the parents in Fig. 1.1 could be taken as children in their own families, and the correlation between them explained by a model of the psychological and sociological mechanisms that result in mates having similar IQs. Or in Fig. 1.3, one could have measured A and B at a preceding time zero, resulting in a diagram in which the correlation between A_1 and B_1 is replaced by a superstructure of causal arrows from A_0 and B_0, themselves probably correlated. There is no hard-and-fast rule in such cases, other than the general maxim that simpler is better, which usually means that if going back entails multiplying variables, do not do it unless you have to. Sometimes, of course, you have to, when some key variable lies back upstream.

Other assumptions in path diagrams

It is assumed in path diagrams that causes are unitary, that is, in a case such as Fig. 1.2, that it is meaningful to think of a single variable T that is the cause of A and B, and not (say) two separate and distinct aspects of a phenomenon T, one of which causes A and one B. In the latter case, a better representation would be to replace T by two different (possibly correlated) variables.

An exception to the rule of unitary causes is residual variables, which typically represent multiple causes of a variable that are external to the path diagram. Perhaps for this reason, path analysts do not always solve for the path coefficients associated with the residual arrows in their diagrams. It is, however, good practice to solve at least for the proportion of variance associated with such residual causes (more on this later). It is nearly always useful to know what proportion of the variation of each downstream variable is accounted for by the causes explicitly included within the path diagram, and what proportion is not.

Another assumption made in path diagrams is that the causal relationships represented by straight arrows are linear. This is usually not terribly restricting--mild departures from linearity are often reasonably approximated by linear relationships, and if not, it may be possible to transform variables so as to linearize their relationships with other variables. The use of log income, rather than income, or reciprocals of latency measures, or arcsine transformations of proportions would be examples of transformations often used by behavioral scientists for this purpose. In drawing a path diagram, one ordinarily does not have to worry about such details--one can always make the blanket assumption that one's variables are measured on scales for which relationships are reasonably linear. But in evaluating the strength of causal effects with real data, the issue of nonlinearity may arise. If variable A has a positive effect on variable B in part of its range and a negative effect in another, it is hard to assign a single number to represent the effect of A on B. However, if A is suitably redefined, perhaps as an absolute deviation from some optimum value, this may be possible. In Chapter 3 we consider some approaches to dealing with nonlinear relationships of latent variables.

Feedbacks and mutual influences

In our examples so far we have restricted ourselves to path diagrams in which, after the source variables, there was a simple downstream flow of causation--no paths that loop back on themselves or the like. Most of the cases we consider in this book have this one-way causal flow, but path representations can be used to deal with more complex situations involving causal loops, as we see in a later chapter. Examples of two such non-one-way cases are shown in Fig. 1.5. In Fig. 1.5(a) there is a mutual causal influence between variables C and D: each affects the other. A causal sequence could go from A to C to D to C to D again

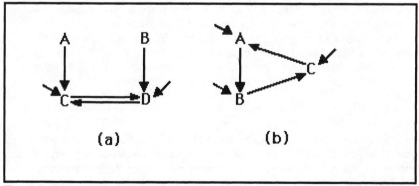

(a)   (b)

Fig. 1.5 Path diagrams with (a) mutual influences and (b) a feedback loop.

and so on. In Fig. 1.5(b) there is an extended feedback loop: A affects B which affects C which in turn affects A.

Direct and indirect causal paths

Sometimes it is useful to distinguish between *direct* and *indirect* causal effects in path diagrams. A direct effect is represented by a single causal arrow between the two variables concerned. In Fig. 1.5(b) variable B has a direct effect on variable C. There is a causal arrow leading from B to C. If B is changed we expect to observe a change in C. Variable A, however, has only an indirect effect on C because there is no direct arrow from A to C. There is, however, an indirect causal effect transmitted via variable B. If A changes, B will change, and B's change will affect C, other things being equal. Thus, A can be said to have a causal effect on C, although an indirect one. In Fig. 1.5(a) variable B has a direct effect on variable D, an indirect effect on variable C, and no causal effect at all on variable A.

Path Analysis

Path diagrams are useful enough as simple descriptive devices, but they can be much more than that. Starting from empirical data, one can solve for a numerical value of each curved and straight arrow in a diagram to indicate the relative strength of that correlation or causal influence. Numerical values, of course, imply scales on which they are measured. For most of this chapter we assume that all variables in the path diagram are expressed in standard score form, that is, with a mean of zero and a standard deviation of one. Covariances and correlations are thus identical. This simplifies matters of presentation, and is a useful way of proceeding in many practical situations. Later, we see how the procedures can be applied to data in original raw score units, and consider some of the situations in which this approach is preferred. We also assume for the present that we are dealing with unlooped path diagrams.

   The steps of constructing and solving path diagrams are referred to collectively as *path analysis,* a method originally developed by the American geneticist Sewall Wright as early as 1920, but only extensively applied in the social and behavioral sciences during the last few decades.

Wright's rules

Briefly, Wright showed that if a situation can be presented as a proper path diagram, then the correlation between any two variables in the diagram can be expressed as the *sum of the compound paths connecting these two points,* where a compound path is a path along arrows that follows three rules:

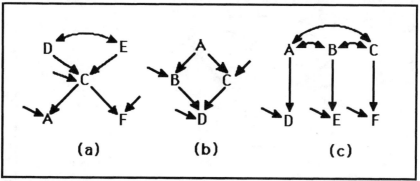

Fig. 1.6 Illustrations of Wright's rules.

(a) no loops;
(b) no going forward then backward;
(c) a maximum of one curved arrow per path.

The first rule means that a compound path must not go twice through the same variable. In Fig. 1.6(a) the compound path ACF would be a legitimate path between A and F, but the path ACDECF would not be because it involves going twice through variable C.

The second rule means that on a particular path, after one has once gone forward along one or more arrows, it is not legitimate to proceed backwards along others. (Going backward first and then forward is, however, quite proper.) In Fig. 1.6(b) the compound path BAC is a legitimate way to go from B to C; the path BDC is not. In the former, one goes backward along an arrow (B to A) and then forward (A to C), which is allowable, but path BDC would require going forward then backward, which is not. This asymmetry may seem a bit less arbitrary if one realizes that it serves to permit events in the diagram to be connected by common causes (A), but not by common consequences (D). The third rule is illustrated in Fig. 1.6(c). DACF is a legitimate compound path between D and F; DABCF is not, because it would require traversing two curved arrows. Likewise, DABE is a legitimate path between D and E, but DACBE is not.

Figure 1.7 serves to provide examples of tracing paths in a path diagram according to Wright's rules. This figure incorporates three source variables, A, B, and C, and three downstream variables, D, E, and F. We have designated each arrow by a lower case letter for convenience in representing compound paths. Each lower case letter stands for the *value* or magnitude of the particular causal effect or correlation. A simple rule indicates how these values are combined: *The numerical value of a compound path is equal to the product of the values of its constituent arrows.* Therefore, simply writing the lower case letters of a path in sequence is at the same time writing an expression for the

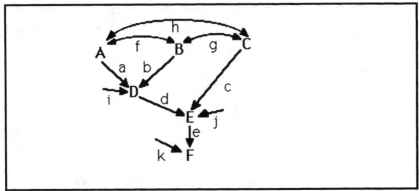

Fig. 1.7 Examples of tracing paths in a path diagram.

numerical value of that path.

For example, what is the correlation between variables A and D in Fig. 1.7? Two paths are legal: *a* and *fb*. A path like *hgb* would be excluded by the rule about only one curved arrow, and paths going further down the diagram like *adcgb* would violate both the rules about no forward then backward and no loops. So the numerical value of r_{AD} can be expressed as *a + fb*. I hope that the reader can see that r_{BD} = *b + fa,* and that r_{CD} = *gb + ha.*

What about r_{AB}? Just *f.* Path *hg* would violate the third rule, and paths like *ab* or *adcg* would violate the second. It is, of course, quite reasonable that r_{AB} should equal *f,* because that is just what the curved arrow between A and B means. Likewise, r_{BC} = *g* and r_{AC} = *h.*

Let us consider a slightly more complicated case: r_{AE}. There are three paths: *ad, fbd,* and *hc.* Note that although variable D is passed through twice, this is perfectly legal, because it is only passed through once on any given path. You might wish to pause at this point to work out r_{BE} and r_{CE} for yourself.

(I hope you got *bd + fad + gc* and *c + gbd + had.*)

Now you might try your hand at some or all of the six remaining correlations in Fig.1.7: r_{DE}, r_{EF}, r_{BF}, r_{CF}, r_{DF}, and r_{AF}. (The answers are not given until later in the chapter, to minimize the temptation of peeking at them first.)

Numerical solution of a path diagram

Given that we can express each of the correlations among a set of observed variables in a path diagram as a sum of compound paths, can we reverse this process and solve for the values of the causal paths given the correlations? The answer is that often we can.

Consider the example of Fig. 1.1, redrawn as Fig. 1.8. Recall that

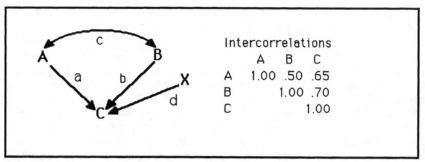

Fig. 1.8 Example of Fig. 1.1, with observed intercorrelations of A, B, and C.

variables A and B were fathers' and mothers' intelligence, and C was children's intelligence. X is a residual variable, representing other unmeasured influences on child's intelligence that are independent of the parents' intelligence.

Suppose that in some suitable population of families we were to observe the correlations shown on the right in Fig. 1.8. We can now, using our newfound knowledge of path analysis (and ignoring X for the moment), write the following three equations:

$$r_{AB} = c$$
$$r_{AC} = a + cb$$
$$r_{BC} = b + ca.$$

Because we know the observed values r_{AB}, r_{AC}, and r_{BC}, we have three simultaneous equations in three unknowns:

$$c = .50$$
$$a + cb = .65$$
$$b + ca = .70.$$

Substitution for c in the second and third equations yields two equations in two unknowns:

$$a + .50b = .65$$
$$.50a + b = .70.$$

These equations are readily solved to yield $a = .40$ and $b = .50$. Thus, if we were to observe the set of intercorrelations given in Fig. 1.8, *and if our causal model is correct*, we could conclude that the causal influences of fathers' and mothers' intelligence on child's intelligence could be represented by values of .40 and .50, respectively, for the causal paths a and b.

What do these numbers mean? They are, in fact, standardized partial regression coefficients--we call them *path coefficients* for short. Because they are *regression coefficients,* they tell us to what extent a change on the variable at the tail of the arrow is transmitted to the variable at the head of the arrow. Because they are *partial* regression coefficients, this is the change that occurs with all other variables in the diagram held constant. Because they are *standardized* partial regression coefficients, we are talking about changes measured in standard deviation units. Specifically, the value of .40 for *a* means that if we were to select fathers who were one standard deviation above the mean for intelligence--but keeping mothers at the mean--their offspring would average four tenths of a standard deviation above the population mean. (Unless otherwise specified, we are assuming in this chapter that the numbers we deal with are population values, so that issues of statistical inference do not complicate the picture.)

Because paths *a* and *b* are standardized partial regression coefficients, also known in multiple regression problems as *beta weights*, one might wonder if we can solve for them as such, by treating the path analysis as a sort of multiple regression problem. The answer is: Yes we can, at least in cases where all variables are measured. In the present example, A, B, and C are assumed known, so we can solve for *a* and *b* by considering this as a multiple regression problem in predicting C from A and B.

Using standard formulas (e.g., McNemar, 1969, p. 192):

$$\beta_1 = (.65 - .70 \times .50)/(1 - .50^2) = .40$$
$$\beta_2 = (.70 - .65 \times .50)/(1 - .50^2) = .50,$$

or exactly the same results as before.

Viewing the problem in this way, we can also interpret the squared multiple correlation between C and A and B as the proportion of the variance of C that is accounted for by A and B jointly. In this case $R^2_{C \cdot AB} = \beta_1 r_{AC} + \beta_2 r_{BC}$ = .40 x .65 + .50 x .70 = .61. Another way in which we can arrive at the same figure from the path diagram is by following a path-tracing procedure.   We can think of the predicted variance of C as that part of its correlation with itself that occurs via the predictors. In this case, this would be *the sum of the compound paths from C to itself via A or B or both.* There is the path to A and back, with value a^2, the path to B and back, with value b^2, and the two paths *acb* and *bca* : $.40^2 + .50^2 + 2 \times .40 \times .50 \times .50 = .16 + .25 + .20 = .61$.

We can then easily solve for the value of the path *d* which leads from the unmeasured residual X. The variance that A and B jointly account for is R^2, or .61. The variance that X accounts for is thus $1 - R^2$, that is, 1 - .61, or .39. The correlation of C with itself via X is the variance accounted for by X, and this is just *dd*. So the value of *d* is $\sqrt{.39}$, or .62.

So long as all variables are measured one can proceed to solve for the

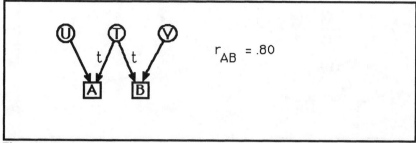

Fig. 1.9 The example of Fig. 1.2, with observed correlation of .80 between alternate forms A and B of a test.

causal paths in a path diagram as beta weights in a series of multiple regression analyses. Thus, in Fig. 1.7 one could solve for *a* and *b* from the correlations among A, B, and D; for *d* and *c* from the correlations among D, C, and E; and for *e* as the simple correlation between E and F. The residuals *i, j,* and *k* can then be obtained as $\sqrt{(1 - R^2)}$ in the various multiple regressions.

In general, however, we must deal with path diagrams involving unmeasured, latent variables. We cannot directly calculate the correlations of these with observed variables, so a simple multiple regression approach does not work. We need, instead, to carry out some variant of the first approach--that is, to solve a set of simultaneous equations with at least as many equations as there are unknown values to be obtained.

Consider the example of Fig. 1.2, test reliability, repeated for convenience as Fig. 1.9. Because this diagram involves both latent variables and observed variables, we have followed a common practice of latent variable modelers by putting the letters representing observed variables in squares (or rectangles), and variables representing latent variables in circles (or ovals).

We wish to solve for the values of the causal paths between the true score T and the observed scores A and B. But T is an unobserved, latent variable; all we have is the observed correlation .80 between forms A and B of the test. How can we proceed? If we are willing to assume that A and B have the same relation to T, which they should have if they are really parallel alternate forms of a test, we can write from the path diagram the equation

$$r_{AB} = t^2 = .80,$$

from which it follows that $t = \sqrt{.80} = .89$. It further follows that t^2 or 80% of the variance of each of the alternate test forms is attributable to the true score on the trait, that 20% is therefore due to error, and that the values of the residual paths from U and V are $\sqrt{.20}$ or .45.

Figure 1.10 (next page) presents another case of a path diagram containing a latent variable. It is assumed that A, C, and D are measured, as shown by the squares. Their intercorrelations are given to the right of the

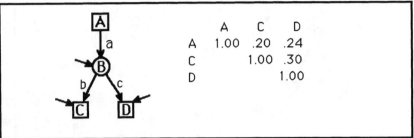

Fig. 1.10 Another simple path diagram with a latent variable.

figure. B, as indicated by the circle, is not measured, so we do not know its correlations with A, C, and D. We can, however, write equations for the three known correlations in terms of the three paths *a, b,* and *c,* and (as it turns out) these three equations can be solved for the values of the three causal paths.

The equations are:

$$r_{AC} = ab$$
$$r_{AD} = ac$$
$$r_{CD} = bc.$$

A solution is:

$$r_{AC}\, r_{CD}/r_{AD} = ab \times bc\,/ac\ = b^2 = .20 \times .30/.24 = .25;\ \ b = .50$$
$$a = r_{AC}/b\ = .20/.50 = .40$$
$$c = r_{AD}/a\ = .24/.40 = .60.$$

Note that another possible solution would be numerically the same, but with all paths negative, because b^2 also has a negative square root. This would amount to a model in which B, the latent variable, is scored in the opposite direction, thus reversing its relationships with the manifest variables.

(By the way, to keep the reader in suspense no longer about the correlations in Fig. 1.7: $r_{DE} = d + ahc + bgc$, $r_{EF} = e$, $r_{BF} = bde + fade + gce$, $r_{CF} = ce + gbde + hade$, $r_{DF} = de + ahce + bgce$, and $r_{AF} = ade + fbde + hce$.)

Underdetermined, overdetermined, and just-determined path diagrams

Figure 1.11(a) shows another simple path diagram. It is somewhat like Fig. 1.10 upside down: Instead of one cause of the latent variable and two effects, there are now two causes and one effect.

However, this change has made a critical difference. There are still just three intercorrelations among the three observed variables A, B, and D, yielding

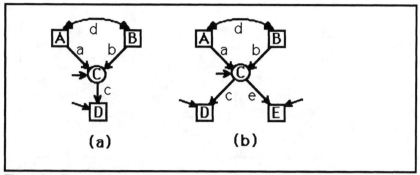

Fig. 1.11 Examples of under- and overdetermined path diagrams.

three equations. But now there are four unknown values to be estimated: *a*, *b*, *c*, and *d*. One observed correlation, r_{AB}, estimates *d* directly. But that leaves only two equations, $r_{AD} = ac + dbc$ and $r_{BD} = bc + dac$, to estimate the three unknowns, *a*, *b*, and *c*, and no unique solution is possible. The path diagram is said to be *underdetermined* (or *unidentified*).

In the preceding problem of Fig. 1.10, there were three equations in three unknowns, and an exact solution was possible. Such a case is described as *just determined* (or *just identified*). Fig. 1.11(b) shows a third case, of an *overdetermined* (or *overidentified*) path diagram. As in the left-hand diagram, C is a latent variable and A and B are source variables, but an additional measured downstream variable E has been added. Now there are six observed intercorrelations among the observed variables A, B, D, and E, yielding six equations, whereas we have only added one unknown, giving five unknowns to be solved for. More equations than unknowns does not guarantee overdetermination, but in this case for most observed sets of correlations there will be no single solution for the unknowns that will satisfy all six equations simultaneously. What is ordinarily done in such cases is to seek values for the unknowns that come as close as possible to accounting for the observed intercorrelations (we defer until the next chapter a consideration of what "as close as possible" means).

It might be thought that just-determined path diagrams, because they permit exact solutions, would be the ideal to be sought for. But in fact, for the behavioral scientist, overdetermined path diagrams are usually much to be preferred. The reason is that the data of the behavioral scientist typically contain sampling and measurement error, and an exact fit to these data is an exact fit to the error as well as to the truth they contain. Whereas--if we assume that errors occur at random--a best overall fit to the redundant data of an overdetermined path diagram will usually provide a better approximation to the underlying true population values. Moreover, as we see later, overdetermined path diagrams permit statistical tests of goodness of fit, which just-determined diagrams do not.

15

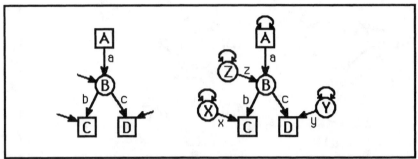

Fig. 1.12 The path model of Fig. 1.10 (left) shown in RAM symbolism (right).

A computer-oriented symbolism for path diagrams--RAM

A way of drawing path diagrams which has advantages for translating them into computer representations has been developed by J. J. McArdle. He calls his general approach to path modeling "Reticular Action Modeling"--RAM for short.

Figure 1.12 shows on the left a path model presented earlier in this chapter, and on the right the same model in a RAM representation. The following points may be noted: (1) Latent variables are designated by placing them in circles, observed variables by placing them in squares, as usual in latent variable modeling. In addition to squares and circles for variables, RAM uses triangles to designate constants--these are important in models involving means, discussed later in this book. (2) Residual variables are represented explicitly as latent variables (X, Y, Z). (3) Two-headed curved arrows leaving and re-entering the same variable are used to represent the variance of source variables. When they are unlabeled, as here, they are assumed to have a value of 1.0--thus these are standardized variables. Curved arrows connecting two different source variables represent their covariance or correlation, in the usual manner of path diagrams.

Although a little cumbersome in some respects, which is why we will not be using it routinely in this book, RAM symbolism, by rendering explicitly a number of things often left implicit in path diagrams, facilitates a direct translation into computer representations. We will see examples in Chapter 2.

Factor Models

An important subdivision of latent variable analysis is traditionally known as factor analysis. In recent discussions of factor analysis, a distinction is often drawn between *exploratory* and *confirmatory* varieties. In exploratory factor analysis, which is what is usually thought of as "factor analysis" if no qualification is attached, one seeks under rather general assumptions for a simple latent variable structure, one with no causal arrows from one latent variable to another, that could account for the intercorrelations of an observed set of variables. In confirmatory factor analysis, on the other hand, one takes a specific hypothesized structure of this kind and sees how well it accounts for the observed relationships in the data.

Traditionally, textbooks on factor analysis discuss the topic of exploratory factor analysis at length and in detail, and then they put in something about confirmatory factor analysis in the later chapters. We, however, find it instructive to proceed in the opposite direction, to consider first confirmatory factor analysis and structural equation modeling more broadly, and to defer an extended treatment of exploratory factor analysis until later (Chapters 5 and 6).

From this perspective, exploratory factor analysis is a preliminary step that one might sometimes wish to take to locate latent variables to be studied via structural modeling. It is by no means a necessary step. Theory and hypothesis may lead directly to confirmatory factor analysis or other forms of structural models, and path diagrams provide a natural and convenient way of representing the hypothesized structures of latent and manifest variables that the analyst wishes to compare to real-world data.

The origins of factor analysis: Charles Spearman and the two-factor theory of intelligence

As it happens, the original form of factor analysis, invented by the British psychologist Charles Spearman shortly after 1900, was more confirmatory than exploratory, in the sense that Spearman had an explicit theory of intellectual performance that he wished to test against data. Spearman did not use a path representation, Wright not yet having invented it, but Fig. 1.13 represents the essentials of Spearman's theory in the form of a path diagram.

Spearman hypothesized that performance on each of a number of intellectual tasks shared something in common with performance on all other intellectual tasks, a factor of general intellectual ability that Spearman called "g." Performance on each task also involved a factor of skills specific to that task, hence the designation "two-factor theory." In Spearman's words: "All branches of intellectual activity have in common one fundamental function (or group of functions), whereas the remaining or specific elements of the activity seem in

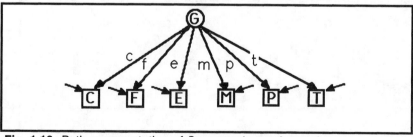

Fig. 1.13 Path representation of Spearman's two-factor theory.

every case to be wholly different from that in all the others" (1904, p. 284).

Spearman obtained several measures on a small group of boys at an English preparatory school: a measure of pitch discrimination, a ranking of musical talent, and examination grades in several academic areas--Classics, French, English studies, and Mathematics. Fig. 1.13 applies his two-factor theory to these data. The letter G at the top of the figure represents the latent variable of general intellectual ability, C, F, E, and M at the bottom represent observed performances in the academic subjects, P stands for pitch discrimination and T for musical talent. General intellectual ability is assumed to contribute to all these performances. Each also involves specific abilities, represented by the residual arrows.

If Spearman's theory provides an adequate explanation of these data, the path diagram implies that the correlation between any two tasks should be equal to the product of the paths connecting them to the general factor: the correlation between Classics and Mathematics should be *cm*, that between English and French should be *ef*, between French and musical talent *ft*, and so on. Because we are attempting to explain 6 x 5/2 = 15 different observed correlations by means of 6 inferred values--the path coefficients *c*, *f*, *e*, *m*, *p*, and *t*--a good fit to the data is by no means guaranteed. If one is obtained, it is evidence that the theory under consideration has some explanatory power.

Fig. 1.14 gives the correlations for part of Spearman's data: Classics, English, Mathematics, and pitch discrimination.

If the single general-factor model fit the data exactly, we could take the intercorrelations among any three variables and solve for the values of the three respective path coefficients, since they would provide three equations in three unknowns. For example:

$$r_{CE} \times r_{CM}/r_{EM} = cecm/em = c^2 = .78 \times .70/.64 = .853; \; c = .92$$
$$r_{EM} \times r_{CE}/r_{CM} = emce/cm = e^2 = .64 \times .78/.70 = .713; \; e = .84$$
$$r_{CM} \times r_{EM}/r_{CE} = cmem/ce = m^2 = .70 \times .64/.78 = .574; \; m = .76.$$

This procedure has been given a name; it is called the *method of triads*. If the data, as here, only approximately fit a model with a single general factor, one

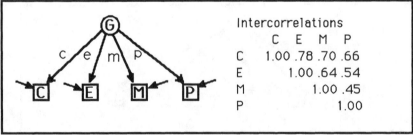

	Intercorrelations			
	C	E	M	P
C	1.00	.78	.70	.66
E		1.00	.64	.54
M			1.00	.45
P				1.00

Fig. 1.14 Data to illustrate the method of triads.

will get slightly different values for a particular path coefficient depending on which triads one uses. For example, we may solve for *m* in two other ways from these data:

$$r_{CM} \times r_{MP}/r_{CP} = cmmp/cp = m^2 = .70 \times .45/.66 = .477; \; m = .69$$
$$r_{EM} \times r_{MP}/r_{EP} = emmp/ep = m^2 = .64 \times .45/.54 = .533; \; m = .73.$$

These three values of *m* are not very different. One might consider simply averaging them to obtain a compromise value. A slightly preferable method, because it is less vulnerable to individual aberrant values, adds together the numerators and denominators of the preceding expressions, and then divides:

$$m^2 = \frac{.70 \times .64 + .70 \times .45 + .64 \times .45}{.78 + .66 + .54} = .531; \; m = .73$$

You may wish to check your understanding of the method by confirming that it yields .97 for *c*, .84 for *e*, and .65 for *p*, for the data of Fig. 1.14. We may get some sense of how accurately our solution can account for the observed intercorrelations among the four variables, by producing the intercorrelation matrix implied by the paths: i.e., *ce, cm, cp*, etc.

$$
\begin{array}{ccc}
.81 & .71 & .63 \\
 & .61 & .55 \\
 & & .47
\end{array}
$$

As is evident, the implied correlations under the model do not differ much from the observed correlations--the maximum absolute difference is .03. The assumption of a single general factor plus a residual factor for each measure does a reasonable job of accounting for the data.

We may as well go on and estimate the variance accounted for by each of the residual factors. Following the path model, the proportion of the variance of each test accounted for by a factor equals the correlation of that test with itself by way of the factor (the sum of the paths to itself via the factor). In this case these have the value c^2, e^2, etc. The variances due to the general factor are thus .93, .70, .53, and .42 for Classics, English, Mathematics, and pitch discrimination, respectively, and the corresponding residual variances due to specific factors are .07, .30, .47, and .58. In traditional factor analytic terminology, the variance a test shares with other tests in the battery is called its *communality*, symbolized h^2, and the variance not so shared is called its *uniqueness*, symbolized u^2. The h^2s of the four measures are thus .93, .70, .53, and .42, and their uniquenesses .07, .30, .47, and .58. Pitch discrimination has the least in common with the other three measures; Classics has the most.

The observant reader will notice that the communality and uniqueness of a variable are just expressions in the factor analytic domain of the general notion of the predicted (R^2) and residual variance of a downstream variable in a path diagram, as discussed earlier in the chapter.

The path coefficients *c*, *e*, *m*, etc. are in factor-analytic writing called the *factor pattern coefficients* (or more simply, the *factor loadings*). The correlations between the tests and the factors, here numerically the same as the pattern coefficients, are collectively known as the *factor structure*.

More than one common factor

As soon became evident to Spearman's followers and critics, not all observed sets of intercorrelations are well explained by a model containing only one general factor; factor analysts soon moved to models in which more than one latent variable was postulated to account for the observed intercorrelations among measures. Such latent variables came to be called *common* factors, rather than *general* factors because, although they were common to several of the variables under consideration, they were not general to all. There remained, of course, *specific* factors unique to each measure.

Figure 1.15 gives an example of a path diagram in which there are two latent variables, E and F, and four observed variables, A, B, C, and D. E is hypothesized as influencing A and B, and F as influencing C and D. In the path diagram there are five unknowns, the paths *a*, *b*, *c*, and *d*, and the correlation *e* between the two latent variables. There are six equations, shown to the right of the diagram, based on the six intercorrelations between pairs of observed variables. Hypothetical values of the observed correlations are given--.60 for r_{AB}, for example. Because there are more equations than unknowns, one might expect that a single exact solution would not be available, and indeed this is the case. An iterative least squares solution, carried out in a way discussed in the next chapter, yielded the values shown to the far right of Fig. 1.15.

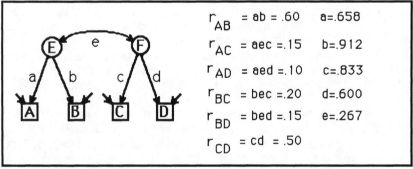

$$r_{AB} = ab = .60 \qquad a=.658$$
$$r_{AC} = aec =.15 \qquad b=.912$$
$$r_{AD} = aed =.10 \qquad c=.833$$
$$r_{BC} = bec =.20 \qquad d=.600$$
$$r_{BD} = bed =.15 \qquad e=.267$$
$$r_{CD} = cd = .50$$

Fig. 1.15 A simple factor model with two correlated factors (E and F).

Table 1-1 Factor solution for the two-factor problem of Fig. 1.15

Variable	Factor pattern		Factor structure		h^2
	E	F	E	F	
A	.66	.00	.66	.18	.43
B	.91	.00	.91	.24	.83
C	.00	.83	.22	.83	.69
D	.00	.60	.16	.60	.36

Factor intercorrelations

	E	F
E	1.00	.27
F	.27	1.00

Reproduced and residual correlations

	A	B	C	D
A		.600	.146	.105
B	.000		.203	.146
C	.004	-.003		.500
D	-.005	.004	.000	

Table 1-1 reports a typical factor analysis solution based on Fig. 1.15. The factor pattern represents the values of the paths from factors to variables; i.e., the paths *a* and *b* and two zero paths from E to A, B, C, and D, and the corresponding paths from F. The factor structure presents the correlations of the variables with the factors: for factor E these have the values *a, b, ec,* and *ed,* respectively, and for factor F, *ea, eb, c,* and *d.* The communalities (h^2) are in this case simply a^2, b^2, c^2, and d^2, because each variable is influenced by only one factor. Finally, the correlation between E and F is just *e*.

The reproduced correlations (those implied by the path values) and the residual correlations (the differences between observed and implied correlations) are shown at the bottom of Table 1-1. The reproduced correlations are obtained by inserting the solved values of *a, b, c,* etc. into the equations of Fig. 1.15: r_{AB} = .658 x .912, r_{AC} = .658 x .267 x .833, and so on. The residual correlations are obtained by subtracting the reproduced correlations from the observed ones. Thus the residual r_{AC} is .15 - .146, or .004.

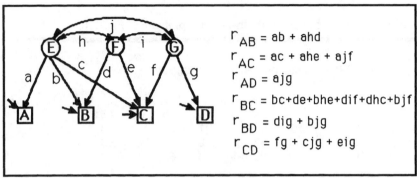

Fig. 1.16 A more complex three-factor model.

A more complex model with three factors is shown in Fig. 1.16. Because this model has 10 unknowns and only 6 equations, it is underdetermined and cannot be solved as it stands. However, if one were to fix sufficient values by a priori knowledge or assumption, one could solve for the remaining values.

The factor solution in symbolic form is given in Table 1-2. By inserting the known and solved-for values in place of the unknowns, one could obtain numerical values for the factor pattern, the factor structure, the communalities, and the factor intercorrelations. Also, one could use the path equations of Fig. 1.16 to obtain the implied correlations and thence the residuals. Notice that the factor pattern is quite simple in terms of the paths, but that the factor structure (the correlations of factors with variables) and the communalities are more complex functions of the paths and factor intercorrelations.

Table 1-2 Factor solution of Fig. 1.16, in symbolic form

Variable	Factor pattern			Factor structure			h^2
	E	F	G	E	F	G	
A	a	0	0	a	ha	ja	a^2
B	b	d	0	b+hd	d+hb	id+jb	b^2+d^2+2bhd
C	c	e	f	c+he	e+hc	f+ie	$c^2+e^2+f^2+2che$
				+jf	+if	+jc	+2eif+2cjf
D	0	0	g	jg	ig	g	g^2

Factor intercorrelations

	E	F	G
E	1.0	h	j
F	h	1.0	i
G	j	i	1.0

Structural Equations

An alternative way of representing a path diagram is as a set of *structural equations*. Each equation expresses a downstream variable as a function of the causal paths leading into it. There will be as many equations as there are downstream variables.

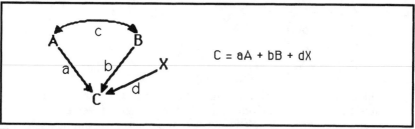

$$C = aA + bB + dX$$

Fig. 1.17 A structural equation based on a path diagram.

Figure 1.17 shows one of the path diagrams considered earlier. It has one downstream variable, hence one structural equation: The score of a person on variable C is an additive function of his scores on A, B, and X. If the variables are obtained in standard-score form for a set of subjects, the values of the weights *a, b,* and *d* required to give a best fit to the data in a least squares sense turn out to be just the standardized partial regression coefficients, or path coefficients, discussed earlier.

Figure 1.18 gives a slightly more complex example, based on the earlier Fig. 1.3. Now there are two downstream variables, A_2 and B_3. A_2 can be expressed as a weighted additive function of the three source variables A_1, B_1, and X, as shown in the first equation, whereas B_3 can be expressed in terms of A_2, B_1, and Y. Note that to construct a structural equation one simply includes a term for every straight arrow leading into the downstream variable. The term

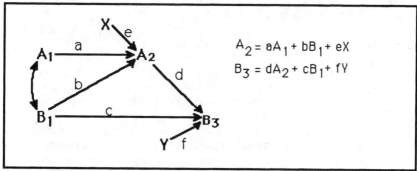

$$A_2 = aA_1 + bB_1 + eX$$
$$B_3 = dA_2 + cB_1 + fY$$

Fig. 1.18 Structural equations based on the path diagram of Fig. 1.3.

consists of the variable at the tail of the arrow times the path coefficient associated with it.

For a final example, consider the factor analysis model of Fig. 1.16 in the preceding section. The structural equations are as follows (X_A, X_B, etc. represent the terms involving the residual arrows):

$$A = aE + X_A$$
$$B = bE + dF + X_B$$
$$C = cE + eF + fG + X_C$$
$$D = gG + X_D$$

Notice that the equations are closely related to the rows of the factor pattern matrix (Table 1-2) with residual terms added. The solution of the set of structural equations corresponds essentially to the solution for the paths in the path diagram and would be similarly underdetermined in this instance. Again, by previously defining a sufficient number of the unknowns, the equations could be solved for those remaining.

The structural equation approach to causal models originated in Economics, and the path approach in biology. For many purposes the two may be regarded simply as alternative representations. Note, however, one difference. Path diagrams explicitly represent the correlations among source variables, whereas structural equations do not. If using the latter, supplementary specifications or assumptions must be made concerning the variances and covariances of the source variables in the model.

Original and Standardized Variables

So far, we have assumed we were dealing with standardized variables. This has simplified the presentation, but is not a necessary restriction. Path, factor, and structural equation analyses can be carried out with variables in their original scale units as well as with standardized variables. In practice, structural equation analysis is usually done in rawscore units, path analysis is done both ways, and factor analysis is usually done with standardized variables. But this is often simply a matter of tradition or (what amounts to much the same thing) of the particular computer program used. There are occasions on which the standardized and rawscore approach each has definite advantages, so it is important to know that one can convert the results of one to the other form and be able to do so when the occasion arises.

Another way of making the distinction between analyses based on standardized and raw units is to say that in the first case one is analyzing correlations, and in the second, covariances. In the first case one decomposes a correlation matrix among observed variables into additive components; in the second case one so decomposes a variance-covariance matrix. The curved arrows in a path diagram are correlations in the first case, covariances in the second. In the first case a straight arrow in a path diagram stands for a standardized partial regression coefficient, in the second case for a rawscore partial regression coefficient. In the first case a .5 beside a straight arrow leading from years of education to annual income means that, other things equal, people in this particular population who are one standard deviation above the mean in education tend to be half a standard deviation above the mean in income. In the second case, if education is measured in years and income in dollars, a 5000 alongside the straight arrow between them means that, other things equal, an increase of 1 year in education represents an increase of $5000 in annual income (in this case, .5 would mean 50 cents!). In each case the arrow between A and B refers to how much change in B results from a given change in A, but in the first case change is measured in standard deviation units of the two variables, and in the second case, in the ratio of their rawscore units (dollars of income per year of education).

Standardized regression coefficients are particularly useful when comparisons are to be made across different variables, unstandardized regression coefficients when comparisons are to be made across different populations.

When comparing across variables, it is difficult to judge the relative importance of education and occupational status in influencing income if the respective rawscore coefficients are 5000 and 300, based on income in dollars, education in years, and occupational status on a 100-point scale. But if the standardized regression coefficients are .5 and .7, respectively, the greater relative influence of occupational status is more evident.

In comparing across populations, rawscore regression coefficients have the merit of independence of the particular ranges of the two variables involved in any particular study. If one study happens to have sampled twice as great a range of education as another, a difference in years of education that is, say, one-half a standard deviation in the first study would be a full standard deviation in the second. A standardized regression coefficient of .3 in one study would then describe exactly the same effect of education on income as a standardized regression coefficient of .6 in the other. This is a confusing state of affairs at best and could be seriously misleading if the reader is unaware of the sampling difference between the studies. A rawscore regression coefficient of $2000 income per added year of education would, however, have the same meaning across the two studies. If the relevant standard deviations are known, a correlation can readily be transformed into a covariance, or vice versa, or a rawscore into a standardized regression coefficient and back, allowing one freely to report results in either or both ways, or to carry out calculations in one mode and report them in the other, if desired. (We qualify this statement later-- model fitting may be sensitive to the scale on which variables are expressed, especially if different paths or variances are constrained to be numerically equal--but it will do for now.)

The algebraic relationships between covariances and correlations are simple:

$$cov_{12} = r_{12}\, s_1 s_2$$
$$r_{12} = cov_{12}/s_1 s_2,$$

where cov_{12} stands for the covariance between variables 1 and 2, r_{12} for their correlation, and s_1 and s_2 for their respective standard deviations.

The relationships between rawscore and standardized path coefficients are equally simple. To convert a standardized path coefficient to its rawscore form, *multiply it by the ratio of the standard deviations of its head to its tail variable.* To convert a rawscore path coefficient to standardized form, invert the process: Multiply by the ratio of the standard deviations of its tail to its head variable.

These rules generalize to a series of path coefficients, as illustrated by Fig. 1.19 and Table 1-3.

The first line in the table shows, via a process of substituting definitions and canceling, that the series of rawscore path coefficients *a*b*c** is equal to the series *abc* of standardized path coefficients multiplied by the ratio of standard deviations of its head and tail variables. The second line demonstrates the converse transformation from rawscore to standardized coefficients.

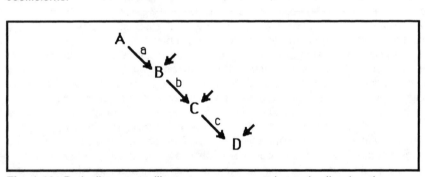

Fig. 1.19 Path diagram to illustrate rawscore and standardized path coefficients.

Table 1-3 Transformation of a sequence of paths from rawscore to standardized form (example of Fig. 1.19)

$a^* b^* c^* = a(s_B/s_A)\, b(s_C/s_B)\, c(s_D/s_C) = abc(s_D/s_A)$
$abc = a^*(s_A/s_B)\, b^*(s_B/s_C)\, c^*(s_C/s_D) = a^*b^*c^*(s_A/s_D)$

Note: Asterisks designate rawscore path coefficients.

The rule for expressing the value of a compound path between two variables in terms of concrete path coefficents (stated for a vertically oriented path diagram) is: *The value of a compound path between two variables is equal to the product of the rawscore path coefficients and the topmost variance or covariance in the path.*

The tracing of compound paths according to Wright's rules, and adding compound paths together to yield the overall covariance, proceed in just the same way with rawscore as with standardized coefficients. The covariance between two variables in the diagram is equal to the sum of the compound paths between them. If there is just a single path between two variables, the covariance is equal to the value of that path. The two path diagrams in Fig. 1.20 illustrate the rule for compound paths headed by a variance and a covariance, respectively. A few examples are given in Table 1-4.

Notice that the rule for evaluating compound paths when using rawscore path coefficients is different from that for standardized coefficients only by the inclusion of one variance or covariance in each path product. Indeed, one can think of the standardized rule as a special case of the rawscore rule, because

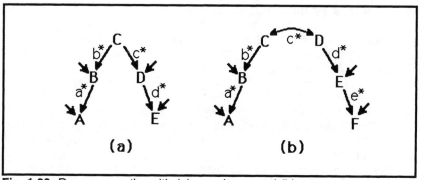

Fig. 1.20 Rawscore paths with (a) a variance and (b) a covariance. (Paths a*, b*, c*, etc. represent rawscore coefficients.)

Table 1-4 Illustrations of rawscore compound path rules, for path diagrams of Fig. 1.20

(a)	(b)
$\text{cov}_{AE} = a^* \, b^* \, s_C^2 \, c^* \, d^*$	$\text{cov}_{AF} = a^* \, b^* \, \text{cov}_{CD} \, d^* \, e^*$
$\text{cov}_{BD} = b^* \, s_C^2 \, c^*$	$\text{cov}_{CF} = \text{cov}_{CD} \, d^* \, e^*$
$\text{cov}_{CE} = s_C^2 \, c^* \, d^*$	$\text{cov}_{DF} = s_D^2 \, d^* \, e^*$

the variance of a standardized variable is 1, and the covariance between standardized variables is just the correlation coefficient.

If we are starting from raw data, standard deviations can always be calculated for observed variables, allowing us to express them in either raw score or standard score units, as we choose. What about the scales of *latent* variables, for which raw scores do not exist? There are two common options. One is simply to solve for them in standard score form and leave them that way. An alternative approach, fairly common among those who prefer to work with covariances and rawscore coefficients, is to assign an arbitrary value, usually 1.0, to a path linking the latent variable to an observed variable, thereby implicitly expressing the latent variable in units based on the observed variable. Several examples of this procedure appear in later chapters.

Differences From Some Related Topics

We need also to be clear about what this book does *not* cover. In this section some related topics, which might easily be confused with latent variable analysis as we discuss it, are distinguished from it.

Manifest versus latent variable models

Many multivariate statistical methods, including some of those most familiar to social and behavioral scientists, do not involve latent variables. Instead, they deal solely with linear composites of *observed* variables. In ordinary multiple regression, for example, one seeks for an optimally weighted composite of measured independent variables to predict an observed dependent or criterion variable. In discriminant analysis, one seeks composites of measured variables that will optimally distinguish among members of specified groups. In canonical analysis one seeks composites that will maximize correlation across two sets of measured variables.

Path and structural equation analysis come in both forms: all variables measured or some not. Many of the earlier applications of such methods in economics and sociology were confined to manifest variables. The effort was to fit causal models in situations where all the variables involved were observed. Biology and psychology, dealing with events within the organism, tended to place an earlier emphasis on the latent variable versions of path analysis. As researchers in all the social sciences become increasingly aware of the distorting effects of measurement errors on causal inferences, latent variable methods have increased in popularity, especially in theoretical contexts. In applied situations, where the practitioner must work with existing measures, errors and all, the manifest variable methods retain much of their preeminence.

Factor analysis is usually *defined* as a latent variable method--the factors are unobserved hypothetical variables that underlie and explain the observed correlations. The corresponding manifest variable method is called *component analysis*--or, in its most common form, the method of *principal components.* Principal components are linear composites of observed variables; the factors of factor analysis are always inferred entities, whose nature is at best consistent with a given set of observations, never entirely determined by them.

Item response theory

A good deal of interest among psychometricians has centered on *item response theory*, sometimes called *latent trait theory,* in which a latent variable is fit to responses to a series of test items. We do not discuss these methods in this book. They typically focus on fitting a single latent variable (the underlying trait being measured) to the responses of subjects to a set of test items, often dichotomous (e.g., right or wrong, true or false), whereas our principal concern is with fitting models involving several latent variables and continuously measured manifest variables. Moreover, the relationships dealt with in item response theory are typically nonlinear: Two- or three-parameter latent curves are fitted, such as the logistic, and this book is primarily concerned with methods that assume linear relationships.

Multilevel models

A number of kinds of multilevel, or hierarchical, models will be discussed in this book, including higher-order factor analysis and latent growth curve modeling. However, the procedures commonly described under the label *multilevel modeling* will not be. This term describes models that are hierarchical in their *sampling design*, not merely their structure. For example, a random sample of U.S. elementary schools might be drawn; within each school a random sample of classrooms; and within each classroom a random sample of students. Variables might be measured at each level--school facilities or principal's attitude at the school level, teacher's experience or class size at the classroom level, student motivation or achievement at the student level. One could then use these data to address effects of higher level variables on lower level outcomes. For example, to what extent do individual students' achievements depend on student-level variables, such as the student's own motivation; to what extent on class-level variables, such as class size, and to what extent on school-level variables, such as budget?

In principle, models of this kind can be analyzed via SEM methods and programs, but in practice specialized software is typically used, and most multilevel modeling research has involved measured rather than latent variables. For these reasons we will not be covering this topic as such in this book, although, as noted, we will discuss some models with a hierarchical structure.

Latent classes versus latent dimensions

Another substantial topic that this book does not attempt to cover is the modeling of latent classes or categories underlying observed relationships. This topic is often called, for historical reasons, *latent structure analysis* (Lazarsfeld, 1950), although the more restrictive designation *latent class analysis* better avoids confusion with the latent variable methods described in this book. The methods we discuss also are concerned with "latent structure," but it is structure based on relations among continuous variables rather than on the existence of discrete underlying categories.

Chapter 1 Notes

Latent variables. Bollen (2002) discusses a number of ways in which latent variables have been defined and distinguished from observed variables.

Cause. Mulaik (1987), Sobel (1995), and Bullock et al. (1994) discuss how this concept is used in causal modeling. A recent effort to put the notion of cause in SEM on a well-defined and scientifically intelligible basis is represented by the work of Judea Pearl (1998, 2000), discussed in Chapter 7. See also Spirtes et al. (1993, 1998) and Shipley (2000).

Path analysis. An introductory account, somewhat oriented toward genetics, is Li (1975). The statement of Wright's rules in this chapter is adapted from Li's. Kenny (1979) provides another introductory presentation with a slightly different version of the path-tracing rules: A single rule--a variable entered via an arrowhead cannot be left via an arrowhead--covers rules 2 and 3. The sociologist O. D. Duncan (1966) is usually credited with rediscovering path analysis for social scientists; Werts and Linn (1970) wrote a paper calling psychologists' attention to the method. For an annotated bibliography on the history of path analysis, see Wolfle (2003).

Factor analysis. Maxwell (1977) has a brief account of some of the early history. Mulaik (1986) updates it; see also Hägglund (2001). See notes to Chapter 5 for books on factor analysis and Cudeck (2000) for a recent overview. For an explicit distinction between the exploratory and confirmatory varieties, see Jöreskog and Lawley (1968), and for a discussion of some of the differences, Nesselroade and Baltes (1984), and McArdle (1996).

Structural equations. These come from econometrics--for some relationships between econometrics and psychometrics, see Goldberger (1971) and a special issue of the journal *Econometrics* edited by de Leeuw et al. (1983). A historical perspective is given by Bentler (1986).

Direct and indirect effects. For a discussion of such effects, and the development of matrix methods for their systematic calculation, see Fox (1980, 1985). See also Sobel (1988). Finch et al. (1997) discuss how sample size and nonnormality affect the estimation of indirect effects.

Under and overdetermination in path diagrams. Often discussed in the structural equation literature as "identification." More in Chapter 2.

"Recursive" and "nonrecursive." In the technical literature, path models with loops are described as "nonrecursive," and path models without loops as "recursive." Beginning students find this terminology confusing, to say the least. It may help to know that "recursive" refers to the corresponding sets of equations and how they can be solved, rather than describing path diagrams.

Original and standardized variables. Their relative merits are debated by Tukey (1954) and Wright (1960), also see Kim and Ferree (1981) and Alwin (1988). See Bielby (1986), Williams and Thomson (1986), and several commentators for a discussion of some of the hazards involved in scaling latent variables. Yuan and Bentler (2000a) discuss the use of correlation versus covariance matrices in exploratory factor analysis. Again, more on this topic in Chapter 2.

Related topics. Several examples of manifest-variable path and structural analysis may be found in Marsden (1981), especially Part II. Principal component analysis is treated in most factor analysis texts (see Chapter 5); for discussions of relationships between factor analysis and principal component analysis, see an issue of *Multivariate Behavioral Research* (Vol. 25, No. 1, 1990), and Widaman (1993). For item response theory, see van der Linden and Hambleton (Eds.) (1997). Reise et al. (1993) discuss relationships between IRT and SEM. For multilevel models (also known as hierarchical linear models) see Goldstein (1995), Bryk and Raudenbush (1992), and Heck (2001). Recent books on the topic include Hox (2002) and Reise and Duan (2003). The relationship between multilevel models and SEM is discussed in McArdle and Hamagami (1996) and Kaplan and Elliott (1997). The basic treatment of latent class analysis is Lazarsfeld and Henry (1968); Clogg (1995) reviews the topic. For a broad treatment of structural models that covers both quantitative and qualitative variables see Kiiveri and Speed (1982); for related discussions see Bartholomew (1987, 2002) and Molenaar and von Eye (1994).

Journal sources. Some journals that frequently publish articles on developments in the area of latent variable models include *Structural Equation Modeling, Psychometrika, Sociological Methods and Research, Multivariate Behavioral Research, The British Journal of Mathematical and Statistical Psychology, Journal of Marketing Research,* and *Psychological Methodology.* See also the annual series *Sociological Methodology.*

Books. Some books dealing with path and structural equation modeling include those written or edited by Duncan (1975), Heise (1975), Kenny (1979), James et al. (1982), Asher (1983), Long (1983a,b, 1988), Everitt (1984), Saris and Stronkhorst (1984), Bartholomew (1987), Cuttance and Ecob (1987), Hayduk (1987, 1996), Bollen (1989b), Bollen and Long (1993), Byrne (1994, 1998, 2001), von Eye and Clogg (1994), Arminger et al. (1995), Hoyle (1995), Schumacker and Lomax (1996), Marcoulides and Schumacker (1996, 2001), Mueller (1996), Berkane (1997), Maruyama (1998), Kline (1998a), Kaplan (2000), Raykov and Marcoulides (2000), Cudeck et al. (2001), Marcoulides and

Moustaki (2002), and Pugasek et al. (2003).

Annotated bibliography. An extensive annotated bibliography of books, chapters, and articles in the area of structural equation modeling, by J. T. Austin and R. F. Calderón, appeared in the journal *Structural Equation Modeling* (1996, Vol. 3, No. 2, pp. 105-175).

Internet resources. There are many. One good place to start is with a web page called SEMFAQ (Structural Equation Modeling: Frequently Asked Questions). It contains brief discussions of SEM issues that often give students difficulty, as well as lists of books and journals, plus links to a variety of other relevant web pages. SEMFAQ's address (at the time of writing) is http://www.gsu.edu/~mkteer/semfaq.html. Another useful listing of internet resources for SEM can be found at http://www.smallwaters.com. A bibliography on SEM is at http://www.upa.pdx.edu/IOA/newsom/semrefs.htm.

There is an SEM discussion network called SEMNET available to those with e-mail facilities. Information on how to join this network is given by E. E. Rigdon in the journal *Structural Equation Modeling* (1994, Vol. 1, No. 2, pp. 190-192), or may be obtained via the SEMFAQ page mentioned above. Searchable archives of SEMNET discussions exist. A Europe-based working group on SEM may be found at http://www.uni-muenster.de/SoWi/struktur.

Chapter 1 Exercises

Note: Answers to most exercises are given at the back of the book, preceding the References. Correlation or covariance matrices required for computer-based exercises are included on the compact disk supplied with the text. There are none in this chapter.

1. Draw a path diagram of the relationships among impulsivity and hostility at one time and delinquency at a later time, assuming that the first two influence the third but not vice versa.

2. Draw a path diagram of the relationships among ability, motivation, and performance, each measured on two occasions.

3. Consider the path diagram of Fig. 1.10 (on page 14). Think of some actual variables A, B, C, and D that might be related in the same way as the hypothetical variables in that figure. (Don't worry about the exact sizes of the correlations.)

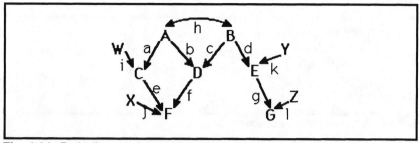

Fig. 1.21 Path diagram for problems 4 to 10 (all variables standardized unless otherwise specified).

4. Identify the source and downstream variables in Fig 1.21.

5. What assumption is made about the causation of variable D?

6. Write path equations for the correlations r_{AF}, r_{DG}, r_{CE}, and r_{EF}.

7. Write path equations for the variances of C, D, and F.

8. If variables A, B, F, and G are measured, and the others latent, would you expect the path diagram to be solvable? (Explain why or why not.)

9. Now, assume that the variables in Fig. 1.21 are *not* standardized. Write path equations, using rawscore coefficients, for the covariances c_{CD}, c_{FG}, c_{AG} and the variances s_G^2 and s_D^2.

10. Write structural equations for the variables D, E, and F in Fig. 1.21.

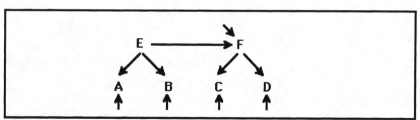

Fig.1.22 Path diagram for problem 11.

11. Redraw Fig. 1.22 as a RAM path diagram. (E and F are latent variables, A through D are observed.)

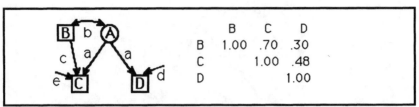

	B	C	D
B	1.00	.70	.30
C		1.00	.48
D			1.00

Fig. 1.23 Path diagram for problem 12.

12. Given the path diagram shown in Fig. 1.23 and the observed correlations given to the right, solve for *a, b, c, d,* and *e.*

13. The following intercorrelations among three variables are observed:

	A	B	C
A	1.00	.42	.12
B		1.00	.14
C			1.00

Solve for the loadings on a single common factor, using the method of triads.

Chapter Two:
Fitting Path Models

In this chapter we consider the processes used in actually fitting path models to data on a realistic scale, and evaluating their goodness of fit. This implies computer-oriented methods. This chapter is somewhat more technical than Chapter 1. Some readers on a first pass through the book might prefer to read carefully only the section on hierarchical χ^2 tests (pp. 61-66), glance at the section on the RMSEA (pp. 68-69), and then go on to Chapters 3 and 4, coming back to Chapter 2 afterwards. (You will need additional Chapter 2 material to do the exercises in Chapters 3 and 4.)

Iterative Solution of Path Equations

In simple path diagrams like those we have considered so far, direct algebraic solution of the set of implied equations is often quite practicable. But as the number of observed variables goes up, the number of intercorrelations among them, and hence the number of equations to be solved, increases rapidly. There are $n(n-1)/2$ equations, where n is the number of observed variables, or $n(n+1)/2$ equations, if variances are solved for as well. Furthermore, path equations by their nature involve product terms, because a compound path is the product of its component arrows. Product terms make the equations recalcitrant to straightforward matrix procedures that can be used to solve sets of linear simultaneous equations. As a result of this, large sets of path equations are in practice usually solved by iterative (= repetitive) trial-and-error procedures, carried out by computers.

The general idea is simple. An arbitrary set of initial values of the paths serves as a starting point. The correlations or covariances implied by these values are calculated and compared to the observed values. Because the initial values are arbitrary, the fit is likely to be poor. So one or more of the initial trial values is changed in a direction that improves the fit, and the process is repeated with this new set of trial values. This cycle is repeated again and again, each time modifying the set of trial values to improve the agreement between the implied and the observed correlations. Eventually, a set of values is reached that cannot be improved on--the process, as the numerical

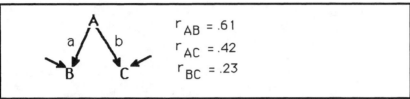

$r_{AB} = .61$

$r_{AC} = .42$

$r_{BC} = .23$

Fig. 2.1 A simple path diagram illustrating an iterative solution.

analysts say, has "converged" on a solution. If all has gone well, this will be the optimum solution that is sought.

Let us illustrate this procedure with the example shown in Fig. 2.1. A simple case like this one might be solved in more direct ways, but we use it to demonstrate an iterative solution, as shown in Table 2-1.

We begin in cycle 1 by setting arbitrary trial values of a and b--for the example we have set each to .5. Then we calculate the values of the correlations r_{AB}, r_{AC}, and r_{BC} that are implied by these path values: they are .50, .50, and .25, respectively. We choose some reasonable criterion of the discrepancy between these and the observed correlations--say, the sum of the squared differences between the corresponding values. In this case this sum is $.11^2 + (-.08)^2 + (-.02)^2$, or .0189.

Next, in steps 1a and 1b, we change each trial value by some small amount (we have used an increase of .001) to see what effect this has on the criterion. Increasing a makes things better and increasing b makes things worse, suggesting that either an increase in a or a decrease in b should improve the fit. Because the change 1a makes a bigger difference than the change 1b does, suggesting that the criterion will improve faster with a change in a, we increase the trial value by 1 in the first decimal place to obtain the new set of trial values in cycle 2. Repeating the process, in 2a and 2b, we find that a change in b now has the greater effect; the desirable change is a decrease.

Decreasing b by 1 in the first decimal place gives the cycle 3 trial values .6 and .4. In steps 3a and 3b we find that increasing either would be beneficial, b more so. But increasing b in the first decimal place would just undo our last step, yielding no improvement, so we shift to making changes in the second place. (This is not necessarily the numerically most efficient way to proceed, but it will get us there.) In cycle 4, the value of the criterion confirms that the new trial values of .6 and .41 do constitute an improvement. Testing these values in steps 4a and 4b, we find that an increase in a is suggested. We try increasing a in the second decimal place, but this is not an improvement, so we shift to an increase in the third decimal place (cycle 5). The tests in steps 5a and 5b suggest that a further increase to .602 would be justified, so we use that in cycle 6. Now it appears that decreasing b might be the best thing to do, cycle 7, but it isn't an improvement. Rather than go on to still smaller changes, we elect to quit at this point, reasonably confident of at least two-place precision in our answer of .602 and .410 in cycle 6 (or, slightly better, the .603 and .410 in 6a).

Table 2-1 An iterative solution of the path diagram of Fig. 2.1

		Trial values		Correlations			Criterion
		a	b	r_{AB}	r_{AC}	r_{BC}	Σd^2
Observed				.61	.42	.23	
Cycle	1	.5	.5	.50	.50	.25	.018900
	1a	.501	.5	.501	.50	.2505	.018701*
	1b	.5	.501	.50	.501	.2505	.019081
	2	.6	.5	.60	.50	.30	.011400
	2a	.601	.5	.601	.50	.3005	.011451
	2b	.6	.501	.60	.501	.3006	.011645*
	3	.6	.4	.60	.40	.24	.000600
	3a	.601	.4	.601	.40	.2404	.000589
	3b	.6	.401	.60	.401	.2406	.000573*
	4	.6	.41	.60	.41	.246	.000456
	4a	.601	.41	.601	.41	.2464	.000450*
	4b	.6	.411	.60	.411	.2466	.000457
	(5)	.61	.41	.61	.41	.2501	.000504
	5	.601	.41	.601	.41	.2464	.0004503
	5a	.602	.41	.602	.41	.2468	.0004469*
	5b	.601	.411	.601	.411	.2470	.0004514
	6	.602	.41	.602	.41	.2468	.0004469
	6a	.603	.41	.603	.41	.2472	.0004459
	6b	.602	.411	.602	.411	.2474	.0004485*
	(7)	.603	.409	.603	.409	.2462	.0004480

*greater change

Now, doing this by hand for even two unknowns is fairly tedious, but it is just the kind of repetitious, mechanical process that computers are good at, and many general and special-purpose computer programs exist that can carry out such minimizations. If you were using a typical general-purpose minimization program, you would be expected to supply it with an initial set of trial values of the unknowns, and a subroutine that calculates the function to be minimized, given a set of trial values. That is, you would program a subroutine that will calculate the implied correlations, subtract them from the observed correlations, and sum the squares of the differences between the two. The minimization program will then proceed to adjust the trial values iteratively, in some such fashion as that portrayed in Table 2-1, until an unimprovable minimum value is reached.

Geographies of search

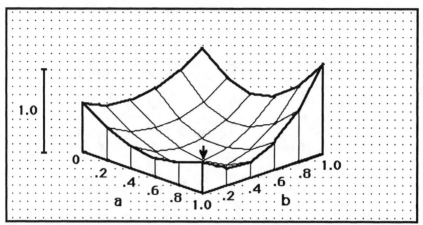

Fig. 2.2 Graphical representation of search space for Fig. 2.1 problem, for values 0 to 1 of both variables. The coordinates a and b refer to the two paths, and the vertical dimension to the value of the criterion.

For the simple two-variable case of Fig. 2.1 and Table 2-1 we can visualize the solution process as a search of a geographical terrain for its lowest point. Values of *a* and *b* represent spatial coordinates such as latitude and longitude, and values of the criterion Σd^2 represent altitudes above sea level. Figure 2.2 is a pictorial representation of the situation. A set of starting trial values represents the coordinates of a starting point in the figure. The tests in steps *a* and *b* in each cycle represent tests of how the ground slopes each way from the present location, which govern the choice of a promising direction in which to move. In each instance we make the move that takes us downhill most rapidly. Eventually, we reach the low point in the valley, marked by the arrow, from which a step in any direction would lead upward. Then we quit and report our location as the solution.

Note that in simple geographies, such as that represented in this example, it doesn't matter what set of starting values we use--we would reach the same final low point regardless of where we start from--at worst it will take longer from some places than from others. Not all geographies, however, are this benign. Figure 2.3 shows a cross-section of a more treacherous terrain. A starting point at A on the left of the ridge will lead away from, not towards, the

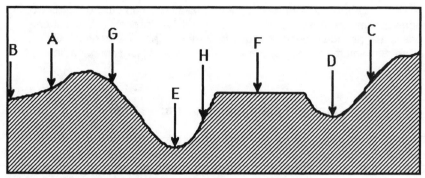

Fig. 2.3 Cross section of a less hospitable search terrain.

solution--the searcher will wind up against the boundary at B. From a starting point at C, on the right, one will see initial rapid improvement but will be trapped at an apparent solution at D, well short of the optimum at E. Or one might strike a level area, such as F, from which no direction of initial step leads to improvement. Other starting points, such as G and H, will, however, lead satisfactorily to E.

It is ordinarily prudent, particularly when just beginning to explore the landscape implicit in a particular path model, to try at least two or three widely dispersed starting points from which to seek a minimum. If all the solutions converge on the same point and it represents a reasonably good fit to the data, it is probably safe to conclude that it is the optimum solution. If some solutions wander off or stop short of the best achieved so far, it is well to suspect that one may be dealing with a less regular landscape and try additional sets of starting values until several converge on the same minimum solution.

It is easy to draw pictures for landscapes in one or two unknowns, as in Fig. 2.3 or 2.2. In the general case of *n* unknowns, the landscape would be an *n*-dimensional space with an *n* + 1st dimension for the criterion. Although such spaces are not easily visualizable, they work essentially like the simple ones, with *n*-dimensional analogues of the valleys, ridges, and hollows of a three-dimensional geography. The iterative procedure of Table 2-1 is easily extended to more dimensions (= more unknowns), although the amount of computation required escalates markedly as the number of unknowns goes up.

Many fine points of iterative minimization programs have been skipped over in this brief account. Some programs allow the user to place constraints on the trial values (and hence on the ultimate possible solutions), such as specifying that they always be positive, or that they lie between +1 and -1 or other defined limits. Programs differ in how they adjust their step sizes during their search, and in their ability to recover from untoward events. Some are extremely fast and efficient on friendly terrain but are not well adapted elsewhere. Others are robust, but painfully slow even on easy ground. Some programs allow the user a good deal of control over aspects of the search process and provide a good deal of information on how it proceeds. Others require a minimum of specification from the user and just print out a final answer.

Matrix Formulation of Path Models

Simple path diagrams are readily transformed into sets of simultaneous equations by the use of Wright's rules. We have seen in the preceding sections how such sets of equations can be solved iteratively by computer programs. To use such a program one must give it a subroutine containing the path equations, so that it can calculate the implied values and compare them with the observed values. With three observed values, as in our example, this is simple enough, but with 30 or 40 the preparation of a new subroutine for each problem can get tedious. Furthermore, in tracing paths in more complex diagrams to reduce them to sets of equations, it is easy to make errors--for example, to overlook some indirect path that connects point A and point B, or to include a path twice. Is there any way of mechanizing the construction of path equations, as well as their solution?

In fact, there are such procedures, which allow the expression of the equations of a path diagram as the product of several matrices. Not only does such an approach allow one to turn a path diagram into a set of path equations with less risk of error, but in fact one need not explicitly write down the path equations at all--one can carry out the calculation of implied correlations directly via operations on the matrices. This does not save effort at the level of actual computation, but it constitutes a major strategic simplification.

The particular procedure we use to illustrate this is one based on a formulation by McArdle and McDonald (1984); an equivalent although more complex matrix procedure is carried out within the computer program LISREL (of which more later), and still others have been proposed (e.g., Bentler & Weeks, 1980; McArdle, 1980; McDonald, 1978). It is assumed that the reader is familiar with elementary matrix operations; if your skills in this area are rusty or nonexistent, you may wish to consult Appendix A or an introductory textbook in matrix algebra before proceeding.

McArdle and McDonald define three matrices, **A**, **S**, and **F**:

A (for "asymmetric" relations) contains paths.
S (for "symmetric" relations) contains correlations (or covariances) and residual variances.
F (for "filter" matrix) selects out the observed variables from the total set of variables.

If there are *t* variables (excluding residuals), *m* of which are measured, the dimensions of these matrices are: **A** = t x t; **S** = t x t; **F** = m x t. The implied correlation (or covariance) matrix **C** among the measured variables is obtained by the matrix equation:

$$C = F (I - A)^{-1} S (I - A)^{-1'} F'.$$

I stands for the identity matrix, and $^{-1}$ and ´ refer to the matrix operations of inversion and transposition, respectively.

This is not a very transparent equation. You may wish just to take it on faith, but if you want to get some sense of why it looks like it does, you can turn to Appendix B, where it is shown how this matrix equation can be derived from the structural equation representation of a path diagram. The fact that the equation can do what it claims to do is shown in the examples below.

An example with correlations

Figure 2.4 and Tables 2-2 and 2-3 provide an example of the use of the McArdle-McDonald matrix equation. The path diagram in Fig. 2.4 is that of Fig. 1.23, from the exercises of the preceding chapter.

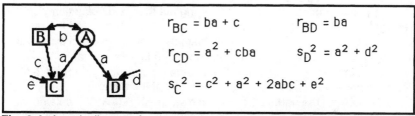

$$r_{BC} = ba + c \qquad r_{BD} = ba$$
$$r_{CD} = a^2 + cba \qquad s_D^2 = a^2 + d^2$$
$$s_C^2 = c^2 + a^2 + 2abc + e^2$$

Fig. 2.4 A path diagram for the matrix example of Tables 2-2 and 2-3.

Variables B, C, and D are assumed to be observed; variable A to be latent, as shown by the squares and the circle. All variables are assumed to be standardized--i.e., we are dealing with a correlation matrix. Expressions for the correlations and variances, based on path rules, are given to the right in the figure. In Table 2-2 (next page), Matrix **A** contains the three straight arrows (paths) in the diagram, the two *as* and the *c*. Each is placed at the intersection of the variable from which it originates (top) and the variable to which it points (side). For example, path *c*, which goes from B to C, is specified in row C of column B. It is helpful (though not algebraically necessary) to group together source variables and downstream variables--the source variables A and B are given first in the Table 2-2 matrices, and the downstream variables C and D last.

Curved arrows and variances are represented in matrix **S**. The top left-hand part contains the correlation matrix among the source variables, A and B. The diagonal in the lower right-hand part contains the residual variances of the

Table 2-2 Matrix formulation of a path diagram by the McArdle-McDonald procedure

A					**S**					**F**			
	A	B	C	D		A	B	C	D		A	B	C	D
A	0	0	0	0	A	1	b	0	0	B	0	1	0	0
B	0	0	0	0	B	b	1	0	0	C	0	0	1	0
C	a	c	0	0	C	0	0	e^2	0	D	0	0	0	1
D	a	0	0	0	D	0	0	0	d^2					

downstream variables C and D, as given by the squares of the residual paths *e* and *d* . (If there were any covariances among residuals, they would be shown by off-diagonal elements in this part of the matrix.)

Finally, matrix **F**, which selects out the observed variables from all the variables, has observed variables listed down the side and all variables along the top. It simply contains a 1 at the row and column corresponding to each observed variable--in this case, B, C, and D.

Table 2-3 demonstrates that multiplying out the matrix equation yields the path equations. First, **A** is subtracted from the identity matrix **I**, and the result inverted, yielding $(I-A)^{-1}$. You can verify that this *is* the required inverse by the matrix multiplication $(I-A)^{-1}(I-A) = I$. (If you want to learn a convenient way of obtaining this inverse, see Appendix B.) Pre- and postmultiplying **S** by $(I-A)^{-1}$ and its transpose is done in this and the next row of the table.

The matrix to the right in the second row, $(I-A)^{-1}S\,(I-A)^{-1\prime}$, contains the correlations among *all* the variables, both latent and observed. The first row and column contain the correlations involving the latent variable. The remainder of the matrix contains the intercorrelations among the observed variables. As you should verify, all these are consistent with those obtainable via path tracing on the diagram in Fig. 2.4 (page 41).

The final pre- and postmultiplication by **F** merely selects out the lower right-hand portion of the preceding matrix, namely, the correlations among the observed variables. This is given in the last part of the table, and as you can see, agrees with the results of applying Wright's rules to the path diagram.

Thus, with particular values of *a*, *b*, *c*, etc. inserted in the matrices, the matrix operations of the McArdle-McDonald equation result in exactly the same implied values for the intercorrelations as would putting these same values into expressions derived from the path diagram via Wright's rules.

Table 2-3 Solution of the McArdle-McDonald equation, for the matrices of Table 2-2

$(I-A)^{-1}$

	A	B	C	D
A	1	0	0	0
B	0	1	0	0
C	a	c	1	0
D	a	0	0	1

$(I-A)^{-1}S$

	A	B	C	D
A	1	b	0	0
B	b	1	0	0
C	a+bc	ab+c	e^2	0
D	a	ab	0	d^2

$(I-A)^{-1'}$

	A	B	C	D
A	1	0	a	a
B	0	1	c	0
C	0	0	1	0
D	0	0	0	1

$(I-A)^{-1}S\ (I-A)^{-1'}$

	A	B	C	D
A	1	b	a+bc	a
B	b	1	ab+c	ab
C	a+bc	ab+c	$a^2+c^2+2abc+e^2$	a^2+abc
D	a	ab	a^2+abc	a^2+d^2

$F(I-A)^{-1}S\ (I-A)^{-1'}F' = C$

	B	C	D
B	1	ab+c	ab
C	ab+c	$a^2+c^2+2abc+e^2$	a^2+abc
D	ab	a^2+abc	a^2+d^2

An example with covariances

The only modification to the procedure that is needed in order to use it with a variance-covariance matrix is to insert variances instead of 1s in the upper diagonal of **S**. The equation will then yield an implied variance-covariance matrix of the observed variables, instead of a correlation matrix, with the path coefficients *a* and *c* in rawscore form.

The procedure is illustrated in Table 2-4 (next page). The example is the same as that in Table 2-3, except that variables A, B, C, and D are now assumed to be unstandardized. The table shows the **S** matrix (the **A** and **F** matrices are as in Table 2-2), and the final result. Notice that these expressions conform to the rawscore path rules, by the inclusion of one variance or covariance in each path, involving the variable or variables at its highest point. (The *b*s are now covariances, and the *a*s and *c*s unstandardized path coefficients.) You may wish to check out some of this in detail to make sure you understand the process.

Table 2-4 Solution for covariance matrix, corresponding to Table 2-3

S

	A	B	C	D
A	s_A^2	b	0	0
B	b	s_B^2	0	0
C	0	0	e^2	0
D	0	0	0	d^2

F(I-A)$^{-1}$S (I-A)$^{-1}$ ´ F´ = C

	B	C	D
B	s_B^2	$ab+c\ s_B^2$	ab
C	$ab+c\ s_B^2$	$a^2 s_A^2 +c^2 s_B^2 +2abc+e^2$	$a^2 s_A^2 +abc$
D	ab	$a^2 s_A^2 +abc$	$a^2 s_A^2 +d^2$

Full-Fledged Model-Fitting Programs

Suppose you were to take a general-purpose minimization program and provide it with a matrix formulation, such as the McArdle-McDonald equation, to calculate the implied correlation or covariance matrices at each step in its search. By describing the matrices **A**, **S**, and **F** in the input to the program, you would avoid the necessity of writing fresh path equations for each new problem.

One might well dress up such a program with a few additional frills: For example, one could offer additional options in the way of criteria for evaluating goodness of fit. In our example, we minimized the sum of squared differences between observed and implied correlations. This least squares criterion is one that is easily computed and widely used in statistics, but there are others, such as maximum likelihood, that might be used and that could be provided as alternatives. (Some of the relative advantages and disadvantages of different criteria are discussed in a later section of this chapter.) While you are at it, you might as well provide various options for inputting data to the program (raw data; existing correlation or covariance matrices), and for printing out various informative results.

In the process, you would have invented a typical structural equation modeling (SEM) program. By now, a number of programs along these general lines exist and can be used for solving path diagrams. They go by such names as AMOS, CALIS, COSAN, EQS, LISREL, MECOSA, Mplus, Mx, RAMONA, and SEPATH. Some are associated with general statistical packages, others are self-contained. The ways of describing the model to the program differ--for some programs this is done via paths, for some via structural equations, for some via matrices. Some programs provide more than one of these options. The styles of output also vary. We need not be concerned here with the details of implementation, but will briefly describe a few representative programs, and illustrate how one might carry out a couple of simple analyses with each. We begin with the best-known member of the group, LISREL, and then describe EQS, Mx, and AMOS, and then others more briefly.

LISREL

This is the father of all SEM programs. LISREL stands for LInear Structural RELations. The program was devised by the Swedish psychometrician Karl Jöreskog, and has developed through a series of versions. The current version is LISREL 8 (Jöreskog & Sörbom, 1993). LISREL is based on a more elaborate matrix formulation of path diagrams than the McArdle-McDonald equation, although one that works on similar principles and leads to the same end result. The LISREL formulation is more complicated because it subdivides the process, keeping in eight separate matrices various elements that are combined in the three McArdle-McDonald matrices.

We need not go into the details of this matrix formulation, since most beginners will be running LISREL via a command language called SIMPLIS, which allows one to describe the problem in terms of a path diagram or a set of structural equations, which the program automatically translates into the matrices required for LISREL. Readers of articles based on earlier versions of LISREL will, however, encounter references to various matrices named LX, TD, GA, BE and so on, and advanced users who wish to go beyond the limitations of SIMPLIS will need to understand their use. Appendix C describes the LISREL matrices briefly.

In the following sections, examples are given of how models may be described in inputs to typical SEM programs. The SIMPLIS example illustrates an input based on the description of paths; EQS illustrates a structural equation representation; Mx illustrates matrix input. Other SEM programs will typically follow one or more of these three modes. A recent trend, led by AMOS, is to enter problems by building a path diagram directly on the computer screen.

An example of input via paths--SIMPLIS/LISREL

An example of SIMPLIS input will be given to solve the path diagram of Fig. 2.5 (next page). This is a simple two-factor model, with two correlated factors, F1 and F2, and four observed variables X1, X2, X3, and X4. We will assume the factors to be standardized (variance = 1.0). Note that the values *w, x, y,* and *z* are placed in the diagram at the *ends* of their respective arrows rather than beside them. We will use this convention to signify that they represent

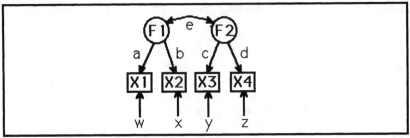

Fig. 2.5 Path diagram for example of Table 2-6.

residual variances rather than path values; this is the form in which LISREL reports them.

Table 2-5 shows the SIMPLIS program. The first line is a title. The next line lists the four observed variables (labels more descriptive than these would normally be used in practice). The third line indicates that the correlation matrix follows, and lines 4 to 7 supply it, in lower triangular form. The next two lines identify the latent variables and specify the sample size. Then come the paths: from F1 to X1 and X2; from F2 to X3 and X4. End of problem. The simplicity of this program illustrates a philosophy of LISREL and SIMPLIS--that things are assumed to be in a typical form by default unless otherwise specified. Thus SIMPLIS assumes that all source latent variables will be standardized and intercorrelated, that there will be residuals on all downstream variables, and that these residuals will be uncorrelated--it is not necessary to say anything about these matters in the program unless some other arrangement is desired. Likewise, it is assumed that LISREL is to calculate its own starting values, and that the default fitting criterion, which is maximum likelihood, is to be used.

Table 2-5 An example of SIMPLIS input for solving the path diagram of Fig. 2.5

```
INPUT FOR FIG. 2.5 PROBLEM
OBSERVED VARIABLES X1 X2 X3 X4
CORRELATION MATRIX
   1.00
    .50   1.00
    .10    .10   1.00
    .20    .30    .20   1.00
LATENT VARIABLES F1 F2
SAMPLE SIZE 100
PATHS
  F1 -> X1 X2
  F2 -> X3 X4
END OF PROBLEM
```

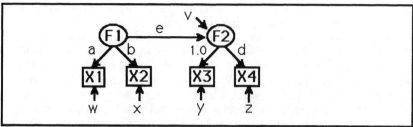

Fig. 2.6 A different model for the data of Fig. 2.5.

Figure 2.6 shows a different model that might be fit to the same data. In this model, we assume again that there are four observed variables, X1 to X4, and two latent variable, F1 and F2, but now there is a causal path, labeled *e*, rather than a simple correlation, between the two latent variables. Thus we have a structural equation model in the full sense, rather than a simple factor analysis model. This leads to two further changes. F2 is now a downstream variable rather than a source variable, so it acquires a residual arrow. This complicates fixing the variance of F2 to a given value (such as 1.0) during an iterative solution, so SEM programs often require users to scale each downstream latent variable via a fixed path to an observed variable, as shown for F2 and X3 (SIMPLIS allows but does not require this). *Source* latent variables may be scaled in either way--we will continue to assume that the variance of F1 is fixed to 1.0. Note that the total number of unknowns remains the same as in Fig 2.5--the residual variance *v* is solved for instead of the path *c,* and there is an *e* to be solved for in either case, although they play different roles in the model. There are now three paths from F1--to X1, X2, and F2--and as there is now only one source latent variable, there is no correlation between such variables to be dealt with.

In the example in Table 2-6, we have assumed that we wish to provide our own starting values for each path to be solved (the parenthesized .5s, followed by the asterisks). The fixed path of 1 from F2 to X3 is represented by a 1 *not* placed in parentheses. We have also assumed that we want to obtain an

Table 2-6 Example of SIMPLIS input for Fig. 2.6 problem

```
INPUT FOR FIG. 2.6 PROBLEM

  [lines 2-9 same as for previous example]

PATHS
  F1 -> (.5)*X1 (.5)*X2 (.5)*F2
  F2 -> 1*X3 (.5)*X4
OPTIONS UL ND=3
END OF PROBLEM
```

ordinary least squares solution (UL, for "unweighted least squares," in the options line), and want to have results given to three decimal places (ND=3).

Many further options are available. For example, one could specify that paths a and b were to be equated by adding the line Let F1 -> X1 = F1 -> X2. As noted, an alternative form of input based on structural equations may be used. The user will need to consult the relevant manuals for further details; these illustrations are merely intended to convey something of the flavor of SIMPLIS/LISREL's style, and to provide models for working simple problems. A number of examples of the use of LISREL in actual research are found in the next two chapters.

An example of input via structural equations--EQS

A rival program along the same general lines as LISREL is EQS by Peter Bentler (1995). Path models are specified to EQS in the form of structural equations. Structural equations were described in Chapter 1. Recall that there is one structural equation for each downstream latent or observed variable in a path model, and that variances and covariances of source variables need also to be specified.

Four kinds of variables are distinguished in EQS: V for observed variables, F for latent variables, E for residuals of observed variables, and D for residuals of downstream latent variables. Each variable is designated by a letter followed by numbers. A typical structural equation for a V variable will include Fs and an E; one for an F variable will include other Fs and a D.

Table 2-7 shows on the left an EQS equivalent of the LISREL program in Table 2-5. In the EQUATIONS section, a structural equation is given for each downstream variable. V1 to V4 stand for the observed variables X1 to X4, F1 and F2 for the two latent source variables, and E1 to E4 for the four residuals. The asterisks designate free variables to be estimated. In the VARIANCES and COVARIANCES sections, the variances of F1 and F2 are fixed at 1 (no asterisk), and E1 to E4 and the covariance of F1 and F2 are to be estimated.

In example (b), corresponding to Table 2-6, the structural relationship of Fig 2.6 is specified between the two latent variables. A structural equation for F2 is added to the list of equations, with a residual D2; the covariance involving the latent variables is dropped; and the path from F2 to V3 is fixed implicitly to 1. Starting values of .5 precede the asterisks. Finally, in the SPEC section, the least squares method is specified by ME = LS (as in the case of LISREL, maximum likelihood is the default method).

Again, many variations are possible in EQS, as in LISREL. A CONSTRAINTS section can impose equality constraints. For example, to require paths a and b in Fig 2.6 to be equal, one would specify /CONSTRAINTS and (V1, F1) = (V2, F1).

Table 2-7 Examples of EQS input for fitting the models in Figs. 2.5 and 2.6

(a)	(b)

```
/TITLE                              /TITLE
   INPUT FOR FIG 2.5 PROBLEM           INPUT FOR FIG 2.6 PROBLEM
/SPECIFICATIONS                     /SPEC
   VAR=4; CAS=100; MA=COR;             VAR=4; CAS=100; MA=COR;
   ANAL=COR;                           ANAL=COR; ME=LS;
/EQUATIONS                          /EQU
   V1 = *F1 + E1;                      V1 = .5*F1 + E1;
   V2 = *F1 + E2;                      V2 = .5*F1 + E2;
   V3 = *F2 + E3;                      V3 =     F2 + E3;
   V4 = *F2 + E4;                      V4 = .5*F2 + E4;
/VARIANCES                             F2 = .5*F1 + D2;
 F1, F2 = 1; E1 TO E4 = *;          /VAR
/COVARIANCES                           F1=1; E1 TO E4 = .5*;
 F1,F2 = *;                            D2 = .5*;
/MATRIX                             /MAT
  1.00                                1.00
   .50 1.00                            .50 1.00
   .10  .10 1.00                       .10  .10 1.00
   .20  .30  .20 1.00                  .20  .30  .20 1.00
/END                                /END
```

An example of input via matrices--Mx

A flexible and powerful SEM program by Michael Neale based on matrix input is called Mx (Neale, 1995). Table 2-8 (next page) gives examples of how one might set up the problems of Fig 2.5 and 2.6 in Mx. Use of the McArdle-McDonald matrix equation is illustrated--recall that any path model can be expressed in this way. (Other matrix formulations can be used in Mx if desired.)

The first line of input is a title. The next provides general specifications: number of groups (NG), number of input variables (NI), sample size (NO for number of observations). Then comes the observed correlation or covariance matrix. In the next few lines the dimensions of the matrices **A, S**, and **F** are specified. Then we have the McArdle-McDonald equation (~ means inverse, and the slash at the end is required). Finally, the knowns and unknowns in **A, S**, and **F** are indicated, as described earlier in the chapter. Zeroes are fixed values, integers represent different values to be solved for (if some of these are to be equated, the same number would be used for both). The VALUE lines at the end put fixed values into various locations: the first such line puts fixed values of 1 into S 1 1 and S 2 2; the others set up the 1s in F.

The righthand part of the table **(b)** shows the modifications necessary for the Fig. 2.6 problem.

Table 2-8 Example of Mx input for Fig. 2.5 and Fig. 2.6 problems

(a)	**(b)**

```
INPUT FOR FIG. 2.5 PROBLEM        INPUT FOR FIG. 2.6 PROBLEM
DATA NG=1 NI=4 NO=100
CMATRIX                           [same as (a) through
   1.00                               COVARIANCES line]
    .50 1.00
    .10  .10 1.00
    .20  .30  .20 1.00
MATRICES
  A FULL 6 6
  S SYMM 6 6
  F FULL 4 6
  I IDENT 6 6
COVARIANCES F*(I-A)~*S*((I-A)~)'*F' /
SPECIFICATION A                   SPECIFICATION A
0 0 0 0 0 0                        0 0 0 0 0 0
0 0 0 0 0 0                        5 0 0 0 0 0
1 0 0 0 0 0                        1 0 0 0 0 0
2 0 0 0 0 0                        2 0 0 0 0 0
0 3 0 0 0 0                        0 0 0 0 0 0
0 4 0 0 0 0                        0 4 0 0 0 0
SPECIFICATION S                   SPECIFICATION S
0                                 0
5 0                               0 3
0 0 6                             0 0 6
0 0 0 7                           0 0 0 7
0 0 0 0 8                         0 0 0 0 8
0 0 0 0 0 9                       0 0 0 0 0 9
VALUE 1 S 1 1 S 2 2               VALUE 1 S 1 1 A 5 2
VALUE 1 F 1 3 F 2 4 F 3 5         VALUE 1 F 1 3 F 2 4 F 3 5
VALUE 1 F 4 6                     VALUE 1 F 4 6
END                               END
```

Note: Mx may give a warning on this problem, but should yield correct results: path a = .59, path b = .85, etc.

An example of path diagram input--AMOS

As mentioned earlier, the program AMOS, designed by James Arbuckle, pioneered a different method for the input of SEM problems: namely, to enter the path model directly. Using AMOS's array of drawing tools, one simply produces the equivalent of Fig. 2.5 or 2.6 on the computer screen, connects it to the correlation matrix or the raw data resident in a data file, and executes the problem. AMOS will supply you with output in the form of a copy of the input diagram with the solved-for path values placed alongside the arrows, or with more extensive tabulated output similar to that of typical SEM programs. The current version is 4.0 (Arbuckle & Wothke, 1999). AMOS can handle most standard SEM problems, and has a reputation for being user-friendly. It and Mx were the first structural modeling programs to utilize the Full Information Maximum Likelihood approach to handling missing data--to be discussed later in this chapter.

Some other programs for latent variable modeling

There is a growing list of programs that can do latent variable modeling. James Steiger's SEPATH (descended from an earlier EzPATH) features a simple path-based input and a number of attractive features. It is associated with the Statistica statistical package. A second program, Wolfgang Hartmann's CALIS, is part of the SAS statistical package. At the time of writing, it does not handle models in multiple groups; otherwise, it is a competent SEM program, and SAS users should find it convenient. It has an unusually broad range of forms in which it will accept input--including the specification of a RAM-type path diagram, matrices, and a structural equation mode similar to EQS's. A third program, Browne and Mel's RAMONA, is associated with the SYSTAT statistical package. It is based on the RAM model discussed earlier, and uses a simple path-based input. It does not yet handle models with means or models in multiple groups, but these are promised for the future.

Other SEM programs, perhaps less likely to be used by beginners in SEM, include Mplus, MECOSA, and COSAN. Bengt Muthén's versatile Mplus has several resemblances to LISREL, although it does not have a SIMPLIS-type input. One notable strength of Mplus is its versatility in handling categorical, ordinal, and truncated variables. (Some other SEM programs can do this to a degree--LISREL by means of a preliminary program called PRELIS.) In addition, Mplus has facilities for analyzing hierarchical models. Gerhard Arminger's MECOSA also covers a very broad range of models. It is based on the GAUSS programming language. An early, flexible program for structural equation modeling is Roderick McDonald's COSAN, which is available in a FORTRAN version (Fraser & McDonald, 1988). This is a matrix-based program, although the matrices are different from LISREL's. They are more akin to the McArdle-McDonald matrices described earlier. Logically, COSAN can be considered as an elaboration and specialization of the McArdle-McDonald model.

Any of these programs should be able to fit most of the latent variable models described in Chapters 2, 3, and 4 of this book, except that not all of them handle model fitting in multiple samples or to means.

Fit Functions

A variety of criteria have been used to indicate how closely the correlation or covariance matrix implied by a particular set of trial values conforms to the observed data, and thus to guide searches for best-fitting models. Four are fairly standard in SEM programs: ordinary least squares (OLS), generalized least squares (GLS), maximum likelihood (ML), and a version of Browne's asymptotically distribution-free criterion (ADF)--the last is called generally weighted least squares in LISREL and arbitrary distribution generalized least squares in EQS. Almost any SEM program will provide at least three of these criteria as options, and many provide all four.

Why four criteria? The presence of more than one places the user in the situation described in the proverb: A man with one watch always knows what time it is; a man with two watches never does. The answer is that the different criteria have different advantages and disadvantages, as we see shortly.

The various criteria, also known as *discrepancy functions*, can be considered as different ways of weighting the differences between corresponding elements of the observed and implied covariance matrices. In matrix terms, this may be expressed as:

$$(s - c)' \; W \; (s - c),$$

where **s** and **c** refer to the nonduplicated elements of the observed and implied covariance matrices **S** and **C** arranged as vectors. That is, the lower triangular elements $\begin{matrix} a \\ b\,c \\ d\,e\,f \end{matrix}$ of a 3 x 3 covariance matrix would become the 6-element vector $(a\,b\,c\,d\,e\,f)'$, and $(s - c)'$ would contain the differences between such elements of the observed and implied covariance matrices. **W** is a weight matrix, and different versions of it yield different criteria. If **W** is an identity matrix, the above expression reduces to $(s - c)'(s - c)$. This is just the sum of the squared differences between corresponding elements of the observed and implied matrices, an ordinary least squares criterion. If the matrices **S** and **C** are identical, the value of this expression will be zero. As **S** and **C** become more different, the squared differences between their elements will increase. The sum of these, call it F, is a discrepancy function--the larger F is, the worse the fit. An iterative model-fitting program will try to minimize F by seeking values for the unknowns which make the implied matrix **C** as much like the observed matrix **S** as possible. In general, an ordinary least squares criterion is most meaningful when the variables are measured on comparable scales. Otherwise, arbitrary differences in the scales of variables can markedly affect their contributions to F.

For ADF, the matrix **W** is based on the variances and covariances among the elements in **s**. If **s** were the 6-element vector of the previous example, **W** would be derived from the inverse of the 6 x 6 matrix of covariances among all possible pairs *aa, ab, ac,* etc., from **s**. The elements of the matrix to be inverted are obtained via the calculation $m_{ijkl} - s_{ij}s_{kl}$, where m_{ijkl} is a fourth-order moment, the mean product of the deviation scores of variables *i, j, k* and *l,* and s_{ij} and s_{kl} are the two covariances in question. This calculation is straightforward; however, as the original covariance matrix **S** gets larger, the vector **s** of its nonduplicated elements increases rapidly in length, and **W**, whose size is the square of that, can become a very large matrix whose storage, inversion, and application to calculations in an iterative procedure are quite demanding of computer resources. In addition, ADF requires very large samples for accuracy in estimating the fourth moments (say 5000 or more), and it tends to behave rather badly in more moderate-sized samples. Since there are other ways of addressing nonnormality, to be discussed shortly, we will not deal with ADF further in this chapter, although in working with very large samples one might still sometimes want to consider its use.

If the observed variables have a distribution that is multivariate normal, the general expression given above can be simplified to:

$$1/2 \ tr \ [(\mathbf{S} - \mathbf{C}) \ \mathbf{V}]^2,$$

where *tr* refers to the trace of a matrix (i.e., the sum of its diagonal elements), and **V** is another weight matrix. This expression involves matrices the size of the original covariance matrix, and hence is computationally more attractive. The choice of weight matrix **V** defines:

$\mathbf{V} = \mathbf{I}$ OLS, ordinary least squares
$\mathbf{V} = \mathbf{S}^{-1}$ GLS, generalized least squares
$\mathbf{V} = \mathbf{C}^{-1}$ ML, maximum likelihood

(The maximum likelihood criterion is typically defined in a different way, as ML = $\ln|\mathbf{C}| - \ln|\mathbf{S}| + tr\mathbf{S}\mathbf{C}^{-1} - m$, which involves the natural logarithms of the determinants of the **C** and **S** matrices, the trace of the product of **S** and $\mathbf{C}^{-1}$, and the number of variables, *m*. The two definitions are not identical, but it has been shown that when the model is correct the estimates that minimize the one also tend to minimize the other.)

In the case of ordinary least squares--as with the general version given earlier--the simplified expression above reduces to a function of the sum of squared differences between corresponding elements of the **S** and **C** matrices. The other criteria, GLS and ML, require successively more computation. GLS uses the inverse of the observed covariance matrix **S** as a weight matrix. This only needs to be obtained once, at the start of the iterative process, because the observed matrix doesn't change. However, the implied matrix **C** changes with each change in trial values, so $\mathbf{C}^{-1}$ needs to be recalculated many times during an iterative ML solution, making ML more computationally costly than GLS. However, with fast modern computers this difference will hardly be noticed on typical small to moderate SEM problems.

If the null hypothesis is true, the assumption of multivariate normality holds, and sample size is reasonably large, both GLS and ML criteria will yield an approximate chi square by the multiplication $(N - 1)F_{min}$, where F_{min} is the value of the discrepancy function at the point of best fit and N is the sample size. All these criteria have a minimum value of zero when the observed and implied matrices are the same (i.e., when $S = C$), and all become increasingly large as the difference between S and C becomes greater.

Table 2-9 illustrates the calculation of OLS, GLS, and ML criteria for two C matrices departing slightly from S in opposite directions. Note that all the goodness-of-fit criteria are small, reflecting the closeness of C to S, and that they are positive for either direction of departure from S. (OLS is on a different scale from the other two, so its size cannot be directly compared to theirs.)

Table 2-9 Sample calculation of OLS, GLS, and ML criteria for the departure of covariance matrices C_1 and C_2 from S

S	2.00	1.00		
	1.00	4.00		
S⁻¹	.5714286	-.1428571		
	-.1428571	.2857143		
	C_1		**C_2**	
C	2.00	1.00	2.00	1.00
	1.00	4.01	1.00	3.99
S - C	.00	.00	.00	.00
	.00	-.01	.00	.01
C⁻¹	.5712251	-.1424501	.5716332	-.1432665
	-.1424501	.2849003	-.1432665	.2865330
(S - C)S⁻¹	.0000000	.0000000	.0000000	.0000000
	.0014286	-.0028571	-.0014286	.0028571
(S - C)C⁻¹	.0000000	.0000000	.0000000	.0000000
	.0014245	-.0028490	-.0014327	.0028653
OLS	.00005000		.00005000	
GLS	.00000408		.00000408	
ML	.00000406		.00000411	

In this example, the ML and GLS criteria are very close in numerical value to each other; as we see later, this is by no means always the case.

Another message of Table 2-9 is that considerable numerical accuracy is required for calculations such as these--one more reason for letting computers do them. In this problem, a difference between **C** and **S** matrices in the second decimal place requires going to the sixth decimal place in the GLS and ML criteria in order to detect its effect. With only, say, 4- or 5-place accuracy in obtaining the inverses, quite misleading results would have been obtained.

Fit criteria serve two purposes in iterative model fitting. First, they guide the search for a best fitting solution. Second, they evaluate the solution when it is obtained. The criteria being considered have somewhat different relative merits for these two tasks.

For the first purpose, guiding a search, a criterion should ideally be cheap to compute, because the function is evaluated repeatedly at each step of a trial-and-error search. Furthermore, the criterion should be a dependable guide to relative distances in the search space, especially at points distant from a perfect fit. For the second purpose, evaluating a best fit solution, the statistical properties of the criterion are a very important consideration, computational cost is a minor issue, and the behavior of the function in remote regions of the search space is not in question.

In computational cost, ordinary least squares is the cheapest, GLS comes next, and then then ML. As we have seen, the latter two criteria have the advantage that when they are multiplied by N - 1 at the point of best fit they can yield a quantity that is approximately distributed as chi square, permitting statistical tests of goodness of fit in the manner described later in the chapter. These statistical properties depend on large samples. It is hard to say how large "large" is, because, as usual, things are not all-or-nothing--approximations gradually get worse as sample size decreases; there is no single value marking a sharp boundary between smooth sailing and disaster. As a rough rule of thumb, one would probably do well to be very modest in one's statistical claims if N is less than 100, and 200 is better.

Finally, the criteria differ in their ability to provide dependable distance measures, especially at points remote from the point of perfect fit. Let us consider an example of a case where ML gives an anomalous solution. The data are from Dwyer (1983, p. 258), and they represent the variance-covariance matrix for three versions of an item on a scale measuring authoritarian attitudes. The question Dwyer asked is whether the items satisfy a particular psychometric condition known as "tau-equivalence," which implies that they measure a single common factor for which they have equal weights, but possibly different residual variances, as shown in the path diagram of Fig. 2.7 (next page). It is thus a problem in four unknowns, *a, b, c,* and *d.* Such a model implies that the off-diagonal elements in **C** must all be equal, and so *a* should be assigned a compromise value to give a reasonable fit to the three covariances. The unknowns *b, c,* and *d* can then be given values to insure a perfect fit to the three observed values in the diagonal.

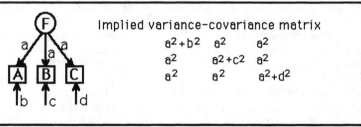

Fig. 2.7 Model of single common factor with equal loadings, plus different specifics ("tau-equivalent" tests).

    This is just what an iterative search program using an OLS criterion does, as shown in the lefthand column of Table 2-10 (Dwyer's observed covariance matrix is at the top of the table, designated **S**). A value of $\sqrt{5.58}$ is found for *a*, and values of $\sqrt{.55}$, $\sqrt{2.71}$, and $\sqrt{1.77}$ for *b*, *c*, and *d*, respectively, yielding the implied matrix $\mathbf{C}_{OLS}$. Dwyer used an ML criterion (with LISREL) and obtained a solution giving the implied matrix on the right in Table 2-10, labeled $\mathbf{C}_{ML}$. Notice that this matrix has equal off-diagonal values, as it must, but that the diagonal values are not at all good fits to the variances in **S**, as shown by the matrix **S-C**. The values of the ML criterion for the fit of the two **C** matrices to **S** are given at the bottom of the table. It is clear that the ML goodness-of-fit

Table 2-10 OLS and ML solutions for Fig. 2.7

S	6.13	6.12	4.78			
	6.12	8.29	5.85			
	4.78	5.85	7.35			
		$\mathbf{C}_{OLS}$			$\mathbf{C}_{ML}$	
C	6.13	5.58	5.58	6.46	5.66	5.66
	5.58	8.29	5.58	5.66	7.11	5.66
	5.58	5.58	7.35	5.66	5.66	8.46
S - C	.00	.54	-.80	-.33	.46	-.88
	.54	.00	.27	.46	1.18	.19
	-.80	.27	.00	-.88	.19	-1.11
ML		.32			.10	
OLS		1.00			2.39	

criterion for C_{ML} is substantially less than that for the solution on the left, which the eye and OLS judge to be superior.

Table 2-11 gives some further examples to illustrate that the criteria do not always agree on the extent to which one covariance matrix resembles another, and that ML and GLS can sometimes be rather erratic judges of distance when distances are not small. In each row of the table, two different **C** matrices are compared to the **S** matrix shown at the left. In each case, which **C** matrix would you judge to be most different from **S**? The OLS criterion (and most people's intuition) judges C_2 to be much further away from **S** than matrix C_1 is in all three examples. GLS agrees for the first two, but ML does not. The third example shows that the shoe is sometimes on the other foot. Here it is ML that agrees with OLS that C_2 is much more different, and it is GLS that does not.

This is not to say that GLS or ML will not give accurate assessments of fit when the fit is good, that is, when **C** and **S** are close to each other. Recall that in Table 2-9 (page 54) the OLS and GLS criteria agreed very well for **C**s differing only very slightly from the **S** of the first Table 2-11 example. But in the early stages of a search when **C** is still remote from **S**, or for problems like that of Table 2-10 where the best fit is not a very good fit, eccentric distance judgments can give trouble. After all, if a fitting program were to propose C_1 as an alternative to C_2 in the first row in Table 2-11, OLS and GLS would accept it as a dramatic improvement, but ML would reject it and stay with C_2.

None of this is meant to imply that searches using the ML or GLS criterion are bound to run into difficulties--in fact, studies reviewed in the next section suggest that ML in practice usually works quite well. I do, however, want to emphasize that uncritical acceptance of any solution a computer program happens to produce can be hazardous to one's scientific health. If in

Table 2-11 How different criteria evaluate the distance of two **C**s from **S**

S		C_1		C_2		GLS says C_1	C_2	ML says C_1	C_2
2	1	1	2	10	9				
1	4	2	5	9	10	.45	10.29	34.00	.86
5	0	5	3	10	-7				
0	5	3	4	-7	10	.38	2.96	3.00	.47
6	5	6	0	2	-1				
5	6	0	7	-1	1	5.80	.73	.59	404.00

doubt, one should try solutions from several starting points with two or three different criteria--if all converge on similar answers, one can then use the ML solution for its favorable statistical properties. If one has markedly non-normal data, one might consider one of the strategies to be described later in the chapter.

Monte Carlo studies of SEM

There have been many studies in which Monte Carlo evaluations have been made of the behavior of SEM programs, studies based on repeated random sampling from artificial populations with known characteristics. Studies by Boomsma (1982, 1985) and Anderson and Gerbing (1984; Gerbing & Anderson, 1985) are representative. These studies manipulated model characteristics and sample sizes and studied the effects on accuracy of estimation and the frequency of improper or nonconvergent solutions.

Anderson and Gerbing worked solely with confirmatory factor analysis models, and Boomsma largely did, so the results apply most directly to models of this kind. Both studies sampled from multivariate normal populations, so questions of the robustness of maximum likelihood to departures from multivariate normality were not addressed. For the most part, both studies used optimum starting values for the iteration, namely, the true population values; thus, the behavior of the maximum likelihood criterion in regions distant from the solution is not at issue. (In one part of Boomsma's study, alternative starting points were compared.)

Within these limitations, a variety of models and sample sizes were used in the two studies combined. The number of latent variables (factors) ranged from 2 to 4, and the correlations between them were .0, .3, or .5. The number of observed indicators per latent variable ranged from 2 to 4, and the sizes of nonzero factor pattern coefficients from .4 to .9, in various combinations. Sample sizes of 25, 50, 75, 100, 150, 200, 300, and 400 were employed.

The main tendencies of the results can be briefly summarized, although there were some complexities of detail for which the reader may wish to consult the original articles.

First, *convergence failures*. These occurred quite frequently with small samples and few indicators per factor. In fact, with samples of less than 100 cases and only two indicators per factor, such failures occurred on almost half the trials under some conditions (moderate loadings and low interfactor correlations). With three or more indicators per factor and 150 or more cases, failures of convergence rarely occurred.

Second, *improper solutions* (negative estimates of residual variance-- so-called "Heywood cases"). Again, with samples of less than 100 and only two indicators per factor, these cases were very common. With three or more indicators per factor and sample sizes of 200 or more, they were pretty much eliminated.

Third, *accuracy*. With smaller samples, naturally, estimates of the population values were less precise--that is, there was more sample-to-sample variation in repeated sampling under a given condition. However, with some exceptions for the very smallest sample sizes (25 and 50 cases), the standard error estimates provided by the SEM program (LISREL) appeared to be dependable--that is, a 95% confidence interval included the population value somewhere near 95% of the time.

Finally, *starting points*. As mentioned, in part of Boomsma's study the effect of using alternative starting values was investigated. This aspect of the study was confined to otherwise favorable conditions--samples of 100 or more cases with three or more indicators per factor--and the departures from the ideal starting values were not very drastic. Under these circumstances, the solutions usually converged, and when they did it was nearly always to essentially identical final values; differences were mostly in the third decimal place or beyond.

Many studies of a similar nature have been carried out. Hoogland and Boomsma (1998) review 34 Monte Carlo studies investigating the effects of sample size, departures from normality, and model characteristics on the results of structural equation modeling. Most, but not all of the studies involved simple confirmatory factor analysis models; a few included structural models as well. Most studies employed a maximum likelihood criterion, but a generalized least squares criterion often gave fairly similar results.

If distributions were in fact close to multivariate normal, sample sizes of 100 were sufficient to yield reasonably accurate model rejection, although larger samples, say 200 or more, were often required for accurate parameter estimates and standard errors. This varied with the size and characteristics of the model: samples of 400 or larger were sometimes needed for accurate results, and in general, larger samples yielded more precision.

With variables that were categorical rather than continuous, or with skewed or kurtotic distributions, larger sample sizes were needed for comparable accuracy. As a rough rule of thumb, one might wish to double the figures given in the preceding paragraph if several of one's variables are expressed in terms of a small number of discrete categories or otherwise depart from normality. Some alternative strategies for dealing with nonnormal distributions are discussed in the next section. In any event, structural equation modeling should not be considered a small-sample technique.

Dealing with nonnormal distributions

If one appears to have distinctly nonnormal data, there are several strategies available. First, and most obviously, one should check for outliers--extreme cases that represent errors of recording or entering data, or individuals that clearly don't belong in the population sampled. Someone whose age is listed as 210 years is probably a misrecorded 21-year-old. Outliers often have an inordinate influence on correlations, and on measures of skewness or kurtosis. Several SEM programs, as well as the standard regression programs in statistical packages such as SAS or SPSS, contain diagnostic aids that can be useful in detecting multivariate outliers, i.e., cases that have unusual combinations of values. In a population of women, sixty-year-old women or pregnant women may not be unusual, but sixty-year-old pregnant women should be nonexistent.

A second option, if one has some variables that are individually skewed, is to transform them to a scale that is more nearly normal, such as logarithms or square roots of the original scores. This is not guaranteed to produce multivariate normality, but it often helps, and may serve to linearize relationships between variables as well. One should always think about the interpretive implications of such a transformation before undertaking it. Log number of criminal acts is likely to be more nearly normally distributed than raw number of criminal acts, but numerically it will be less intelligible. However, if one believes that the difference between 2 and 4 criminal acts is in some sense comparable to the difference between 10 and 20 such acts in its psychological or sociological implications, then a logarithmic transformation may be sensible.

A third option is to make use of a *bootstrap* procedure. A number of SEM programs include facilities for doing this. The bootstrap is based on a simple and ingenious idea: to take repeated samples from one's own data, taken as representative of the population distribution, to see how much empirical variation there is in the results. Instead of calculating (say) the standard error of a given path value based on assumed multivariate normality, one simply has the computer fit the model several hundred times in different samples derived from the observations. One then takes the standard deviation of these estimates as an empirical standard error--one that reflects the actual distribution of the observations, not the possibly hazardous assumption that the true distribution is multivariate normal. In practice, if one's data contains *n* cases, one selects samples of size *n* from them *without ever actually removing any cases.* Thus each bootstrap sample will contain a different selection from the original cases, some appearing more than once, and others not at all. It may be helpful to look at this as if one were drawing repeated samples in the ordinary way from a population that consists of the original sample repeated an indefinitely large number of times. Because it is assumed that the sample distribution, whatever it is, is a reasonably good indicator of the population distribution, bootstrapping of this kind should not be undertaken with very small samples, whose distribution may depart by chance quite drastically from that of the population. With fair-sized samples, however, bootstrapping can provide an attractive way of dealing with nonnormal distributions.

Still other approaches to nonnormality, via several rescaled and robust statistics, show promise and are available in some SEM programs. (See the Notes to this chapter.)

Hierarchical χ^2 Tests

As noted earlier, for GLS or ML one can multiply the criterion at the point of best fit by N - 1 to obtain an approximate χ^2 in large samples. (Some programs provide a χ^2 for OLS as well, but it is obtained by a different method.) The χ^2 can be used to test the fit of the implied **C** to **S**. The degrees of freedom for the comparison are the number of independent values in **S** less the number of unknowns used in generating **C**.

For example, in the problem of tau-equivalence discussed earlier in the chapter (Fig. 2.7 on page 56), there were m $(m + 1)/2 = 6$ independent values in **S** (the three variances in the diagonal and the three covariances on one side of it). There were four unknowns being estimated, a, b, c, and d. So there are two degrees of freedom for a χ^2 test. The minimum value of the ML criterion was .10 (Table 2-10). As it happens, the data were gathered from 109 subjects, so $\chi^2 =$ 108 x .10 = 10.8. From a χ^2 table (see Appendix G), the χ^2 with 2 df required to reject the null hypothesis at the .05 level is 5.99. The obtained χ^2 of 10.8 is larger than this, so we would reject the null hypothesis and conclude that the model of tau-equivalence did not fit these data; that is, that the difference between **C** and **S** is too great to be likely to result from sampling error.

Notice that the χ^2 test is used to conclude that a particular model *does not* fit the data. Suppose that χ^2 in the preceding example had been less than 5.99; what could we then have concluded? We could not conclude that the model is correct, but merely that our test had not shown it to be incorrect. How impressive this statement is depends very much on how powerful a test we have applied. By using a sufficiently small sample, for instance, we could fail to reject models that are grossly discrepant from the data. On the other hand, if our sample is extremely large, a failure to reject the model would imply a near-exact fit between **C** and **S**. Indeed, with very large samples we run into the opposite embarrassment, in that we may obtain highly significant χ^2s and hence reject models in cases where the discrepancies between model and data, although presumably real, are not large enough to be of any practical concern. It is prudent always to examine the residuals **S** - **C**, in addition to carrying out a χ^2 test, before coming to a conclusion about the fit of a model.

It is also prudent to look at alternative models. The fact that one model fits the data reasonably well does not mean that there could not be other, different models that fit better. At best, a given model represents a tentative explanation of the data. The confidence with which one accepts such an explanation depends, in part, on whether other, rival explanations have been tested and found wanting.

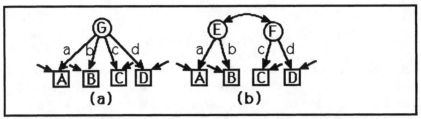

Fig. 2.8 Path models for the χ^2 comparisons of Table 2-12.

Figure 2.8 and Table 2-12 provide an example of testing two models for fit to an observed set of intercorrelations among four observed variables A, B, C, and D. Model (a) is a Spearmanian model with a single general factor, G. Model (b) has two correlated common factors, E and F. In both models, each observed variable has a residual, as indicated by the short unlabeled arrows.

A hypothetical matrix of observed correlations is given as **S** at the top of Table 2-12. Fits to the data, using an iterative solution with a maximum likelihood criterion, are shown for each of the Fig. 2.8 models. If we assume that the correlations in **S** are based on 120 subjects, what do we conclude? As the individual χ^2s for the two models indicate, we can reject neither. The correlation matrix **S** could represent the kind of chance fluctuation to be expected in random samples of 120 cases drawn from populations where the true underlying situation was that described by either model (a) or model (b).

Suppose that the correlations had instead been based on 240 subjects. Now what conclusions would be drawn? In this case, we could reject model (a) because its χ^2 exceeds the 5.99 required to reject the null hypothesis at the .05 level with 2 df. Model (b), however, remains a plausible fit to the data.

Does this mean that we can conclude that model (b) fits significantly better than model (a)? Not as such--the fact that one result is significant and another is nonsignificant is *not* the same as demonstrating that there is a significant difference between the two, although, regrettably, one sees this error made fairly often. (If you have any lingering doubts about this, consider the case where one result is just a hairsbreadth below the .05 level and the other just a hairsbreadth above--one result is nominally significant and the other not, but the difference between the two is of a sort that could very easily have arisen by chance.) There is, however, a direct comparison that can be made in the case of Table 2-12 because the two models stand in a *nested*, or hierarchical, relationship. That is, the model with the smaller number of free variables can be obtained from the model with the larger number of free variables by fixing one or more of the latter. In this case, model (a) can be obtained from model (b) by fixing the value of the interfactor correlation *e* at 1.00--if E and F are standardized and perfectly correlated, they can be replaced by a single G. Two such nested models can be compared by a χ^2 test: The χ^2 for this test is just the

Table 2-12 Comparing two models with χ^2

S	1.00	.30	.20	.10
	.30	1.00	.20	.20
	.20	.20	1.00	.30
	.10	.20	.30	1.00

	model (a)	(b)	difference
χ^2, N = 120	4.64	.75	3.89
χ^2, N = 240	9.31	1.51	7.80
df	2	1	1
$\chi^2_{.05}$	5.99	3.84	3.84

difference between the separate χ^2 s of the two models, and the df is just the difference between their dfs (which is equivalent to the number of parameters fixed in going from the one to the other).

In the example of Table 2-12, the difference between the two models turns out in fact to be statistically significant, as shown in the rightmost column at the bottom of the table. Interestingly, this is true for either sample size. In this case, with N = 120 either model represents an acceptable explanation of the data, but model (b) provides a significantly better one than does model (a).

Chi-square difference tests between nested models play a very important role in structural equation modeling. In later chapters we will encounter a number of cases like that of Table 2-12, in which two models each fit acceptably to the data, but one fits significantly better than the other. Moreover, where two nested models differ by the addition or removal of just one path, the chi-square difference test becomes a test of the significance of that path. In some ways, a chi-square difference test is more informative than an overall chi-square test of a model because it is better focused. If a model fails an overall chi-square test, it is usually not immediately obvious where the difficulty lies. If a chi-square difference test involving one or two paths is significant, the source of the problem is much more clearly localized.

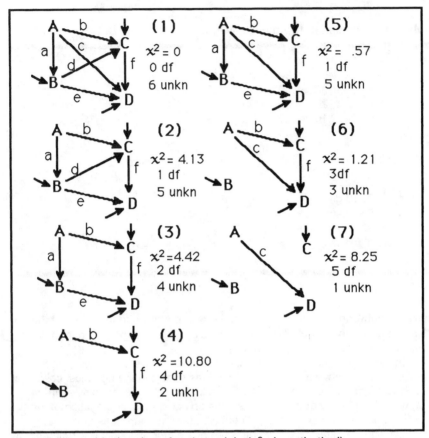

Fig. 2.9 Hierarchical series of path models (χ^2s hypothetical).

Figure 2.9 further illustrates the notion of nested models. Models 1, 2, 3, and 4 represent such a hierarchical series because 2 can be obtained from 1 by setting path *c* to the fixed value of zero, 3 from 2 by similarly fixing *d*, and 4 from 3 by fixing *a* and *e* to zero. Obviously, in such a series any lower model can be obtained from any higher one by fixing paths--e.g., model 4 can be obtained from model 1 by setting paths *a, c, d,* and *e* to zero. Thus tests based on differences in χ^2 can be used to compare the fit of any two models in such a nested series. In the last described case such a test would have four degrees of freedom, corresponding to the four paths fixed in going from model 1 to model 4.

However, models 5, 6, and 7 in Fig. 2.9, while hierarchically related to model 1 and each other, are not in the same series as 2, 3, and 4. Thus, model 6 could not be compared with model 3 by taking the difference in their respective χ^2s. Although model 6 has fewer paths than model 3, they are not included within those of model 3--model 6 has path c as an unknown to be solved for, whereas model 3 does not. Assuming that the four variables A, B, C, and D are all measured, model 1 is a case with $m (m - 1)/2 = 6$ observed correlations and 6 unknowns to be solved for. A perfect fit will in general be achievable, χ^2 will be 0, and there will be 0 df. Obviously, such a model can never be rejected, but then, because it can be guaranteed to fit perfectly, its fit provides no special indication of its merit. The other models in Fig. 2.9 do have degrees of freedom and hence can potentially be rejected. Notice that the direct χ^2 tests of these models can be considered as special cases of the χ^2 test of differences between nested models because they are equivalent to the test of differences between these models and model 1.

Table 2-13 gives some examples of nested χ^2 tests based on the models of Fig. 2.9. The test in the first line of the table, comparing models 2 and 1, can be considered to be a test of the significance of path c. Does constraining path c to be zero significantly worsen the fit to the data? The answer, based on $\chi^2 = 4.13$ with 1 df, is yes. Path c makes a difference; the model fits significantly better with it included. Another test of the significance of a single path is provided in line 6 of the table, model 5 versus model 1. Here it is a test of the path d. In this case, the data do not demonstrate that path d makes a significant contribution: $\chi^2 = .57$ with 1 df, not significant. A comparison of model 3 with model 1 (line 2) is an interesting case. Model 2, remember, did differ significantly from model 1. But model 3, with one less unknown, cannot be judged significantly worse than model 1 ($\chi^2 = 4.42$, 2df, NS). This mildly paradoxical situation arises occasionally in such χ^2 comparisons. It occurs because the increase in χ^2 in going from model 2 to model 3 is more than offset

Table 2-13 Some χ^2 tests for hierarchical model comparisons of Fig. 2.9

	Model comparison	χ^2 1st	χ^2 2nd	df 1st	df 2nd	χ^2_{diff}	df_{diff}	p
1.	2 vs 1	4.13	0	1	0	4.13	1	<.05
2.	3 vs 1	4.42	0	2	0	4.42	2	NS
3.	3 vs 2	4.42	4.13	2	1	.29	1	NS
4.	4 vs 3	10.80	4.42	4	2	6.38	2	<.05
5.	4 vs 1	10.80	0	4	0	10.80	4	<.05
6.	5 vs 1	.57	0	1	0	.57	1	NS
7.	6 vs 1	1.21	0	3	0	1.21	3	NS
8.	7 vs 6	8.25	1.21	5	3	7.04	2	<.05

by the increase in degrees of freedom. Thus whereas the additional restriction on model 3 caused by setting path *d* to zero makes it fit worse than model 2 in an absolute sense, relative to the degrees of freedom one is less confident that the difference from model 1 is real.

Eliminating paths *a* and *e* in addition to *d* and *c* (model 4) is clearly going too far, whether the comparison is made with the full model (line 5), or with a model with *c* and *d* removed (line 4). However, if *c* is present *a* and *e* can be dispensed with--or at any rate, they cannot be demonstrated to be essential (line 7). Nevertheless, as line 8 indicates, *c* alone cannot do the job--deleting *b* and *f* leads to a significant worsening of fit ($\chi^2 = 7.04$, 2 df, p < .05).

Figure 2.9 also illustrates that the fact that a given model cannot be rejected does not mean that one should conclude that it represents the truth. Consider model 3. One cannot reject it as a plausible explanation of the data ($\chi^2 = 4.42$, 2 df, p > .10--line 2). But this does not mean that other models might not do at least as well. Indeed, we have one in model 6 that with fewer parameters actually achieves a smaller χ^2. To be sure, we cannot carry out a direct statistical test of the relative goodness of fit of models 3 and 6 because they are not nested, but one would hardly wish to cheer very loudly about model 3 if one were aware that model 6 was lurking in the wings. The moral is that it pays to do some exploring of alternative models before going too far out on a limb on the basis of a significance test of any one. Otherwise, one risks the embarrassment of an unsuspected model 6 turning up.

This is not an empty threat. As we see later, in SEM analyses it is very frequently the case that there are alternative models out there, often many of them, that fit the data as well as does the particular model under consideration.

Standard errors

Model-fitting programs usually provide approximate standard errors for path and variance estimates, either routinely or on request. This saves having to carry out χ^2 difference tests to assess the significance of individual paths, a fact that is particularly helpful if one is scanning a large model with a view to dropping a number of possibly superfluous paths. A single χ^2 difference test can then be carried out to see if the selected paths are jointly dispensible. (In EQS, a test called the Wald test is available for this.)

If one is revising models one is in an exploratory mode; therefore the reported standard errors should be treated as guidelines, not as a serious basis for the assignment of probability values. If many tests are being made, some may well be "significant" merely by chance. Nor should one feel compelled to drop every path that is nonsignificant, especially when the sample size is small. With small samples, a path that is numerically appreciable may not exceed twice its standard error; yet its removal may materially affect the solution. If the path was theoretically justified in the first place, it is often wiser to leave it in the model until cross-validation confirms that it is trivial and can safely be dropped.

Descriptive Criteria of Model Fits

A χ^2 test provides a useful basis for making decisions about the fit of a model, or the relative fits of different models. Moreover, for reasonable sample sizes, a χ^2 roughly equal to its degrees of freedom is an instant definition of satisfactory fit. A glance at Appendix G will show that $\chi^2 \approx$ df means $p \approx .50$, for df not too small (and even for small df, $p > .30$). Nevertheless, χ^2 has limitations as a descriptive index of model fit.

For one thing, χ^2 is sensitive to sample size. With large enough samples, substantively trivial discrepancies can lead to rejection of an otherwise highly satisfactory model; with small enough samples, χ^2 can be nonsignificant even in the face of gross misfits. As a consequence, a variety of proposals have been made as to how one might derive an index, perhaps on a scale of 0 to 1, that would describe how well, in a metric rather than in a null-hypothesis sense, a given model fits the data.

The various overall fit indices that have been proposed tend to fall into two categories: those that simply describe goodness of fit, and those that involve considerations of parsimony--i.e., that take into account the number of unknowns used to achieve that fit. A model reaching a particular level of fit while solving for fewer free parameters would show as superior on an index of the latter kind.

Fit indices differ in other ways as well. Some are *normed* to fall in the range 0 to 1, others are not. Some describe fit directly, and others describe fit relative to a *baseline model* (sometimes called a *null model*)--i.e., some simple model that any reasonable model should be able to improve on. These indices are often referred to as *incremental fit indices*, because they assess improvements in fit. A typical baseline against which improvement is assessed is that the observed variables are uncorrelated. A perennial problem with fit indices using baseline models is that a mediocre fit can be made to appear a good one by choosing a baseline that is bad enough. For example, if many high correlations are built into a measurement model by using a large number of nearly-synonymous indicators of its latent variables, the model will fit vastly better than a null model which assumes zero correlations among the indicators --almost irrespective of the fit of its structural part.

A more recent distinction is between *sample-based* and *population-based* fit indices. The former describes how well the model fits in the present sample. The latter estimates how well it would fit in the population. The latter approach recognizes that no model should be expected to fit exactly in the population--that all models represent simplifications of reality. This means that the lack of fit of any particular model to sample data can conceptually be broken into two parts--that due to the *error of approximation* of the population data by the model, and that due to the *error of estimation* in sampling. The former is independent of sample size, the latter is not, decreasing as sample size increases. Population-based indices are based on estimates of the error of approximation. Normally, an estimate of how well the model can account for variation in the population is of more interest than how well it fits in the sample. Population-based indices make use of a distribution called "noncentral χ^2," which is the distribution that the minimized fitting function follows when a model fits only approximately in the population. This distribution is characterized by a quantity called the noncentrality parameter, which depends on the degree of misfit. The noncentrality parameter can be estimated by the best-fit χ^2 minus its degrees of freedom. If χ^2 is less than df, as can happen by chance with close model fits or in small samples, the noncentrality parameter is taken as zero--that is, the noncentral χ^2 distribution becomes the ordinary χ^2 distribution.

The fact that different investigators have considered the various factors mentioned to be of different importance has led to a large number of proposed goodness-of-fit indices, even though virtually all of them are derived in one way or another from the value of the fitting function F at the point of best fit--or N - 1 times that value, χ^2. Remember that F is the quantity that the model-fitting program works to minimize, the value that describes how close the implied covariance or correlation matrix is to the observed matrix. A fit index based on F (or, equivalently, χ^2) represents an estimate of how well the program has succeeded in this effort. A number of these indices are described and compared briefly in Appendix D. We focus here on one, a population index based on noncentral χ^2 that has a number of virtues and is coming into increasingly widespread use among latent variable modelers. This is the Root Mean Square Error of Approximation, or RMSEA.

A population-based index of fit: RMSEA

The Root Mean Square Error of Approximation (RMSEA) is a population-based index, which means that it is relatively insensitive to sample size. It has an explicit parsimony adjustment, does not require specification of a baseline model, and one can obtain confidence intervals for it or use it to carry out statistical tests.

If we rescale the noncentrality parameter, χ^2 - df, by dividing it by N - 1, we obtain a quantity *d* which we can use to define RMSEA:

$$\text{RMSEA} = \sqrt{(d/df)}.$$

Thus if a χ^2 of 15.00 were obtained with 8 df in a sample of 201 cases, the rescaled noncentrality parameter *d* would be (15 - 8)/200, or .035, and RMSEA would be $\sqrt{(.035/8)}$, or .066.

Thus RMSEA is based on the ratio of the rescaled noncentrality parameter to the model's degrees of freedom. It is zero when the noncentrality parameter is zero, and for a given positive value is lower if the model involves fewer free parameters (i.e., has more df). Browne and Cudeck have suggested the following guidelines for interpreting RMSEAs: "Practical experience has made us feel that a value of the RMSEA of about .05 or less would indicate a close fit of the model in relation to the degrees of freedom . . . . We are also of the opinion that a value of .08 or less for the RMSEA would indicate a reasonable error of approximation and would not want to employ a model with a RMSEA greater than .1" (1993, p. 144). Its originator, Steiger, considers values below .10 "good" and below .05 "very good" (1989, p. 81).

It is possible to obtain confidence limits for RMSEA via the noncentral χ^2 distribution, and typical SEM programs will provide these. The 90% confidence interval in the preceding example goes from .00 to .11. Thus, although the best estimate from our data is that the fit of this model is reasonably good in the population, this is an estimate subject to a fair amount of uncertainty--the actual fit in the population might plausibly be anywhere from perfect to less-than-acceptable.

Later in the chapter, we consider the use of RMSEA in evaluating the power of a test in SEM.

Finally, the confidence interval of RMSEA can be used to test a null hypothesis of *poor* fit. If the upper limit of the 90% confidence interval lies below whatever cutoff one has selected as marking unacceptable fit--say .10--one can reject the hypothesis that the fit of the model in the population is that or worse. In other words, one can conclude at the specified level of confidence that the present model fits acceptably in the population. Clearly, this is a more meaningful conclusion for most applications of SEM than the one from the usual χ^2 test of fit, which is that an exact fit can't be ruled out. Moreover, this approach has the advantage of not tempting the user to draw positive conclusions from a failure to reject a null hypothesis (or, worse yet, to hold down the sample size to encourage this result). By stating the null hypothesis in terms of poor fit, so that its rejection leads to the positive substantive conclusion, the use of large samples and other good scientific behavior is encouraged.

Thus RMSEA is a goodness-of-fit index with a number of scientific merits. However, neither RMSEA nor any of the other similar indices is immune to statistical problems stemming from nonnormality, too-small samples, or the like. The presence of conditions such as these should lead any goodness-of-fit index to be interpreted with caution. If data are decidedly not normal, approaches such as the normalizing transformations or bootstrap evaluations mentioned earlier in this chapter may be worth considering.

Examination of residuals

Goodness-of-fit indices should not blind us to a way of evaluating the fit of a model that can always be employed, and nearly always should be--the direct inspection of the residuals **S - C**. Not only does the smallness of these residuals give an absolute sense of the goodness of the fit, but the location of the larger residuals can suggest which aspects of the data are least well captured by the model. Model-fitting programs typically provide such residual matrices either routinely or on request. Residuals from analyzing correlation matrices are relatively easy to evaluate, since all variables are on comparable scales. Those from analyzing covariance matrices, especially if the variables are on quite different scales, can be harder to interpret, but most programs can provide some form of standardized residuals to facilitate comparisons across variables on different scales. Most can also supply an overall average of the size of residuals, such as the SRMR (standardized root mean residual). Hu and Bentler (1999) suggest using a double criterion to evaluate goodness of fit: first, that a goodness-of-fit index, such as RMSEA, indicates a satisfactory fit, and second, that an average of the residuals, such as SRMR, is small. (A combination of RMSEA of .06 with SRMR of .08 worked well in their study.)

In addition, an informed user will not stop with evaluating overall model fit. Any goodness-of-fit index is a kind of average for the model as a whole, and a moderately good overall fit might result from an excellent fit for relatively unimportant parts of the model offsetting a serious misfit at one or more theoretically crucial points. Examination of the residuals may be helpful here. In addition, the parameter estimates themselves should always be scrutinized to be sure they all make sense--an excellent fit that requires bizarre parameter values to produce it is hardly cause for much rejoicing, although it may sometimes provide clues toward a better model.

The Power to Reject an Incorrect Model

When fitting models using a chi-square criterion, large samples are desirable for statistical accuracy. Perhaps an even more important reason for using large samples is statistical power--to have a good chance of rejecting a model if it is wrong. If the acceptance of a model is to have any real meaning, there must have been a reasonable chance of rejecting it if it were false. The sample size one needs in order to reject an incorrect model depends on several things, including the nature of the misspecification involved and how confident one wants to be of detecting it.

Generally speaking, the power of a test of a hypothesis is the probability that one will reject it if it is false. To determine the power of a test in model fitting requires four things:

1. A model.
2. An alternative to the model that one would want to be able to discriminate from it.
3. The desired level of significance.
4. The sample size, N.

We will consider two situations in which we might wish to evaluate power, one in which the alternative to the model is specified in terms of some

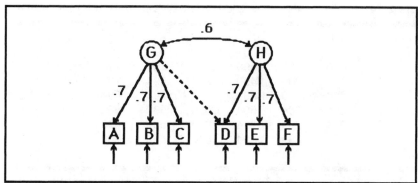

Fig 2.10 Simple factor analysis model for power example. Dashed arrow--additional path to be detected.

particular variation on the model, such as an extra path, that we would like to have a good probability of detecting, the other in which the alternative is expressed as a given level of the root mean square error of approximation (RMSEA) discussed in the preceding section. In the first situation, we will distinguish two cases. In both we will assume that a particular extra path is present. However, in one we will assess our chances of detecting that path when we are testing specifically for it, and in the other our chances of detecting it when fitting an overall model.

Power to detect an added path

Consider the simple factor analysis model shown in Fig. 2.10. What is our power to reject the basic model in favor of one with an added path indicated by the dashed line, assuming a .05 significance level and a sample size N = 500?

To begin with, we need to assume a specific value for the added path--its detection will be relatively easy if it is large, because then it will have a substantial effect on the correlations, and difficult if it is small, because then it will not. We can estimate the power for any specified value of the path: let us use .30 as an example. Now the procedure requires three steps (Satorra & Saris, 1985):

1. Obtain the implied covariance or correlation matrix *under the alternative hypothesis*, i.e., with the extra path included. This matrix is shown below the diagonal in Table 2-14 (next page). It can be obtained either directly from Fig. 2.10 via the path rules, or by specifying the model to the model-fitting program with all paths fixed to the desired values.

2. Use this obtained matrix as input to a model-fitting run *using the original model*, i.e., without the added path, and obtain the value of chi square. This will be an approximation to a noncentral chi square. In the example, this comes out to be 14.93, with 8 degrees of freedom.

Table 2-14. Implied correlations under alternative models in power example

	A	B	C	D	E	F
A	1.000	.490	.490	.364	.294	.294
B	.490	1.000	.490	.364	.294	.294
C	.490	.490	1.000	.364	.294	.294
D	.504	.504	.504	1.000	.532	.532
E	.294	.294	.294	.616	1.000	.490
F	.294	.294	.294	.616	.490	1.000

Note: The implied correlations for the model of Fig. 2.10 with extra path of .30 are shown below the diagonal; with path of .10, above the diagonal.

3. Consult a table of noncentral chi square to obtain the desired estimate of power. A condensed version of such a table is given as Appendix H, which gives for various dfs the noncentral chi square required for various levels of power. The df to be used in this step depends on the particular case being considered. If we are asking what our chance is of detecting this particular path when we are testing specifically for it, a difference chi square with a single df is involved, and we look across the first row of the table.

Our power in this case turns out to be excellent--we have somewhere between a 90% and a 99% probability of rejecting the original model at the .05 level if the path is present.

Suppose, however, that we are in the situation where we would like to be able to detect the effect produced by such an extra path, but without knowing in advance exactly which path it will be. Now the overall df for a test of the model is the appropriate one to use. This is the df provided by the program in step 2 above.

Looking across the row df = 8 in the power table for a value close to 14.93, we find that the power is approximately .80. That is, there is about an 80% chance that if the true model contains the dotted path with a value of .30, we would reject the originally proposed model.

Suppose that in this situation we had wished to detect a smaller departure from the original model, say an added path of .10 instead of .30. The implied matrix for this case is shown above the diagonal in Table 2-14. Step 2 now yields a chi square of 1.95, still with 8 df, and consultation of the noncentral chi square table shows that the power is well below .50--that is, the odds would be against our being able to detect a misspecification of this magnitude, using an N of 500. How large a sample would be needed to raise our power to .80, a level which has been suggested as a desirable minimum (Cohen, 1977)? The chi square in step 2 increases roughly proportionately with N--it is N - 1 times the minimum value of the fitting function, which is constant for a given model and covariance matrix. Dividing the chi square of 15.03 required for a power of

.80 by the obtained 1.95 yields a factor of 7.7--that is, we would need a sample size of about 7.7 x 500 or 3850 to do the job. For the test of a single path known a priori, the required chi square for a power of .80 is 7.85, and the sample size needed is approximately (7.85/1.95) x 500 = 2013.

How does one obtain values for the paths to include in the original and alternative models? In planning a study, one simply chooses plausible values based on one's knowledge of prior research in the area--if in doubt, several possibilities may be tried. In evaluating an existing study, the path values from the original study can be used, along with an additional path or paths, to obtain the implied matrix.

Overall power to reject a model

By the preceding approach, one assesses the power of a model by evaluating effects for a few typical or theoretically critical paths. Alternatively, an overall assessment of power may be made via RMSEA and the test of poor fit described earlier. Again one must specify a null and an alternate hypothesis-- let us take .10 as the lower boundary of the "poor fit" range, and .05 as the upper boundary of "good fit." Then the question is: If the fit is actually good in the population (RMSEA $\leq$ .05), do we have a high probability with our sample size of being able to reject the hypothesis that it is bad (RMSEA $\geq$ .10)?

A table of power values and required sample sizes for this situation is given in Appendix I. The lefthand part of the table contains power values for various combinations of sample size and degrees of freedom; the righthand columns give the minimum sample sizes required to achieve powers of .80 and .90. It is evident from the table that with a sample of 100 cases and few df one doesn't have much power--with 20 df or less and N = 100 the odds are worse than 50-50 that the data will rule out a poor fit (RMSEA of .10) even if the model fits adequately in the population (RMSEA of .05). With 1 or 2 df, sample sizes in the thousands are required for 80% power. With 20 or more df, samples in the 200-100 range have acceptable power. With large numbers of degrees of freedom, even samples below 100 may provide adequate power; however, with samples under 100 one begins to worry about other statistical difficulties.

Power calculations with latent variable models, as in other research designs, are frequently sobering. Nevertheless, as with other research designs, the estimation of power should routinely be a part of the planning of an SEM study. Power calculations may also be useful in evaluating the claims of existing studies in the literature. If a given study had very little chance of rejecting substantively important departures from the accepted model, this should be taken into account in assessing the author's conclusions.

Identification

In Chapter 1 we encountered the distinction between underdetermined, just-determined, and overdetermined models, and indicated that underdetermined models have no unique solution, and overdetermined models are generally desirable. How does one determine in practice that a model is not underdetermined--or in the language of structural modelers, that it is *identified*?

The simplest test is to count the unknown parameters to be solved for, to make sure that they do not exceed the number of observed values to be fitted. The latter is the number of unduplicated variances and covariances in the covariance matrix, which is $p(p + 1)/2$, for p observed variables. Thus if one is fitting a five-variable covariance matrix (= 15 data points) and a count of the model yields 16 parameters to be solved, one need go no further--the solution will be underdetermined.

The converse is not true, unfortunately--a model can pass this test and still be unidentified. For one thing, a complex model may be overdetermined in one part and underdetermined somewhere else, which means, of course, that the model as a whole is not identified. For another, even a model that appears to be adequately identified may not be so for certain values of its unknown parameters--this is referred to as *empirical underidentification.* To take a simple example, the two-factor model from Fig. 2.5, repeated for convenience as Fig. 2.11, has 10 observations and 9 unknowns and is in general solvable--but it will not be if the correlation e between latent variables turns out to be zero, because then the model will in effect break apart into two two-variable single-factor problems, neither with a unique solution (any product of a and b that equals r_{AB} will fit the data, and similarly for c and d).

How can we be sure that neither of these sorts of things has happened to us? One fairly simple test is to run the model with two different sets of start values. If it arrives at two solutions that are identical in chi square, but have different values for one or more parameters, you are quite likely dealing with an underidentified model. Another test is to take the final implied matrix and input it

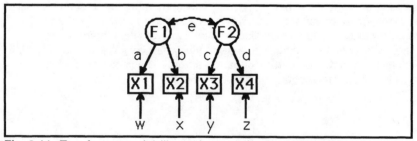

Fig. 2.11 Two-factor model illustrating empirical underidentification.

to the program as an observed matrix, and see if you get the same parameter estimates again. In addition, a number of SEM programs provide warnings of possible underidentification based on the behavior of a matrix used in the fitting process.

As is often true in life, prevention is better than cure. The most common sources of identification problems are (1) too few indicators for one or more of the latent variables in the model, (2) the presence of such features as reciprocal paths, feedback loops, and correlated residuals, and (3) mistakes--such as neglecting to fix the scale of a latent variable. As to (1), if you always have four or more indicators per latent variable, which is a good idea anyway, you should rarely be in trouble. A case to watch out for is a latent variable measured by a single indicator. Sometimes, for example with a variable like sex or age, this is a perfectly reasonable thing to do, but in most such cases it is necessary to assign the error variance of such a variable a fixed value--zero if perfect reliability is assumed, or one minus the reliability if it is not (multiplied by the variance of the variable, if unstandardized). As to (2), features like these are sometimes of central theoretical interest, and if so, they should be included in the model. But modelers who toss them in with too much abandon can expect pretty often to have to deal with identification problems. Finally, (3), mistakes. Well, they will get made. One thing always to check if it appears that you may have a problem with identification is that the model you have actually specified is the model you intended to run. Another is to check that each latent variable has its scale determined by fixing either its variance or a path to an observed variable (if your SEM program doesn't handle this automatically).

Matters concerning model identification have received a good deal of attention from SEM specialists, and the discussions can sometimes get quite technical. For most SEM practitioners, most of the time, identification problems, if they arise at all, can be dealt with fairly readily. However, if your modeling frequently involves the kinds of features described under (2) above, you may find helpful an article by Rigdon (1995), which describes how to break down SEM models to locate the sources of identification difficulties due to feedback loops, correlated residuals, and the like. Although correlated errors are often a source of identification problems, they aren't always. Brito and Pearl (2002) provide a simple rule that holds for path diagrams without loops: So long as the correlated errors do not involve variables at the head and tail of a single causal arrow, they will not prevent identification. Thus error correlations involving indirect effects should not present a problem.

Missing Data

A perennial problem arising in latent variable modeling, particularly of data gathered in natural settings, is that of missing data. Participants omit items in questionnaires, either because they are invited to skip items they don't wish to respond to, or by error, or for other reasons. In studies involving repeated measurement, not everyone shows up for every testing. Longitudinal studies, in which the same individuals are measured on repeated occasions, perhaps years apart, may wind up with only a small fraction of the sample with which they began. The unhappy prospect is a covariance matrix based on small numbers or different numbers of cases. What's a modeler to do?

There has been a lot of attention paid to this issue by statisticians over the years. The short answer is that there are several ways of dealing with missing data, some are more effective than others, and none can work magic.

Listwise and pairwise deletion

Most statistical packages offer at least two simple options. In listwise deletion, also called complete-case analysis, the covariance (or correlation) matrix is calculated using only those cases for which the data are complete. In pairwise deletion, also called available-case analysis, each covariance is calculated on all cases having data for both variables--this means that different covariances may reflect different subsamples of the data, and have different Ns. Basing different covariances on different cases leads to the possibility of mathematically inconsistent--or even impossible--covariance matrices. Moreover, if the model-fitting program asks for a single N, what should that N be? The smallest of those present? The largest? Some average, such as the mean or the median?

Listwise deletion escapes these difficulties, providing an internally consistent covariance matrix and a single N, but often at a terrible price. If there are many items of missing data and they are scattered about in a data set, there may only be a few subjects with complete data, and the result is that one winds up using only a tiny subset of the data that actually exist--and a biased subset, at that. Suppose that the relevant variables for your study include a trait such as conscientiousness. Is it plausible to believe that the subjects that fill out every item or who return for every session represent a random selection on this trait?

If samples are large and there are only a few items of data missing more or less at random, it won't make much practical difference whether listwise or pairwise deletion is used. However, if there are many subjects who have missing data, pairwise deletion will usually be preferable. The issue of what N to use with pairwise deletion has not been extensively investigated, but one recent study (Marsh, 1998) slightly favored the use of mean N.

However, although listwise or pairwise deletion often work tolerably well in practice, better methods exist, and they are becoming increasingly accessible to latent variable modelers. We consider three: multiple-group approaches, full information maximum likelihood, and multiple imputation.

Multiple-group approaches

These are useful in situations where only a small number of patterns of missing data occur. For example, missingness may be planned: all participants may receive part A of the questionnaire, but only subsets receive parts B, C, and D. Or it may be unplanned, but occur in only a few ways: In a study done over three sessions, participants may fall into three groups--those who were present at all three sessions, those who showed up only for the first two, and those who dropped out after one. In such cases, we can treat the participants with each missing-data pattern as a separate group, and equate the parameters we are solving for across these groups. Most model-fitting programs allow simultaneous model fitting in several groups. The usual use of this facility is to allow comparisons across existing groups such as males and females, or different social classes--we will consider a number of examples of this sort in Chapter 4--but it can be used for missing data patterns as well, provided there are only a few such patterns and each occurs reasonably often, so that the subgroups which they define are not too small.

Much more common, however, are situations in which many different missing data patterns occur. For these, we can use either of our remaining two alternatives, full information maximum likelihood or multiple imputation.

Full information maximum likelihood

Full information maximum likelihood, FIML for short, is available in some SEM programs--AMOS, Mx, and Mplus are examples. Essentially, with FIML the model is fit to the raw data rather than to the covariance matrix, using a maximum likelihood criterion. This allows fitting to all the data that are present-- thus the "full information" part of the name. The requirement for iteratively returning to the full data set rather than just to the covariance matrix makes FIML computationally more intensive than the simpler methods, but with powerful modern computers this is seldom a bar, except perhaps in very large problems.

Multiple imputation

The strategy here is a little different. Missing scores in the data matrix are filled in or "imputed" by a method that randomly selects values from the scores that other cases like this case have. This is done several times (say, 3 to 10 times), and the SEM analysis is carried out on each of the resulting complete data matrices. At the end, the results for all of the solutions are averaged to give a final estimate of each parameter that is solved for. The variance of the separate estimates gives an idea of how robust the final estimate is--i.e., how much it varies as a result of the imputation process. "Other cases like this" may be defined in various ways--for example, as a member of a specified subgroup, or in terms of scores on other variables that are predictive of the variable on which the data are missing.

Are data missing at random?

Discussions of the preceding methods often use a terminology of "missing at random" (MAR) and "missing completely at random" (MCAR). MCAR means roughly what its name suggests--that the fact that an item is missing is completely unrelated to the value that item would have if we knew it. This is a fairly strong assumption. It means, for example, that if income is omitted on a questionnaire this will have nothing to do with whether the income is large or small. For some kinds of data we may be willing to make such an assumption, and if so, we can use any of the five methods we have described, including the two simpler ones, without fear of introducing systematic bias. The methods will still differ in precision, from listwise deletion (least) to the three complex methods (most).

The other term, MAR, is perhaps a little misleading--it might be better described as MARC, "missing at random, conditionally." It means that once we have taken into account other information in the data matrix, the missingness may be considered random. This could be the case, for example, if we have measured social class, and within a given social class the unreported incomes do not differ systematically from the ones that are reported. Listwise and pairwise deletion may be biased for data that are MAR but not MCAR, the other three methods are unbiased for data that are MAR or better.

What about data which we cannot confidently assume to be either MAR or MCAR--that is, most data? Sometimes information about the mechanisms by which data become missing can be helpful, although solutions here tend to be somewhat specialized and ad hoc. It may be useful to compare cases having missing data to cases without, as a check. Sometimes it is possible to learn something about why data are missing by intensive follow-up of a few cases. But often we wind up using one or more of the available methods, cross-checking our results against those from other data obtained under different conditions, and hoping for the best. We may take comfort in the opinion of some experts that the more sophisticated methods often do reasonably well even in . the face of moderate departures from MAR assumptions. But in any case, when there is a good deal of missing data, and a strong possibility of bias in its missingness, one does well to be modest in one's statistical claims whatever one's strategy has been.

Correlations Versus Covariances in Model Fitting

Earlier, in discussing the use of standardized versus unstandardized variables in path models, it was noted that one often had a choice as to which scaling was used. What are some of the considerations in making such a choice, apart from the greater familiarity of correlations to many readers, and the relative ease of comparison of effects across standardized variables?

A fairly obvious point is that if one is comparing different groups, different times, etc., and one wants to take variance differences into account, one should analyze a covariance matrix; on the other hand, if one wishes to ignore variance differences, one might elect to analyze standardized variables, i.e., a correlation matrix.

In making such a decision, one should always consider the inadvertent changes in scale that the calculation of correlations may bring about. Suppose that the effect of education in years on income in dollars is being compared in two populations for which one or both of these variables differs in variance. If an added year of education is worth $5000 in income in both populations, the unstandardized regression coefficients obtained in an analysis using covariances will be equal, but the standardized regression coefficients obtained in an analysis of correlations will not be. If one specifies parameters in a model to be equal across groups or across time, the automatic changes of scale involved in the calculation of correlations separately in the different groups or for the different times will defeat one's purpose. One should specify the equality on the scale for which it is expected to hold--in this case the rawscore scale-- and thus one should analyze covariances. If one elects to standardize variables for other reasons, the standardization should be across the combined groups or occasions to preserve the uniformity of scale.

This may not always be the case. If one's theory indicates that equality should be defined relative to the variability in each population--that an extra year of education has more effect on income in a group where education tends not to vary much--then standard score regressions may be more nearly constant than raw score regressions, and correlation matrices calculated within groups a better choice for analysis. Or if one desires to equate factor loadings or residual variances across variables within a sample, standardization may often make sense. The important thing is that one think about which scale the equality is expected on, and make sure that one's constraints are imposed as intended.

In addition, there are statistical issues. The statistical theory underlying maximum likelihood and generalized least squares solutions has mostly been developed for the case of covariance matrices rather than correlation matrices. Since correlation matrices *are* covariance matrices--of standardized variables-- one might wonder why a problem arises. One answer is that statistical constraints are introduced when the same sample is used both to standardize the variables and calculate the covariances. However, if one is dealing with large samples, as is highly desirable on other grounds, the slight bias involved in using the sample standard deviation to determine the rescaling of a variable will probably not have serious consequences (assuming that such rescaling is substantively appropriate).

A more problematic issue of degrees of freedom arises when fitting correlation matrices in multiple groups, since the variances are inherently constrained to be equal across groups (because all are 1.0). Neale and Cardon (1992, p. 256) propose a simple df adjustment, which amounts, in typical cases, to not counting the diagonal elements in groups after the first. However, some simulations (unpublished) suggest that this procedure tends to overcorrect in practice.

A different kind of statistical constraint arises if one requires that values of parameters be restricted to those that yield a proper correlation matrix, i.e., one with exact unities in the diagonal. A few SEM programs are equipped to do statistical inference with correlation matrices as such--RAMONA and SEPATH are examples. The more typical practice, however, is not to do this, but simply to analyze correlation matrices as covariance matrices which have been calculated using standardized variables. This is what usually happens by default when one inputs a correlation matrix to a model-fitting program.

To summarize: Model fitting to covariance matrices is statistically the standard procedure, but the substitution of correlation matrices (i.e., the prior standardization of variables) is often feasible, and in some cases may have advantages. However, in instances where one is equating parameters across groups or over time one should not use correlation matrices without very careful thought about the implications of doing so.

"Standardized" solutions

Most SEM programs, after fitting to a covariance matrix, will provide a standardized solution on request, as a convenience in interpreting the results. It should be kept in mind that this will not always give the same results as standardizing the variables beforehand (i.e., analyzing a correlation matrix). This is particularly true for models that contain equality constraints. Paths constrained to be equal will be equal in the original raw-score metrics in which the solution was carried out, not in the standardized metric in which the results are reported. Inferential aspects of the solution--standard errors, fit indices, chi squares--also are appropriate to the original, not the standardized, metric.

A caution

In using any of the methods described in this chapter, we encounter the usual dilemma confronting the individual who would like to be both statistical purist and practical researcher. Few, if any, users of chi square tests or standard error estimates are in a position to fully justify the probability values they report. Nearly always, the strongest appropriate claim would be something like: "To the extent that the underlying assumptions hold, we can conclude that. . . . " Or, perhaps more frankly: "The statistical tests and probability values in this paper are reported in a mainly descriptive spirit, to help orient the reader among the various models we present."

Some such statement should be taken as appended to every substantive study described in this book. I have not ordinarily made it explicitly. To do it only on occasion would be invidious. To do it every time would be an unkindness to the reader.

Chapter 2 Notes

Search methods. Various procedures go by such names as steepest descent, Fletcher-Powell, Gauss-Newton, Newton-Raphson, Levenberg-Marquardt, the Fisher scoring method, the EM algorithm, etc. LISREL uses a Fletcher-Powell variant, but offers other options; EQS uses a Gauss-Newton algorithm. Schoenberg and Richtand (1984) discuss the use of the EM method for estimating factor analysis and measurement models.

Matrix formulations. McArdle and McDonald (1984) discuss some relationships among such formulations; Bentler and Weeks (1985) comment.

SEM programs. An article in which the authors of seven SEM programs describe their programs is Kano (1997). Earlier comparative reviews, some dated in some respects but still useful, include comparisons of seven programs by Waller (1993), three programs by Hox (1995), and two programs by Howell (1996). For two recent comparisons of three of the four programs featured in this chapter--AMOS, EQS, and LISREL--see Kline (1998b) and von Eye and Fuller (2003). Both conclude that all three are fine programs. For those for whom cost is a major consideration, the excellent--and free--program Mx should also prove attractive--find it at http://www.vcu.edu/mx.

Reviews of SEM software are a regular feature of the journal *Structural Equation Modeling.* Current information on SEM programs is accessible via the internet—e.g., via the SEMFAQ home page described in the notes to Chapter 1; it is also possible to search the SEMNET archives for comments by users (both happy and disgruntled) of particular programs. SEM software is a fluid market--changes in distribution arrangements, program features, and prices are frequent. As noted, one of the programs described in this chapter, Mx, is available free via the internet. For some of the others, free demonstration versions are available which can be used for small problems. If you need to fit nonstandard SEM models, you might want to consider AUFIT (Browne & du Toit, 1992), which provides a central model-fitting core to which the user adds specialized subroutines. Software designed for RAM-type path modeling rather than model-fitting is McArdle and Boker's RAMpath (1990).

Fitting criteria. Bollen (2001) describes a 2-stage least squares alternative to ML or GLS that can be used with nonnormal distributions, and which is also relatively robust to misspecification, in that the effects of errors in the model tend to remain localized. Olsson et al. (1999) compare ML and GLS criteria in SEM. See also ADF, below.

ADF. See Browne (1984). For examples of applications see Huba and Harlow (1983), Tanaka and Huba (1987), and Windle et al. (1989). For its poor performance at any but very large sample sizes, see Hu, Bentler, and Kano (1992) and Boomsma and Hoogland (2001).

Start values. Work by Hendricks and Boomsma (see Boomsma & Hoogland, 2001) suggests that when models are misspecified, convergence problems may result, but that these can often be dealt with by the use of different start values.

Assumptions. For a general discussion of statistical assumptions in SEM, see Bentler and Dudgeon (1996); for reviews of Monte Carlo studies see Hoogland and Boomsma (1998) and Powell and Schafer (2001). For a discussion of the statistical impact of sample size, see Tanaka (1987) and Boomsma and Hoogland (2001); for outliers, Yuan and Bentler (2001b) and Bollen (1987); for categorical and ordinal data, Babakus et al. (1987) and Muthén (1984, 1993; Muthén & Kaplan, 1985). The effects of selection are considered by Muthén and Jöreskog (1983), Muthén (1989a,b), and Meredith (1993), among others.

The robustness of model-fitting methods to departures from multivariate normality are considered by Browne (1987), Huba and Harlow (1987), Berkane and Bentler (1987), Sharma et al. (1989), Satorra (1990), Benson and Fleishman (1994), Chou and Bentler (1995), West et al. (1995), Wang et al. (1996), Olsson et al. (2000), and Boomsma and Hoogland (2001). There seems to be some consensus that parameter estimates can often be robust in the face of departures from assumptions that have severe consequences for chi squares and standard errors. Satorra and Bentler have proposed a scaled statistic for dealing with nonnormality which has shown promise in simulation studies by Chou et al. (1991), Hu et al. (1992), Anderson (1996), and Fouladi (2000); see also Satorra (2001). It is provided in EQS; matrix methods for calculating it for use with other programs are also available (Bentler & Dudgeon, 1996). Several additional statistics for dealing with nonnormal distributions are proposed by Yuan and Bentler (1997, 1998). Another idea: Yuan et al. (2000) suggest applying a multivariate normalizing transformation to the covariance matrix prior to carrying out SEM. This can minimize the effects of outliers, as well as other sources of nonnormality.

Bootstrap. Stine (1989) provides a general introduction to bootstrap methods. Discussions of bootstrapping in SEM include Bollen and Stine (1993), Yung and Bentler (1996), and Nevitt and Hancock (2001); all note its promise, but warn of potential pitfalls (such as its use with too-small samples). An application of bootstrap-based corrections to ADF is provided by Yung and Bentler (1994), and Raykov (2001) applies the bootstrap to obtaining confidence intervals for the difference in fit between two structural equation models. Many SEM programs, including LISREL, EQS, Mx, SEPATH, and AMOS, provide bootstrapping or other Monte Carlo facilities.

Non-nested models. For methods of comparing the fits of models that are *not* nested, see Rust et al. (1995) and McAleer (1995). The latter reviews the topic broadly, not just with respect to SEM. See also Oczkowski (2002).

Descriptive fit indices. For trends in goodness-of-fit indices, see Tucker and Lewis (1973), Bentler and Bonett (1980), Tanaka and Huba (1985,1989), Akaike (1987), Bozdogan (1987), Bollen and Liang (1988), Marsh et al. (1988), Bollen (1989a), McDonald (1989), Mulaik et al. (1989), Steiger (1989, 1990), La Du and Tanaka (1989, 1995), Bentler (1990), McDonald and Marsh (1990), Maiti and Mukherjee (1990), Cudeck and Henly (1991), Browne and Cudeck (1993), Bandalos (1993), Gerbing and Anderson (1993), Goffin

(1993), Sugawara and MacCallum (1993), Tanaka (1993), Williams and Holahan (1994), Ding et al. (1995), Hu and Bentler (1995, 1998, 1999), Marsh et al. (1996), Rigdon (1996), Anderson (1996), Weng and Cheng (1997), Fan et al. (1999), Breivik and Olsson (2001), and Tanguma (2001).

The value of consulting residuals in addition to using fit indices is underscored by Browne et al. (2002), who describe situations in which fit indices and residuals can give very different indications of goodness of fit. Widaman and Thompson (2003) argue that many SEM programs use an inappropriate null model to calculate incremental fit indices when models involve constraints.

RMSEA. A criticism of RMSEA, and a reply to it, may be found in Hayduk and Glaser (2000) and Steiger (2000). For a discussion of potential biases in the estimation of the noncentrality parameter used in RMSEA (and an argument that its confidence intervals may be less problematic), see Raykov (2000). Nevitt and Hancock (2000) evaluate two ways of adjusting RMSEA for nonnormality, and Hancock and Freeman (2001) examine its power in a test of not-close fit. In a Monte Carlo study, Curran et al. (2002) found RMSEA to be accurate for moderately misspecified models when sample sizes were reasonably large (i.e., 200 or more), and MacCallum and Hong (1997) found RMSEA to be more satisfactory than GFI or AGFI for power analysis and model evaluation. However, RMSEA may be more vulnerable than GFI to the effects of model size (Breivik & Olsson, 2001), with large models appearing to yield better fits than otherwise comparable small ones. Steiger (1998) discusses the extension of RMSEA to multiple samples.

Power. The classic treatment of power in SEM is Satorra and Saris (1985)--see also Saris and Satorra (1993). A review of power evaluation in SEM, focusing on single-df tests, is Kaplan (1995). The reasons why power may be different for discrepancies in different parts of a model are discussed by Kaplan and Wenger (1993). Muthén and Muthén (2002) describe how to use a Monte Carlo study to decide on sample size and estimate power.

Power in connection with the RMSEA is discussed in an important paper by MacCallum, Browne, and Sugawara (1996). In the text, I suggest a test of poor fit, contrasting null and alternate RMSEAs of .10 and .05, whereas MacCallum et al. focus on a test of not-close fit, based on RMSEAs of .05 and .01. The test of poor fit advocated here was inspired by MacCallum et al.'s approach, and the values for Table I were calculated using their program. It is my belief that rejecting a hypothesis of poor fit will be more useful to typical SEM users, and easier for their readers to understand, than rejecting a hypothesis of not-close fit, as proposed by MacCallum et al.

A facility for calculating values of the noncentral chi-square distribution (and other probability distributions) is available on the internet at http://calculators.stat.ucla.edu/cdf.

Identification. Some of the issues are discussed in Rindskopf (1984a), Bollen and Jöreskog (1985), Bollen (1989b), Seidel and Eicheler (1990), and Rigdon (1995). An extensive, rather technical treatment is given by

Bekker et al. (1994). The choice of identifying the scale of latent variables by setting a path to 1.0 or the variance to 1.0 is often an arbitrary one, but not always, especially when equality constraints are present--O'Brien and Reilly (1995) discuss the matter. For examples of cases in which the placement of constraints makes a difference, see Millsap (2001).

Missing data. The standard treatment is Little and Rubin's (1987) book *Statistical analysis with missing data*. Other recent books include Allison (2002) and Schafer (1997). Rovine (1994), Arbuckle (1996), Graham and Hofer (2000), Little and Schenker (1995), and Wothke (2000) have chapters on the treatment of missing data in SEM; Enders (2001) also provides an overview of the topic. See also empirical comparisons of several methods by Brown (1994), Allison (2000), Enders and Bandalos (2001), Wiggins and Sacker (2002), and Gold and Bentler (2000). Schafer's website (http://www.stat.psu.edu/~jls) contains a (free) program called NORM for doing multiple imputation; it is available in an S-Plus version and as a stand-alone Windows program. Release 8.2 of SAS contains a multiple imputation procedure, PROC MI (for details, see http://support.sas.com/rnd/app/papers/multipleimputation.pdf.) The methods discussed in the present chapter generally assume multivariate normality. For dealing with missing data when variables are nonnormal, see Yuan and Bentler (2000b), and Gold et al. (2003), and for a statistical test of whether missing data are in fact MCAR, see Kim and Bentler (2002).

Correlations and covariances. See Cudeck (1989) and Browne and Arminger (1995) for some of the relevant theory.

Chapter 2 Exercises

Note: The correlation matrices required for problems 5 and 9 (and similar problems in subsequent chapters) are on the compact disk supplied with this book. They are in simple text format, with one row per line, no tabs, and one or more spaces between entries, and each is in the form of a full symmetric matrix. A title line and variable labels are also supplied. The file on the CD can be read into a word processor and the matrices copied as necessary into your SEM program or into a file readable by it.

1. Apply the iterative procedure of Table 2-1 to the path model of Fig. 2.12, for the correlations shown to its right (see pages 36-37). Begin with trial values of .5, .5, .5, and carry out 4 cycles of the search.

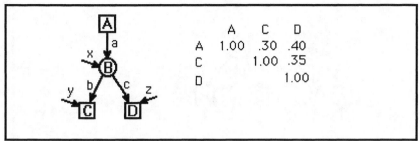

Fig. 2.12 Path model and correlations for Problem 1.

2. Solve directly for the paths a, b, and c in Fig. 2.12, using the methods of the previous chapter (page 14). How do the results of problem 1 compare with these?

3. Draw a cross-section of a perverse terrain in which very good solutions exist but a simple iterative search program would have a poor chance of finding them.

4. Set up the three McArdle-McDonald matrices for the path diagram of problem 1.

5. (See Note at beginning of exercises.) An investigator believes that ambition, of which he has three measures, is a cause of achievement, for which he has two measures. In a sample of 100 subjects, the following correlations were observed. Use an SEM program to solve for the (standardized) path values, using a maximum likelihood criterion. Interpret the results.

	Ach1	Ach2	Amb1	Amb2	Amb3
Ach1	1.00				
Ach2	.60	1.00			
Amb1	.30	.20	1.00		
Amb2	.20	.30	.70	1.00	
Amb3	.20	.10	.60	.50	1.00

6. Four nested models based on a 4 x 4 variance-covariance matrix have 3, 5, 6, and 9 unknowns and yield χ^2s of 16.21, 8.12, 2.50, and 1.28, respectively. What conclusions about models or the differences between models could you draw at the .05 level of significance?

7. Compute RMSEA for the data of problem 6, assuming a sample size of 100 and a baseline model with no free parameters and $\chi^2 = 25.00$. What interpretations would you make?

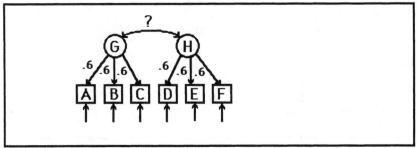

Fig. 2.13 Path model for problem 8.

8. You want to decide if G and H, in Fig. 2.13, are correlated. If N = 50, what would be your power to detect a correlation of .5 between G and H (as against a correlation of zero)? What N would give you 80% power to detect a correlation of .5?

9. (See Note at beginning of exercises.) Four measures of creativity, tests W, X, Y, and Z, were given to 500 high school students. The intercorrelations among the tests were:

	W	X	Y	Z
W	1.00	.40	.50	.30
X		1.00	.55	.35
Y			1.00	.40
Z				1.00

Solve for the loadings of the measures on a single factor, using an SEM program and a least squares criterion. Fix one path to 1.0 and free the variance of the latent variable. Obtain a standardized as well as the unstandardized solution (if your program permits).

10. Convert the unstandardized solution of problem 9 by hand to a standardized solution, using the rules for standardized and unstandardized path coefficients from Chapter 1. Compare the results to those obtained in problem 9.

11. Suppose that you were fitting the model in problem 9 using a maximum likelihood criterion. Use the Appendix I table to determine what your power would be to reject a hypothesis of poor fit if the approximation is actually good in the population. What sample size would you need in order to have a power of .80 in this situation?

Chapter Three:
Fitting Path and Structural Models to Data from a Single Group on a Single Occasion

In this chapter and the next we consider a number of different applications of path and structural models. This serves two purposes. First, it gives some sense of various ways in which these methods can be employed, as well as practice in applying and interpreting them. Second, it introduces additional concepts and techniques useful in dealing with path and structural models, both in general and in some important special cases. One caution: Several of the examples in this and the following chapters are classics from the SEM literature that are included for their pedagogical clarity rather than as ideal exemplars of power, sample size, or measurement technique. You might find it instructive to apply the power calculations of the preceding chapter to a few of them.

Structural and Measurement Models

Most structural modelers, following Jöreskog, distinguish between two conceptually distinct parts of path models, namely, a *structural* part and a *measurement* part. The structural part of a model specifies the relationships among the latent variables, and the measurement part specifies the relationship of the latent to the observed variables.

An example from a desegregation study

Figure 3.1 (next page) gives an example. This is a path diagram of part of a study of school desegregation. The diagram follows the convention of representing latent variables by circles or ovals, and observed variables by squares or rectangles. This is helpful in keeping things straight in complicated models.

There are five latent variables, listed beside the diagram. Each is indexed by two or three observed variables, identified below the diagram. Collectively, these constitute the measurement model, shown in the top part of Fig. 3.2 (page 89). The structural model consists of the relationships among the five latent variables, shown at the bottom of that figure.

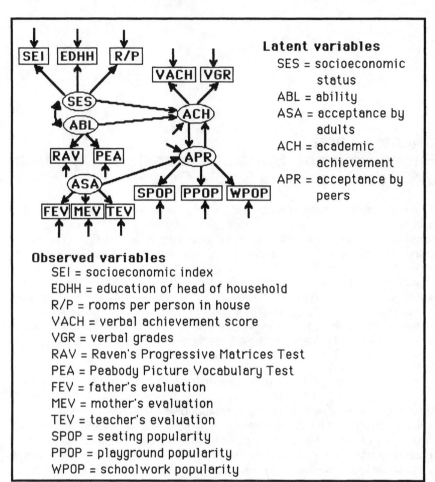

Latent variables
SES = socioeconomic status
ABL = ability
ASA = acceptance by adults
ACH = academic achievement
APR = acceptance by peers

Observed variables
SEI = socioeconomic index
EDHH = education of head of household
R/P = rooms per person in house
VACH = verbal achievement score
VGR = verbal grades
RAV = Raven's Progressive Matrices Test
PEA = Peabody Picture Vocabulary Test
FEV = father's evaluation
MEV = mother's evaluation
TEV = teacher's evaluation
SPOP = seating popularity
PPOP = playground popularity
WPOP = schoolwork popularity

Fig. 3.1 Path model used in a desegregation study (Maruyama & McGarvey, 1980).

Note that the structural and measurement models play rather distinct roles in the overall path model. One could very easily alter either without changing the other. Thus, one might maintain the same structural model of relationships among the latent variables but change the measurement model by using different tests or measurements to index the latent variables. Alternatively, one could keep the same measures but change the structural model by making different assumptions about the relationships among the latent variables--one could assume, say, that the child's academic achievement influences peer approval but not vice versa, or that acceptance by adults is

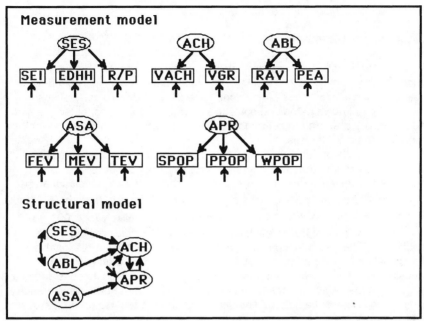

Fig. 3.2 Measurement and structural components of path model of Fig. 3.1.

affected by the child's academic achievement.

The measurement model is a variant of confirmatory factor analysis. One could consider the top part of Fig. 3.2 to consist of five small Spearman general-factor problems: In each case the latent variable can be seen as a factor general to the tests that measure it, with the residual arrows--shown here below the squares--representing influences specific to the tests. This would not, however, be an altogether satisfactory way to proceed, because it is not only the correlations of, say, SEI, EDHH, and R/P among themselves that provide information concerning the paths between them and SES; such information is also supplied in the relative correlations of these variables with others in the model. In fact, a direct Spearman approach would not work at all for the latent variables with only two indicators, which require at least some additional correlations in order to obtain a unique solution. It is more appropriate, therefore, to think of the measurement model as a single, multiple-factor confirmatory factor analysis. So far as the measurement model is concerned, the relationships among the factors are unanalyzed correlations. It is the structural model that interprets these correlations as resulting from a particular set of causal relationships among the latent variables.

In practice, the usual procedure is to solve the measurement and structural models simultaneously because, in so doing, one brings to bear all information available about each path. In Chapter 7 we discuss situations in which one might wish to solve them separately.

A solution of the model

Maruyama and McGarvey present correlations among the 13 observed variables for a sample of 249 children--the correlations given in Table 3-1. One could in principle write path expressions for each of these 78 correlations in terms of the unknown paths and solve them for the path values, but Maruyama and McGarvey preferred to set up the appropriate LISREL matrices and let the program handle the details.

The results are shown in Figure 3.3, in which all latent variables are standardized, so that these numbers are ordinary path coefficients and correlations. Residual variances are shown at the ends of the residual arrows.

The χ^2 for testing the goodness of fit of the model is 140.30, based on 59 degrees of freedom. A χ^2 of 140.30 based on 59 df is unlikely (p < .001) to occur with a sample of this size if the model of Fig. 3.1 holds exactly in the population. Thus, we may conclude that it does not. But is it a reasonable approximation? The root mean square error of approximation (RMSEA; discussed in the last chapter) is .074; this may be interpreted as constituting a marginally acceptable, but not an outstanding, level of fit. Further exploration might, of course, yield a better fitting version of the model. However, Maruyama and McGarvey did not pursue matters further at this point.

One feature of this model, the reciprocal paths between ACH and APR, represents a step beyond the models that we have so far considered. We look further at such looped models later in the chapter; for the moment we need

Table 3-1 Correlations among observed variables in desegregation study (data from Maruyama & McGarvey, 1980), N = 249

	SEI	EDH	R/P	VACH	VGR	RAV	PEA	FEV	MEV	TEV	SP	PP	WP
SEI	1.00												
EDHH	.56	1.00.											
R/P	.17	.10	1.00										
VACH	.17	.30	.19	1.00									
VGR	.16	.21	-.04	.50	1.00								
RAV	.06	.15	-.00	.29	.28	1.00							
PEA	.16	.21	.28	.40	.19	.32	1.00						
FEV	.01	-.04	-.04	.01	.12	.10	-.06	1.00					
MEV	-.07	-.05	.00	.13	.27	.16	-.07	.42	1.00				
TEV	-.02	-.01	.04	.21	.27	.14	.08	.18	.31	1.00			
SPOP	.05	.04	.02	.28	.24	.08	.13	.07	.15	.25	1.00		
PPOP	.10	.10	-.04	.23	.18	.09	.17	.02	.08	.08	.59	1.00	
WPOP	.10	.17	-.03	.32	.40	.14	.17	.08	.17	.33	.55	.49	1.00

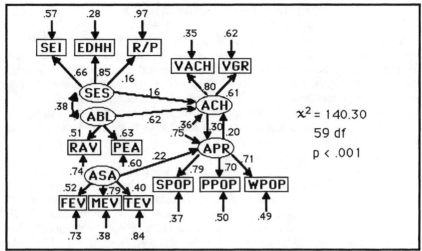

Fig. 3.3 Standardized solution to path diagram of Fig. 3.1 from correlations of Table 3-1.

merely note that in the present example the solution in LISREL presented no special problems.

We need not go into all the details of Maruyama and McGarvey's solution procedure, but a few points may be helpful. First, as is usual with LISREL, the correlation matrix was treated as if it were a variance-covariance matrix, with $n(n + 1)/2 = 91$ distinct observed values--the 13 variances plus the 78 covariances on one side of the diagonal. Maruyama and McGarvey employed a mixed technique for scaling the latent variables. On the source variable side they specified standardized latent variables, leaving 16 unknowns to be solved for in the measurement model: the $3 + 2 + 3 = 8$ paths from the latent variables SES, ABL, and ASA to the eight manifest variables measuring them, plus the corresponding 8 residual paths. On the downstream variable side of the measurement model, they fixed one path from each of the latent variables to 1.0, leaving only $1 + 2 = 3$ paths to be solved, plus the 5 residual paths, or 8 unknowns. Altogether, then, there are a total of $16 + 8 = 24$ unknown paths to be solved for in the measurement model.

In the structural model there are a total of 8 unknowns: one correlation among source latent variables, three paths from source to downstream latent variables, two reciprocal paths between the latter, and two residuals for the downstream latent variables. Thus, there are altogether $24 + 8 = 32$ unknowns to be solved for; and 91 observed values minus 32 unknowns yields the 59 df.

The initial solution provided by LISREL (using a maximum likelihood criterion) was thus standardized on the source variable side but not on the downstream variable side; however, one can also request a fully standardized solution, and it is that which is reported in Fig. 3.3.

91

Confirmatory Factor Analysis

Traditionally, a latent variable analysis that is called a *factor analysis* is one in which a model containing latent variables is fit to a correlation matrix, the model being mainly a measurement model with the structural model confined to simple correlations among the latent variables. The use of correlation matrices, though common, is not essential--covariance matrices can be factor analyzed, and sometimes are, especially in that class of factor analyses called *confirmatory factor analyses*, in which a specifically hypothesized set of latent variables is fit to a covariance or correlation matrix (the latter, of course, being a covariance matrix among standardized variables).

The main result of any factor analysis, as noted in Chapter 1, is a table showing the *factor pattern*, or values of the paths between the latent and observed variables. If the latent variables are correlated, there will also be a table of their intercorrelations (*factor intercorrelation matrix*). In the case of correlated factors, there may also be reported a table of the correlations between observed and latent variables (*factor structure matrix*).

A study of attitudes toward police

In Chapter 1 we considered some simple artificial examples of confirmatory factor analysis. Here we look at a case (McIver, Carmines & Zeller, 1980) in which several hypotheses were fit to correlations based on a large real-life data set.

The correlations, from a study of attitudes toward police, are given in Table 3-2. They are based on telephone interviews with a total of some 11,000 respondents in 60 neighborhoods in three U.S. metropolitan areas. Included in the table are the intercorrelations among six items reflecting attitudes toward the

Table 3-2 Correlations among nine items in police survey (data from McIver, Carmines, & Zeller, 1980)

	1	2	3	4	5	6	7	8	9
1. Police service	1.00	.50	.41	.33	.28	.30	-.24	-.23	-.20
2. Responsiveness	.02	1.00	.35	.29	.26	.27	-.19	-.19	-.18
3. Response time	-.01	-.02	1.00	.30	.27	.29	-.17	-.16	-.14
4. Honesty	-.01	-.01	.04	1.00	.52	.48	-.13	-.11	-.15
5. Courtesy	-.03	-.02	.03	.01	1.00	.44	-.11	-.09	-.10
6. Equal treatment	.01	.01	.06	-.01	.00	1.00	-.15	-.13	-.13
7. Burglary	.00	.02	.01	.01	.02	-.03	1.00	.58	.47
8. Vandalism	-.01	.00	.01	.02	.03	-.02	.00	1.00	.42
9. Robbery	-.02	-.02	.00	-.04	.00	-.04	.00	-.01	1.00

Note: Original correlations are above diagonal; residuals from 3-factor solution are below it.

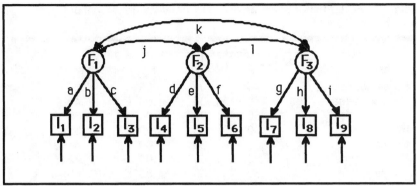

Fig. 3.4 Simple three-factor model for data of Table 3-2 from survey on attitudes toward police (McIver et al., 1980).

quality of police services, plus three items having to do with the likelihood of burglary, vandalism, and robbery in the neighborhood.

The authors had originally surmised that the six attitude items might form a single general dimension of attitude toward police, and indeed they are all mutually positively intercorrelated in Table 3-2. But inspection of the table suggested that there might be two distinct subclasses of attitude items, judging from somewhat higher correlations within than across item subsets. The first three items, having to do with the general quality of police services, their responsiveness to citizen needs, and the rapidity with which the police answered a call, seemed to go together, as did the second three, having to do with the personal qualities of the police--their honesty, courtesy, and fairness. The three items concerning likelihood of various kinds of crime also seemed to group together and to be mildly negatively correlated with the first six items having to do with the perceived quality of the police service.

Consequently, a hypothesis of three correlated factors was fit to the data. (The fact that this hypothesis was arrived at on the basis of preliminary inspection of the data means that the chi-square tests should not be regarded as yielding strict probabilities, but rather as more informal indices of goodness of fit.)

Table 3-3 (next page) gives the results of fitting the hypothetical three-factor model shown in Fig. 3.4. Each item has a substantial loading on its corresponding factor. The first two factors of police attitudes are substantially correlated ($r = .62$), and the third, crime factor, is negatively correlated with both, somewhat more highly with the first factor (police service) than with the second (personal qualities of the police). The communalities (h^2)--which in this case are simply equal to the squares of the individual paths a, b, c, etc., because each item reflects only one factor--suggest that only around half the item variances are being accounted for by the common factors, with the rest presumably due to specific factors and error.

Table 3-3 Factor pattern and factor intercorrelations for model of Fig. 3.4 (McIver et al., 1980)

	Factor	**pattern**		
Item	F_1	F_2	F_3	h^2
1. Police service	.74	.00	.00	.55
2. Responsiveness	.65	.00	.00	.43
3. Response time	.56	.00	.00	.32
4. Honesty	.00	.75	.00	.56
5. Courtesy	.00	.68	.00	.46
6. Equal treatment	.00	.65	.00	.42
7. Burglary	.00	.00	.80	.63
8. Vandalism	.00	.00	.72	.52
9. Robbery	.00	.00	.59	.35

Factor intercorrelations

	F_1	F_2	F_3
F_1	1.00	.62	-.41
F_2		1.00	-.24
F_3			1.00

$\chi^2 = 226.21$, 24 df, $p < .001$

The three common factors were assumed to be in standard-score form. Forty-five observed variances and covariances (9 x 10/2) were fit using 21 unknowns (*a* through *l*, in Fig. 3.4, plus the 9 residuals), leaving 24 df for the χ^2 test. The obtained χ^2, with this huge sample, is a highly significant 226.21. Nevertheless, the solution does a fairly good job of accounting for the data. The RMSEA of .028, with a 90% confidence interval of .024 to .031, suggests that the factor model represents an excellent approximation. The narrow confidence interval reflects the large sample, and means that we can confidently reject either a null hypothesis of perfect fit or one of poor fit. The residuals, the differences between the observed correlations and the correlations implied by the solution of Table 3-3, are shown in Table 3-2 below the principal diagonal. (An example of the calculation: the implied correlation between item 1, Police service, and item 2, Responsiveness, is *ab* in Fig. 3.4, or .74 x .65 = .48, using the path values from the Table 3-3 solution. The observed correlation is .50; .50 - .48 = .02.) The residuals are small. The largest absolute discrepancy between observed and expected correlations is .06, and the majority are .02 or less. For many purposes one might be perfectly content with this good a fit. However, the discrepancies of .04, .03, and .06 of item 3 (police response time) with items 4 through 6 (personal qualities) suggest that the fit might be improved a little if F_2 as well as F_1 were allowed to influence item 3. Such a solution yielded a reduction of χ^2 from 226.21 to 127.31, at the cost of one degree of freedom--a highly significant improvement. Substantively, however, the change makes little difference except in the paths to item 3 (the path from F_1 drops from .57 to .45 as that from F_2 rises from 0 to .15; the estimated correlation of F_1 and F_2 also drops slightly, from .62 to .58).

The authors went on to test models allowing the residuals to be correlated for a couple of pairs of variables, 4 and 9, and 2 and 7, further reducing the χ^2 to 83.60. This is still a highly significant improvement, if one takes the χ^2s seriously, but as this amounts to introducing new factors to explain the discrepancies of single correlations, it is not very helpful from the point of view of parsimony.

The overall χ^2 is still highly significant with 21 df, despite the fact that at this stage the data are being fit very much ad hoc. With very large samples one needs to be careful not to confuse statistical with practical significance. Some of the small deviations of the data from the model may indeed not be due to chance, but to introduce a hypothetical variable to account for each one of them is unlikely to be of much value for either science or practice.

Some Psychometric Applications of Path and Structural Models

A number of problems in psychometrics lend themselves to latent variable methods. We considered an example involving test reliability in Chapter 1. In the present section, we look at examples involving parallel and congeneric tests, and the separation of trait and method variance.

Parallel and congeneric tests

First, some definitions: Two tests are said by psychometricians to be *parallel* if they share equal amounts of a common factor, and each also has the same amount of specific variance. Consider Fig. 3.5 (next page). If tests A and B are parallel, *a* and *b* would be equal, and so would *c* and *d*. V would represent the common factor the two tests share.

Tests are said to be *congeneric* if they share a common factor, but not necessarily to the same degree. Tests A and B would still be congeneric-- because they share V--even though *a* were not equal to *b*, nor *c* to *d*. (We encountered also in Chapter 2 a third, intermediate condition, *tau-equivalence*, in which *a* = *b*, but *c* ≠ *d*; however, this will not be involved in the present example.)

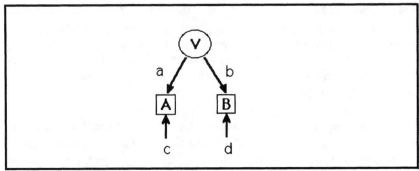

Fig. 3.5 Parallel or congeneric tests.

    Jöreskog provides a structural analysis of some data gathered by F. M. Lord on four vocabulary tests. Tests A and B were short tests given under leisurely conditions, whereas C and D were longer tests given under time pressure. The variance-covariance matrix of the four tests is given in Table 3-4.

    Jöreskog carried out tests of four hypotheses, which can be expressed in terms of Fig. 3.6 by imposing the conditions noted in parentheses:

    H1: Tests A and B are parallel, as are C and D, and all four tests are congeneric. ($a = b$, $e = f$; $c = d$, $g = h$; the correlation $i = 1.0$--that is, V_1 and V_2 are identical except possibly for scale.)

    H2: Both test pairs are parallel, as in H1, but the two pairs are not necessarily congeneric. ($a = b$, $e = f$; $c = d$, $g = h$.)

    H3: All four tests are congeneric but are not necessarily parallel. ($i = 1.0$.)

    H4: A and B are congeneric, as are C and D, but the two pairs need not be congeneric with each other. (Fig. 3.6 as it stands.)

    Note that these hypotheses form two nested series, H1, H2, H4, and H1, H3, H4, within which χ^2 comparisons may be made.

Table 3-4 Covariance matrix for four vocabulary tests (data from Lord; Jöreskog & Sörbom, 1979, p. 55), N = 649

Test	A	B	C	D
A	86.40			
B	57.78	86.26		
C	56.87	59.32	97.28	
D	58.90	59.67	73.82	97.82

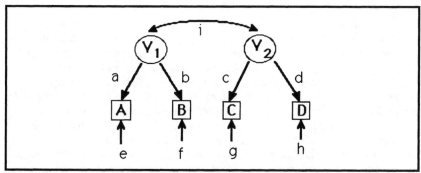

Fig. 3.6 Hypotheses about parallel and congeneric tests.

Table 3-5 shows the results of several χ^2 tests. In the upper part of the table the models representing the four hypotheses are tested individually. By χ^2 test, the hypothesis of perfect fit can be rejected for models H1 and H3 but not for models H2 and H4. H1 and H3 also have mediocre to poor RMSEAs, with upper confidence limits above .10. H2 and H4 have chi squares less than their degrees of freedom, and hence RMSEA estimates of zero. More to the point, the substantial sample allows us to reject the hypothesis of poor fit in both cases (the upper limits of the 90% CI for RMSEA fall below .10--they are .029 and .097, respectively).

The unacceptable models H1 and H3 contain the assumption that all four tests are congeneric, whereas the acceptable models H2 and H4 do not contain

Table 3-5 Hypothesis tests for problem of Fig. 3.5 with data of Table 3-4 (after Jöreskog & Sörbom, 1979, p. 55)

Model	χ^2	df	p	RMSEA	LCL	UCL
H1	37.34	6	<.01	.090	.063	.118
H2	1.93	5	.86	.000	.000	.029
H3	36.22	2	<.01	.162	.119	.211
H4	.70	1	.70	.000	.000	.097

Model comparison	χ^2_{diff}	df	p			
H2 vs H1	35.41	1	<.01			
H4 vs H3	35.52	1	<.01			
H3 vs H1	1.12	4	>.80			
H4 vs H2	1.23	4	>.80			

Note: LCL, UCL = lower and upper limits of 90% confidence interval for RMSEA

this assumption.

The specific comparisons of H2 versus H1 and H4 versus H3 (bottom part of Table 3-5) represent pairs of models that are equivalent except for the assumption that tests A and B are congeneric with tests C and D. Both comparisons show that this assumption is not tenable. The other two comparisons shown, H3 versus H1, and H4 versus H2, test whether A is parallel to B and C is parallel to D. These assumptions remain quite tenable.

Note that the sample size is fairly large (N = 649). Although A and B have been shown to be noncongeneric with C and D, the two pairs of tests are not in fact *very* different. The correlation *i* was estimated in the solution to model H2 as approximately .90, suggesting that although the speeded and unspeeded vocabulary tests are not measuring quite the same thing, what they measure does not differ much for practical purposes.

Fitting one of these psychometric models is equivalent to carrying out a confirmatory factor analysis. Another psychometric model that shares this character is the multitrait-multimethod model, to which we now turn.

Multitrait-multimethod models

The multitrait-multimethod model (Campbell & Fiske, 1959) is an approach to psychological measurement that attempts to separate out true variance on psychological traits from variance due to measurement methods. The basic strategy is to measure each of several traits by each of several methods. Correlations among these measurements are arranged in a multitrait-multimethod matrix that enables one to assess *convergent validity*, the tendency for different measurement operations to converge on the same underlying trait, and *discriminant validity*, the ability to discriminate among different traits.

Table 3-6 is an example of a multitrait-multimethod correlation matrix. It is based on part of a study by Bentler and McClain (1976) in which 68 fifth-grade girls were measured in each of three ways on four personality variables: impulsivity, extraversion, academic achievement motivation, and test anxiety.

For the self-rating measure, each of the girls filled out four standard personality questionnaires, one for each trait. For the teacher ratings, teachers were asked to rank the children in their class on each of the four variables under consideration. Their ratings were converted to scores using a normalizing transformation. The peer ratings were obtained by a sociometric procedure, in which children in the class were asked to write the names of children who fit various descriptions. Four to eight items were used per trait. An example of an item for extraversion was: "Which children like to be with other children a lot?"

The off-diagonal elements in a multitrait-multimethod matrix such as Table 3-6 can be classified into three groups. In the triangles adjacent to the main diagonal are *within-method, cross-trait* correlations. They are underlined in Table 3-6. An example would be the .42 at the start of the third row, the correlation between extraversion and impulsivity, both measured by peer ratings. In the diagonals of the square blocks in the rest of the table, given in boldface type, are the *within-trait, cross-method* correlations, also known as the *validity diagonals.* An example would be the .64 at the start of the fifth row, the correlation between peer and teacher assessments of extraversion. The remaining, unmarked off-diagonal elements are the *cross-trait, cross-method* correlations. High correlations in the validity diagonals are evidence of *convergent validity,* the agreement of different methods of measuring the same trait. Low correlations elsewhere provide evidence of *discriminant validity,* that the putatively different traits really are distinct. Within-method, cross-trait correlations in excess of cross-method, cross-trait correlations are evidence of the presence of *method variance,* associations among measures stemming from properties of the measurement methods used.

    In Table 3-6 the correlations in the validity diagonals are generally positive and appreciable in size (.30 to .66, with a mean of .51), suggesting reasonable convergent validity. They tend to be decidedly higher than the cross-method, cross-trait correlations (mean absolute value of .20), indicating some degree of discriminant validity. However, the latter correlations are by no means always negligible (they range up to about .50), suggesting some overlap

Table 3-6 Multitrait-multimethod correlation matrix for four traits measured by peer, teacher, and self-ratings (data from Bentler & Lee, 1979), N = 68

	Trait and method of measurement											
	Ep	Ap	Ip	Mp	Et	At	It	Mt	Es	As	Is	Ms
Ep	1.00											
Ap	-.38	1.00										
Ip	.42	-.21	1.00									
Mp	-.25	.54	-.54	1.00								
Et	.64	-.15	.26	-.05	1.00							
At	-.29	.66	-.19	.44	-.25	1.00						
It	.38	-.09	.56	-.19	.59	-.14	1.00					
Mt	-.22	.51	-.33	.66	.06	.62	-.05	1.00				
Es	.45	-.05	.12	.10	.50	-.05	.36	.17	1.00			
As	.04	.38	-.03	.14	.08	.30	.09	.16	.02	1.00		
Is	.33	-.13	.35	-.18	.41	-.14	.45	-.13	.43	.16	1.00	
Ms	-.21	.37	-.44	.58	-.01	.41	-.10	.62	.06	.04	-.37	1.00

Note: Trait: E = extraversion, A = test anxiety, I = impulsivity, M = academic achievement motivation. Rater: p = peer, t = teacher, s = self. Correlations: underlined = within-method, cross-trait; boldface = within-trait, cross-method.

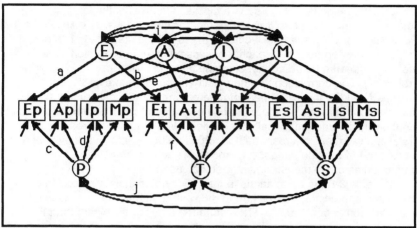

Fig. 3.7 Path model of multitrait-multimethod matrix of Table 3-6.

among the traits. The within-method, cross-trait correlations (mean absolute value of .28) are slightly higher than the cross-method, cross-trait correlations; thus there appears to be some method variance.

Such a multitrait-multimethod matrix can be represented by a path model in the manner shown in Fig. 3.7. The 12 observed variables are shown in the center row of the figure. Four latent variables representing true scores on the four traits are shown in the circles at the top of the diagram. Three latent variables representing the effects of the three methods are shown in the circles at the bottom. Each observed measurement is determined by a trait and a method (e.g., arrows *a* and *c* for *Ep*), plus a residual. The traits may be intercorrelated--for example, extraversion and impulsivity might be related (arrow *i*). So might the methods--for example, peer and teacher ratings (arrow *j*). However, it is assumed in this particular diagram that the design of the experiment has insured that there will be no systematic correlations between methods and traits (no curved arrows connecting the top and bottom circles).

Within-trait, cross-method correlations are produced by direct paths via the trait in question, and possibly by indirect paths via the correlations among methods. For example, the correlation between peer and teacher ratings of extraversion may be expressed as:

$$r_{EpEt} = ab + cjf.$$

Within-method, cross-trait correlations are the other way around--direct paths via methods and indirect paths via possible correlations among traits. For example, the correlation between peer ratings of extraversion and impulsivity may be expressed as:

$r_{Eplp} = cd + aie.$

Cross-method, cross-trait correlations are produced only via indirect paths of both kinds. For example:

$r_{lpEt} = eib + djf.$

The model of Fig. 3.7 involves 12 paths from traits to measures, 12 paths from methods to measures, 12 residuals, 6 intercorrelations among traits, and 3 intercorrelations among measures, a total of 45 unknowns to be estimated from 78 observed variances and covariances (12 x 13/2), leaving 33 degrees of freedom for a χ^2 goodness-of-fit test. (Or one could set 1 path per factor to 1.0, and solve instead for the 7 factor variances, leaving the number of df still 33.)

A solution of the path model by Bentler and Lee (1979) is in Table 3-7. The values of the 12 paths from the trait factors to the measurements are shown in the first subtable. Obviously, the measurements are substantially determined by the traits--somewhat more so for the peer and teacher ratings than for the self-ratings.

Determination of the measurements by the methods is shown in the second subtable. On the whole, these numbers are a bit lower than those in the first part of the table, but they are by no means all low--measurements of impulsivity, for example, seem to be about as much determined by methods (third column of second table) as by the trait (third row of first table).

Table 3-7 Solution to model of Fig. 3.7 for data of Table 3-6 (data from Bentler & Lee, 1979, Table 7)

	Peer	Ratings Teacher	Self	
1. Trait factors	Peer	Teacher	Self	
Extraversion	.98	.62	.42	
Anxiety	.77	.91	.35	
Impulsivity	.78	.64	.42	
Motivation	.72	.89	.66	
		Traits		
2. Method factors	E	A	I	M
Peer ratings	.15	-.25	.32	-.68
Teacher ratings	.74	-.19	.49	.13
Self ratings	.34	.17	.89	-.22

Table 3-7 (cont.)

3. Trait factor intercorrelations

	E	A	I	M
Extraversion	1.00	-.35	.52	-.24
Anxiety		1.00	-.26	.74
Impulsivity			1.00	-.48
Motivation				1.00

4. Method factor intercorrelations

	P	T	S
Peer ratings	1.00	.08	.04
Teacher ratings		1.00	.32
Self ratings			1.00

The trait factors are substantially interrelated (third subtable). Test anxiety and academic achievement motivation tend to go together, as do extraversion and impulsivity, with the two pairs negatively related to each other. The method factors (fourth subtable) are fairly independent of one another, except for a modest correlation between teacher and self-ratings.

Bentler and Lee fit their model using a maximum likelihood criterion, obtaining a χ^2 of 43.88 with 35 df, indicating a tolerable fit (p > .10, RMSEA = .062). They had 35 df rather than 33 because they additionally set the unique variances of two variables, Mp and Is, to zero. (This was done to forestall a tendency for these variances to go negative during the solution, an awkward event known in factor analytic circles as a "Heywood case.") Negative variances of any kind are, of course, not possible in the real world. Empirical measures with no unique variance are also implausible, because this implies, among other things, the absence of errors of measurement. Fortunately, fixing the parameters in question to plausible values (error variances of .10) does not lead to a significant worsening of fit. (Bentler and Lee also fit several other models to these data--the interested reader can consult their article for details.)

Structural Models--Controlling Extraneous Variables

The technique of partial correlation, and the related method of analysis of covariance, are often used by social scientists to examine relationships between certain variables when other, potentially distorting variables are held statistically constant. Users of these methods sometimes do not realize that the partialed variable or covariate is assumed to be measured without error, and that if this is not the case, very misleading conclusions may be drawn.

Figure 3.8 provides a simple example. A correlation between latent variables A and B is assumed in the model to be due wholly to a third variable C

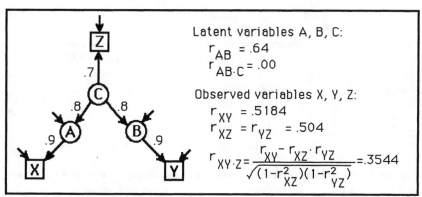

Fig. 3.8 Example of misleading partial correlation when partialed variable C is imperfectly measured by Z.

that influences them both; removing the effect of this third variable should, therefore, result in a partial correlation $r_{AB \cdot C} = 0$. But see what happens when C is measured with considerable error, and one applies the traditional formula for partial correlation. An observed correlation of .52 between X and Y is reduced only to .35, perhaps leading an unsuspecting reader to believe that A and B are connected in other ways than through C. A structural analysis based on an appropriate path model, even with quite rough estimates of the reliabilities of measurement of A, B, and C, should provide a much less misleading picture.

Mediation

The role of an intermediate variable in transmitting effects from one variable to another is often discussed in the literature under the heading of "mediation"-- e.g., Judd and Kenny (1981). Mediation is a variant of the situation in Fig. 3.8, with the arrow between A and C reversed in direction so that the causal path runs from A to C to B, with C acting as mediator between A and B. The correlations among the observed variables are not affected by this change, so the analysis to the right in Fig. 3.8 still applies. A study based on the observed variables X, Y, and Z would conclude that mediation by C was only partial, although complete mediation in fact occurs among the latent variables.

Analyzing a quasi-experiment--the effect of Head Start

Table 3-8 (next page) presents some data from a study on the effects of a Head Start program on children's cognitive skills. Two measures of the latter were used--the Illinois Test of Psycholinguistic Abilities and the Metropolitan

Table 3-8 Correlations among variables in Head Start evaluation (data from Bentler & Woodward, 1978), N = 303

	MEd	FEd	FOc	Inc	HS	ITPA	MRT
Mother's education	1.00	.47	.24	.30	-.12	.26	.28
Father's education	.00	1.00	.28	.21	-.08	.25	.22
Father's occupation	-.03	.04	1.00	.41	-.22	.22	.26
Income	.01	-.02	.00	1.00	-.18	.12	.19
Head Start participation	-.02	.03	-.01	.00	1.00	-.10	-.09
ITPA score	.00	.01	-.03	-.03	.00	1.00	.65
MRT score	.02	-.02	.01	.04	-.01	.00	1.00

Note: ITPA = Illinois Test of Psycholinguistic Abilities, MRT = Metropolitan Readiness Test. Original correlations are above diagonal, residuals from fitted model are below it.

Readiness Test, both taken after completion of the Head Start program, as well as being given to a control group of nonparticipants.

As you can see from Table 3-8, the correlations between participating in Head Start and scores on the two tests assessing cognitive ability are, on the face of it, a little embarrassing to proponents of Head Start--although they are small, they are in the wrong direction: Participants in the program did a little worse than members of the control group. But there were also negative correlations between Head Start participation and various parental educational and economic measures--apparently the control group members were selected from families somewhat better off than those from which the Head Start children came. Could this account for the results?

Figure 3.9 represents a path model proposed by Bentler and Woodward (1978). (It is actually only one of several considered in their article, but we confine ourselves to this one.) The model involves five latent variables. The four main source variables include the independent variable, Head Start participation, and three variables describing family background--a general socioeconomic status variable (SES) common to all four of the observed socioeconomic indicators, and two variables capturing specific aspects of education and economic circumstances. (As the diagram indicates, Bentler and Woodward assumed that these latter two might be correlated with each other, and that all three might be correlated with Head Start participation.) Other assumptions made in the diagram were that general SES and Head Start participation were the avenues of any influence of the source variables on cognitive skills, that cognitive skills were equally well measured by the two tests, and that Head Start participation and family income were measured without error. (One could certainly argue with some of these assumptions, but we proceed with the example. You might find it instructive to try fitting some other variations of the model to the data.)

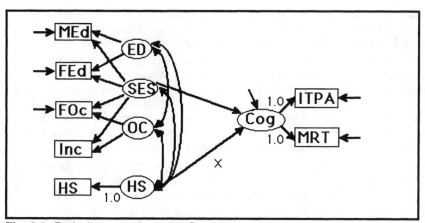

Fig. 3.9 Path diagram of a Head Start evaluation. x = path showing effect of Head Start participation on cognitive skills.

The latent variables were taken as standardized except for *Cog*, which was assigned arbitrary paths of 1.0 to the observed variables (themselves standardized).

The crucial path, marked *x* in Fig. 3.9, describes the direct influence of Head Start on cognitive skills when the other variables are held constant. Is it positive (Head Start helps) or negative (Head Start hinders), and--in either case--does it differ significantly from zero?

Figure 3.10 shows the values of the paths and the variance of the latent variable Cognitive Skills that were obtained in a solution using LISREL with the

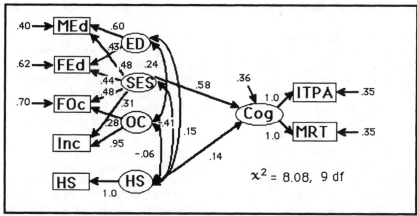

Fig. 3.10 Path diagram of Fig. 3.9 with values from solution including Head Start effect.

data of Table 3-8. Observe that when the socioeconomic statuses of the participants and the controls are taken into account, the estimate of the effect of Head Start participation on cognitive skills is slightly positive (.14).

The obtained χ^2 of 8.08 with 9 degrees of freedom represents a reasonably good fit to the data for the model as a whole, a fact that is also indicated by an estimated RMSEA of zero and the small residual correlations, which are shown below the diagonal in Table 3-8. Bentler and Woodward therefore went on to test whether the particular path representing Head Start effects differed significantly from zero, by comparing a model with this path free to one with it set to zero. The obtained χ^2 for the latter model is 9.93. The difference between the two χ^2s, 1.85, when tested as a χ^2 with 1 df, is well short of conventional levels of statistical significance (p > .10). Bentler and Woodward concluded, accordingly, that these data could not be said to demonstrate any effect of Head Start, positive or negative.

A note on degrees of freedom may be helpful. The model was treated as a covariance model with standardized latent independent variables. Twenty-eight (7 x 8/2) observed variances and covariances were fitted. Nineteen unknowns were solved for: 4 correlations among the source variables; 2 paths from source variables to *Cog* and 8 to the observed variables; the residual to *Cog*; and 4 different residuals to observed variables (those to ITPA and MRT are forced by the model to be the same). Twenty-eight data points minus 19 unknowns equals 9 degrees of freedom. In the second model, with one less path to be solved for, there are 10 df. Note also that one of the variables, Head Start participation, is dichotomous, so that the normality assumptions would come into question.

Models With Reciprocal Influences and Correlated Errors

Most of the models considered so far have been unlooped, that is, they have no causal sequences that loop back on themselves either remotely (A causes B causes C causes A) or immediately (A causes B causes A). The latter are usually described as models with reciprocal influences, because A influences B and B influences A. Also, most of the models considered so far have uncorrelated residuals; that is, the miscellaneous unspecified residual causes that influence a given variable are assumed uncorrelated with any other specific or residual causes in the diagram.

Violations of either of these conditions create problems for Wright's rules and for path analyses carried out by ordinary regression methods, although it is possible to deal with them by various special techniques, such as two-stage least squares (e.g., James & Singh, 1978). However, these conditions do not present any special difficulties for the general iterative model-fitting procedures described in this book, provided that the latent variables in the models are sufficiently well rooted in data to yield definite solutions. In practice, such models often do give trouble--assuring identification is sometimes not easy when loops or correlated errors are present, and convergence on a solution may be more difficult to attain--but, typically, one simply specifies the model in the normal way and presents it to the iterative program. It will solve it or it won't. As an extra precaution, however, one might want to obtain solutions from different sets of starting values as a clue to possible identification problems.

A study of career aspirations

Table 3-9 presents a set of data from a classic and much analyzed study by Duncan, Haller, and Portes (1968), in which both reciprocal influences and correlated residuals are involved. The original data were gathered in a study of career aspirations (Haller & Butterworth, 1960) in which 442 seventeen-year-old boys in a southern Michigan county were given tests and questionnaires. There were 329 boys in the sample naming at least one other boy also in the sample as one of their best friends. Thus, there were 329 instances of a boy and a close friend, on both of whom similar data on abilities, background, and career aspirations were available. (There are some subtle statistical issues raised by taking both boys and friends from the same sample, but we ignore them here.)

Five variables were measured for each boy: (1) his perception of what his parents' aspirations were for his further education and occupational status; (2) his intelligence (measured by his score on a nonverbal IQ test); (3) his family's socioeconomic status (as measured by parental income and material

Table 3-9 Correlations among variables related to career aspirations of boys and their friends (data from Duncan, Haller, & Portes, 1968), N = 329

	Respondent					Friend				
	PA	IQ	SES	EA	OA	PA	IQ	SES	EA	OA
Respondent										
Parent aspiration	1.00	.18	.05	.27	.21	.11	.08	.02	.11	.08
Intelligence		1.00	.22	.40	.41	.10	.34	.19	.29	.26
Family SES			1.00	.40	.32	.09	.23	.27	.31	.28
Educ. aspiration				1.00	.62	.07	.29	.24	.37	.33
Occup. aspiration					1.00	.08	.30	.29	.33	.42
Friend										
Parent aspiration						1.00	.21	-.04	.28	.20
Intelligence							1.00	.30	.52	.50
Family SES								1.00	.41	.36
Educ. aspiration									1.00	.64
Occup. aspiration										1.00

possessions);   (4) the amount of further education that he expected to obtain; and (5) the level of occupation to which he aspired. Figure 3.11 shows a version of one model proposed by Duncan, Haller and Portes. In the left-hand part of the diagram are six source variables. Three represent the respondent's intelligence, his family's socioeconomic status, and his perception of his parents' aspirations for him; the other three represent the same measures for the respondent's friend. To the right in the diagram are two downstream latent variables representing the level of ambition of the respondent and his friend. It is assumed that an individual's ambition for educational and economic success will be influenced by his parents' aspirations for him, by his intelligence, and by his family's socioeconomic status. It is also assumed (path marked *w*) that his friend's family's socioeconomic status might affect the level of education and occupation to which he himself aspires, but that his friend's intelligence and parental aspirations will not, except by way of the effect they might have on the friend's own ambition.

The latent variable of ambition is indexed by the two observed variables of educational aspiration and occupational aspiration, for both the respondent and his friend.

Additional possibilities are considered, as shown on the path diagram:

1. Reciprocal influence, as indicated in Fig. 3.11 by the paths marked *x*. Does one's boy's ambition regarding educational and occupational achievement influence the ambition of his friend?

2. Correlated residual influences on the two friends' ambition, as indicated by the path marked *y*. It is possible that factors not included in the diagram that are shared in common by the two friends might influence their levels of ambition (in addition to whatever direct influence the boys have on each other). These might include, for example, the effect of teachers, or of other peers.

3. Correlated errors of measurement, as indicated by the paths marked *z*. There might be shared effects on the specifics of a particular measurement instrument, in addition to the true correlations of the common factors being measured. For example, two friends might have discussed particular colleges and jobs, in addition to whatever general resemblance there was in their overall levels of ambition.

Previous analyses of these data have usually omitted the extreme left-hand part of the path diagram, i.e., the paths from the latent variables intelligence, SES, etc. to the observed measures of them. This is equivalent to assuming that these variables are perfectly measured--an unlikely assumption. If the reliabilities of the measurements were known, the square roots of these reliabilities could be entered as the values of the paths from the latent variables representing the true scores to the fallible observed scores (compare the example of Fig. 1.9, Chapter 1). For the purpose of illustration, we will arbitrarily

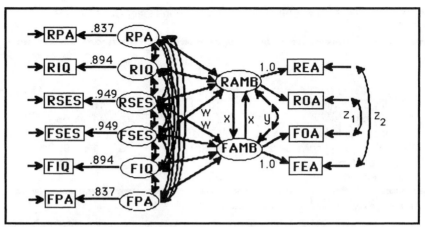

Fig. 3.11 Path model for study of career aspirations. R = respondent, F = friend; PA = parental aspirations; IQ = intelligence; SES = socioeconomic status; AMB = ambition; EA = educational aspirations; OA = occupational aspirations; w, x, y, z = paths tested. Path values fixed by assumption are shown.

assume that the reliabilities of measurement of parental aspiration, intelligence, and socioeconomic status are .7, .8, and .9, respectively, in this population, and hence that the square roots of these numbers, .837, .894, and .949, are the values of the corresponding paths in the measurement model.

A preliminary question we may ask is whether we need to maintain a distinction between corresponding paths for respondents and their friends. After all, these are drawn from the same population, and it would not be at all surprising if they would agree within sampling error. If so, we need only solve for a single unknown value for each such set of paired paths, increasing the number of degrees of freedom and the general robustness of the analysis.

The first χ^2 test shown in Table 3-10 (next page) investigates this possibility. The first row of the table shows a χ^2 of 11.60, with 13 degrees of freedom, for the full model of Fig. 3.11. The second shows the results of assuming 15 equalities between respondent and friend: 3 in the correlations among the source variables for each individual (e.g., $r_{RPA,RIQ} = r_{FPA,FIQ}$); 3 in the correlations across pairs (e.g., $r_{RPA,FIQ} = r_{FPA,RIQ}$); 4 in the paths from source variables to Ambition (e.g., RPA to RAMB = FPA to FAMB); 1 in the reciprocal paths (RAMB to FAMB = FAMB to RAMB); 1 in the paths from the latent to the observed variables (RAMB to ROA = FAMB to FOA); and 3 in the residuals from occupational and educational aspirations and ambition.

The difference in χ^2 between the model with and without these equality constraints is 7.29; with 15 degrees of freedom this does not come even close

Table 3-10. Tests of hypotheses for the Duncan-Haller-Portes career aspiration model (Fig. 3.11)

	χ^2	df	χ^2_{diff}	df_{diff}	p
1. Unconstrained model	11.60	13			
2. Equality constraints only	18.89	28	7.29	15	>.90
3. No SES path (w)	23.07	29	4.18	1	<.05
4. No reciprocal influence (x)	20.81	29	1.92	1	>.10
5. No AMB residual correlation (y)	18.89	29	.00	1	>.95
6. Both 4 and 5 (no x or y)	25.67	30	6.78	2	<.05
7. No correlated errors (z)	32.21	30	13.32	2	<.01

Note: line 2 tested against 1, and lines 3-7 against 2.

to statistical significance. Thus, we might as well simplify matters by making the symmetry assumptions, which we do in the remainder of the analysis.

Line 3 asks whether we really need a path w. Is it necessary to postulate a direct influence of his friend's family's status on a boy's ambition? The result of the test is that the model fits significantly better with such a path than without it ($\chi^2 = 4.18$, 1 df, p < .05). However, the estimated value of the path (.09--see Table 3-12, model 2) suggests that it is not a major contributor to ambition. Line 4 asks the same question about reciprocal influences, the paths x in the figure. The model is judged not to fit significantly worse when they are omitted ($\chi^2 = 1.92$, 1 df, p > .10). The same conclusion can be drawn in line 5 about a possible correlation y between the residual factors lying back of the two latent dependent variables ($\chi^2 = .00$, 1 df, p > .95). Thus we cannot show that either of these features of the model--the influence of one friend's ambition on the other, or shared influences among the unmeasured variables affecting each--is necessary to explain the data. If, however, we exclude both of these at once (the analysis of line 6) we *do* get a significant χ^2 (6.78, 2 df, p < .05), suggesting that the two may represent alternative ways of interpreting the similarity between friends' aspirations which our design is not sufficiently powerful to distinguish. As can be seen in Table 3-12, when both are fit, the residual correlation y is negligible (model 2), but when the reciprocal paths are set to zero (model 4), the correlation y becomes appreciable (.25). Setting y to zero (model 5) has little effect, as one would expect from its trivial value in model 2.

Finally, the analysis in line 7 of Table 3-10 asks if the specific measures of educational and occupational aspirations might have errors that are correlated for the two friends. The substantial χ^2 (13.32, 2 df, p < .01) suggests that it is indeed a plausible assumption that such correlated errors exist.

This example, then, illustrates the application of a path diagram with somewhat more complex features than most of those we have considered

Table 3-11 Estimated values of the paths and correlations for three models from Table 3-10

	Model 2	Model 4	Model 5
Paths			
PA to AMB	.19	.19	.19
IQ to AMB	.35	.38	.35
SES to AMB	.24	.26	.24
FSES to AMB (w)	.09	.12	.09
AMB to AMB (x)	.12	.00	.12
AMB to OA	.91	.91	.91
Correlations			
AMB residuals (y)	-.00	.25	.00
OA residuals (z_1)	.26	.26	.26
EA residuals (z_2)	.07	.07	.07

Note: Paths are unstandardized, but covariances have been standardized to correlations. Models correspond to the lines in Table 3-10.

previously. It is clear that further testable hypotheses could be stated for this model: For just one example, the diagram assumes that the respondent's own aspiration level and his estimate of his parents' aspirations for him are not subject to correlated errors. (Is this a reasonable assumption? How would you test it?) This case also suggests that tests of different hypotheses may not be independent of one another (x and y). In addition, if many hypotheses are tested, particularly if some are suggested by inspection of the data, one should remember that the nominal probability levels can no longer be taken literally, though the differential χ^2s may still serve as a general guide to the relative merits of competing hypotheses.

Another point worth noting about this example is that *none* of the overall models tested in Table 3-10 can be rejected; that is, if one had begun with any one of them and tested only it, the conclusion would have been that it represented a tolerable fit to the data. It is only in the comparisons among the models that one begins to learn something of their relative merits.

Nonlinear Effects Among Latent Variables

The relationships expressed in path models are linear. Path models are, after all, a special application of linear regression. However, it is well known that in linear regression one can express nonlinear and interactive relationships by the device of introducing squares, products, etc. of the original variables. Thus, to deal with a curvilinear prediction of Y from X we might use the prediction equation:

$$Y = aX + bX^2 + Z.$$

Or we could deal with an interactive effect of X and Z on Y with an equation such as:

$$Y = aX + bZ + cXZ + W.$$

These equations represent nonlinear relationships among observed variables by the use of linear regressions involving higher order or product terms. Can the same thing be done with *latent* variables? Kenny and Judd (1984) explore this question and conclude that the answer is: Yes. We follow their strategy.

Suppose we wish to represent the first nonlinear relationship above, but X is an unobserved, latent variable, indexed by two observed variables, call them A and B. In structural equation form:

$$A = aX + U$$
$$B = bX + V$$
$$Y = cX + dX^2 + Z.$$

The first two equations constitute the measurement model, the third the structural model. (For simplicity we are treating Y as an observed variable, but it could be a latent variable as well, with its own indexing measures.)

But how is X^2 to be linked to the data? Kenny and Judd point out that the preceding equations imply relationships of X^2 to A^2, B^2 and the product AB. For example, by squaring the equations for A and B we obtain the first two of the following equations, and by taking the product of the equations for A and B we obtain the third:

$$A^2 = a^2X^2 + 2aXU + U^2$$
$$B^2 = b^2X^2 + 2bXV + V^2$$
$$AB = abX^2 + aXV + bXU + UV.$$

Figure 3.12 represents these various relationships in the form of a path diagram. Notice that X, X^2, XU, and XV are shown as uncorrelated. This will be the case if X, U, and V are normally distributed and expressed in deviation score form. Kenny and Judd also show that given these assumptions, expressions can be derived for the variances of the square and product terms. Under these conditions the following relations hold:

$$V_{X^2} = 2(V_X)^2; \quad V_{XU} = V_X V_U.$$

The first of these expressions means that the variance of X^2 equals two times the square of the variance of X. The second, that the variance of the product XU equals the product of the variances of X and U. Similar relationships hold for

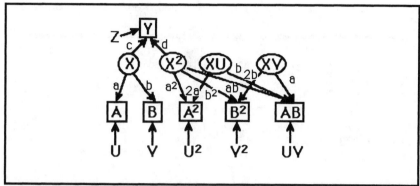

Fig. 3.12 Path diagram for nonlinear effect of X on Z.

V_{U^2}, V_{UV}, etc. This means that we can write equations for the observed variances and covariances of A, B, A^2, B^2, AB, and Y in terms of a moderate number of parameters. If we set to 1.0 one of the paths from X to an observed variable, say a, we have left as unknowns the paths b, c, d, the variance of X, and the variances of the residuals U, V, and Z. The remaining values can be obtained from these. The equivalences are given in Table 3-12.

Table 3-12 Equivalence constraints for Kenny-Judd solution

Variances:	Paths:
$V_{X^2} = 2(V_X)^2$	$X^2 \rightarrow A^2 = 1$
$V_{XU} = V_X V_U$	$\rightarrow B^2 = b^2$
$V_{XV} = V_X V_V$	$\rightarrow AB = b$
$V_{U^2} = 2(V_U)^2$	$XU \rightarrow A^2 = 2$
$V_{V^2} = 2(V_V)^2$	$\rightarrow AB = b$
$V_{UV} = V_U V_V$	$XV \rightarrow B^2 = 2b$
	$\rightarrow AB = 1$

Note: Path a is set to 1.0 throughout.

Kenny and Judd present illustrative variances and covariances for simulated data from a sample of 500 subjects. These are given in Table 3-13 (next page). There are $6 \times 7/2 = 21$ observed variances and covariances and 7 parameters, so there are 14 degrees of freedom for the solution.

There are a couple of difficulties in fitting this model with standard SEM programs. We wish to fix paths and variances in such relations as b and b^2, or b and $2b$, and some programs do not provide for other than equality constraints.

Table 3-13 Covariance matrix of observed values (Kenny & Judd simulated data, N = 500)

	A	B	A^2	B^2	AB	Y
A	1.150					
B	.617	.981				
A^2	-.068	-.025	2.708			
B^2	.075	.159	.729	1.717		
AB	.063	.065	1.459	1.142	1.484	
Y	.256	.166	-1.017	-.340	-.610	.763

In a pinch, one might circumvent this by a creative use of what are called "phantom variables" (see Appendix E) but a more generally satisfactory solution would usually be to seek out a program that allows one to impose such constraints directly. A second difficulty concerns the use of a fitting criterion such as maximum likelihood, because some of our variables are not normally distributed. We have assumed, for example, that X is normal, but that means that X^2 will not be.

Kenny and Judd fit their model with the program COSAN mentioned in Chapter 2 that is extremely flexible in allowing the user to specify relationships among paths. They also used a generalized least squares fitting criterion that they believed to be less vulnerable to multivariate nonnormality than is maximum likelihood.

Their solution is shown in Table 3-14, along with the values used to generate the simulated data. It is clear that their procedure has essentially recovered these values.

Table 3-14 Solutions of Fig. 3.12 model for data of Table 3-13

Parameter	Original	COSAN	LISREL 8
b	.60	.62	.63
c	.25	.25	.25
d	-.50	-.50	-.50
x	1.00	.99	1.00
u	.15	.16	.16
v	.55	.54	.55
z	.20	.20	.20

Note: COSAN solution from Kenny and Judd (1984).

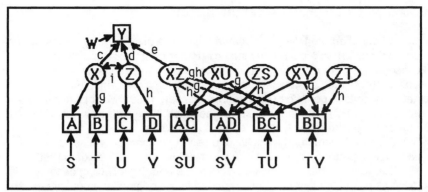

Fig. 3.13 Path diagram for interactive effect of X and Z on Y. Unlabeled paths set to 1.0.

A study by Jaccard and Wan (1995) has suggested that solutions of nonlinear models of this sort may be fairly robust to the lack of multivariate normality in derived variables, provided the original variables are normal. Indeed, in their study the violations of multivariate normality had much less adverse consequences than an attempt to use the distribution-free criterion, ADF, with moderate-sized samples. A solution to the Kenny-Judd data using LISREL 8 with a maximum likelihood criterion is also shown in Table 3-14. It is evident that the COSAN and LISREL solutions have done about equally well in recovering the values used to generate the data.

Kenny and Judd went on to carry out a similar analysis for the case of an interactive relationship between two variables, as represented in the second equation given at the beginning of this section. The general principles involved are the same. A path diagram for an example is shown in Fig. 3.13; as you can see, each of the latent variables X and Z is indexed by two observed variables, and there are a number of additional product and residual terms. The 9 observed variables provide 45 variances and covariances, and there are 13 parameters to be solved for (the variances of X and Z, their covariance i, the paths $g, h, c, d,$ and e, and the residual variances S, T, U, V, and W).
Again, Kenny and Judd were reasonably successful in recovering the values used to generate their simulated data.

Obviously, the possibility of constructing and solving path models of nonlinear and interactive relationships broadens considerably the range of latent variable problems that can be dealt with. It may be expected, however, that models involving such relationships will tend to be fairly demanding in the quantity and quality of data that are required in order to arrive at dependable solutions.

This is an active area of investigation, and quite a few different strategies have been suggested for modeling nonlinear and interactive relationships among latent variables--see the Notes to this chapter.

Chapter 3 Notes

Structural equation modeling has been applied to a diverse array of topics: for example, health problems in early infancy (Baker et al. 1984), political alienation (Mason et al. 1985), university teaching evaluations (Marsh & Hocevar, 1983), attitudes toward natural foods (Homer & Kahle, 1988), the female orgasmic experience (Newcomb & Bentler, 1983), Machiavellian beliefs (Hunter et al. 1982), rat neural systems (McIntosh & Gonzalez-Lima, 1991), and the effect of special promotions on supermarket sales (Walters & MacKenzie, 1988). A list of 72 structural modeling studies in personality and social psychology appearing between 1977 and 1987 is given in Breckler (1990).

Caution: Numerical results given in this and the following chapter sometimes differ slightly from those reported in the original sources, presumably because of differences in rounding, slight convergence discrepancies, minor misprints in correlation tables, or the like. I have not recomputed everything, but if a study forms the basis of an exercise, I have tried to provide consistent figures. RMSEAs were generally not reported in the original studies, most of which predate the widespread use of this index.

Maruyama-McGarvey study. There is some inconsistency in the labeling of variables in the original paper. I have followed the identifications in their Table 2, which according to Maruyama (personal communication) are the correct ones.

Multitrait-multimethod models. K. F. Widaman (1985) discusses hierarchically nested models for MTMM data, and Schmitt and Stults (1986) look at different methods of analyzing MTMM matrices. General reviews include chapters by Marsh and Grayson (1995) and by Wothke (1996). MTMM models that multiply the effects of traits and methods instead of adding them have been discussed by a number of authors, including Cudeck (1988), Wothke and Browne (1990), and Verhees and Wansbeek (1990). Wothke and Browne show how multiplicative models can be fit using standard SEM programs such as LISREL. There is mixed evidence concerning the relative merits of additive and multiplicative models in practical application. Some reviews have reported additive ones to be more often successful (Bagozzi & Yi, 1990), but other authors have disagreed (Goffin & Jackson, 1992; Coovert et al., 1997), or found the evidence to be mixed (Byrne & Goffin, 1993). A recent study involving 79 data sets found the additive model to work better for 71 of them (Corten et al., 2002). Saris and Aalberts (2003) look at different interpretations of correlated disturbance terms in MTMM studies. Differences in how convergent and discriminant validity are manifested in the two kinds of models are pointed out by Reichardt and Coleman (1995). The fitting of MTMM models within and across groups is discussed by Marsh and Byrne (1993).

Mediation. Shrout and Bolger (2002) recommend bootstrap methods for the evaluation of direct and indirect effects in mediation studies in SEM. Hoyle and Kenny (1999) stress the value of using a latent variable in mediation research when variables are imperfectly measured.

Models with loops. Heise (1975) provides a good introduction to this topic, including the modifications of path rules required to deal with looped models.

Nonlinear relationships. See also Busemeyer and Jones (1983) on handling multiplicative effects. Jöreskog and Yang (1996) argue that for correct inference means must be included in such models. Other recent suggestions for dealing with quadratic and interaction effects include a two-step strategy suggested by Ping (1966) and a simple two-stage least squares method proposed by Bollen (1995), in which various empirical square and product terms are treated as instrumental variables. Applied to the data of Table 3-13, Bollen's method yields estimates for c and d of .25 and -.49, respectively, as accurately recovering the underlying values as the COSAN and LISREL 8 solutions in Table 3-14. Interest in such effects continues. Moulder and Algina (2002) present a Monte Carlo comparison of several methods, and Schumacker (2002) suggests a simple strategy based on first estimating latent variable scores and then multiplying these. Computational issues in the estimation of nonlinear structural equation models are addressed by Lee and Zhu (2000, 2002). Neale (1998) shows how to implement the Kenny-Judd models in Mx. Li et al. (2000) extend Jöreskog and Yang's method to deal with interactions in latent curve models, but Wen et al. (2002) suggest that they may not have got it quite right yet. Yang-Wallentin (2001) compares Bollen's 2SLS with Kenny-Judd solved via maximum likelihood, and concludes that both have merits but require samples of 400+. Contributions from a number of workers in this area may be found in a volume edited by Schumacker and Marcoulides (1998), which contains useful summaries by Rigdon et al. and Jöreskog, and new strategies by Laplante et al. and Schermelleh-Engel et al. For yet another approach, see Blom and Christoffersson (2001).

Chapter 3 Exercises

1. Can you conclude that tests T1 to T3, whose covariance matrix is given below, are not parallel tests? (N = 35) How about tau-equivalent?

	T1	T2	T3
T1	54.85		
T2	60.21	99.24	
T3	48.42	67.00	63.81

2. In McIver et al.'s police survey model (Fig. 3.4), can we conclude that the paths from F_2 to its three indicators are really different from one another? (State and test an appropriate null hypothesis).

3. Part of Campbell and Fiske's original multitrait-multimethod matrix is given in Table 3-15. These are ratings of clinical psychology trainees by staff members, fellow trainees, and themselves. Tabulate and compare the correlations in the three principal categories (within trait, across method; within method, across trait; and across both method and trait).

Table 3-15 Multitrait-multimethod matrix (data from Campbell & Fiske, 1959), N = 124

	StA	StC	StT	TrA	TrC	TrS	SeA	SeC	SeS
Ratings:									
Staff									
Assertive	1.00								
Cheerful	.37	1.00							
Serious	-.24	-.14	1.00						
Trainee									
Assertive	.71	.35	-.18	1.00					
Cheerful	.39	.53	-.15	.37	1.00				
Serious	-.27	-.31	.43	-.15	-.19	1.00			
Self									
Assertive	.48	.31	-.22	.46	.36	-.15	1.00		
Cheerful	.17	.42	-.10	.09	.24	-.25	.23	1.00	
Serious	-.04	-.13	.22	-.04	-.11	.31	-.05	-.12	1.00

Trait and method

4. Estimate a multitrait-multimethod model for the data of Table 3-15, using an SEM program (if using LISREL you may need to set AD=OFF to obtain a solution). Assume that the methods are uncorrelated, and that the traits are uncorrelated with the methods. Compare to the results of models using trait factors only and method factors only.

5. Calculate the original and partial correlations r_{XY} and $r_{XY \cdot Z}$--see Fig. 3.8--for the following additional values of the path from C to Z: .9, 1.0, .5, .0. Comment on the results.

6. Keep the measurement model from Maruyama and McGarvey's desegregation study but make one or more plausible changes in the structural model. Fit your model, using an SEM program, and compare the results to those in Fig. 3.3.

7. Construct a different path model for the Head Start evaluation data (Table 3-8), with different latent variables and hypothesized relations among them. Retain in your model the dependent latent variable of cognitive skills and a path x to it from Head Start participation. Fit your model and make a χ^2 test for the significance of path x.

8. Repeat the test of the basic Duncan-Haller-Portes model of Fig. 3.11 (use the version with equality constraints--line 2 of Table 3-10). Then test to determine if each of the paths z_1 and z_2 makes a separate significant contribution to the goodness of fit of the model. (Note: Fitting this model has caused difficulties for some SEM programs. If yours acts up, try fixing the residual variances to .3, .2, .1, etc., and leaving the paths between latent and observed RPA, RIQ, etc., free. Also, some programs may not permit specifying all the 15 equalities in the example. Specify as many as you can--the results should be similar and the conclusion the same.)

9. In the text, a question was raised about assuming uncorrelated errors between a boy's own educational and occupational aspirations and his estimate of his parents' aspiration for him. How might this assumption be tested?

10. Write the path equations for V_A, $C_{B,AC}$, $C_{AC,AD}$, and V_Y, from Fig. 3.13.

Chapter Four:
Fitting Models Involving Repeated Measures or Multiple Groups

In this chapter we continue our survey of a variety of applications of path and structural models. The models considered introduce some additional features over those discussed in Chapter 3. We begin by considering several models dealing with the covariances among measures that are repeated over time. Then we look at models fitted simultaneously in two or more groups. Finally, we consider models that compare means as well as covariances, either for different groups or over time.

Models of Events Over Time

Latent variable causal models are often used to analyze situations in which variables are measured over a period of time. Such situations have the advantage of permitting a fairly unambiguous direction of causal arrows: If event A precedes event B and there is a direct causal connection between them, it is A that causes B and not vice versa. If, on the other hand, A and B were measured more or less contemporaneously, a distinction between the hypotheses "A causes B" and "B causes A" must be made on other grounds--not always a simple matter.

This is not to say that variables sequenced in time never give trouble in assigning cause. Even though B follows A, it is always possible that B might reflect some third variable C that precedes and is a cause of A, and therefore one might be less wrong in calling B a cause of A than the reverse. Of course, one would be still better off with C in the model as a cause of both A and B, with no causal arrow between A and B at all. Nonetheless, the presence of temporal ordering often lends itself naturally to causal modeling, and we examine some examples in the next few sections.

A minitheory of love

Tesser and Paulhus (1976) carried out a study in which 202 college students filled out a 10-minute questionnaire on attitudes toward dating. The

Table 4-1 Correlations among four measures of "love" on two occasions (data from Tesser & Paulhus, 1976), N = 202

	T1	L1	C1	D1	T2	L2	C2	D2
Occasion 1								
Thought	1.000	.728	.129	.430	.741	.612	-.027	.464
Love		1.000	.224	.451	.748	.830	.094	.495
Confirmation			1.000	.086	.154	.279	.242	.104
Dating				1.000	.414	.404	.108	.806
Occasion 2								
Thought					1.000	.764	.161	.503
Love						1.000	.103	.505
Confirmation							1.000	.070
Dating								1.000
S D	3.59	19.49	1.80	2.87	3.75	20.67	1.72	3.16
Mean	9.83	50.66	5.08	3.07	9.20	49.27	4.98	2.95

questionnaire contained several subscales having to do with attitudes and behavior toward a particular member of the opposite sex "where there is some romantic interest involved on somebody's part." Four measures were obtained: (T) how much the respondent thought about the other person during the last 2 weeks; (L) a 9-item love scale; (C) to what extent were the respondent's expectations concerning the other person confirmed by new information during the past 2 weeks; and (D) number of dates with the other person during the same 2-week period.

Two weeks later the subjects filled out the questionnaire again, with respect to the same person, for events during the 2 weeks between the two questionnaire administrations. Table 4-1 presents Tesser and Paulhus' basic results, which they subjected to a simple path analysis and which were later reanalyzed by Bentler and Huba (1979) using several different latent variable models.

Figure 4.1 (next page) shows a slightly modified version of one of Bentler and Huba's models. Basically, the four scales are shown as reflecting a common factor of attraction at each time period; attraction at the second period is explainable by a persistence of attraction from the first (path *m*) plus possible new events (path *n*). It is assumed that the measurement model (*a, b, c, d* ; *e, f, g, h*) is the same on both occasions of measurement. It is also assumed that the specifics of a particular behavior or attitude may show correlation across the two occasions. For example, an individual's frequency of dating a particular person is influenced by a variety of factors other than general attraction, and these might well be similar at both times--as might also be various measurement artifacts, such as the tendency of a person to define "dates" more or less broadly, or to brag when filling out questionnaires.

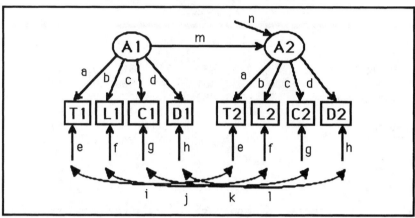

Fig. 4.1 A model for the "love" data of Tesser and Paulhus (Table 4-1). A = general attraction; T, L, C, D = four measures of specific attitudes and behavior (see text); 1, 2 = two occasions.

Table 4-2 shows the results of fitting the model of Fig. 4.1 to the correlations in Table 4-1. The paths reported are from an unstandardized solution (using LISREL); however, the measured variables are implicitly standardized by the use of correlations, the variance of the latent variable A1 is set to 1.0, and that of A2 does not differ much from 1.0, so the results in the table can pretty much be interpreted as though they were from a standardized path model. Thinking about a person and the love questionnaire are strong measures of the general attraction variable, dating is a moderate one, and confirmation of expectations is a very weak one. The residual variances reflect these inversely--the love score is least affected by other things, and the confirmation score is nearly all due to other factors. The general factor of attraction toward a particular person shows a strong persistence over the 2 weeks (m = .94, standardized, .92).

The residual covariances suggest that for thought and love the correlation between the two occasions of measurement is mostly determined by the persistence of the general factor, whereas for dating there is a large cross-occasion correlation produced by specific factors. On the whole, the measure of confirmation of expectations does not relate to much of anything else within occasions, and only quite moderately to itself across occasions. It was based on only one item; one might speculate that it may not be a very reliable measure. The measure of dating frequency may suffer from some psychometric problems as well--it appears to be markedly skewed (SD ≈ mean in Table 4-1). One might wish in such a case to consider preliminary transformation of the scale (say to logarithms) before embarking on an analysis that assumes multivariate normality. Or one should hedge on one's probability statements.

Table 4-2 Solution of path model of Fig. 4.1 for data of Table 4-1: Tesser and Paulhus study

Variable	Paths		Residual variances		Residual covariances	
Thought	a	.83	e^2	.31	i	.11
Love	b	.88	f^2	.20	j	.09
Confirmation	c	.17	g^2	.97	k	.21
Dating	d	.53	h^2	.70	l	.53
Attraction	m	.94	n^2	.15		

Note: Paths unstandardized; variance of A1 set at 1.0, variance of A2 = 1.043. χ^2 = 45.87, 22 df, p < .01. Residual variances are squares of path values e, f, g, etc.

As a matter of fact, based on the obtained χ^2 of 45.87 with 22 degrees of freedom, if one takes the statistics seriously one would conclude that the present model does not fit exactly in the population (a conclusion that Bentler and Huba also arrived at from an analysis based on covariances using a similar model). Judged by the RMSEA, the approximation is acceptable, but somewhat marginal (RMSEA = .074), and one cannot reject the hypothesis of poor fit (upper limit of interval = .103). If one calculates the correlations implied by the solution of Table 4-2 and compares them to the observed correlations, the largest discrepancies are for the correlation between T1 and C2, which the model predicts to be about .13 but which was observed as -.03, and for the correlation between C1 and L2, which was predicted as .14 but observed as .28. If one includes ad hoc paths for these in the model, the fit becomes statistically acceptable (χ^2 = 26.34, 20 df, p > .15)--Bentler and Huba obtained a similar result in their analysis. Because in doing this one is likely to be at least in part fitting the model to the idiosyncrasies of the present data set, the revised probability value should be taken even less seriously than the original one. The prudent stance is that paths between T1 and C2 and C1 and L2 represent hypotheses that might be worth exploring in future studies but should not be regarded as established in this one.

Should one analyze correlations or covariances? As we have seen, in the present example, the results come out pretty much the same whether correlations were analyzed, as described, or whether covariances were, as in Bentler and Huba's analysis of these data. Both methods have their advantages. It is easier to see from the .83 and .88 in Table 4-2 that paths *a* and *b* are roughly comparable, than to make the same judgment from the values of 3.18 and 16.16 in Bentler and Huba's Table 1. On the other hand, the statistical theory underlying maximum likelihood and generalized least squares model fitting is based on covariance matrices, and application of these methods to correlation matrices, although widely practiced, means that the resulting χ^2s will contain one step more of approximation than they already do.

One further consideration, of minor concern in the present study, will sometimes prove decisive. If the variances of variables are changing markedly over time, one should be wary of analyzing correlations because this in effect restandardizes all variables at each time period. If one does not want to do this, but does wish to retain the advantages of standardization for comparing different variables, one should standardize the variables once, either for the initial period or across all time periods combined, and compute and analyze the covariance matrix of these standardized variables.

The simplex--growth over time

Suppose you have a variable on which growth tends to occur over time, such as height or vocabulary size among schoolchildren. You take measurements of this variable once a year, say, for a large sample of children. Then you can calculate a covariance or correlation matrix of these measurements across time: Grade 1 versus Grade 2, Grade 1 versus Grade 3, Grade 2 versus Grade 3, and so on.

In general, you might expect that measurements made closer together in time would be more highly correlated--that a person's relative standing on, say, vocabulary size would tend to be less different on measures taken in Grades 4 and 5 than in Grades 1 and 8. Such a tendency will result in a correlation matrix that has its highest values close to the principal diagonal and tapers off to its lowest values in the upper right and lower left corners. A matrix of this pattern is called a simplex (Guttman, 1954).

Table 4-3 Correlations and standard deviations across grades 1-7 for academic achievement (Bracht & Hopkins, 1972), Ns = 300 to 1240

Grade	Correlations						
	1	2	3	4	5	6	7
1	1.00	.73	.74	.72	.68	.68	.66
2		1.00	.86	.79	.78	.76	.74
3			1.00	.87	.86	.84	.81
4				1.00	.93	.91	.87
5					1.00	.93	.90
6						1.00	.94
7							1.00
SD	.51	.69	.89	1.01	1.20	1.26	1.38

Table 4-3 provides illustrative data from a study by Bracht and Hopkins (1972). They obtained scores on standardized tests of academic achievement at each grade from 1 to 7. As you can see in the table, the correlations tend to show the simplex pattern by decreasing from the main diagonal toward the upper right-hand corner of the matrix. The correlations tend to decrease as one moves to the right along any row, or upwards along any column. The standard deviations at the bottom of Table 4-3 show another feature often found with growth data: The variance increases over time.

Figure 4.2 represents a path diagram of a model fit by Werts, Linn, and Jöreskog (1977) to these data. Such a model represents one possible way of interpreting growth. It supposes that the achievement test score (T) at each grade level is a fallible measure of a latent variable, academic achievement (A). Achievement at any grade level is partly a function of achievement at the previous grade, via a path w, and partly determined by other factors, z. Test score partly reflects actual achievement, via path x, and partly random errors, u. Because variance is changing, it is appropriate to analyze a covariance rather than a correlation matrix. Covariances may be obtained by multiplying each correlation by the standard deviations of the two variables involved.

Figure 4.2 has 7 xs, 7 us, 6 ws, 6 zs, and an initial variance of A for a total of 27 unknowns. There are 7 x 8/2 = 28 variances and covariances to fit. However, as Werts et al. point out, not all 27 unknowns can be solved for: There is a dependency at each end of the chain so that two unknowns--e.g., two us--must be fixed by assumption. Also, they defined the scale of the latent variables by setting the xs to 1.0, reducing the number of unknowns to 18--5 us, 6 ws, 6 zs, and an A--leaving 10 degrees of freedom.

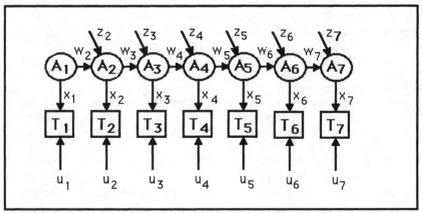

Fig. 4.2 Path model of growth over time. A = academic achievement; T = test score; 1-7 = grades.

Table 4-4 Solution of path diagram of Fig. 4.2 for data of Table 4-3 (growth over time)

Grade	w	z	A	u
1			.184	.076[a]
2	1.398	.041	.400	.076
3	1.318	.049	.743	.049
4	1.054	.137	.962	.058
5	1.172	.051	1.372	.068
6	1.026	.104	1.548	.040
7	1.056	.138	1.864	.040[a]

Note: w, z, A, u as in Fig. 4.2. Values u[a] set equal to adjacent value of u. A, z, u expressed as variances, w as an unstandardized path coefficient. $A_n = V_n - u_n$, where V_n is the variance of test at Grade n.

Table 4-4 shows estimates of the unknown values. The simplex model provides a reasonable fit to the data, if N is taken equal to its median value, which is 795. It is not an exact fit ($\chi^2 = 28.57$, 10 df, p < .01), but it is a decent one (RMSEA = .048). The hypothesis of poor fit can be rejected (upper limit of confidence interval for RMSEA = .069, which is < .10). The variance of academic achievement, A, increases steadily and substantially over the grades, whereas trends for *w*, *z*, and *u* are much less marked, especially if one discounts the first 2 or 3 years.

A point of mild interest in this solution is that the *w* parameters, which represent the effect of academic achievement in one grade on that in the next, are slightly greater than 1.0. Does this mean that academic skill persists without loss from one year to the next, indeed with enhancement? Are students who think they forget things over the summer really mistaken? Alas, more likely it means that what happens to a student between one year's measurement and the next is correlated with his or her standing the preceding year, so that the academically rich get richer and the poor lag further behind them. A suitable latent variable analysis taking additional variables into account would provide a way to clarify this issue.

Finally, could we fit an even simpler model to these data, one that has *w*, *z*, and *u* constant, and only A varying? The answer can be obtained by fitting a model with just four unknowns A, *z*, *w*, and *u*. The resulting χ^2 with 24 df is 200.91. The χ^2 difference of 172.34 with 14 degrees of freedom says: No, we cannot. The grade-to-grade differences in these parameters are too large to be attributable merely to chance.

Liberal-conservative attitudes at three time periods

Judd and Milburn (1980) used a latent variable analysis to examine attitudes in a nationwide sample of individuals who were surveyed on three occasions, in 1972, 1974, and 1976. Table 4-5 shows a portion of their data, based on three topics related to a liberal-conservative dimension of attitude (actually, Judd and Milburn studied five such topics). These particular data are from a subsample of 143 respondents who had attended 4 or more years of college. The numbers in the table mean, for example, that these respondents' attitudes toward busing in the 1972 and 1974 surveys were correlated .79, and their attitude toward busing in 1972 was correlated .39 with their attitude toward criminal rights in 1974.

The authors postulated that the interrelationships among these attitude measurements would largely be accounted for by a general factor of liberalism-conservatism, to which all three of the attitudes would be related at each of the three time periods, plus a specific factor for each attitude that would persist across time. (Actually, the main focus of Judd and Milburn's interest was to compare these features of attitude in a relatively elite group, the present sample, with those in a non-elite group, consisting of respondents who had not attended college. We look at this aspect of the study later in this chapter, in the context of cross-group comparisons.)

Table 4-5 Correlations among attitudes at three time periods (Judd & Milburn, 1980), N = 143, 4 years college

		B_{72}	C_{72}	J_{72}	B_{74}	C_{74}	J_{74}	B_{76}	C_{76}	J_{76}
1972	Busing	1.00	.43	.47	.79	.39	.50	.71	.27	.47
	Criminals		1.00	.29	.43	.54	.28	.37	.53	.29
	Jobs			1.00	.48	.38	.56	.49	.18	.49
1974	Busing				1.00	.46	.56	.78	.35	.48
	Criminals					1.00	.35	.44	.60	.32
	Jobs						1.00	.59	.20	.61
1976	Busing							1.00	.34	.53
	Criminals								1.00	.28
	Jobs									1.00
	SD	2.03	1.84	1.67	1.76	1.68	1.48	1.74	1.83	1.54

Note: Busing = bus to achieve school integration; Criminals = protect legal rights of those accused of crimes; Jobs = government should guarantee jobs and standard of living.

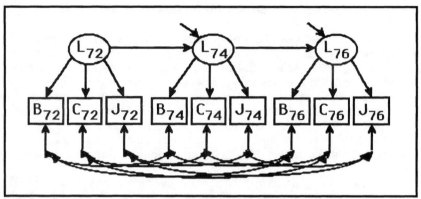

Fig. 4.3 Path model for attitudes measured in 1972, 1974, and 1976. L = general factor; B, C, J = specific attitudes; 72, 74, 76 = years.

Figure 4.3 represents their hypothesis. Liberalism in 1974 is partly predictable from liberalism in 1972, and partly by unrelated events; and similarly for 1976. The general degree of a person's liberalism in any year is reflected in his or her specific attitudes toward busing, the rights of criminals, and guaranteed jobs. A person's attitudes on one of these specific topics in one survey is related to his or her attitude on this same topic in another survey, but not with specific attitudes on other subjects, except by way of the common liberalism-conservatism factor. (Actually, Judd and Milburn worked with a slightly different, but essentially equivalent, model.)

Table 4-6 presents an analysis of the Judd and Milburn data using LISREL and a covariance matrix based on Table 4-5. On the whole, the model fits very well ($\chi^2 = 11.65$, 16 df, p > .70; RMSEA = 0). Liberalism is most strongly defined by attitudes toward busing, with attitudes toward guaranteed jobs ranking slightly ahead of attitudes toward justice for accused criminals. Not surprisingly, the three attitudes tend to fall in the reverse order with respect to unexplained variance, as well as the amount of specific association with the same attitude in other years.

A question one might ask is whether liberal-conservative attitudes in 1972 would have any effect on those in 1976 except via 1974; i.e., could there be a delayed effect of earlier on later attitudes? This can be tested by fitting a model with an additional direct path from L_{72} to L_{76}. This yields a χ^2 of 11.56 for 15 df. The difference, a χ^2 of .09 with 1 df, is far short of statistical significance. There is thus no evidence of such a delayed effect on attitudes, sometimes called a "sleeper effect," in these data.

Table 4-6 Solution of path model of Fig. 4.4 representing liberal-conservative attitudes at three time periods

	Path from L	Residual variance	Specific covariance with 1974	Specific covariance with 1976
1972 Busing	1.00[a]	1.51	.58	.29
Criminals	.58	2.52	.88	1.21
Jobs	.63	1.74	.41	.37
1974 Busing	1.00[a]	.92		.23
Criminals	.62	2.00		1.22
Jobs	.68	1.18		.48
1976 Busing	1.00[a]	.72		
Criminals	.49	2.82		
Jobs	.61	1.49		

Note: Unstandardized coefficients. Paths marked[a] arbitrarily set at 1.00. $\chi^2 = 11.65$, 16 df, $p > .70$. Additional paths in structural model: L_{72} to $L_{74} = .86$, L_{74} to $L_{76} = .99$; L_{72} variance = 2.60; residual variances, $L_{74} = .24$, $L_{76} = .18$.

Models Comparing Different Groups

The general approaches described in this and the preceding chapter are readily extended to the case of model fitting in several independent groups of subjects. In the fitting process, one combines the fit functions from the separate groups and minimizes the total. For statistical tests, one obtains an overall χ^2 for the combined groups, with an appropriate df which is the difference between the number of empirical values being fitted and the number of unknowns being solved for, taking into account any constraints being imposed within or across groups.

Again, differences in χ^2s for different nested solutions can be compared, using the differences between the associated degrees of freedom. Thus, for example, if one were solving for five unknowns in each of three groups, one could compare a solution that allowed them all to differ in each group with one that required them all to be constant across groups. There would be 15 unknowns to be solved for in the first case, and only 5 in the second, so the increase in χ^2 between the two would be tested as a χ^2 with 15 - 5 = 10 df.

Attitudes in elite and non-elite groups

Earlier we discussed a set of data by Judd and Milburn involving the structuring of attitudes with respect to a dimension of liberalism-conservatism. These attitudes were measured in three different years for a sample of 143 college-educated respondents. Responses were also available from the same nationwide surveys for a group of 203 individuals who had not attended college. Table 4-7 shows the data for the noncollege group, corresponding to Table 4-5 for the college group. (An intermediate group who had attended college, but for less than 4 years, was excluded to sharpen the contrast between the "elite" and "non-elite" groups.)

As we have seen, a model of a general attitude at each time period and specific attitudes correlated across time periods fits the data for college graduates quite well. Would it do as well for a less elite group? If it did, would there be differences between the groups in the parameters of the model?

One can fit the model of Fig. 4.3 (page 128) simultaneously to the data from both groups. If the same model fits in both but with different values for the paths, one can conclude that the same general sort of explanation is applicable in both groups, although with quantitative differences. Or one can go further and ask if the same model with the same values will fit both sets of data. And, of course, one can take intermediate positions and constrain the values of certain paths to be the same in both groups, but allow others to vary.

Table 4-7 Correlations among attitudes at three time periods (Judd & Milburn, 1980), N = 203, no college

		B_{72}	C_{72}	J_{72}	B_{74}	C_{74}	J_{74}	B_{76}	C_{76}	J_{76}
1972	Busing	1.00	.24	.39	.44	.20	.31	.54	.14	.30
	Criminals		1.00	.25	.22	.53	.21	.21	.40	.25
	Jobs			1.00	.22	.16	.52	.22	.13	.48
1974	Busing				1.00	.25	.30	.58	.13	.33
	Criminals					1.00	.21	.25	.44	.16
	Jobs						1.00	.21	.23	.41
1976	Busing							1.00	.17	.28
	Criminals								1.00	.14
	Jobs									1.00
	S D	1.25	2.11	1.90	1.31	1.97	1.82	1.34	2.00	1.79

Note: Busing = bus to achieve school integration; Criminals = protect legal rights of those accused of crimes; Jobs = government should guarantee jobs and standard of living.

If one fits the path model of Fig. 4.3 to the data of both the college and noncollege groups, without additional cross-group constraints, one obtains a χ^2 of 24.56 with 32 df, representing an excellent fit to the data (p > .80; RMSEA = 0). This in effect represents a separate solution for the same model in each group, and one can indeed do the solutions separately and add the χ^2s and dfs: fitting the model in the noncollege group alone gives a χ^2 of 12.91 with 16 df; taken together, 11.65 + 12.91 = 24.56 and 16 + 16 = 32. (Such simple additivity will not hold if there are cross-group constraints.)

If one goes to the opposite extreme and requires that both the model and quantitative values be the same in both groups, one obtains a χ^2 of 153.98 with 61 df, p < .001--thus, one can confidently reject the hypothesis of no quantitative differences between the samples.

One particular intermediate hypothesis, that quantities in the structural model are the same in both groups but the measurement models may be different, leads to a χ^2 of 26.65 with 34 degrees of freedom. This does not represent a significant worsening of fit from the original solution in which both structural and measurement models are allowed to differ (χ^2_{diff} = 2.09, 2 df, p > .30). Thus, the difference between the two groups appears to lie in the measurement rather than the structural model.

Table 4-8 compares the solutions for the college and noncollege groups.

Table 4-8 Solution for the paths from liberalism to specific attitudes, for college and noncollege groups

		Unstandardized		Standardized	
		College	Noncollege	College	Noncollege
1972	Busing	1.00[a]	1.00[a]	.80	.63
	Criminals	.58	1.12	.51	.42
	Jobs	.63	1.40	.61	.58
1974	Busing	1.00[a]	1.00[a]	.84	.55
	Criminals	.62	.96	.54	.35
	Jobs	.68	1.44	.68	.58
1976	Busing	1.00[a]	1.00[a]	.87	.47
	Criminals	.49	.90	.41	.28
	Jobs	.61	1.65	.60	.58

Note: Paths marked[a] fixed at 1.0. Standard deviation for latent variable of liberalism from fitted solution: College--72 = 1.614, 74 = 1.475, 76 = 1.519; Noncollege--72 = .789, 74 = .727, 76 = .633.

The absolute values of paths from the latent variables to the observed variables are different for the two samples, but this is primarily a matter of the arbitrary scaling: attitude toward busing happens to be a relatively strong indicator of liberalism for the college group and a relatively weak one for the noncollege group, so that scalings based on this attitude will look quite different in the two cases. The standardized paths in the right-hand part of Table 4-8, obtained by multiplying the unstandardized paths by the ratio of standard deviations of their tail to their head variables (see Chapter 1) provide a better comparison. Since the two samples are not very different in the overall level of variance of the observed variables (median SD across the 9 scales is 1.74 for college and 1.82 for noncollege), these values suggest a lesser relative contribution of the general liberalism-conservatism factor in the noncollege group.

Table 4-9 compares the paths between the latent variables across time. For both groups the analysis suggests a relatively high degree of persistence of liberal-conservative position, particularly between the 1974 and 1976 surveys. Again, the greater ease of interpretation of the standardized variables is evident.

Table 4-9 Solution for the paths connecting liberalism across years, for college and noncollege groups

	Unstandardized		Standardized	
	College	Noncollege	College	Noncollege
1972 to 1974	.86	.77	.94	.84
1974 to 1976	.99	.86	.96	.99

The genetics of numerical ability

Some problems in behavior genetics can be treated as straightforward intercorrelation or covariance problems involving multiple groups, and solved with SEM programs, although sometimes explicit models are written and solved with general fitting programs. We consider an example of each approach.

Table 4-10 gives correlations for three subscales of the Number factor in Thurstone's Primary Mental Abilities battery, in male and female identical and fraternal twin pairs. Correlations for male twins are shown above the diagonal in each matrix, and those for female twins are shown below. The data are from studies by S. G. Vandenberg and his colleagues in Ann Arbor, Michigan, and Louisville, Kentucky; the studies and samples are described briefly in Loehlin and Vandenberg (1968).

Table 4-10 Within-individual and cross-pair correlations for three subtests of numerical ability, in male and female identical and fraternal twin pairs (numbers of pairs: Identicals 63, 59; Fraternals 29, 46)

	Ad1	Mu1	3H1	Ad2	Mu2	3H2
Identical twins						
Addition 1	1.000	.670	.489	.598	.627	.456
Multiplication 1	.611	1.000	.555	.499	.697	.567
3-Higher 1	.754	.676	1.000	.526	.560	.725
Addition 2	.673	.464	.521	1.000	.784	.576
Multiplication 2	.622	.786	.635	.599	1.000	.540
3-Higher 2	.614	.636	.650	.574	.634	1.000
Fraternal twins						
Addition 1	1.000	.664	.673	.073	.194	.379
Multiplication 1	.779	1.000	.766	.313	.380	.361
3-Higher 1	.674	.679	1.000	.239	.347	.545
Addition 2	.462	.412	.500	1.000	.739	.645
Multiplication 2	.562	.537	.636	.620	1.000	.751
3-Higher 2	.392	.359	.565	.745	.603	1.000
Standard deviations						
Identicals, male	7.37	13.81	16.93	8.17	13.33	17.56
Identicals, female	8.00	12.37	15.19	6.85	11.78	14.76
Fraternals, male	9.12	16.51	17.20	7.70	14.52	14.74
Fraternals, female	8.99	15.44	16.98	7.65	14.59	18.56

Note: In the correlation tables, males are shown above and females below the diagonal. 1 and 2 refer to scores of the first and second twin of a pair.

Figure 4.4 (next page) gives a path model for genetic influences on the correlations or covariances within and across twins. The latent variable N refers to a general genetic predisposition to do well on numerical tests. It is assumed to affect performance on all three tests, but perhaps to different degrees, as represented by paths *a*, *b*, *c*. These are assumed to be the same for both twins of a pair (designated 1 and 2). The genetic predispositions N are assumed to be perfectly correlated for identical twins, who have identical genotypes, but to be correlated .5 for fraternal twins, who are genetically ordinary siblings.

The bottom part of Fig. 4.4 allows for nongenetic sources of correlation among abilities within individuals and across pairs. Again, corresponding covariances are assumed to be equal--not all these are marked on the figure, but two examples are given. The residual covariance *d* between the addition

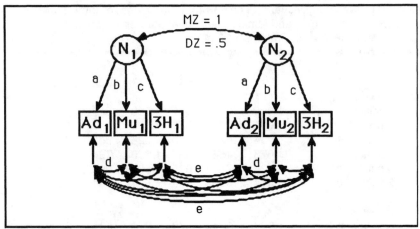

Fig. 4.4 Twin correlations on three subscales of numerical ability. MZ, DZ = identical and fraternal twins; N = genetic component of numerical ability; Ad, Mu, 3H = subscales; 1, 2 = first and second twin of a pair.

and multiplication scales is assumed to be the same in those individuals designated "twin 2" as it is in those individuals designated "twin 1," and a covariance such as e between twin 1's score on "3-Higher" and twin 2's score on "Addition" is assumed to be the same as that between twin 2's "3-Higher" score and twin 1's "Addition."

Altogether, there are 15 unknowns to be solved for: the 3 paths a, b, c, 3 residual variances, 3 within-person covariances across traits (d is an example), 3 different across-person covariances across traits (e is an example), and 3 across-person covariances for the same trait. There are $4 \times 6 \times 7/2 = 84$ data points , leaving $84 - 15 = 69$ df for testing the fit of the model to the data from the four groups at once.

The obtained value of χ^2 is 92.12 ($p = .03$; RMSEA = .083), indicating that the model doesn't hold exactly in the population, and provides a somewhat marginal approximation. With these sample sizes, neither a fairly good approximation nor a fairly poor one can be ruled out (90% CI for RMSEA = .025 to .125).

Could we improve matters by fitting the model for the males and females separately? This would involve 30 unknowns and $84 - 30 = 54$ df. The obtained χ^2 is 73.28, so the difference in χ^2 is 18.84 for 15 df, which does not represent a statistically significant improvement in fit ($p > .10$). We may as well go with the same result for both sexes, keeping in mind that the marginal fit suggests that our model may not be correct in all respects.

Table 4-11 shows the estimates (from a standardized solution). The genetic paths have values from .61 to .82; the squares of these represent the proportion of variance attributable to the common genetic factor (if the model is

Table 4-11 Solution of model of Fig. 4.4 with data of Table 4-10 for genetics of numerical ability

	Genetic path	Residual variance	Residual same-trait cross-person covariance
Addition	.664	.559	.147
Multiplication	.821	.326	.093
3-Higher	.610	.628	.345

	Other residual covariances	
	Within-person	Cross-person
Ad-Mu	.146	.059
Ad-3H	.233	.153
Mu-3H	.136	.136

correct), namely, from 37% to 67% for these three measures. The rest, the residual variances, are attributable to non-genetic factors, including errors of measurement, or to genetic factors specific to each skill. Whereas the trait variances include a component due to errors of measurement, the trait covariances do not. Here the genes show up more strongly, although the environmental contributions are still evident. The genetic contributions to the within-person correlations among the tests are .55, .41, and .50 (calculated from the path diagram as, for example, .664 x .821 = .55). The environmental contributions are .15, .23, and .14 (bottom left of Table 4-11). The genetic plus the environmental covariance is approximately equal to the phenotypic correlation: for the addition-multiplication correlation this sum is .55 + .15 = .70; the mean of the 8 within-person Ad-Mu correlations in Table 4-10 is .68. Looked at another way, about 79% of the correlation between addition and multiplication skills in this population is estimated to be due to the shared effects of genes.

Heredity, environment, and sociability

In the previous section we discussed fitting a model of genetic and environmental influences on numerical ability, treated as an SEM problem involving multiple groups--namely, male and female identical and fraternal twins. In this section we consider a model-fitting problem in which data from two twin samples and a study of adoptive families are fit using a general-purpose model-fitting program. It may serve as a reminder that latent variable models are a broader category than "problems solved by LISREL and EQS."
    The data to be used for illustration are correlations on the scale "Sociable" of the Thurstone Temperament Schedule. The correlations,

Table 4-12 Correlations for the trait *Sociable* from the Thurstone
Temperament Schedule in two twin studies and an adoption study

	Pairing	Correlation	Number of pairs
1.	MZ twins: Michigan	.47	45
2.	DZ twins: Michigan	.00	34
3.	MZ twins: Veterans	.45	102
4.	DZ twins: Veterans	.08	119
5.	Father-adopted child	.07	257
6.	Mother-adopted child	-.03	271
7.	Father-natural child	.22	56
8.	Mother-natural child	.13	54
9.	Adopted-natural child	-.05	48
10.	Two adopted children	-.21	80

Note: Michigan twin study described in Vandenberg (1962), and Veterans twin study in Rahe, Hervig, and Rosenman (1978); correlations recomputed from original data. Adoption data from Loehlin, Willerman, and Horn (1985).

in Table 4-12, are between pairs of individuals in the specified relationships. The first four pairings are for identical (MZ) and like-sexed fraternal (DZ) twins from two twin studies. The first study, done at the University of Michigan, involved highschool-age pairs, both males and females (see Vandenberg, 1962, for details). The second study was of adult pairs, all males, who had served in the U.S. armed forces during World War II and were located through Veterans Administration records (Rahe, Hervig, & Rosenman, 1978). The remaining pairings in the table are from a study of adoptive families in Texas (Loehlin, Willerman, & Horn, 1985).

Figure 4.5 shows a generalized path diagram of the causal paths that might underlie correlations such as those in Table 4-12. A trait S is measured in each of two individuals 1 and 2 by a test T. Correlation on the trait is presumed to be due to three independent sources: additive effects of the genes, G; nonadditive effects of the genes, D; and the environment common to pair members, C. A residual arrow allows for effects of the environment unique to each individual and--in all but the MZ pairs--for genetic differences as well.

Table 4-13 shows equations for the correlation $r_{T_1 T_2}$ between the test scores of members of various kinds of pairs. The equations are derived from the path model of Fig. 4.5. The assumptions inherent in the genetic correlations at the top of Fig. 4.5 are that mating is random with respect to the trait; that all nonadditive genetic variance is due to genetic dominance; and that there is no selective placement for the trait in adoptions. Doubtless none of these is exactly true (for example, the spouse correlation in the adoptive families for sociability

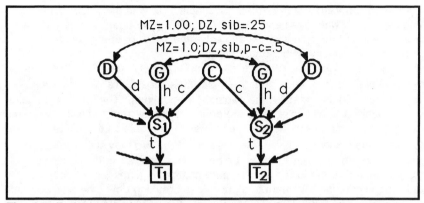

Fig. 4.5 Path model of genetic and environmental sources of correlation between two individuals. G = additive genes; D = nonadditive genetic effect; C = shared environment; S = sociability; T = test score; 1, 2 = two individuals.

was .16, which is significantly different from zero with 192 pairs but is certainly not very large). However, minor departures from the assumptions should not seriously compromise the model. The Table 4-13 equations allow (via c_1, c_2, c_3) for differentiating among the degrees of shared environment in the cases of identical twins, ordinary siblings, and parents and their children. The equations do not attempt to discriminate between the environmental relationships of parents and adopted or natural children, or of DZ twins and other siblings; obviously, one might construct models that do, and even--with suitable data-- solve them.

The path *t* in Fig. 4.5 is taken as the square root of the reliability of test T (the residual represents error variance). The reliability (Cronbach's alpha) of

Table 4-13 Equations for correlations between pairs of individuals in different relationships

Relationship	Table 4-12 pairings	Equation for correlation
MZ twins	1,3	$(h^2 + d^2 + c_1^2)\, t^2$
DZ twins	2,4	$(.5h^2 + .25d^2 + c_2^2)\, t^2$
Parent, adopted child	5,6	$(c_3^2)\, t^2$
Parent, natural child	7,8	$(.5h^2 + c_3^2)\, t^2$
Adoptive siblings	9,10	$(c_2^2)\, t^2$

Note: h, c, d, t as in Fig. 4.5.

the TTS scale Sociable in the Veterans sample, .76, was assumed to hold for all samples. Thus, *t* was taken as $\sqrt{.76}$ = .87 in solving the equations. A general-purpose iterative program was used to solve the set of path equations in Table 4-13 for the unknown parameters.

There are 10 observed correlations in Table 4-12; models with 1 to 4 unknowns were tested, allowing 6 to 9 df for the χ^2 tests. Table 4-14 gives χ^2s from several models based on the Table 4-13 equations. The first row contains a "null model"--that all correlations are equal. It can be rejected with confidence (p < .001). The models in the remaining lines of the table all constitute acceptable fits to the data ($\chi^2 \approx$ df, or less, p > .30). We may still, however, compare them to see if some might be better than others. Adding a single environmental or nonadditive genetic parameter to *h* (lines 3 or 4) does not yield a significant improvement in fit; nor does breaking down the environmental parameter into MZ twins versus others (line 5). A three-way breakdown of environment (line 6), into that for parent and child, siblings and MZ twins, does somewhat better, although the improvement is not statistically significant (χ^2_{diff} of 6.49 from line 2, 5.87 from line 3, and 3.58 from line 5, all p > .05). Although with larger samples a model like that of line 6 might be defensible, for the moment we may as well stay with the parsimonious one-parameter model of line 2. This model estimates that approximately half of the variance of sociability (h^2 = 52%) is genetic in origin. The rest is presumably attributable to environment; this is not, however, the environment common to family members, but that unique to the individual. A result of this kind is fairly typical in behavior genetic studies of personality traits (Bouchard & Loehlin, 2001).

Table 4-14 Solutions of Table 4-13 equations for various combinations of parameters

	Model	χ^2	df	χ^2_{diff}	df_{diff}
1.	all rs equal (null)	36.02	9		
2.	h only	9.09	9		
3.	h + c	8.47	8	.62	1
4.	h + d	7.60	8	1.49	1
5.	h + c_1 + c_2	6.18	7	2.91	2
6.	h + c_1 + c_2 + c_3	2.60	6	6.49	3

Note: Model comparisons are with line 2 model.

Fitting Models to Means as well as Covariances

The models we have discussed so far in this chapter have been fitted to correlation or covariance matrices. However, in comparisons involving different groups or different occasions, means are likely to be of at least as much interest to an investigator as covariances. Fortunately, latent variable models, with fairly minor elaboration, can be fitted to means as well as covariance matrices from multiple groups or multiple occasions. Does the mean score on some latent variable differ between men and women? Before and after some treatment? Fitting latent variable models that incorporate means will let us address such questions--even though the theoretical variables of principal interest remain themselves unobserved, as in other latent variable models.

A simple example

Figure 4.6 provides a simple, hypothetical, exactly-fitting example to illustrate the principles involved. There are two groups, Group 1 and Group 2, each measured on manifest variables X, Y, and Z--the means on these variables are shown at the bottom of the figure. Just to keep things as simple as possible, assume that both groups have identical covariance matrices of standardized variables with off-diagonal elements of .48, .42, and .56, leading in the usual way to the values of the paths and residual variances shown in the figure.

This is all familiar ground. What's new is the triangle at the top of the figure with a "1" in it, and the paths a through e leading from it to the latent and

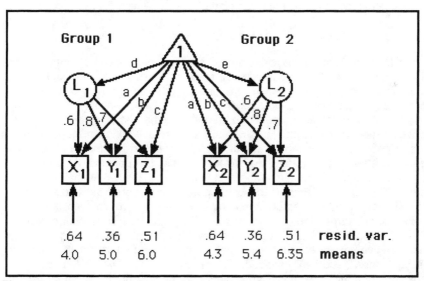

Fig. 4.6 A two-group path model incorporating means.

manifest variables. The triangle represents a constant, in this case 1.0. Because it is a constant, its variance is zero, and according to the path rules of Chapter 1, the paths *a*, *b*, *c*, *d*, and *e* leading from it will contribute nothing to the variances and covariances of the Ls or the Xs, Ys, and Zs. But they do affect the means of the variables to which they point, and this allows us to make inferences from the observed means concerning the latent ones.

We proceed as follows. We select one group as a reference group: let's say Group 1. We fix to zero the path from the constant to the latent variable(s) in this group (i.e., path *d* in the figure). This means that paths *a*, *b*, and *c* must account for the means in the left-hand group, since with *d* = 0 there is no contribution to them via L_1. That implies, in this exactly-fitting example, that *a* = 4.0, *b* = 5.0, and *c* = 6.0. The paths *a*, *b*, and *c* are specified to be equal in both groups. Thus they provide the same initial values 4.0, 5.0, and 6.0; the higher observed values of 4.3, 5.4, and 6.35 must come via *e* and L_2. That is, *e* must equal .5 so that .5 x .6 will equal the .3 to be added to 4.0 to give 4.3, and so on. Of course, in the real world it won't all be so exact, and we will use a model-fitting program to get estimates of *a*, *b*, *c*, and *e* and the paths in the original model--estimates that will come as close as possible to fitting the observations, given the model.

The values of *a*, *b*, and *c* are baseline values for the manifest variable means. What is *e*? It represents the difference between the means of the latent variables in the two groups: that is, in this example, L_2 is .5 higher than L_1 in standard-score units. To test if this constitutes a significant difference, we could set *e* to zero also, and test the worsening of fit as a χ^2 with 1 df.

Stress, resources, and depression

Let us look at a more realistic example involving a comparison of group means. Holahan and Moos (1991) carried out a study of life stressors, personal and social resources, and depression, in adults from the San Francisco Bay Area. Participants were asked to indicate which, if any, of 15 relatively serious negative life events had happened to them during the last 12 months. The list included such things as problems with supervisors at work, conflicts with friends and neighbors, and unemployment or financial troubles. On the basis of these responses, subjects were divided into two groups: 128 persons who reported two or more such events during the past year were classified as the "high-stressor" group, and 126 persons who reported none were classified as the "low-stressor" group. (Persons reporting just one negative life event were excluded, to sharpen the contrast between the high and low stressor groups.)

The participants also responded to a questionnaire containing scales to measure five variables: depressed mood, depressive features, self-confidence, easygoingness, and family support. The first two of these were taken to be indicators of a latent variable Depression, and the second three to be indicators

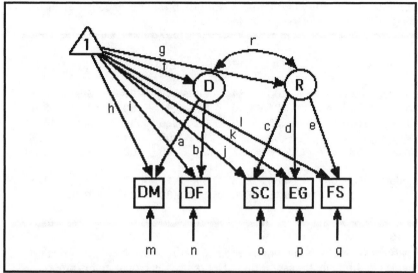

Fig. 4.7 Path diagram for the high-stressor group, initial testing. (The diagram for the low-stressor group is the same, except that the paths *f* and *g* from the constant to D and R are fixed to zero.) Latent variables: D = Depression and R = Resources. Observed variables: DM = depressed mood, DF = depressive features, SC = self-confidence, EG = easygoingness, FS = family support.

of a latent variable Resources. Holahan and Moos followed up their subjects four years later, and fitted models involving coping styles and changes in depression in the two groups over time, but we will ask a simpler question of just the first-occasion data: How do the high-stressor and the low-stressor groups compare on the two latent variables? Figure 4.7 gives the path diagram for the high-stressor group; the diagram for the low-stressor group, taken as the reference group, would be the same, except that the two paths from the constant to the latent variables are fixed to zero.

Table 4-15 (next page) contains the correlations, means, and standard deviations for the five measured variables; those for the high-stressor group are shown above the diagonal, and those for the low-stressor group below. The results of the model fitting are shown in Table 4-16. As indicated in the footnote to Table 4-16, the model fits reasonably well to the data from the two groups: the chi-square is nonsignificant, and the RMSEA of .059 falls in the acceptable range. However, the sample sizes are not quite large enough to rule out the possibility of a poor fit in the population (the upper 90% confidence limit of RMSEA is .105).

Table 4-15 Correlations, standard deviations, and means for high-stressor group (above diagonal) and low-stressor group (below diagonal) at initial testing. (Data from Holahan and Moos, 1991)

	DM	DF	SC	EG	FS	SD	M
Depressed mood	1.00	.84	-.36	-.45	-.51	5.97	8.82
Depressive features	.71	1.00	-.32	-.41	-.50	7.98	13.87
Self-confidence	-.35	-.16	1.00	.26	.47	3.97	15.24
Easygoingness	-.35	-.21	.11	1.00	.34	2.27	7.92
Family support	-.38	-.26	.30	.28	1.00	4.91	19.03
Standard deviation	4.84	6.33	3.84	2.14	4.43	N	128
Mean	6.15	9.96	15.14	8.80	20.43	126	

Of primary interest are the means and standard deviations of the two latent variables in the high-stressor group. Depression is higher in this group, and Resources lower; the variability is higher for both, to about the same degree. The difference in means is estimated as slightly larger for Depression than for Resources, but not significantly so: refitting the model with the two means required to be numerically equal does not lead to a significant increase in chi-square (χ^2_{diff} = .571, 1 df, p > .30). Not surprisingly, the two latent variables are negatively correlated, -.72 and -.78 in the two groups.

As expected, the baseline means *h* through *l* roughly follow the observed means in the low-stressor reference group. The differences in the latent variables predict that the means for the indicator variables for Depression should be higher in the high-stressor group and those for Resources should be lower. The observed means in Table 4-15 show this pattern with one interesting exception: Self-confidence isn't lower in the high-stressor group as the model predicts--in fact, there is a slight difference in the other direction. Clearly, the model doesn't explain everything.

Note that it was possible to equate the measurement models across the two groups. If it had not been possible to equate at least the factor loadings (paths *a* through *e*), this would have presented a problem for interpreting the group differences on the latent variables: Are they the same variables in the two groups, or not? To argue that they are the same variables, one would have to go beyond the model fitting and provide a theoretical argument that the same latent variables should be differently related in the appropriate way to their indicators in the high- and low-stressor groups.

Table 4-16 Solution of the path model of Fig. 4.7

Latent variables			Measurement model					
			Paths		Residual variances		Baseline means	
Low stressor group								
mean, Depression	f.	[0.00]	a.	4.44	m.	2.94	h.	6.08
mean, Resources	g.	[0.00]	b.	5.25	n.	16.17	i.	10.26
SD, Depression		[1.00]	c	1.56	o.	11.85	j	15.58
SD, Resources		[1.00]	d.	1.01	p	3.64	k.	8.61
Correlation	r.	-.72	e.	2.68	q	12.35	l.	20.40
High stressor group								
mean, Depression	f.	.63						
mean, Resources	g.	-.50						
SD, Depression		1.30			[same as low-stressor group]			
SD, Resources		1.29						
Correlation	r.	-.78						

Note: χ^2 = 26.965, 19df, p = .10-5. RMSEA = .059; 90%CI = .00 to .105. Values in square brackets fixed.

Changes in means across time—latent curve models

Changes in behaviors and attitudes across time are often of interest to social scientists. Means may be directly incorporated into some of the temporal models discussed earlier in the chapter--for example, simplexes. Here we discuss a different approach, the fitting of *latent curve* models (Meredith & Tisak, 1990). Basically, these models assume that changes in any individual's behavior over time may be described by some simple underlying function, plus error. The model is the same for everyone, but the parameters may differ from person to person. Any curve capable of being described by a small number of parameters could be used; for simplicity we use a straight line in our example. Such a line may be identified by two parameters, its intercept and its slope. That is, one individual may have a steeper rate of increase than another (a difference in slope); or one may begin at a higher or lower level (a difference in intercept).

Our example involves attitudes of tolerance toward deviant behaviors (stealing, cheating, drug use, etc.), measured annually in a sample of young adolescents. (The example is adapted from Willett and Sayer, 1994).

Table 4-17 Tolerance of deviant behaviors at four ages and exposure to deviant peers

| | Tolerance for deviance at age | | | | Age 11 |
	11	12	13	14	exposure
Means	.2008	.2263	.3255	.4168	-.0788
Covariances					
11	.0317				
12	.0133	.0395			
13	.0175	.0256	.0724		
14	.0213	.0236	.0531	.0857	
Age 11 exposure	.0115	.0133	.0089	.0091	.0693

Note: Data from Willett and Sayer (1994). N = 168. Log scores.

Means and covariances for the tolerance measure for ages 11 to 14 are given in Table 4-17. Also included in the table is a measure of the exposure of the individual at age 11 to peers who engage in such activities. A question of interest is whether exposure to such peers at age 11 affects either the initial level or the subsequent rate of increase in tolerance for behaviors of this kind. Both measures were transformed by the authors to logarithms to reduce skewness.

A path model is shown in Figure 4-8. The measures of tolerance at ages 11 to 14 are represented by the four squares at the bottom of the figure. The latent variables I and S represent the intercept and slope that characterize an individual's pattern of response. Note that these have been assigned fixed paths to the measures. These paths imply that an individual's response at age

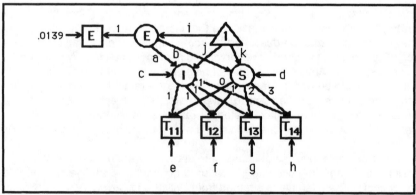

Fig. 4-8 Path model of change in tolerance for deviant behaviors.

11 will be determined by his intercept parameter, plus zero units of slope, plus a residual (*e*). His response at age 12 will be the intercept parameter, plus one unit of slope, plus error. At 13, intercept plus two units, plus error. And so on.

In the upper part of the figure there is a latent variable E, representing exposure to deviant peers. This is assumed to contribute via paths *a* and *b* to the intercept and slope of an individual's growth curve. The measured variable E is taken to be an imperfect index of this latent variable; in the absence of information about the actual reliability of measurement, we have assigned a numerical value for illustrative purposes using an arbitrarily assumed reliability of .80 (i.e., error variance = .20 x .0693 = .0139).

Again, the triangle in the diagram with a 1 in it represents a constant value of 1. Recall that because it is a constant, the paths *i*, *j*, and *k* leading from it do not contribute to the variances of the latent variables to which they point, or their covariances, but they provide a convenient way of representing effects on means. Fitting the model (via LISREL and a maximum likelihood criterion) yields the values in Table 4-18. The parameter *i* merely reflects the mean log exposure score of -.0788. The intercept parameter *j* gives the initial level of tolerance for deviant behavior, and *k* the yearly increment, yielding approximate predicted values of .20, .27, .34, and .41 for the four ages. ("Approximate," because this neglects small additional effects via the paths *ia* and *ib*--the actual predicted values run about .01 lower.) The paths *a* and *b* indicate the effects of exposure to delinquent peers on tolerance: There is an appreciable effect on level but essentially none on slope (the small negative value of *b* is less than half its standard error). That is, children who were exposed to more delinquent peers at age 11 show higher levels of tolerance for deviant behavior, but the rate of increase over age in all groups appears to be about the same.

A linear latent growth curve does not, however, fit these data particularly well. The overall chi square is a highly significant 26.37 for 8 df. The RMSEA is an unsatisfactory .117. Inspection of the means in Table 4-17 suggests that it is the first one that is chiefly out of line--the increases from ages 12 to 13 to 14 are close to 1.0 per year, but the increase from 11 to 12 is only about .2. One can't, of course, know from these data whether this might represent a genuine

Table 4-18 Results from fitting path model of Fig. 4.8 to data of Table 4-17

Means		Paths (std.)		Residual variances (std.)			
i	-.08	a	.42	c	.82	e	.54
j	.20	b	-.05	d	.99+	f	.66
k	.07					g	.41
						h	.26

Note: Paths and residual variances are standardized.

145

discontinuity due (let us say) to hormonal or ecological factors entering the picture at around age 12, or a measurement artifact such as a floor effect. A log score of .2008 corresponds to a raw score value of 1.22, and the minimum possible raw score (if a child indicates that all the deviant behaviors are "very wrong") is 1.00. We can easily enough ask "what if." Suppose the mean at the first measurement had been, say, .1200 instead of .2008--i.e., roughly in line with the others--would the model have fit acceptably? The answer is, better but still not wonderfully. The chi square is substantially lower, 16.27, but one would still reject the hypothesis of perfect fit. The RMSEA drops to a marginally acceptable .079, but one could still not reject the hypothesis that the fit is poor in the population (upper 90% confidence limit for RMSEA is .134). Would the substantive interpretation be any different? Not much. Lowering the first point would give us a lower intercept parameter ($j = .14$) and a higher estimate of the slope ($k = .10$), but the conclusions about the effect of peers (parameters a and b) would be essentially unchanged. Of course this remains speculation, but it and other "what if"s that one might consider may be helpful in planning the next experiment, or may give some idea as to which results from this one are likely to prove robust. (For another "what if" in this case, see the exercises at the end of the chapter.)

Factorial equivalence

As mentioned earlier, an issue arises when a model is fitted in two or more groups: Are the latent variables the same in both groups? The issue is salient in cross-cultural comparisons. If we want to claim (for example) that family loyalty is more strongly related to conservatism in Mexico than in the United States, we must first be able to show that our measures of the latent variables family loyalty and conservatism are equivalent in both cultures. Otherwise, it makes little sense to compare the correlations between them. The same issue arises in making comparisons in distinct subgroups within one society, such as males and females, or different ethnic groups. What does it mean to say that women are more anxious than men, or less anxious, if our measure of anxiety does not have the same meaning in the two sexes?

In SEM terms, if we want to make comparisons involving latent variables in two or more groups, we are asking questions of the form: Are the means of the latent variables equal? Are their variances equal? Are the relations between Latent Variable A and Latent Variable B the same in the different groups? To be able to answer such questions requires that we first demonstrate the invariance across groups of the measurement part of our model. Meredith (1993) has distinguished between *strict* factorial invariance and *strong* factorial invariance in this situation. Strict factorial invariance requires equivalence of all the elements of the measurement model--the factor loadings, the specific means for each of the manifest variables (i.e., those to which the effects of the latent variables are added), and the specific variances. Strong factorial variance merely requires equivalence for the first two, allowing

146

the possibility that measurement error, for example, might differ from group to group. For making cross-group comparisons of latent variables, strict factorial invariance in the measurement model is the scientific ideal. However, with due caution in interpretation within a substantive framework, strong factorial invariance may be adequate, and in some cases even weaker factorial invariance, in the form of identity or similar configuration of just the factor loadings, may permit drawing useful conclusions. The fitting to the data of models involving means is an essential step in making cross-group inferences about latent variables, but we must be able to say that they are the same variables in each group.

The Versatility of Multiple-Group Designs

One use of a multiple-group model is to deal with interactions. In one of his short stories, F. Scott Fitzgerald said of the very rich that "They are different from you and me." If the very rich are only different in that they have more money, and, accordingly, differ in attitudes that tend to vary with money, one could include wealth as a variable in an ordinary path model along with attitude measures. A good fit of this model would be testimony to the accuracy of such an interpretation. On the other hand, if the very rich are categorically different, that is, have attitudes that vary in distinctively different ways from yours and mine, a better solution would be to fit a two-group model, in which measures could be related in different ways among the very rich and the rest of us.

If one is in doubt as to whether the very rich are fundamentally different, a natural approach would be to see if the same model could be fit in both groups-- does constraining them to be the same lead to a significant increase in chi square? If so, one could pursue further model fitting to ascertain which differences between the rich and the rest of us are essential and which are not.

This logic can be extended to many different kinds of interaction. Are individuals low, medium and high in the strength of an attitude susceptible to different forms of persuasion? Do men and women achieve economic success by different routes? Do paranoid and non-paranoid schizophrenics show a different pattern of physiological response to a sudden noise? Fit multiple group models and see.

Experiments and data summary

Latent variable models need not be confined to correlational settings, but can provide an effective and flexible way of analyzing the data from experiments. In the simplest case, where one could use SEM but probably wouldn't, there is an experimental group and a control group, and one tests for a difference between means in a two-group design. In more complex cases, one may have multiple experimental and control groups, various covariates, unequal sample sizes, a desire to equate or leave free various parameters across groups, and so on, and an approach via SEM may be quite attractive.

In Chapter 2 we discussed multiple groups as a way of handling missing data. Another possible application is as a method of data summary. If the same model is fit in a number of data samples, the parameters that can and can't be equated represent an economical way of describing the areas of agreement among the samples, and of testing for differences. Where applicable, this may sometimes have advantages over meta-analysis or similar techniques.

A Concluding Comment

The examples we have considered in this and the preceding chapter represent a variety of applications of path and structural equation analysis to empirical data in the social and behavioral sciences. Most of these models were originally fit using LISREL, but as we noted earlier, this fact reflects the widespread availability of this particular program rather than any inherent feature of these problems.

In the next two chapters we turn temporarily away from models like these to consider the important class of latent variable methods known as exploratory factor analysis. In the final chapter we return to consider some strategic issues in the use of latent variable models in scientific research.

Chapter 4 Notes

Some of the kinds of models described in this chapter are discussed in a special section of *Child Development* (Connell & Tanaka, 1987) dealing with structural modeling over time. See also edited books by Collins and Horn (1991), Collins and Sayer (2001), and Gottman (1995). For latent variable growth curve modeling, see Duncan et al. (1999). For a general view of the multivariate modeling of changes over time, see Nesselroade (2002). For behavior genetic models, which inherently involve model fitting in multiple groups, see a special issue of the journal *Behavior Genetics* (Boomsma et al. 1989), and a book by Neale and Cardon (1992).

Statistical issues with multiple groups. Yuan and Bentler (2001a) discuss multigroup modeling in the presence of nonnormality or similar problems. Steiger (1998) deals with extension of the RMSEA to the multiple group situation.

Simplexes. Guttman (1954) originally proposed the simplex model for the case of a series of tests successively increasing in complexity, such that each required the skills of all the preceding tests, plus some new ones--an example would be addition, multiplication, long division. But simplex correlation patterns may occur in many other situations, such as the growth process considered in the chapter. The Bracht and Hopkins example was slightly simplified for purposes of illustration by omitting data from one grade, the ninth. Jöreskog (Jöreskog & Sörbom, 1979, Chapter 3) discusses model-fitting involving a number of variants of the simplex.

Latent traits and latent states. The distinction is discussed by Steyer and Schmitt (1990); Tisak and Tisak (2000) explore how this tradition relates to the latent growth curve ideas discussed in this chapter.

Modeling the individual and the group. Molenaar et al. (2003) emphasize that the two are not the same. Mehta and West (2000) show how to use individual-growth-curve-based SEM to deal with the effects of measuring different individuals at different ages.

Genetic assumptions. The value of .5 for the genetic correlation between dizygotic twins (numerical-ability example) assumes that assortative mating (the tendency for like to marry like) and genetic dominance and epistasis (nonadditive effects of the genes on the trait) are negligible in the case of numerical ability, or at least that to the extent they occur they offset one another. The first process would tend to raise the genetic correlation for fraternal twins, and the latter two would tend to lower it. Assortative mating tends to be substantial for general intelligence and verbal abilities but is usually modest for more specialized abilities, such as numerical and spatial skills (DeFries et al., 1979). In the sociability example, a path allowing for nonadditive genetic effects is included in the model.

Models involving means. Willett and Sayer's (1994) example given in the present chapter has been simplified for illustrative purposes by dropping one age (15) and one predictor variable (gender). A basic paper on latent curve analysis is Meredith and Tisak (1990). For a technical summary of the fitting of mean and covariance structures, see Browne and Arminger (1995); a basic paper is Sörbom (1974). Hancock (1997) compares the group mean differences approach described in the text to an alternative strategy of carrying out the analysis within a single group but adding a variable that codes for group identification (*cf.* Head Start example in Chapter 3). Dolan (1992) and Dolan and Molenaar (1994) consider group mean differences in a selection context. A cross-cultural application is discussed by Little (1997). The varying of means over groups and over time are brought into a common SEM framework by Meredith (1991). Three different ways of representing changes in means in SEM are described by Browne and du Toit (1991). For a readable exposition of latent growth modeling, see Lawrence and Hancock (1998). For further examples of its use, see Duncan and Duncan (1994) and Stoolmiller (1994, 1995). Extensions of such models to multiple groups and several trait domains are discussed by Willett and Sayer (1996). Reasons for preferring these models to an alternative, direct arrows connecting measures repeated over time, are given by Stoolmiller and Bank (1995). Cheong et al. (2003) discuss representing mediational processes in latent growth curve models, and Muthén (1997) the use of latent growth curve models with multilevel data. McArdle (e.g., 2001) describes an approach to change over time via latent difference scores. Kaplan et al. (2001) ask what happens when the model is dynamic and you model it as static. For modeling of time series, see du Toit and Browne (2001).

Longitudinal behavior-genetic growth curve models. Genetic and environmental effects on a trait over time may be modeled using twin or other behavior genetic multiple group models (McArdle, 1986; Neale & McArdle, 2000). Examples using large longitudinal twin samples include McGue and Christensen (2003) and Finkel et al. (2003). See also Heiman et al. (2003). McArdle and Hamagami (2003) discuss several different model-fitting approaches to inferring how genes and environment contribute to trait changes over time.

Factorial equivalence. The issue of practical versus statistical significance arises in this context as well. With very large samples, failures of chi-square tests may occur with discrepancies from factorial invariance that are too small to make a practical difference. Cheung and Rensvold (2002) explore the use of differences in goodness-of-fit indices in this situation. Steenkamp and Baumgartner (1998) discuss various kinds of invariance in cross-national research, and Lubke and Dolan (2003) look specifically at the requirement that residual variances be equal across groups. Millsap (1998) discusses invariance of intercepts. Rivera and Satorra (2002) compare several SEM approaches to group differences with nonnormal data in a large multi-country data set. A number of issues in establishing cross-cultural equivalence are discussed in Harkness et al. (2003).

Analyzing experiments. See, for example, Bagozzi and Yi (1989), Kühnel (1988), Muthén and Speckart (1985), and Kano (2001). Cole et al. (1993) discuss the relative merits of SEM and MANOVA for analysis in experimental (and nonexperimental) designs. A combination of experiment and SEM is discussed by du Toit and Cudeck (2001).

Fitzgerald quotation. From his story "The rich boy" (1982, p. 139).

Multiple-group analysis as data summary. For a number of examples, see Loehlin (1992).

Chapter 4 Exercises

1. Fit the Tesser and Paulhus correlations (Table 4-1) as a confirmatory factor analysis involving five uncorrelated factors: a general attraction factor on which all eight measurements are loaded, and four specific factors, one for each test. Assume equal loadings across the two occasions for the general and the specific factors and the residuals.

2. For the model in problem 1, relax the requirement that the loadings on the general factor are equal on the two occasions. Does this significantly improve the goodness of fit?

3. Test the hypothesis for the Judd-Milburn data (Tables 4-5 and 4-7) that the measurement model is the same across groups, although the structural model may differ. (Note that covariances are analyzed, not correlations.)

4. Set up and solve the path problem for the genetics of numerical ability as in the text (sexes equal), using correlations rather than covariances. Still using correlations, test the additional hypothesis that the three subscales are parallel tests of numerical ability (i.e., have a single common parameter in each of the five sets in Table 4-11).

Table 4-19 Data for problem 5 (women above diagonal, men below)

Scale		A	B	C	D	M	SD
	A	1.00	.48	.10	.28	.98	5.2
	B	.50	1.00	.15	.40	1.00	7.0
	C	.12	.16	1.00	.12	.99	6.1
	D	.45	.70	.17	1.00	1.03	8.3
SD		1.08	1.15	1.01	1.18	N	208
M		7.5	10.2	7.0	11.1	200	

5. Table 4-19 shows means, standard deviations, and correlations on four hypothetical masculinity-femininity scales in samples of 200 men (below diagonal) and 208 women (above diagonal). Is it reasonable to conclude that there is a general masculinity-femininity latent variable that accounts both for the interrelationships among the measures and the differences in mean and variance between the samples? Are there differences between the sexes in how the tests measure this factor?

6. Would the latent curve model of growth (Fig. 4-8) fit better if the growth curve were quadratic rather than linear in this age range? (*Hint:* Set the paths from S to values 0, 1, 4, 9 instead of 0, 1, 2, 3.)

Chapter Five:
Exploratory Factor Analysis--Basics

So far, we have been discussing cases in which a specific hypothesized model is fit to the data. Suppose that we have a path diagram consisting of arrows from X and Y pointing to Z. The theory, represented in the path diagram, indicates that X and Y are independent causes, and the sole causes, of Z. The qualitative features of the situation are thus spelled out in advance, and the question we ask is, does this model remain plausible when we look at the data? And if so, what are the quantitative relationships: What is our best estimate of the relative strengths of the two causal effects?

In this chapter we turn to another class of latent variable problems, the class that has been widely familiar to psychologists and other social and biological scientists under the name *factor analysis*, but which we are calling *exploratory factor analysis* to distinguish it from confirmatory factor analysis, which we have treated as an example of the kind of model fitting described in the preceding paragraph.

In exploratory factor analysis we do not begin with a specific model, only with rather general specifications about what kind of a model we are looking for. We must then find the model as well as estimate the values of its paths and correlations.

One can do a certain amount of exploration with general model-fitting methods, via trial-and-error modification of an existing model to improve its fit to data. But the methods we cover in this chapter and the next start out de novo to seek a model of a particular kind to fit to a set of data.

One thing that makes this feasible is that the class of acceptable models in the usual exploratory factor analysis is highly restricted: models with no causal links among the latent variables and with only a single layer of causal paths between latent and observed variables. (This implies, among other things, that these models have no looped or reciprocal paths.) Such models are, in the terminology of earlier chapters, mostly measurement model, with the structural model reduced to simple intercorrelations among the latent variables.

Indeed, in the perspective of earlier chapters, one way to think of exploratory factor analysis is as a process of discovering and defining latent variables and a measurement model that can then provide the basis for a causal analysis of relations among the latent variables.

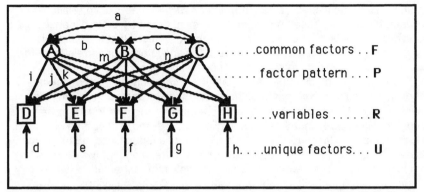

Fig. 5.1 Example of a factor analysis model. A, B, C = factors; D, E, F, G, H = observed variables; a, b, c = factor intercorrelations; d, e, f, g, h = specifics; i, j, k, m, n, etc. = factor pattern coefficients.

The latent variables in factor analysis models are traditionally called *factors*. Most often, in practice, both observed and latent variables are kept in standardized form; that is to say, correlations rather than covariances are analyzed, and the latent variables--the factors--are scaled to unit standard deviations. We mostly follow this procedure in this chapter. However, it is important to be aware that this is *not* a necessary feature of factor analysis--that one can, and in certain circumstances should, keep data in its rawscore units and analyze covariances rather than correlations, and that some factor analytic methods scale factors to other metrics than standard deviations of 1.0.

Figure 5.1 shows an example of a factor analysis model that reintroduces some of the factor analysis terminology that was earlier presented in Chapter 1 and adds a few new matrix symbols. A, B, and C are the three *common factors.* Their intercorrelations are represented by the curved arrows *a, b,* and *c,* which collectively form the *factor intercorrelation matrix,* which we designate **F.** D, E, F, G, and H are the *observed variables,* the tests or measures or other observations whose *intercorrelation matrix,* **R,** we are analyzing. The arrows *i, j, k,* etc. represent paths from latent to observed variables, the *factor pattern coefficients.* Collectively, these paths are known as the *factor pattern,* in matrix form **P.** Finally, paths *d, e, f,* etc. represent residual or *unique factors,* also called *specific factors.* They are expressed in matrix form as a diagonal matrix **U,** or as variances U^2. The *communalities,* the share of the variance of the variables explained by the factors, are equal to $I - U^2$, where **I** is the identity matrix.

In the example, the dimensions of matrix **F** would be 3 x 3, matrices **R** and **U** would be 5 x 5 (although only the five nonzero diagonal values of **U** would be of interest), and **P** would be 5 x 3; conventionally, **P** is arranged so that the rows represent the observed variables and the columns the factors.

Another matrix mentioned earlier, the *factor structure* matrix of correlations between factors and observed variables, is symbolized by **S**; its dimensions are also variables by factors, or 5 x 3 in the example. Recall that the elements of this matrix are a complex function of the paths and interfactor correlations--for example, the correlation between A and D is $i + bm + an$.

For a factor model, one can obtain the correlations implied by the model either by tracing the appropriate paths in the diagram according to Wright's rules, or, more compactly, by the matrix operations $_{imp}\mathbf{R} = \mathbf{PFP}' + \mathbf{U}^2$, where the $_{imp}$ before **R** indicates that these are implied or predicted, rather than observed, values of the correlations. (**PFP**′ by itself yields communalities in the diagonal instead of total variances--a so-called *reduced* correlation matrix that we symbolize by **R**$_r$.) The reader may wish to satisfy him- or herself, by working through an example or two, that path tracing and matrix calculation indeed give identical results.

Now it is in general the case that there are an infinite number of possible path models that can reproduce any given set of intercorrelations, and this is still true even if we restrict ourselves to the class of factor models. To give our search any point we must redefine it more narrowly. Let us invoke parsimony, then, and say that we are looking for the *simplest* factor model that will do a *reasonable* job of explaining the observed intercorrelations.

How does one determine whether a particular model does a reasonable job of explaining observed correlations? This is by now a familiar problem with a familiar solution: One generates the correlations implied by the model and then uses a formal or informal criterion of goodness of fit to assess their discrepancy from the observed correlations. Smallest absolute differences, least squares and maximum likelihood have all been used for this purpose.

What is meant by a *simple* model? Factor analysts typically use a two-step definition: (1) a model that requires the *smallest number of latent variables* (factors); (2) given this number of factors, the model with the *smallest number of nonzero paths* in its pattern matrix. Additional criteria are sometimes invoked, such as (3) uncorrelated factors or (4) equal distribution of paths across variables or factors, but we focus on the first two, which are common to nearly all methods of exploratory factor analysis.

Applications of the first two criteria of simplicity correspond to the two main divisions of an exploratory factor analysis, *factor extraction* and *rotation*.

In the first step, factor extraction, methods are employed to yield models having the smallest number of factors that will do a reasonable job of explaining the correlations, although such methods typically produce models that are highly unsatisfactory according to the second criterion. Then in the second step, rotation, these models are transformed to retain the same small number of factors, but to improve them with respect to the second criterion of nonzero paths.

154

Factor Extraction

One straightforward procedure goes as follows, beginning with the reduced correlation matrix R_r (a correlation matrix with estimated communalities replacing the 1s in the diagonal):

> Step 1. Solve for a general factor of R_r.
>
> Step 2. Obtain the matrix impR implied by the obtained general factor.
>
> Step 3. Subtract impR from the matrix used in Step 1, leaving a residual matrix that we designate resR.
>
> Step 4. Examine the residual matrix resR; are you willing to regard it as trivial? If so, stop. If not, put resR in place of R_r in Step 1, and repeat.

This account glosses over some details, but it gives the essentials of a procedure that will produce a series of factors of decreasing magnitude, each of which is uncorrelated with all the others. This facilitates reaching the first goal of simplicity, the smallest number of factors necessary to fit the data reasonably well, because if factors are solved for in order of size, when one cuts off the process in Step 4, one knows that no potential factor remains unconsidered whose contribution toward explaining R would exceed that of the least important factor examined so far. And because the factors are independent, each obtained factor will make a unique and nonoverlapping contribution to the explanation of R.

The factors resulting from the process described, being general factors, will tend to have many nonzero paths and thus not be simple according to the second of our two criteria; we deal with this problem later when we discuss the second stage of exploratory factor analysis known as "rotation."

Extracting successive general factors

An example of a general factor is shown in Table 5-1 (next page). On the left in the table is an intercorrelation matrix, with communalities (in parentheses) replacing the 1s in the diagonal; thus, it is a reduced correlation matrix R_r. For purposes of the example, we have inserted exact communalities in the diagonal--ordinarily, one would not know these, and would have to begin with estimates of them (we discuss some methods later in this chapter).

Shown to the right in Table 5-1 are general factors extracted from the same correlation matrix by two methods. The column labeled *Principal factor* contains values obtained by an iterative search for a set of path coefficients which would yield the best fit of implied to observed correlations according to a least squares criterion. The column labeled *Canonical factor* contains values obtained by a similar search using a maximum likelihood criterion instead. (The searches were carried out via LISREL, specifying one standardized latent variable and residuals fixed to U^2.) Note that although each method leads to

Table 5-1 Extraction of an initial general factor by two methods (hypothetical correlations with exact communalities)

R_r							First general factor	
							Principal	Canonical
	D	E	F	G	H		factor	factor
D	(.16)	.20	.24	.00	.00	D	.170	.065
E	.20	(.74)	.58	.56	.21	E	.782	.685
F	.24	.58	(.55)	.41	.21	F	.649	.525
G	.00	.56	.41	(.91)	.51	G	.857	.939
H	.00	.21	.21	.51	(.36)	H	.450	.507

slightly different estimates of the paths from the factor to the variables, the solutions are generally similar, in that G is largest, D is smallest, with E then F and H falling between.

As we see later, there are other methods for obtaining principal and canonical factor loadings via the matrix attributes known as eigenvalues and eigenvectors, but those methods yield results equivalent to these.

Table 5-2 carries the process through successively to a second and third factor, using the principal factor method. In the first row of Table 5-2 are shown the correlation matrix, the same as in Table 5-1, with communalities in the diagonal. On the right, in the columns of factor pattern matrix **P**, the loadings of the three factors are entered as they are calculated. The first column, labeled I, is the first principal factor from Table 5-1, the single factor that by a least squares criterion comes closest to reproducing R_r. Below this, on the right in the second row of matrices, are shown impR, the correlations (and communalities) implied by the first general factor. They are obtained via **pp´** (e.g., $.170^2 = .029$; .170 x .782 = .133; etc.). On the left in this row is what is left unexplained--the residual matrix resR, obtained by subtracting impR from R_r (e.g., .16 - .029 = .131; .20 - .133 = .067; etc.)

The basic principal factor procedure is then applied to this residual matrix, to find the single general factor best capable of explaining these remaining correlations: The result is the second principal factor, labeled II in the matrix **P**. (This was again obtained by LISREL, with the residuals now fixed at 1-.131, etc.)

In the third row of matrices, these various steps are repeated. The matrix implied by factor II is $impR_2$, and the still unexplained correlations, $resR_2$, are obtained by subtracting $impR_2$ from $resR_1$. Clearly, not very much is left unexplained--the largest numbers in $resR_2$ are on the order of .03 or .04. In

Table 5-2 Extraction of three successive general factors by the principal factor method (data of Table 5-1)

R_r

	D	E	F	G	H
D	(.16)	.20	.24	.00	.00
E	.20	(.74)	.58	.56	.21
F	.24	.58	(.55)	.41	.21
G	.00	.56	.41	(.91)	.51
H	.00	.21	.21	.51	(.36)

P

	I	II	III	h²
D	.170	.325	.161	.160
E	.782	.302	-.193	.740
F	.649	.330	.142	.550
G	.857	-.413	-.071	.910
H	.450	-.337	.208	.360

resR₁

(.131)	.067	.130	-.146	-.076
.067	(.128)	.072	-.111	-.142
.130	.072	(.129)	-.146	-.082
-.146	-.111	-.146	(.175)	.124
-.076	-.142	-.082	.124	(.157)

impR₁

(.029)	.133	.110	.146	.076
.133	(.612)	.508	.671	.352
.110	.508	(.421)	.556	.292
.146	.671	.556	(.735)	.386
.076	.352	.292	.386	(.203)

resR₂

(.025)	-.031	.023	-.012	.034
-.031	(.037)	-.028	.013	-.040
.023	-.028	(.020)	-.010	.029
-.012	.013	-.010	(.005)	-.015
.034	-.040	.029	-.015	(.043)

impR₂

(.106)	.098	.107	-.134	-.110
.098	(.091)	.100	-.124	-.102
.107	.100	(.109)	-.136	-.111
-.134	-.124	-.136	(.170)	.139
-.110	-.102	-.111	.139	(.114)

resR₃

(-.001)	.000	.000	-.001	.001
.000	(.000)	-.001	-.001	.000
.000	-.100	(.000)	.000	-.001
-.001	-.001	.000	(.000)	.000
.001	.000	-.001	.000	(.000)

impR₃

(.026)	-.031	.023	-.011	.033
-.031	(.037)	-.027	.014	-.040
.023	-.027	(.020)	-.010	.030
-.011	.014	-.010	(.005)	-.015
.033	-.040	.030	-.015	(.043)

many practical situations we might well decide that the small values left in resR₂ are attributable to sampling or measurement error, poor estimation of the communalities, or the like, and stop at this point. But in our hypothetical exact example we continue to a third factor, III, which, as shown in resR₃ in the bottom row, explains (except for minor rounding errors) everything that is left.

Note that the contributions of the three factors, that is, impR₁ + impR₂ + impR₃, plus the final residual matrix resR₃, will always add up to the starting matrix R_r. This is a consequence of these being independent factors: Each explains a unique and nonoverlapping portion of the covariation in $\mathbf{R_r}$. Note also that the sizes of the pattern coefficients in $\mathbf{P}$ tend on the whole to decrease as we move from I to II to III: Successive factors are less important; $_{imp}\mathbf{R_1}$ explains more of $\mathbf{R_r}$ than does $_{imp}\mathbf{R_2}$, and $_{imp}\mathbf{R_2}$ more than $_{imp}\mathbf{R_3}$.

Notice further that the total explained correlation $\mathbf{R_r}$ can be obtained either by $_{imp}\mathbf{R_1} + {_{imp}}\mathbf{R_2} + {_{imp}}\mathbf{R_3}$ or by $\mathbf{PP'}$. This equivalence is not surprising if one traces the steps of matrix multiplication, because exactly the same products are involved in both instances, and only the order of adding them up differs.

Finally, notice the column at the top right of Table 5-2 labeled h^2, the communalities implied by the solution. They are obtained as the diagonal of $\mathbf{PP'}$, or, equivalently, as the sums of the squared elements of the rows of $\mathbf{P}$ (to see this equivalence, go mentally through the steps of the matrix multiplication $\mathbf{PP'}$). In this case, because true communalities were used to begin with and the solution is complete, the implied communalities agree with the diagonal of $\mathbf{R_r}$.

Figure 5.2 compares the preceding solution, expressed in path diagram form, with the causal model which in fact was used to generate the correlation matrix analyzed in Table 5-2.

First, by the appropriate path tracing, either diagram yields the same correlations among variables and the same communalities. The communality of G in the top diagram is the sum of the squares of the paths to B and C, plus twice the product of these paths and the correlation r_{BC}; i.e., $.5^2 + .6^2 + 2 \times .5 \times .5 \times .6 = .91$. The communality of G in the bottom diagram is just the sum of the squared paths to I, II, and III, because the latter are all uncorrelated; i.e., $.86^2 + (-.41)^2 + (-.07)^2 = .91$. The correlation between D and E in the top diagram is $.4 \times .5 = .20$. That between D and E in the bottom diagram is $.17 \times .78 + .32 \times .30 + .16 \times (-.19)$, which also equals .20.

Both of these three-factor models, then, explain the data equally well: They imply the same correlations and communalities (and hence the same specific variances). The one explains the data with a smaller number of paths (9) and has two of its factors correlated. The other explains the data with three uncorrelated general factors of decreasing magnitude, involving a total of 15 paths, one from every factor to every variable.

Most factor analysts believe that the action of causes in the real world is better represented by models like (a) than by models like (b). Causes typically have a limited range of effects--not every cause influences everything. And real-life causal influences may often be correlated. Nevertheless, a model like (b) has two great merits: (1) It can be arrived at by straightforward procedures from data, and (2) it establishes how many factors are necessary to explain the data to any desired degree of precision. As noted earlier, methods exist for transforming models like (b) into models more like (a), so that a model like (b) can be used as a first step in an exploratory analysis.

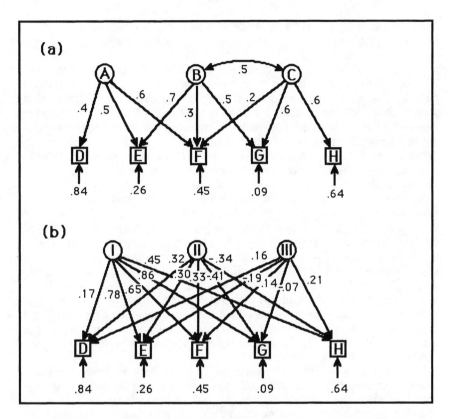

Fig. 5.2 Path models for Table 5-1. (a) Model used to generate correlations. (b) Model representing initial principal factor solution.

Direct calculation of principal factors

We have considered one way of arriving at an initial factor solution: by the successive extraction of independent general factors from a correlation matrix with communalities in the diagonal. In practice, however, a direct calculation can be used to obtain loadings for all the principal factors simultaneously. By this method, the principal factor pattern is obtained via the eigenvalues and eigenvectors of the reduced correlation matrix; i.e., the matrix R_r . (Readers unfamiliar with the concepts of eigenvalues and eigenvectors should consult Appendix A or a matrix algebra text.) If we arrange the eigenvectors in the columns of a matrix **V** and the square roots of the eigenvalues from large to small in a diagonal matrix **L**, we can obtain the principal factors by the matrix multiplication **P = VL.** Put another way, the principal factor pattern is a rescaling of the eigenvectors by the square roots of the eigenvalues. Postmultiplying a matrix by a diagonal matrix rescales its columns by the values in the diagonal matrix.

Given the eigenvalues and eigenvectors, then, the principal axis solution is simple. This just sweeps the computational effort under the rug, of course, by pushing it back into the chore of computing the eigenvalues and vectors. This is a very substantial computation, if carried out by hand for a large correlation matrix--think in terms of days or weeks, not minutes or hours. But fast and efficient computer routines exist for calculating the eigenvalues and vectors of symmetric matrices, and are widely available. If for any reason you wish to solve for eigenvalues and vectors by hand, which is feasible for small examples, standard textbooks (e.g., Morrison, 1976) will show you how.

The eigenvalues corresponding to the principal factors are of interest in their own right--they represent the variance of observed variables explained by the successive factors. If we sum the squares of the factor loadings **P** in Table 5-2 by columns rather than rows, we will obtain the eigenvalues. They are, respectively, 2.00, .59, and .13. Their sum, 2.72, is the same as the sum of the communalities; it is the total explained variance. The first factor accounts for a substantial part of the total communality (2.00/2.72 of it, or about 74%). The second factor accounts for about 22%, and the third for 5%. Another way of looking at the three eigenvalues is as the sums of the diagonal elements (traces) of the three implied matrices in Table 5-2. (Can you see why these are algebraically equivalent?) Again, the eigenvalues reflect the relative contributions of the three factors.

We need now to return to two matters that we have so far finessed in our examples: namely, (1) estimating the communalities, and (2) deciding at what point the residuals become negligible. In real-life data analyses we do not usually have advance knowledge of how much of a variable's variance is shared with other variables and how much is specific. And in real life, we will usually have many trivial influences on our variables in addition to the main causes we hope to isolate, so that after the factors representing the latter are extracted we still expect to find a certain amount of residual covariance. At what point do we conclude that all the major factors have been accounted for, and what is left in the residual matrix is just miscellaneous debris? We consider these topics in turn.

Estimating Communalities

As we have seen, an exploratory factor analysis begins by removing unique variance from the diagonal of the correlation or covariance matrix among the variables. Because one rarely knows in advance what proportion of the variance is unique and what is shared with other variables in the matrix (if one did, one would probably not need to be doing an exploratory analysis), some sort of estimate must be used. How does one arrive at such an estimate? How important is it that the estimate be an accurate one?

The answer to the second question is easy: The larger the number of variables being analyzed, the less important it is to have accurate estimates of the communalities. Why? Because the larger the matrix, the less of it lies in the diagonal. In a 2 x 2 matrix, half the elements are diagonal elements. In a 10 x 10 matrix, only one tenth are (10 diagonal cells out of a total of 100). In a 100 x 100 matrix, 1% of the matrix is in the diagonal, and 99% consists of off-diagonal cells. In a 2 x 2 matrix, an error in a communality would be an error in one of two cells making up a row or column total. In a 100 x 100 matrix, it would be an error in one of a hundred numbers entering into the total, and its effect would be greatly attenuated. In factoring a correlation matrix of more than, say, 40 variables, it hardly matters what numbers one puts into the principal diagonal, even 1s or 0s--although since it is very easy to arrive at better estimates than these, one might as well do so. Many different methods have been proposed. We discuss two in this chapter, plus a strategy for improving any initial estimate via iteration.

Highest correlation of a variable

A very simpleminded but serviceable approach in large matrices is to use as the communality estimate for a given variable the highest absolute value of its correlation with any other variable in the matrix; that is, the largest off-diagonal number in each row in the matrix is put into the diagonal with positive sign.

The highest correlation of a variable with another variable in the matrix *isn't* its communality, of course, but it will in a general way resemble it: Variables that share much variance with other variables in the matrix will have high correlations with those variables and hence get high communality estimates, as they should, whereas variables that don't have much in common with any other variables in the matrix will have low correlations and hence get low communality estimates, again correctly. Some cases won't work out quite so well--e.g., a variable that has moderate correlations with each of several quite different variables might have a high true communality but would receive only a moderate estimate by this method. Nevertheless, in reasonably large matrices, or as a starting point for a more elaborate iterative solution, this quick and easy method is often quite adequate.

Squared multiple correlations

A more sophisticated method, but one requiring considerably more computation, is to estimate the communality of a given variable by the squared multiple correlation of that variable with all the remaining variables in the matrix. In practice, this is usually done by obtaining R^{-1}, the inverse of the (unreduced) correlation matrix R. The reciprocals of the diagonal elements of R^{-1}, subtracted from 1, yield the desired squared multiple correlations (often called SMCs for short); that is, for the i th variable:

161

$$\text{SMC}_i = 1 - 1/k_{ii},$$

where k_{ii} is the ith element of the main diagonal of $\mathbf{R}^{-1}$.

Table 5-3 illustrates the calculation of SMCs for the example of Table 5-1. $\mathbf{R}$ is the correlation matrix; $\mathbf{R}^{-1}$ is its inverse, calculated by a standard computer routine. The bottom part of the table shows the steps in obtaining the SMCs.

SMCs are not communalities either; in fact, they are systematically lower than (at most equal to) the true communalities. Nevertheless, they are related to the communalities in a general way, in that if a variable is highly predictable from other variables in the matrix, it will tend to share a good deal of variance in common with them, and if it is unpredictable from the other variables, it means that it has little common variance. In large matrices, the SMCs are often only slightly below the theoretical true communalities.

Table 5-3 Calculation of squared multiple correlations of each variable with all others (data of Table 5-1)

$\mathbf{R}$	1.00	.20	.24	.00	.00
	.20	1.00	.58	.56	.21
	.24	.58	1.00	.41	.21
	.00	.56	.41	1.00	.51
	.00	.21	.21	.51	1.00

$\mathbf{R}^{-1}$	1.096	-.204	-.230	.219	-.021
	-.204	1.921	-.751	-.869	.197
	-.230	-.751	1.585	-.189	-.079
	.219	-.869	-.189	1.961	-.778
	-.021	.197	-.079	-.778	1.372

	diagonal	1/diag.	SMC
D	1.096	.912	.088
E	1.921	.521	.479
F	1.585	.631	.369
G	1.961	.510	.490
H	1.372	.729	.271

Iterative improvement of the estimate

The basic idea is that one makes an initial communality estimate somehow, obtains a factor pattern matrix **P**, and then uses that to obtain the set of communalities implied by the factor solution. In the usual case of uncorrelated initial factors, these are just the sums of the squares of the elements in the rows of **P**; more generally, they may be obtained as the diagonal of **PFP′**, where **F** is the matrix of factor intercorrelations. One can then take these implied communalities, which should represent a better estimate than the initial ones, put them in place of the original estimates in R_r, and repeat the process. The **P** from this should yield still better estimates of the communalities, which can be reinserted in R_r, and the process repeated until successive repetitions no longer lead to material changes in the estimates. Such a process involves a good deal of calculation, but it is easily programmed for a computer, and most factor analysis programs provide iterative improvement of initial communality estimates as an option.

Table 5-4 shows several different communality estimates based on the artificial example of Table 5-1. The first column gives the true communality. The first estimate, highest correlation in the row, shows a not-atypical pattern for this method of overestimating low communalities and underestimating high ones. The second, SMCs, shows, as expected, all estimates on the low side. The third shows the outcome of an iterative solution starting with SMCs. (We discuss the fourth shortly). No solution recovers the exact set of communalities of the model generating the correlations, but for this small matrix the iterative solution comes much closer than either of the one-step estimates, and the total estimated communality is also fairly close to that of the theoretical factors.

Table 5-4 Comparison of some communality estimates for the correlation matrix of Table 5-1

Variable	h²	h² estimate 1	2	3	4
C	.16	.24	.09	.19	.18
D	.74	.58	.48	.73	.66
E	.55	.58	.37	.52	.53
F	.91	.56	.49	.81	.72
G	.36	.51	.27	.46	.40
Sum	2.72	2.47	1.70	2.71	2.49

Note: h² = communality from model which generated *r*s. Estimates: (1) highest r in row; (2) SMC; (3) SMC with iteration (3 principal factors); (4) SMC with limited iteration (same, 3 cycles).

One disadvantage of iterative solutions for the communalities is that they will sometimes lead to a "Heywood case"; a communality will converge on a value greater than 1.0. This is awkward; a hypothetical variable that shares more than all of its variance with other variables is not too meaningful. Some factor analysis computer programs will stop the iterative process automatically when an offending communality reaches 1.0, but this isn't much better, because a variable with no unique variance is usually not plausible either. A possible alternative strategy in such a case might be to show, e.g., by means of a χ^2 test, that the fit of the model with the communality reduced to a sensible value is not significantly worse than it is with the Heywood case communality. If this proves *not* to be the case, the model is unsatisfactory and something else must be considered--extracting a different number of factors, rescaling variables to linearize relationships, eliminating the offending variable, or the like. Another strategy is to limit the number of iterations--two or three will often produce a substantial improvement in communality estimates without taking one across the line into Heywood territory. An illustration of the effects of limited iteration (3 cycles) is shown in column 4 of Table 5-4. It will be seen that most of the communality estimates have moved substantially toward their true values in the first column from the SMCs in column 2.

If you are a very alert reader, it may have occurred to you that there is another potential fly in the ointment in using iterative approaches. In order to use such an approach to improving communality estimates, one must first know how many factors to extract--because using a different number of columns in **P** will result in different implied communalities. In the case of our hypothetical example, we used the three factors known to account for the data as the basis of our iterative improvement, but in real life one must first decide how many factors to use to obtain the implied communality estimates that are to be iteratively improved. To this problem of determining the number of factors we now turn.

Determining the Number of Factors

In practice, deciding on the number of factors is a much stickier problem than communality estimation. As mentioned in the last section, with reasonably large correlation matrices even quite gross errors in estimating the communalities of individual variables will usually have only minor effects on the outcome of a factor analysis. Not so with extracting too many or too few factors. This will not make too much difference in the initial step of factor extraction, other than adding or subtracting a few columns of relatively small factors in the factor pattern matrix **P**. But it will often make a material difference when the next, transformation stage is reached. Admitting an additional latent variable or two into rotations often leads to a substantial rearrangement of paths from existing latent variables; trying to fit the data with one or two fewer latent variables can also lead to a substantial reshuffling of paths. Such rearrangements can lead to quite different interpretations of the causal structure underlying the observed correlations.

So the problem is not a trivial one. What is its solution? In fact, many solutions have been proposed. We describe three in this chapter, the Kaiser-Guttman rule, the scree test, and parallel analysis, and others in the next.

The Kaiser-Guttman rule

This is easily stated: (1) Obtain the eigenvalues of the correlation matrix **R** (*not* the reduced matrix **R**$_r$); (2) ascertain how many eigenvalues are greater than 1.0. That number is the number of nontrivial factors that there will be in the factor analysis. Although various rationales have been offered for the choice of the particular value 1.0, none is entirely compelling, and it is perhaps best thought of as an empirical rule that often works quite well. Because it is easy to apply and has been incorporated into various popular computer programs for factor analysis, it has undoubtedly been the method most often used to answer the question "How many factors?" in factor analyses during recent decades.

It is not, however, infallible. If you apply it, for example, to a set of eigenvalues obtained by factoring the intercorrelations of random data, the Kaiser-Guttman rule will not tell you that there are no interpretable factors to be found. On the contrary, there will typically be a sizeable number of factors from such data with eigenvalues greater than 1.0, so the rule will tell you to extract that many factors. (To see that there must be eigenvalues greater than 1.0, consider that their sum must be *m* for an *m*-variable matrix. When you extract them in order of size, there will be some larger than 1.0 at the beginning of the list and some smaller than 1.0 at the end.)

Table 5-5 (next page) provides an example, in which eigenvalues from the correlations of random scores and real psychological test data are compared. If one were to apply the Kaiser-Guttman rule to the random data, it would suggest the presence of 11 meaningful factors; there are, of course, actually none. For the real psychological data, the rule would suggest 5 factors, which is not unreasonable--factor analysts, using various criteria, have usually argued for either 4 or 5 factors in these particular data. (Note that the 5th eigenvalue is only just slightly above 1.0, which suggests another difficulty with a Kaiser-Guttman type of rule: Chance fluctuations in correlations might easily shift a borderline eigenvalue from, say, .999 to 1.001, leading to a different decision for the number of factors, but would one really want to take such a small difference seriously?)

Presumably, one does not often factor correlations based on random data intentionally, but one may occasionally want to factor analyze something similar--say, intercorrelations of measures of quite low reliability, such as individual questionnaire items, which could involve a substantial influence of random measurement error. In such cases one could be led badly astray by blind reliance on the Kaiser-Guttman rule.

Table 5-6. Eigenvalues from random and real data

Rank in size	Random data	Real data		Rank in size	Random data	Real data
1	1.737	8.135		13	.902	.533
2	1.670	2.096		14	.850	.509
3	1.621	1.693		15	.806	.477
4	1.522	1.502		16	.730	.390
5	1.450	1.025		17	.717	.382
6	1.393	.943		18	.707	.340
7	1.293	.901		19	.672	.334
8	1.156	.816		20	.614	.316
9	1.138	.790		21	.581	.297
10	1.063	.707		22	.545	.268
11	1.014	.639		23	.445	.190
12	.964	.543		24	.412	.172

Note: Random data = correlation matrix of random scores on 24 variables for 145 cases. Real data = Holzinger-Swineford data on 24 ability tests for 145 7th- and 8th-grade children, from Harman (1976, p. 161).

The scree test

This procedure also employs eigenvalues. However, instead of using a 1.0 cutoff, the user plots successive eigenvalues on a graph and arrives at a decision based on the point at which the curve of decreasing eigenvalues changes from a rapid, decelerating decline to a flat gradual slope.

The nature of this change can be best illustrated by an example. The eigenvalues for the real data from Table 5-5 are plotted in Fig. 5.3. Notice how the first few eigenvalues drop precipitously, and then after the fourth, how a gradual linear decline sets in. This decline is seldom absolutely linear out to the last eigenvalue--often, as here, it may shift to a more gradual slope somewhere en route. This linear or near-linear slope of gradually declining eigenvalues was called the *scree* by R. B. Cattell (1966a), who proposed this test. He arrived at this name from the geological term for the rubble of boulders and debris extending out from the base of a steep mountain slope. The idea is that when you climb up to the top of the scree, you have reached the real mountain slope--or the real factors. Below that, you have a rubble of trivial or error factors. The scree test would suggest four factors in this example, for the four eigenvalues rising above the scree.

Figure 5.4 shows the scree test applied to the eigenvalues from random data. In this case, there are no true factors arising above the rubble of the scree, which begins with the first eigenvalue. Again, the scree has an initial, approximately linear segment, and then further out another section of slightly lesser slope. In this example, the scree test would provide much better

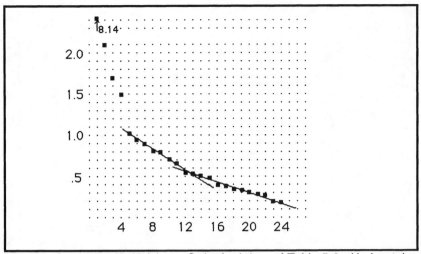

Fig. 5.3 Scree test for Holzinger-Swineford data of Table 5-6. Horizontal axis: eigenvalue number; vertical axis: eigenvalue size.

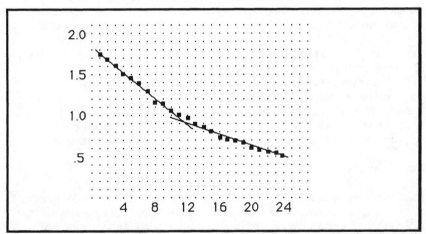

Fig. 5.4 Scree test for random data of Table 5-6. Horizontal axis: eigenvalue number; vertical axis: eigenvalue size.

guidance to the number of factors than would the Kaiser-Guttman rule--although either approach would work fairly well for the data of Fig. 5.3.

Figure 5.5 (next page) applies the scree test to the artificial example of Table 5-1. This illustrates a difficulty of applying the scree test in small problems: There is not enough excess of variables over factors to yield

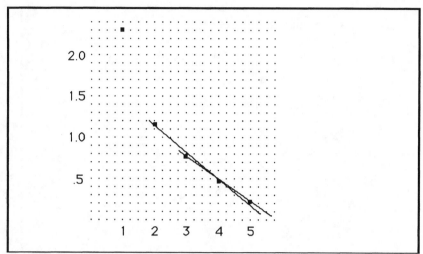

Fig. 5.5 Scree test for data of sample problem of Table 5-1. Horizontal axis: eigenvalue number; vertical axis: eigenvalue size.

sufficient rubble for a well-defined scree. The Kaiser-Guttman rule would suggest two factors in this case. A scree test would indicate the presence of at least one real factor and would not be very compelling after that--one could make a case for one, two, three, or more factors. The graph is *consistent* with the presence of three factors, but one's confidence in the true linearity of a slope defined with just two points cannot be very high!

Most users of the scree test inspect visual plots of the eigenvalues in the manner we have described. However, a computer-based version also exists (Gorsuch, 1983, p. 168), and Bentler and Yuan (1998) have proposed a statistical test for the linearity of the eigenvalues remaining after the extraction of a given number of factors--that is, a statistical version of the scree test.

Parallel analysis

Another eigenvalue-based procedure, parallel analysis (Horn, 1965), does not rely on eigenvalues greater than 1.0, but uses the number of eigenvalues that are greater than those which would result from factoring random data. For example, in Table 5.5, only the first three real-data eigenvalues exceed the corresponding random-data eigenvalues. The fourth is close, but thereafter the random ones are clearly larger. Thus the indication would be for the extraction of three, or possibly four, factors. In this case, three might represent underextraction; four or five factors is the usual choice for these data (Harman, 1976, p. 234). Also, in practice, one normally does the random factoring several times, rather than just once, to get a better estimate of the random-data curve.

168

Rotation

Up to this point, we have pursued one approach to simplicity: to account adequately for the data with the smallest number of latent variables, or factors. The strategy was to solve for a series of uncorrelated general factors of decreasing size, each accounting for as much as possible of the covariation left unaccounted for by the preceding factors.

As noted earlier, the typical next step is to transform such solutions to simplify them in another way--to minimize the number of paths appearing in the path diagram. This process is what factor analysts have traditionally called *rotation*. It received this name because it is possible to visualize these transformations as rotations of coordinate axes in a multidimensional space. A serious student of factor analysis will certainly want to explore this way of viewing the problem, but we do not need to do so for our purposes here. References to the spatial approach crop up from time to time in our terminology --uncorrelated factors are called *orthogonal* (at right angles), and correlated factors are called *oblique*, because that is the way they looked when the early factor analysts plotted them on their graph paper. But for the most part we view the matter in terms of iterative searches for transformation matrices that will change initial factor solutions into final ones that account just as well for the original correlations but are simpler in other ways.

Consider the path diagram in Fig. 5.6. It represents two factors, A and B, which are correlated .5, and which affect the observed variables C through H via the paths shown, leaving unexplained the residual variances given at the bottom of the figure. By now you should be able to verify readily that the path diagram would produce the correlation matrix and the communalities h^2 shown in the top part of Table 5-6 (next page).

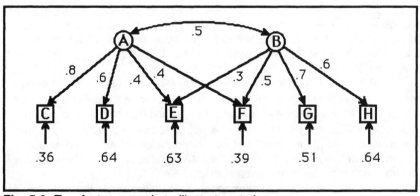

Fig. 5.6 Two-factor example to illustrate rotation.

Table 5-6 Example of rotated two-factor solution (artificial data based on Fig. 5.6; exact communalities)

R

	C	D	E	F	G	H	h^2
C	1.00	.48	.44	.52	.28	.24	.64
D	.48	1.00	.33	.39	.21	.18	.36
E	.44	.33	1.00	.47	.35	.30	.37
F	.52	.39	.47	1.00	.49	.42	.61
G	.28	.21	.35	.49	1.00	.42	.49
H	.24	.18	.30	.42	.42	1.00	.36

P_0

	I	II
C	.704	-.379
D	.528	-.284
E	.607	-.032
F	.778	.073
G	.596	.368
H	.510	.315

T

	A	B
I	.607	.547
II	-.982	1.017

$F = (T'T)^{-1}$

	A	B
A	1.00	.50
B	.50	1.00

P

	A	B
C	.80	-.00
D	.60	-.00
E	.40	.30
F	.40	.50
G	.00	.70
H	.00	.60

Note: **R** = correlation matrix; **P_0** = initial principal factor pattern; **T** = transformation matrix; **P** = transformed factor pattern; **F** = factor intercorrelations.

The matrix **P_0** represents principal factors obtained from the eigenvalues and vectors of **R_r** (using the exact communalities shown), in the manner outlined earlier. It is simple in the first sense we have considered: **$P_0 P_0'$** reconstructs **R_r** exactly (within rounding error); i.e., the two factors account for all the common variance and covariance in the matrix, and the first accounts for as much as possible by itself. The factor pattern is not, however, simple in the second sense. Only one, or at most two, paths (from the second factor to E and F) are small enough to plausibly be considered negligible.

Next to **P_0** in the table is a matrix **T**. For the moment we will not worry about how it was obtained--by magic, perhaps. But what it does is to produce by the matrix multiplication **$P_0 T$** a new matrix **P**, one that has several zero paths, four, in fact, and whose remaining paths--to two decimal places--agree perfectly with those of the model that generated the data. As shown below **T**, one can also obtain as a function of **T** the intercorrelation matrix of the factors, **F**, again in agreement with the model of Fig. 5.6.

The factor pattern **P** is "just as good as" **P_0** in the sense that both can reconstruct the original (reduced) correlation matrix **R_r** with two factors--

although because the factors represented by **P** are correlated, we must take this into account. For P_0, we can use $P_0 P_0'$ to yield the matrix R_r. With **P**, we use **PFP'**, where **F** is the factor intercorrelation matrix. This is the more general formulation and includes $P_0 P_0'$ as a special case: Because the initial factors are uncorrelated, their intercorrelation matrix is an identity matrix and can be dropped from the expression.

If we know **T**, then, we can transform P_0 to the simpler pattern **P** that we seek (assuming that such a simpler pattern exists). How can we find **T**? In some very simple cases it can be obtained by direct calculation, but in general it is pursued by a process of iterative trial and error, and nowadays a computer usually carries out the search.

A variety of different procedures exist for this purpose, going by such exotic names as Varimax, Quartimax, Oblimin, Orthoblique, and Promax, to name just a few of the more popular ones. (Gorsuch, 1983, gives a table listing 19 such procedures and describes it as a "sample.") We will say something later about the differences among the methods, but for the moment let us consider them as all doing the same thing: modifying some initial arbitrary **T** (such as an identity matrix) by some form of systematic trial and error so that it yields a **P** which, while retaining its capacity to reconstruct R_r, gets progressively simpler and simpler in the second sense of containing an increasing number of zero or near-zero paths.

For the present, we discuss two rotation methods: Varimax, which produces orthogonal factors, and Oblimin, which allows factors to be correlated. In the next chapter we consider some others.

An orthogonal transformation procedure--Varimax

Varimax, derived by Henry Kaiser (1958) from an earlier procedure called Quartimax (Neuhaus & Wrigley, 1954), seeks for a **T** that will produce factors uncorrelated with one another; that is, after the transformation the factors remain independent, but are simpler in the sense of having more zero or near-zero paths.

Both Quartimax and Varimax use a criterion of simplicity of **P** that is based on the sum of the fourth powers of the pattern coefficients, and both modify **T** in an iterative fashion until a **P** is reached for which the criterion cannot be improved. In both, the changes in **T** are introduced in such a way that $(T'T)^{-1}$, the factor intercorrelation matrix **F**, always remains an identity matrix. The criteria used, and hence the properties of the solutions, are, however, a little different. Quartimax uses as a criterion just the sum of the fourth powers of the elements of **P**: in symbols,

$$\Sigma\Sigma p^4,$$

where p represents a pattern coefficient, and the $\Sigma\Sigma$ means to sum over both rows and columns.

Varimax subtracts from this sum a function of the sum of squared coefficients within columns of **P**. The Varimax criterion may be given as

$$\Sigma\Sigma p^4 - {}^1/_k \Sigma_f(\Sigma_v p^2)^2,$$

where Σ_f and Σ_v indicate summing across factors and variables, respectively, and k is the number of variables.

The sums of fourth powers of the coefficients in a **P** matrix will tend to be greater when some coefficients are high and some are low than when all are middling (given that in both cases the correlation matrix is equally well reconstructed, and the factors remain orthogonal). Thus, the iterative process will tend to move toward a **P** matrix with a few high values and many near-zero values, if such a matrix can be found that continues to meet the other requirements.

The Quartimax criterion is indifferent to where the high values are located within the **P** matrix--many of them could be on a single general factor, for example. The Varimax modification awards a bonus to solutions in which the variance is spread out more evenly across the factors in **P**, so Varimax tends to avoid solutions containing a general factor.

Varimax is usually applied to variables that have first been rescaled so their communality equals 1.0. This tends to prevent the transformation process from being dominated by a few variables of high communality. Varimax applied to variables rescaled in this way is called "normal" or "normalized" Varimax--as opposed to "raw" Varimax, in which the criterion is calculated on coefficients in their ordinary scaling. The rescaling is easily accomplished by dividing every coefficient in a row of the factor pattern matrix by the h^2 of that variable before beginning the rotational process, and then scaling back by multiplying by h^2 at the end. This procedure is also sometimes referred to as "Kaiser normalization," after its inventor.

Varimax is a relatively fast and robust procedure, and is widely available in standard computer factor analysis packages. It can be used with confidence whenever conditions are suitable (i.e., where the causal factors underlying the observed correlations are expected to be independent of one another, or nearly so, and one expects to find the variance spread out among the factors). Even when moderately correlated factors are expected, Varimax is sometimes still used because of its other virtues. Even with somewhat correlated factors it will often identify the main factors correctly. If an orthogonal procedure is used when factors are in fact correlated, the low coefficients will only be relatively low, not near zero as they would be with an oblique factor solution, but which coefficients are high and which low will often agree fairly well between the two solutions.

Table 5-7 gives examples of Quartimax and Varimax solutions based on the sample problem of Fig. 5.6. An initial principal factor solution was

Table 5-7 Factor pattern matrices, factor intercorrelations, and transformation matrices for Quartimax and Varimax transformations of an initial principal factor solution (example problem of Fig. 5.6)

P	Initial		Quartimax		Varimax		Paths	
	I	II	A	B	A	B	A	B
C	.70	-.38	.78	-.17	.78	.20	.80	.00
D	.53	-.28	.59	-.13	.58	.15	.60	.00
E	.61	-.03	.59	.13	.47	.39	.40	.30
F	.78	.07	.73	.28	.52	.58	.40	.50
G	.60	.37	.47	.52	.19	.67	.00	.70
H	.51	.32	.41	.44	.16	.58	.00	.60

F		I	II		A	B		A	B		A	B
I		1.00	.00	A	1.00	.00	A	1.00	.00	A	1.00	.50
II		.00	1.00	B	.00	1.00	B	.00	1.00	B	.50	1.00

T			A	B		A	B
I			.962	.273		.736	.677
II			-.273	.962		-.677	.736

Criteria:				
Quartimax	1.082		1.092		1.060
Varimax	.107		.204		.389

Note: Communalities for initial solution iterated from SMCs. Raw Quartimax and Varimax transformations. Paths from path diagram.

transformed so as to maximize the Quartimax or Varimax criterion. The raw versions were used to keep the examples simple. Note that the **T** matrices for orthogonal rotations are symmetrical, apart from signs.

It will be observed that the Varimax **P** approximates the values of the original path model fairly well in its larger coefficients, but that the small ones are systematically overestimated. The Quartimax **P** assigns relatively more variance to the first factor, making it a fairly general factor.

From the values of the Quartimax and Varimax criteria given at the bottom of the table, you can see that each criterion is highest for its own solution (as it should be). The initial principal factor solution is not too bad by the Quartimax criterion because it does have some high and some low loadings, but it is unsatisfactory to Varimax because the principal factor solution maximizes the difference in variance between the two factors.

In this example, Varimax does better than Quartimax at approximating the paths of the original model, and either one does better than the initial principal factor solution. The advantage Varimax has here results from the fact that the model to be approximated has two roughly equal factors--that is, there is no general factor present.

An oblique transformation procedure--Oblimin

When the true underlying factors are substantially correlated, orthogonal rotations such as those of Varimax cannot achieve ideal solutions. A variety of methods have been proposed for locating good solutions when factors are correlated with one another ("oblique"). Because the factor intercorrelations represent additional free variables, there are more possibilities for strange things to happen in oblique than in orthogonal solutions. For example, two tentative factors may converge on the same destination during an iterative search, as evidenced by the correlation between them becoming high and eventually moving toward 1.00--this cannot happen if factors are kept orthogonal. Despite their real theoretical merits, oblique solutions tend to be more difficult to compute, more vulnerable to idiosyncrasies in the data, and generally more likely to go extravagantly awry than orthogonal ones. There is no one oblique procedure that works well in all situations, hence the proliferation of methods. We describe here one widely used procedure, Direct Oblimin, and will briefly discuss some others in the next chapter. Direct Oblimin uses an iterative procedure based on improving a criterion, as in Quartimax or Varimax, except that the requirement that factors be uncorrelated is dropped.

The criterion used in the Direct Oblimin procedure (Jennrich & Sampson, 1966) is as follows--the criterion is minimized rather than maximized:

$$\Sigma_{ij} (\Sigma_v p_i^2 p_j^2 - w \, {}^1/_k \, \Sigma_v p_i^2 \, \Sigma_v p_j^2).$$

Σ_{ij} refers to the sum over all factor pairs ij ($i < j$), and the other symbols are as used for the Varimax criterion. The weight w (sometimes given as δ) specifies different variants of Oblimin that differ in the degree to which correlation among the factors is encouraged. If $w = 0$, only the first part of the expression, the products of the squared pattern coefficients on different factors, is operative. This variant is sometimes given a special name, Direct Quartimin. It tends to result in solutions with fairly substantial correlations among the factors. By making the weight w negative, high correlations among factors are penalized. Most often, zero weights or modest negative weights (e.g., $w = -.5$) will work best. Large negative weights (e.g., $w = -10$) will yield essentially orthogonal factors. Positive weights (e.g., $w = .5$) tend to produce over-oblique and often problematic solutions.

174

The term *direct* in the title of Direct Oblimin indicates that the criterion is applied directly to the factor pattern matrix **P**. (There also exists an Indirect Oblimin in which the criterion is applied to a different matrix). Again, as in the case of Varimax, the transformation may be carried out on a factor matrix rescaled so that all the communalities are equal to 1.0, with a return to the original metric at the end.

Table 5-8 presents a Direct Oblimin solution for the sample 2-factor problem. (The Quartimin version--$w = 0$--was used.) Observe that the pattern coefficients approximate the paths of the original model quite well, except that the near-zero loadings are slightly negative. The correlation between factors is a little on the high side (.57 vs. .50), but on the whole the solution has recovered quite well the characteristics of the path diagram that generated the correlations.

Below the **F** in the table is the **T**, the transformation matrix that produces the Oblimin **P** from the **P₀** of the initial solution. It is this **T**, of course, that has

Table 5-8 Factor pattern matrix, factor intercorrelations, and transformation matrix for an Oblimin transformation of an initial principal factor solution (example problem of Fig. 5.6)

	Initial		Oblimin		Original	
P	I	II	A	B	A	B
C	.70	-.38	.81	-.02	.80	.00
D	.53	-.28	.61	-.01	.60	.00
E	.61	-.03	.38	.30	.40	.30
F	.78	.07	.37	.51	.40	.50
G	.60	.37	-.05	.73	.00	.70
H	.51	.32	-.04	.62	.00	.60

F	I	II		A	B		A	B
I	1.00	.00	A	1.00	.57	A	1.00	.50
II	.00	1.00	B	.57	1.00	B	.50	1.00

T		A	B
I		.575	.555
II		-1.071	1.081

Criterion:
Oblimin   .172   .051

Note: Same initial solution as Table 5-7. Oblimin is Direct Quartimin (w = 0), unnormalized.

resulted from iterative modifications by the computer program until the resulting **P** has as low a score as possible on the Oblimin criterion. In the bottom row of the table are given values of the Oblimin criterion for the initial solution and for the Oblimin solution, which has succeeded in reducing it considerably.

Factor pattern and factor structure in oblique solutions

As mentioned previously, two matrices relating the observed variables to the latent variables are frequently reported. One is the factor pattern matrix **P** that we have already discussed. The other is the factor structure matrix **S**, which is a matrix giving the correlations between the factors and the variables. When factors are uncorrelated (orthogonal), there is just a single path from any factor to any variable, and hence the correlation between them is numerically equal to the path coefficient. In this case, therefore, **S** equals **P** and only one need be reported. However, in an oblique solution, there will be additional compound paths between factors and variables via correlations with other factors, and **S** will in general not be equal to **P**. However, **S** may readily be calculated from **P** and the factor intercorrelations **F** by the equation:

$$S = PF.$$

Table 5-9 gives an example based on the paths from Fig. 5.6 (labeled "original paths" in Table 5-8). Note that the **S** matrix does not have the zero paths of the **P** matrix; because the factors are correlated, each is correlated with variables on which it has no direct causal influence. (The reader should verify that the matrix multiplication that

Table 5-9 Factor structure, for the factor pattern of Table 5-8

	Factor pattern P			Factor intercorrelations F			Factor structure S	
	A	B		A	B		A	B
C	.80	.00	A	1.00	.50	C	.80	.40
D	.60	.00	B	.50	1.00	D	.60	.30
E	.40	.30				E	.55	.50
F	.40	.50				F	.65	.70
G	.00	.70				G	.35	.70
H	.00	.60				H	.30	.60

yields **S** is equivalent to determining the correlations from tracing the paths in the path diagram of Fig. 5.6.)

An Example: Thurstone's Box Problem

In this section, we carry through an exploratory factor analysis from raw scores to rotated factors. We use as an example a demonstration problem originally devised by Thurstone (1947) and later modified by Kaiser and Horst (1975). The intent is to illustrate exploratory factor analysis in a situation in which the true underlying latent variables are known, so we can check our results.

Thurstone began with a hypothetical population of 20 rectangular boxes; the first three are illustrated at the top of Table 5-10. For each box, a number of "scores" were derived, as mathematical functions of one or more of its three dimensions length (= X), width (= Y), and height (= Z). Thus, the first box, which was 3 units long by 2 wide by 1 high, had a score on the first variable (X^2) of 9, on the second (Y^2) of 4, and so on. The fourth, fifth, and sixth variables are products of two dimensions each, the seventh through ninth are natural logarithms, and the tenth is the triple product XYZ. (Thurstone actually created 20 variables, but we are using only 10 of them to keep the example more manageable.)

Table 5-10 Scores on 10 variables for first three boxes, Thurstone's box problem (data from Kaiser & Horst, 1975)

Variable	Box 1 True	Box 1 Observed	Box 2 True	Box 2 Observed	Box 3 True	Box 3 Observed
1. X^2	9.0	8.9	9.0	9.4	9.0	6.9
2. Y^2	4.0	5.0	4.0	4.5	9.0	10.2
3. Z^2	1.0	2.7	4.0	3.8	1.0	.7
4. XY	6.0	5.6	6.0	5.4	9.0	10.3
5. XZ	3.0	3.4	6.0	8.1	3.0	4.2
6. YZ	2.0	2.1	4.0	3.4	3.0	3.2
7. ln X	1.1	1.1	1.1	1.1	1.1	1.1
8. ln Y	.7	.8	.7	.6	1.1	1.1
9. ln Z	.0	.3	.7	.4	.0	.0
10. XYZ	6.0	2.3	12.0	9.8	9.0	9.9

Kaiser and Horst added 5% random error to Thurstone's scores, in the interest of greater realism, and doubled the number of boxes from 20 to 40 by using each twice (with different random errors). The resulting scores for the first three boxes, rounded to one decimal place, are given in the columns labeled *observed* in Table 5-10. The full data matrix is in Appendix F, and the matrix of score intercorrelations in Table 5-11.

Table 5-11 Correlation matrix, Thurstone box problem

	V1	V2	V3	V4	V5	V6	V7	V8	V9	V10
V1	1.00	.23	.08	.64	.42	.15	.92	.10	.10	.46
V2		1.00	.17	.84	.21	.57	.37	.93	.13	.53
V3			1.00	.14	.85	.84	.16	.27	.91	.77
V4				1.00	.34	.50	.73	.76	.12	.65
V5					1.00	.78	.50	.22	.87	.87
V6						1.00	.30	.64	.81	.91
V7							1.00	.28	.18	.59
V8								1.00	.21	.58
V9									1.00	.76
V10										1.00

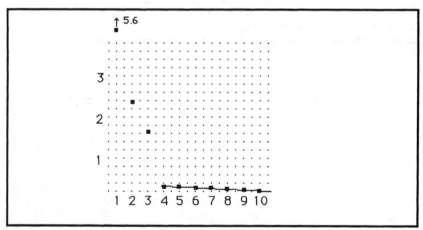

Fig. 5.7 Scree test for Thurstone box problem.

The eigenvalues are given in Table 5-12 and a scree test in Fig. 5.7. Clearly, by either the Kaiser-Guttman rule or the scree test, a three-factor solution is indicated. Table 5-13 shows three principal factors based on the (unrounded) correlation matrix, using iterated communality estimates

178

Table 5-12 Eigenvalues, Thurstone box problem

1.	5.621	6.	.079
2.	2.348	7.	.072
3.	1.602	8.	.049
4.	.100	9.	.025
5.	.088	10.	.015

Table 5-13 Unrotated principal factors, Thurstone box problem

Variables	F1	F2	F3	h^2
V1	.503	.468	.683	.938
V2	.649	.506	-.499	.925
V3	.732	-.615	-.020	.914
V4	.736	.647	-.056	.963
V5	.834	-.400	.282	.934
V6	.904	-.280	-.252	.959
V7	.633	.470	.558	.933
V8	.664	.382	-.604	.951
V9	.717	-.627	.045	.909
V10	.971	-.108	.047	.956

starting from SMCs. As you can see, the communality estimates are all quite high, in the range .90 to .97, consistent with the fact that the variables contain around 5% random error.

   Table 5-14 (next page) shows two transformed solutions and a direct confirmatory maximum likelihood solution. The first solution is an orthogonal rotation using Varimax. For most practical purposes, this would be quite adequate: it correctly identifies the three factors as respectively reflecting the latent dimensions Z, Y, and X that underlie the manifest measurements, as one may verify by comparing the rotated factor pattern to the path diagram of Fig. 5.8 (p. 181). Nevertheless, because nearly all the minor loadings in the Varimax solution are positive, there is an indication that the underlying dimensions X, Y, and Z are slightly correlated with one another; i.e., that there is a general size factor in the population of boxes. Therefore, an oblique solution (Direct Oblimin; $w = 0$) was carried out; it is also shown in Table 5-14. This yields a slightly cleaner solution; whereas the Varimax factor pattern had several of its minor loadings in the .15 to .25 range, the oblique solution has all its near-

Table 5-14 Final factor solutions, Thurstone box problem

	Varimax			Direct Oblimin			Confirmatory		
	F1	F2	F3	F1	F2	F3	F1	F2	F3
V1	.08	.06	.96	-.00	-.08	.99	.00	.00	.96
V2	.11	.94	.16	-.03	.96	.03	.00	.96	.00
V3	.95	.08	-.02	.98	-.04	-.11	.95	.00	.00
V4	.10	.77	.60	-.05	.72	.51	.00	.70	.53
V5	.90	.05	.36	.90	-.12	.29	.85	.00	.36
V6	.84	.50	.05	.80	.41	-.09	.79	.48	.00
V7	.17	.22	.93	.07	.08	.92	.00	.00	.95
V8	.20	.95	.02	.08	.98	-.12	.00	.95	.00
V9	.95	.02	.02	.99	-.10	-.07	.95	.00	.00
V10	.79	.43	.39	.73	.30	.28	.71	.36	.36
F1	1.00	.00	.00	1.00	.28	.22	1.00	.15	.11
F2		1.00	.00		1.00	.29		1.00	.25
F3			1.00			1.00			1.00

Note: Kaiser normalization used for Varimax and Oblimin solutions.

zero loadings .12 or less in absolute value. The correlations among the factors are modest--in the .20s. There is, however, a suggestion that this solution may be a little too oblique: 11 of the 15 near-zero loadings are negative.

On the far right in Table 5-14 is a confirmatory maximum likelihood analysis of the correlation matrix via LISREL, based on the path diagram of Fig. 5.8: The zero values shown were fixed, and the nonzero values solved for. Note that this solution is a trifle less oblique than the Oblimin solution but agrees with it in finding the three dimensions to be slightly correlated in these data, suggesting the presence of a (modest) general size factor. We can compare the factor intercorrelations with the true correlations among the length, width, and height dimensions, calculated for Thurstone's original population of boxes: $r_{XY} = .25$, $r_{YZ} = .25$, $r_{XZ} = .10$. Obviously, the two oblique factor solutions have come reasonably close--the Oblimin, as suspected, has slightly overestimated the correlations.

Thus, a factor analysis *can* correctly recover information about known latent variables, even in the face of a certain amount of random error and nonlinearities of relationship between the latent and observed variables. However, a caution: It is not always this easy. This is, after all, an example in which three and only three major latent dimensions are present. In most real-life data sets confronting social and behavioral

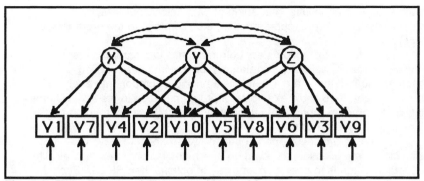

Fig. 5.8 Path diagram of Thurstone box problem.

scientists, there are likely to be numerous lesser causal factors in addition to the few major factors the analyst is interested in. The smaller of these extraneous factors can usually be safely lumped together under the heading of random error--this means, incidentally, that the communalities are likely to be considerably lower than the .95s of the box example. But in addition there are likely to be some appreciable nuisance factors present, not quite large enough to isolate successfully, yet sufficiently large to distort the picture presented by the main variables. The investigator may be deemed fortunate who encounters a situation as clear-cut as Thurstone's boxes.

Factor Analysis Using Packaged Programs-- SPSS and SAS

Several widely used statistical program packages contain facilities for doing factor analysis, and two are described briefly here. Additional information may be found in a paper by MacCallum (1983), which compares several factor analysis programs in some detail. Two cautions: Programs are not static entities--they get revised by their makers from time to time; and program packages are not monolithic--sometimes different subprograms within a package do things differently. There is no substitute for a direct test to determine what the version of program X currently on your local computer actually does in situation Y.

Here we consider the SPSS program called FACTOR (SPSS Inc., 1990), and the SAS program PROC FACTOR (SAS Institute, 1990). These two programs are generally similar in what they do, but not identical. In ease of use, the overriding consideration is familiarity with the general system: Someone who knows other SAS or SPSS programs should find the corresponding factor analysis program easy to learn and use, whereas someone coming as a complete stranger to a system must acquire a considerable baggage of information about forms of data input, handling of missing values, managing of data and output files, conventions for program representation, etc., common to the programs in that system.

In the factor extraction step, both programs can carry out a simple principal factor analysis of a correlation matrix, with user-supplied communalities. (If these are 1.0, this is a principal components analysis.) Table 5-15 and 5-16 show examples of program setups in the two systems that will accomplish a principal factor analysis with Varimax rotation for the correlation matrix of Table 5-1.

Both programs allow many options--with respect to ways of estimating communalities, deciding on how many factors to extract, etc. In general, SAS tends to offer a wider array of options than SPSS. Each

Table 5-15 SPSS FACTOR

```
TITLE   'CHAPTER 5 EXAMPLE'
MATRIX DATA   VARIABLES=D E F G H /CONTENTS=CORR
BEGIN DATA
 1.00
  .20  1.00
  .24   .58  1.00
  .00   .56   .41  1.00
  .00   .21   .21   .51  1.00
END DATA
LIST
FACTOR   MATRIX=IN (COR=*)
    /DIAGONAL=.16 .74 .55 .91 .36
    /CRITERIA=FACTORS (3)
    /EXTRACTION=PAF
    /ROTATION=VARIMAX
```

Table 5-16 SAS PROC FACTOR

```
DATA EXAMP(TYPE=CORR);
_TYPE_ ='CORR';
INPUT _NAME_ $ D E F G H;
CARDS;
D 1.0 . . . .
E .20 1.0 . . .
F .24 .58 1.0 . .
G .00 .56 .41 1.0 .
H .00 .21 .21 .51 1.0
    ;
PROC FACTOR   METHOD=PRIN  NFACT=3 ROTATE=VARIMAX;
    PRIORS .16 .74 .55 .91 .36;
    TITLE 'CHAPTER 5 EXAMPLE';
RUN;
```

package provides a number of methods of factor extraction--most of the methods described in this book are available in both. In either system, one may begin an analysis from raw data or from a matrix entered directly or produced by other programs in the series. Following factor extraction, one may proceed immediately to the factor rotation step, or save the results of the extraction for entry into different rotation procedures.

In current versions, both packages provide the basic orthogonal rotation procedures Varimax and Quartimax, either raw or normalized; SAS also provides a more general Orthomax procedure of which Varimax and Quartimax are special cases. For oblique rotation methods, both packages offer Oblimin, described in the present chapter, and a program called Promax, described in the next. SAS also offers Procrustes and Orthoblique, programs described briefly in the next chapter, and several others (the options available in earlier versions of the two packages may vary). SAS and SPSS differ in what they do if no specification is made concerning rotation. SPSS rotates automatically, using its default rotation procedure, which is Varimax; in order not to rotate, the user must specify a no-rotation option. In SAS the default is for no rotation, so if the user wishes to rotate, a particular rotation procedure must be specified.

If you are familiar with one system, but switch to the other to obtain some particular feature--a word of caution: read the manual carefully, and make some checks. Some of the little things are done differently in SPSS and SAS, and an unwary user can easily wind up with a different analysis than the one intended.

Chapter 5 Notes

There are a number of excellent books on factor analysis in which you can pursue further the topics of this and the next chapter. Examples include:

Harman, H. H. (1976). *Modern factor analysis* (3rd ed.). Probably the best systematic treatment of the many variants of factor analysis. Extensive worked examples.

Mulaik, S. A. (1972). *The foundations of factor analysis.* A well-regarded general text.

Gorsuch, R. L. (1983). *Factor analysis* (2nd ed.). Broad and readable, with a practical research emphasis. Less formal than Harman or Mulaik.

Lawley, D. N., & Maxwell, A. E. (1971). *Factor analysis as a statistical method* (2nd ed.). An emphasis on statistical inference and the use of maximum likelihood methods.

Cattell, R. B. (1978). *The scientific use of factor analysis.* A rich but opinionated discussion by a creative contributor to the field.

McDonald, R. P. (1985). *Factor analysis and related methods.* Good on relationships between factor analysis and other latent variable modeling.

Many references to the research literature using exploratory factor analysis can be found in the texts just listed. Harman (1976, pp. 7-8), for example, cites studies in fields as diverse as economics, medicine, geology, meteorology, political science, sociology, biological taxonomy, anthropology, architecture, human engineering, communication, and the study of lightplane accidents. If you want to get really serious, Hinman and Bolton (1979) give short descriptions of approximately 1000 factor analytic studies published in the areas of experimental, animal, developmental, social, personality, clinical, educational, and industrial psychology during just the 5-year period 1971-1975! Fabrigar et al. (1999) evaluate the use of exploratory factor analysis in contemporary research.

Sample size. MacCallum et al. (1999) found little support for commonly suggested rules of thumb regarding sample sizes in exploratory factor analysis. With high communalities, a small number of factors, and a relatively large number of indicators per factor, Ns of 100 or less yielded good recovery of factors; with lower communalities, more factors, and fewer indicators per factor, Ns of 300 or even 500 might be required for comparable results.

Factor analysis model. MacCallum and Tucker (1991; see also MacCallum et al., 2001) suggest that the factor analysis model be reformulated to take explicit account of the fact that it is only expected to be an approximation in the population, due to the presence of minor undetected factors, nonlinearities, and the like. Increasing sample size will diminish misfit due to random error, but not misfit due to elements such as these.

Communality estimation. Kaiser (1990) suggests the *square* of the highest correlation of a variable as a starting point for iterative estimation.

Number of factors. Zwick and Velicer (1986) compared five methods, including the three described in this chapter, for determining the number of factors to extract (actually, in their case, principal components). Of the three, parallel analysis came off the best, the scree test also did quite well, and the Kaiser-Guttman rule was least satisfactory. Schweizer (1992) also found the Kaiser-Guttman rule to perform less well than the scree test and parallel analysis. In the Zwick and Velicer study, a fourth method, Velicer's (1976) minimum average partial correlations (MAP) also performed well. Humphreys and Montanelli (1975), Lautenschlager (1989), and Turner (1998) discuss parallel analysis; the latter suggests a modification to correct a slight tendency to underextract. Lawrence and Hancock (1999) explore the consequences of extracting too many factors in a factor analysis. Wood et al. (1996) look at both over- and under-extraction--they find the latter to have more serious consequences.

Kaiser normalization. An alternative procedure proposed by Cureton and Mulaik is discussed by Browne (2001). It gives greater weight to tests loading on a single factor, and less weight to tests loading on two or more factors. Either procedure may sometimes lead to difficulties in small samples.

Other model data sets. Other sets of data with known underlying properties that can be used to try out exploratory factor analysis methods include populations of real measured boxes (Thurstone, 1947, p. 369; Gorsuch, 1983, p. 11), chicken eggs (Coan, 1959), and cups of coffee (Cattell & Sullivan, 1962). An elaborate artificial data set is provided by Cattell and Jaspers (1967).

Chapter 5 Exercises

Problems 1 and 2 involve the following correlation matrix **R** (N = 200):

	A	B	C	D
A	1.00	.28	-.14	.42
B	.28	1.00	-.08	.24
C	-.14	-.08	1.00	-.12
D	.42	.24	-.12	1.00

1. Obtain eigenvalues and eigenvectors of **R**, using any available computer program that yields normalized eigenvectors ($\mathbf{V'V = I}$). Rescale the eigenvectors to principal factor pattern coefficients, **P**, by **VL**, where **L** is a diagonal matrix of the square roots of the eigenvalues. Show that, by using 1, 2, 3, and 4 factors (i.e., 1 to 4 columns of **P**), **PP′** gives increasingly accurate reconstructions of **R** (but comment).

2. If $\mathbf{U}^2$ is a diagonal matrix of uniquenesses with elements .51, .84, .96, and .64, obtain $\mathbf{R}_r$ as $\mathbf{R} - \mathbf{U}^2$. Obtain the eigenvalues and eigenvectors of $\mathbf{R}_r$, and convert to **P** (set any small imaginary square roots to zero). Use the first column of **P** to reconstruct $\mathbf{R}_r$. Comment.

Problems 3 to 5 involve the following **R** matrix of five socioeconomic variables for 25 Los Angeles census tracts (Harman, 1976, p. 14).

Variable	Pop	Sch	Emp	Pro	Hou
Total population	1.00	.01	.97	.44	.02
Median school years		1.00	.15	.69	.86
Total employment			1.00	.51	.12
Professional services				1.00	.78
Median house value					1.00
Standard deviations	3440	1.8	1241	115	6368

3. Estimate the communalities of **R** by squared multiple correlations, using any available matrix inversion program.

4. How many factors would be indicated for **R** by the Kaiser-Guttman rule? By the scree test?

5. Use an SEM program to test the hypothesis that a single common factor would fit these data. (Hint: fix residuals to U^2 and analyze **R** matrix.) Would you accept or reject the hypothesis of a single common factor?

Given the initial pattern matrix P_0 below for two tests of verbal ability and two tests of mechanical aptitude, and the transformation matrix **T**:

P_0	I	II		**T**	A	B
V1	.8	.2		I	.75	.36
V2	.8	.3		II	.96	-1.16
M1	.6	-.4				
M2	.4	-.4				

6. Calculate the rotated factor pattern **P**. Obtain the factor intercorrelations **F**, and the factor structure **S**.

7. Draw the path diagrams for the rotated and unrotated factors, omitting any paths less than .10 in absolute value.

8. Calculate the communalities from the path diagram for the rotated factors, and as the sum of the squares of the rows of P_0. Comment.

9. If your factor analysis program will let you enter P_0 directly, carry out a Varimax and a Direct Oblimin ($w = 0$) or other oblique rotation of P_0. Use Kaiser normalization. Compare the orthogonal and oblique solutions to each other and to the problem 6 solution.

10. Verify by direct matrix calculation (**PFP′**) that both rotated solutions imply the same R_r, and that this is the same as that implied by the unrotated matrix P_0.

Chapter Six:
Exploratory Factor Analysis--Elaborations

Rescalings--Alpha and Canonical Factors

We saw in Chapter 5 that general factors may be obtained using a maximum likelihood rather than a least squares criterion, and we called these Canonical factors. It turns out that Canonical factors (Rao, 1955; Harris, 1962), and yet another variety, Alpha factors (Kaiser & Caffrey, 1965) can be obtained via the same basic eigenvalue-eigenvector procedure as principal factors, by rescaling the starting correlation or covariance matrix before carrying out the calculation.

The two methods use different preliminary scalings: Alpha analysis rescales variables so that they have equal communalities of 1.0, whereas the Canonical factor approach rescales variables so that they have equal uniquenesses of 1.0.

A numerical example of Alpha and Canonical factor analysis, based on the correlation matrix of Table 5-1, is given in Table 6-1(next page). Formally, the Alpha method rescales variables by $H^{-1}R_rH^{-1}$, where H^{-1} is a diagonal matrix of the reciprocals of the square roots of the commmunalities, and the Canonical method rescales by $U^{-1}R_rU^{-1}$, where U^{-1} contains the reciprocals of the square roots of the uniquenesses. (Recall that one obtains the inverse of a diagonal matrix by taking reciprocals of its elements.) The Alpha rescaling results in a matrix in which differences along the diagonal are eliminated, whereas the Canonical rescaling results in a matrix in which they are enhanced.

Table 6-1 illustrates the process with the same reduced correlation matrix used for the principal factor solution in Chapter 5; it is shown in the center of the top row. To its left is a column vector of the reciprocals of the square roots of the communalities (e.g., $1/\sqrt{.16} = 2.5$). These are used in the diagonal matrix H^{-1} which pre and postmultiplies R_r to yield the matrix shown on the left in the second row. Note that this has rescaled all the diagonal elements to 1.0, and the other elements proportionately (zeroes, of course, stay zero).

To the right is the Canonical factor solution. At the top are the u^{-1} (e.g.,

Table 6-1 Alpha and Canonical factor solutions (correlation matrix of Table 5-1, exact communalities)

h^{-1}		R_r				u^{-1}
2.500	.16	.20	.24	.00	.00	1.091
1.162	.20	.74	.58	.56	.21	1.961
1.348	.24	.58	.55	.41	.21	1.491
1.048	.00	.56	.41	.91	.51	3.333
1.667	.00	.21	.21	.51	.36	1.250

$H^{-1}R_rH^{-1}$					$U^{-1}R_rU^{-1}$				
1.000	.581	.809	.000	.000	.190	.428	.390	.000	.000
.581	1.000	.909	.682	.407	.428	2.846	1.696	3.661	.515
.809	.909	1.000	.580	.472	.390	1.696	1.222	2.037	.391
.000	.682	.580	1.000	.891	.000	3.661	2.037	10.111	2.125
.000	.407	.472	.891	1.000	.000	.515	.391	2.125	.562

Alpha factors			Canonical factors		
I	II	III	I	II	III
.586	.770	.253	.071	.383	.198
.918	.174	-.357	1.344	.992	-.236
.948	.315	.044	.783	.720	.301
.808	-.577	-.115	3.130	-.560	-.038
.694	-.638	.333	.634	-.270	.295

Rescaled Alpha factors			Principal factors			Rescaled Canonical factors		
I	II	III	I	II	III	I	II	III
.23	.31	.10	.17	.32	.16	.06	.35	.18
.79	.15	-.31	.78	.30	-.19	.69	.51	-.12
.70	.23	.03	.65	.33	.14	.53	.48	.20
.77	-.55	-.11	.86	-.41	-.07	.94	-.17	-.01
.42	-.38	.20	.45	-.34	.21	.51	-.22	.24

1-.16 = .84; 1/√.84 = 1.091). In the second row is the rescaled R_r matrix. Note that the differences are now exaggerated: The high values tend to be scaled up much more than the low values--.16 becomes .19, whereas .91 becomes 10.11. This is because the uniqueness for the first variable is already large (.84) and only needs to be increased a little to equal 1.0, whereas the small uniqueness in the second case (.09) must be increased manyfold.

In the third row of the table are the factor patterns, obtained via **VL** from the eigenvalue-eigenvector solutions of the matrices above them, as with principal factors. Finally, the factors are returned to their original metric (the standardized variables of the correlation matrix) by the rescalings **HP** and **UP**, respectively. A general similarity to the principal factor solution (bottom row, center) is evident, although there are differences in the sizes of coefficients. Those for the principal factor method tend to lie between the values derived from the two rescalings.

Rao arrived at his formulation of Canonical factor analysis via an attempt to define factors that would have maximum generalizability to other samples of subjects. Kaiser and Caffrey arrived at their formulation of Alpha factor analysis via an attempt to define factors that would have maximum generalizability to other measures of the underlying variables. Although it is not necessarily the case that transformed versions of these solutions would retain these properties for individual factors, one might perhaps still choose one of these two approaches if one's primary concern lay with the one or the other kind of generalization.

Both the Alpha and Canonical factor methods can be said to be "scale free," in the sense that they yield the same factors when starting from differently scaled variables: for example, from a covariance matrix of variables in their original raw units, or from a correlation matrix, where the variables are implicitly standardized. The principal factor approach will give different factor solutions in these two cases. The Alpha and Canonical approaches, because of their preliminary rescaling of both the correlation and covariance matrices to the same standard form, will not, arriving at the same solution in each case. These factors--as in Table 6-1--are often scaled back to an ordinary standard-score metric at the end for interpretability. However, the basic properties of the solutions--maximum accounting for communality by each factor, and so on-- apply to the scaling in which the eigenvalue solution is actually carried out.

From a more general perspective, we may speak of various possible alternative scalings of variables for a factor analysis: (1) Leave the variables in their original rawscore metrics, i.e., do a principal factor analysis of the covariance matrix **C** (actually, of the reduced covariance matrix $\mathbf{C_r}$, with common variances in the diagonal); (2) scale the variables by the square roots of their variances (their standard deviations), by factoring the correlations $\mathbf{R_r}$; (3) scale the variables by the square roots of the common portions of their variances, i.e., do an Alpha analysis; or, (4) scale the variables by the square roots of the unique portions of their variances, i.e., do a Canonical analysis.

Alternative 2, the factor analysis of ordinary correlations, is by far the most widely used in practice. It might perhaps be regarded as a compromise between 3 and 4 when one is concerned, as one usually is, with generalizing across both subjects and variables. Alternative 1, the factoring of covariances, may suffer excessively from arbitrariness of scale: A variable, e.g., annual income, can have a quite different effect on the factor analysis if it is expressed in dollars or in thousands of dollars, because of the huge difference in the size of the variance and covariances in the two cases. However, when differing sizes of variances are at the heart of the issue, as may be the case in comparing factor analyses across different groups (e.g., different cultures, different ages, or the like), one would not want to lose the differences among the groups by restandardizing for each, and hence would prefer to work with the covariance matrices directly. As we have noted earlier, a possible way to eat one's cake and have it too is to standardize all one's variables over the combined groups, to deal with the problem of noncomparable units of the different variables, and then to factor analyze covariance matrices for the separate groups using this common metric.

Alternative Stopping Criteria

Chi-square test of residuals

As noted, the Canonical factors are maximum likelihood factors, that is, each factor represents the best possible fit to the residual correlations, according to a maximum likelihood criterion. This presents the possibility of a χ^2 test after the addition of each factor, as to whether the correlations implied by the factors extracted so far constitute an adequate account of the original correlations.

Table 6-2 Chi-square test of residuals after each factor (sample problem of Table 5-1, with communalities assumed known), N = 100

	Factor pattern		
	I	II	III
D	.06	.35	.18
E	.69	.51	-.12
F	.53	.48	.20
G	.94	-.17	-.01
H	.51	-.22	.24
χ^2	94.67	3.16	0.00
df	10	5	0
p	< .001	> .50	--

Note: Maximum likelihood factors extracted successively via LISREL. Chi-square test is for the significance of residuals after the extraction of the given factor (= test of goodness of fit of impR to R_r based on all factors so far).

Such a test may be thought of either as a test of the goodness of fit of the model to the data, or as a test for the insignificance of the residuals left when the correlations implied by the model are subtracted from the observed correlations.

The calculations for the example problem of Table 5-1 are shown in Table 6-2. The maximum likelihood factors were obtained by successive extractions of a single factor using LISREL; as can be seen, they are the same as the rescaled canonical factors calculated via eigenvalues and vectors in Table 6-1. Chi squares were obtained on the assumption that the correlations were based on 100 subjects. As can be seen, a statistical test at a conventional significance level would have concluded that two factors, plus sampling error, provide a plausible explanation of the data--agreeing, in this case, with the Kaiser-Guttman rule. Only if the expected sampling error were considerably decreased, e.g., if a sample size of upwards of 400 were assumed, would a χ^2 test suggest the extraction of a third factor from this particular matrix of correlations. (Note that such "what if" questions are easily answered because the χ^2s go up proportionally to N - 1.)

Cross-validation

The ultimate test of any method of choosing the number of factors to extract is that it selects factors that will be found again in new samples of subjects and new sets of tests covering the same domain. If the ultimate criterion is cross-validation, why not use it as the immediate criterion? Indeed, several such procedures have been suggested. One such method, which cross-validates across subject samples, has been proposed by Cudeck and Browne (1983).

The method goes as follows:

1. Split the subjects randomly into two equal subsamples, call them A and B.
2. Take one subsample, say A, and factor with increasing numbers of factors, 1, 2, 3, . . . , k.
3. After each factor is extracted, apply a goodness-of-fit test, such as maximum likelihood, to the discrepancy between the correlations implied by the factors extracted in A and the observed correlations *in the other subsample*, B.
4. Repeat, factoring in B and testing against A.
5. Take as the optimum number of factors the one that yields the best cross-validation indices of fit. Ideally, this number will turn out to be the same for both directions of cross-validation. If it is not, one could argue either for taking the smaller of the two, or an intermediate number. In Cudeck and Browne's examples (discussed shortly), if the number was not the same in both directions it was usually close.

The fit of the model to the correlations in the original subsample necessarily improves as the number of factors increases. But the fit to the correlations in the opposite subsample typically improves and then deteriorates, suggesting that after awhile the factoring in the first subsample is merely fitting idiosyncrasies of sampling error, making the fit in the second sample get worse instead of better.

Table 6-3 provides some examples from Cudeck and Browne. The data were subsamples drawn from a large study in which six ability tests were given on three occasions to a large group of high school students. There were thus 18 measures intercorrelated for each subsample, from which 9 factors were extracted using a maximum likelihood procedure. After each factor, the maximum likelihood criterion was calculated for the fit to the opposite subsample correlations; these numbers are presented in the table. As you can see, for the smallest subsample size (75 subjects apiece), the best cross-validation in each direction was for a 3-factor solution. For the 200-subject subsamples, 4 or 5 factors represented the best cross-validation, and for 800-subject subsamples, 8 or 9 factors were optimum.

The authors also reported the number of factors that would have been chosen in each case based on a χ^2 test in the original sample. These χ^2s are not shown in the table, but a § symbol marks the smallest number of factors that yielded an acceptable solution (p > .05). For the smaller samples, the number of factors cross-validating tended to be less than the number that were statistically significant in the original sample (3 factors versus 5 factors for

Table 6-3 Using a cross-validation criterion in choosing the number of factors, for three sample sizes (data from Cudeck & Browne, 1983)

Number of factors	N = 75		N = 200		N = 800	
	A	B	A	B	A	B
1	5.02	4.99	2.56	2.52	1.75	1.82
2	4.94	5.14	2.05	2.13	1.31	1.34
3	4.91*	4.71*	1.85	1.87	.92	.97
4	5.30¶	5.05	1.83*	1.90	.81	.81
5	5.55§	5.20§¶	1.90	1.66*	.72	.73
6	5.72	5.37	1.83§¶	1.77§	.69	.68
7	5.97	5.61	1.86	1.74¶	.61	.68
8	5.88	5.79	1.88	1.79	.56*	.64§
9	--	5.70	1.91	1.75	.58¶§	.64*¶

* best cross-validation criterion.
§ smallest number of factors with p > .05.
¶ number of factors chosen by Akaike's criterion.

N = 75). For large samples, the two criteria tended to yield comparable numbers of factors. Cudeck and Browne studied other sample sizes as well as those shown; they also demonstrated that their procedure can be used with other structural models besides factor models.

In addition, Cudeck and Browne report results for Akaike's information criterion (see Appendix D) based on the χ^2 in the original sample. The number of factors yielding the most parsimonious solution based on this criterion is shown by the ¶ symbol in Table 6-3. In general, the parsimonious solution by Akaike's criterion corresponded quite well with the first solution acceptable at the .05 level of significance. Both methods slightly overfactored relative to the cross-validation criterion in smaller samples but tended to agree with it in large ones.

Alternative Rotation Methods

As mentioned in Chapter 5, many methods of factor rotation exist. Why? Several reasons might be mentioned. First, some procedures incorporate particular constraints. For example, some seek the best solution with uncorrelated factors, others allow factors to become correlated. Some procedures allow a general factor to emerge, others avoid one. Second, the different procedures differ in such practical characteristics as how widely they are available, how difficult they are to use, how robust they are in the face of various adversities, and so on. And finally, none of them works best on all problems. On a particular correlation matrix, method A finds a simple **P** that method B does not; on another matrix, method B goes to an elegant solution like a hot knife through butter, whereas method A bogs down hopelessly. Of course, on many problems with fairly simple and clear-cut structure, any of a variety of procedures will locate that structure and yield basically similar results.

Orthomax

The Varimax and Quartimax procedures discussed in the last chapter can be considered special cases of a general class of orthogonal transformations called Orthomax, whose criterion can be written:

$$\Sigma\Sigma p^4 - w\, {}^1\!/_k \Sigma_f (\Sigma_v p^2)^2 .$$

The weight w determines the particular criterion. If $w = 0$, the second part of the expression vanishes, and we have the Quartimax criterion. With $w = 1$, we have Varimax. Intermediate values of w would yield solutions with intermediate properties. A negative value of w would award a bonus to solutions with unequal factors, instead of a penalty, and so on.

Promax

The Promax solution (Hendrickson & White, 1964) is an oblique solution that proceeds in two steps. First an orthogonal Varimax solution is obtained. Then it is transformed to an oblique solution that has the same high and low loadings, but with the low loadings reduced (if possible) to near-zero values. The second step is done by direct calculation, not iteration, so that if an orthogonal solution can correctly identify the factors, Promax provides an efficient route to an oblique solution.

The second step of a Promax solution is a variant of a procedure called Procrustes (Hurley & Cattell, 1962), which forces a factor pattern matrix to a best least squares fit to a predesignated target matrix. It gets its name from the legendary Greek who forced travelers to fit his guest bed by stretching or lopping them as necessary.

In Promax, the target matrix is obtained by raising the elements of the Varimax-rotated pattern matrix to a higher power--usually the third or fourth-- and restoring minus signs if the power is even. By raising the pattern coefficients to a higher power, the low values go essentially to zero, while the high values, although they are lowered, remain appreciable, so the contrast between high and low values is sharpened. For example, at the fourth power all loadings of .26 or less become zero to two decimal places, whereas loadings of .70 and .80 remain appreciable at .24 and .41.

Call the target matrix P_t. Then an initial transformation matrix T_i is obtained by a least squares matrix solution of an overdetermined set of simultaneous equations:

$$T_i = (P_0{}'P_0)^{-1}P_0{}'P_t ,$$

where P_0 is the initial unrotated factor pattern matrix. This is the first part of the Procrustes solution. The second part is to rescale T_i to its final form T by postmultiplying it by a diagonal matrix D, chosen to make the factor intercorrelation matrix $(T'T)^{-1}$ have diagonal elements equal to 1.0. The necessary D may be obtained as the square roots of the diagonal elements of $(T_i{}'T_i)^{-1}$.

Table 6-4 illustrates a Promax solution to the rotation problem of the previous chapter, based on the Varimax solution of Table 5-7 (page 173). At the left of the table is P_t, obtained from the Varimax solution by raising its elements to the fourth power (because they were all initially positive, no restoration of minus signs is required). In the center of the table, T_i, $(T_i{}'T_i)^{-1}$, D, and T are successively calculated. At the right, T is applied to the unrotated solution to yield a Promax solution, which is quite similar to the Oblimin solution of Table 5-8 in the preceding chapter.

Table 6-4 Calculation of a Promax solution via Procrustes, from the Varimax solution of Table 5-7

P_t		T_i		D		$P = P_0 T$	
A	B	A	B	A	B	A	B
.37	.00	I .171	.115	A 3.253	.000	.84	-.06
.11	.00	II -.362	.247	B .000	4.779	.62	-.04
.05	.02					.37	.30
.07	.11	$(T_i \,' T_i)^{-1}$		$T = T_i D$		.35	.51
.00	.20	A	B	A	B	-.10	.77
.00	.11	A 10.583	9.947	I .556	.549	-.09	.66
		B 9.947	22.842	II -1.176	1.180		

Note: P_t is target factor pattern = Varimax solution of Table 5-7 with elements raised to 4th power. $T_i = (P_0\,'P_0)^{-1}P_0\,'P_t$ = transformation matrix before rescaling. D = square roots of diagonal elements of $(T_i\,'T_i)^{-1}$. T = rescaled transformation matrix. P_0 = unrotated factor pattern. P = rotated factor pattern.

Other oblique rotation methods

As noted earlier, a large number of different methods for oblique factor rotation have been proposed. Some represent slight variations on those discussed in this book; the reader can consult other sources (such as Gorsuch, 1983) for more details and citations to original articles. Two methods operating on rather different principles may be worth mentioning briefly. One is the method called Orthoblique (Harris & Kaiser, 1964). This procedure, like Promax, reaches an oblique solution via an orthogonal rotation, but the strategy is a slightly different one. The first k eigenvectors of the correlation matrix (where k is the desired number of factors) are subjected to an orthogonal rotation (originally, raw Quartimax, although others can also be used). The transformation matrix developed in this step is then rescaled in its rows or columns or both by suitable diagonal matrices, to become the final transformation matrix **T**, the matrix that transforms an initial principal factor solution into the final rotated oblique solution.

The other principle to be considered is embodied in procedures such as Maxplane (Cattell & Muerle, 1960) and the KD transformation (Kaiser & Madow, 1974). These methods focus specifically on low pattern coefficients and work at transforming factors to get as many pattern coefficients close to zero as possible. Methods such as these strive directly for the second kind of simplicity in a pattern matrix--a large number of near-zero paths. They are most often used to apply final touches to an approximate solution arrived at by another procedure. As a case in point, the KD procedure applied following an Orthoblique rotation yielded a solution to the Table 5-6 rotation problem that was an almost exact reproduction of the underlying path model, differing from it by no more than .01 in any correlation or path coefficient.

Estimating Factor Scores

Given a factor solution, and the scores of individuals on the observed variables, can we determine the individuals' scores on the latent variables, the factors? This would be attractive to do, if we assume the latent variables to represent fundamental causal influences underlying the interrelations of the superficial measures we actually observe.

The answer is, in general: No we cannot, although we can provide *estimates* of such scores. These estimates may be quite good if the observed variables are strongly related to the latent variables, or quite poor if they are not.

A number of different methods have been proposed and are discussed in standard factor analysis texts such as Gorsuch (1983) or Harman (1976). One simple one is to add together with equal weight the scores on the observed variables that are most highly correlated with the factor--a robust approach that has a good deal to be said for it. However, the most widely used method is to recognize that we are dealing with a prediction situation, in which we want to predict the latent variable, the factor, from the set of observed variables. An accepted way of making predictions of a given variable from a set of related variables is by carrying out a multiple regression.

Recall that in multiple regression one solves for a set of weights (called "beta weights"), which can be applied to the observed variables to predict the unknown variable. To solve for such weights, one needs to know the correlations among the predictor variables, and the correlations of these with the variable being predicted. Then the vector of beta weights may be obtained by premultiplying the latter by the inverse of the former. The matrix of correlations among the predictors (the observed variables) is of course obtainable--it is just the correlation matrix $\mathbf{R}$. The correlations of the observed variables with a factor is a column of the factor structure matrix $\mathbf{S}$; let's call this $\mathbf{s}$. So we can get the desired beta weights $\mathbf{b}$ for estimating a factor as follows:

$$\mathbf{b} = \mathbf{R}^{-1}\mathbf{s} \, .$$

These weights $\mathbf{b}$, applied to the observed variables in standard-score form, will yield the best prediction, in the least squares sense, of this factor from these variables. The equation

$$\mathbf{B} = \mathbf{R}^{-1}\mathbf{S}$$

will give the beta weights, as columns of **B**, for the whole set of factors simultaneously.

One can work with raw instead of standard scores by rescaling the betas appropriately and supplying an additive constant, but we need not deal with such complications here. Any standard text on multiple regression will supply the details.

All the other paraphernalia of regression analysis apply. The vector multiplication **b´s** gives the square of the multiple correlation of the factor with the predictors and thus represents the proportion of variance of the factor that is predictable from the observed variables. This will give one some notion of how well the factor scores are estimated in the present set of data. To get an idea of how well these factor estimation weights will transfer to new samples, a cross-validity coefficient can be calculated (Rozeboom, 1978):

$$R_c^2 = 1 - (1 - R^2)(N + m)/(N - m) .$$

The R^2 inside the parentheses is the squared multiple correlation, N is the sample size, and m is the number of predictors (observed variables). The corrected value R_c^2 is an estimate of how well the beta weights calculated in the given sample will predict in the population (and hence, on average, in new random samples from that population). If the measurement is good--that is, the obtained multiple correlation is high--and if the ratio of subjects to variables is large, one would not expect much falling-off of prediction in a new sample. For instance, in a 6-variable problem based on 100 subjects in which the obtained multiple correlation is .90, the expected drop-off when using the factor estimation weights in a new sample is only to a correlation of .89: $R_c^2 = 1 - (1 - .81)$ 106/94 = .786; $\sqrt{.786} = .89$. If one were to do a 17-variable factor analysis on 50 subjects and obtain a multiple correlation of .70, the expected drop would be all the way to zero (try it in the formula and see), and the factor score estimation would be completely worthless.

The factor scores estimated by regression using beta weights and standardized predictors will have a mean of zero and a variance equal to R^2. If it is desired to produce the factor scores in standard score form, which is customary, the beta weights can simply be multiplied by 1/R before applying them to the (standardized) predictors. (A little reflection should show why this is so. Hint: What is the standard deviation of the initial set of estimated factor scores?)

Table 6-5 (next page) shows the calculation of factor scores for our two-factor example. At the top of the table are R^{-1}, the inverse of the correlation matrix, and **S**, the factor structure matrix (from Table 5-9). $R^{-1}S$ yields the beta weights, **B**. **B´S** yields a matrix that has the squared multiple correlations from the regressions in its principal diagonal; the reciprocals of their square roots are in the rescaling matrix $D^{-1/2}$, which rescales **B** to **W**. **W** contains the coefficients that produce standardized estimates of the factor scores.

The final step is taken in the bottom row of the table. Hypothetical data for three subjects on the six variables are shown in the rows of **Z**. Postmultiplied by **W**, these yield the estimates (in standard-score form) of scores for these three individuals on the two factors A and B.

The correlation among these factor estimates can be obtained, if desired, by pre- and postmultiplying **B′S** by $D^{-1/2}$. The estimates for the two factors turn out to be correlated .67, somewhat higher than the correlation of .50 between the factors themselves. This is a typical result when estimating factor scores by this method.

Table 6-5 Estimating factor scores by regression (two-factor example of Tables 5-6 and 5-9)

R^{-1}	Inverse of correlation matrix							**S**	Factor structure	
	C	D	E	F	G	H			A	B
C	1.64	-.48	-.32	.52	.01	.00		C	.80	.40
D	-.48	1.36	-.14	-.22	.00	.00		D	.60	.30
E	-.32	-.14	1.43	-.31	-.18	-.12		E	.55	.50
F	-.52	-.22	-.31	1.88	-.48	-.33		F	.65	.70
G	.01	.00	-.18	-.48	1.44	-.35		G	.35	.70
H	.00	.00	-.12	-.33	-.35	1.32		H	.30	.60

B	Beta weights					**W**	Factor score weights	
	A	B	**B′S**				A	B
C	.51	-.01	.769	.502		C	.58	-.01
D	.22	-.00	.502	.725		D	.25	-.00
E	.15	.13				E	.17	.15
F	.23	.35	$D^{-1/2}$			F	.27	.41
G	-.00	.38	1.140	.000		G	-.00	.44
H	-.00	.26	.000	1.174		H	-.00	.30

Z	Data (standard scores)						Z_F	Factor scores	
	C	D	E	F	G	H		A	B
	1.2	.6	1.5	.8	.1	1.1		1.31	.92
	-1.0	-1.6	-.1	.0	.8	-1.4		-.99	-.07
	-.7	1.2	.9	-1.0	-1.3	.7		-.23	-.64
	.	.	.	.	.	.		.	.
	.	.	.	.	.	.		.	.

Note: **B = R⁻¹S**; **D** = diag **B′S**; **W = BD⁻¹/²**; **Z_F = ZW**.

As another illustration, Table 6-6 shows factor scores for the first three boxes in Thurstone's box problem (see Table 5-10, last chapter; the factor scores are based on the Direct Oblimin solution in Table 5-14). Comparison to standardized values of the true scores suggests that, with the high communalities of this example, the factor scores do a reasonable (although not a perfect) job of estimating the true-score values.

Table 6-6 Theoretical true standard scores compared to factor scores, first three boxes in Table 5-10 (Direct Oblimin solution of Table 5-14)

	Original			Standardized			Factor scores		
	X	Y	Z	X	Y	Z	F3	F2	F1
Box 1	3	2	1	-1.43	-1.29	-1.17	-1.47	-1.05	-.93
Box 2	3	2	2	-1.43	-1.29	.13	-1.26	-1.40	-.26
Box 3	3	3	1	-1.43	.00	-1.17	-1.42	.13	-1.05

Note: Means for original scores over population of 40 boxes: 4.1, 3.0, 1.9; SDs: .768, .775, .768; factors reordered for ease of comparison.

Factor score indeterminacy

It is tempting to interpret the factor score estimation problem as though there were a "real" set of factor scores out there somewhere, and our difficulty is in not being able to estimate them accurately. But in a sense, the fundamental problem is not really one of estimation, it is that a given factor solution (**P**, **S**, and **F**) just doesn't define factors uniquely. For any given **P**, **S**, and **F** there is a range of potential factors that are equally compatible with the obtained results. If the communalities of the original variables are high, these potential factors will tend to be highly correlated, much like one another, and the choice among them may not be crucial. But if the communalities are low, some potential factors may actually have zero correlations with others (McDonald & Mulaik, 1979). In short, if we hope to score subjects accurately on latent variables, they should be latent variables with strong and preferably multiple links to data. If there are important aspects of our latent constructs that are not well reflected in our measurements, and many aspects of our measures unrelated to the latent constructs, we should not be surprised if there is ambiguity in trying to assess the one from the other.

Extension analysis

Suppose we carry out an exploratory factor analysis on a set of variables, and have available the scores of additional variables for the same subjects. Can we extend the factor solution to these new variables? The answer is: Yes, we can, but subject to the same limitation as with calculating scores on the factors.

The simplest way, conceptually, is just to obtain the estimated scores on a factor and correlate these scores with the scores on the additional variables. This will provide the matrix **S** for the new variables, their correlations with the (estimated) factors. One can then obtain the factor pattern matrix **P** for the new variables by the relationship $P = SF^{-1}$, the inverse of the relationship $S = PF$ given earlier for getting the factor structure from the factor pattern matrix. Again, this is the factor pattern for the new variables with respect to the estimated factors, and the utility of an extension analysis thus is dependent to a considerable degree on the presence of conditions that minimize factor indeterminacy and lead to accurate estimation of factor scores.

In practice we do not actually have to go through the step of calculating factor scores for individuals--a matrix shortcut exists. To obtain the estimated correlations of a factor with the new variables, one may multiply the matrix of correlations of the new variables with the old ones, call it **Q**, times the vector of beta weights scaled to produce standardized factor scores, call it **w**; that is,

$$s = Qw.$$

If **W** is a matrix with rescaled beta weights as its columns, the equation becomes:

$$S = QW,$$

providing a convenient way of calculating **S**, and thence **P**.

Table 6-7 illustrates the extension of the example two-factor analysis to

Table 6-7 Extension of factor analysis of Table 5-6 to two new variables I and J

Q	Correlations of new variables with original variables						W Factor score weights		
	C	D	E	F	G	H		A	B
I	.60	.40	.50	.60	.50	.40	C	.58	-.01
J	.20	.10	-.10	-.30	-.10	-.20	D	.25	-.00
							E	.17	.15
S	Factor structure		P		Factor pattern		F	.27	.41
	A	B			A	B	G	-.00	.44
I	.69	.66	I		.48	.42	H	-.00	.30
J	.05	-.24	J		.22	-.36			

Note: $S = QW$; $P = SF^{-1}$. Factor score weights from Table 6-5.

two new variables, I and J. Hypothetical correlations of the two new variables with the original six variables are shown as **Q**, as well as the factor score coefficients **W** from Table 6-5. The factor structure matrix **S** for the new variables is obtained by the matrix multiplication **QW**, and the factor pattern matrix **P** by $\mathbf{SF^{-1}}$, where $\mathbf{F^{-1}}$ is the inverse of the factor intercorrelation matrix **F** from Table 5-6. The matrix **S** gives the estimated correlations of the new variables with the two factors A and B, and **P** gives estimates of the paths from the factors to the new variables.

There is a question that might have occurred to some readers: If one has scores on the additional variables for the same subjects, why weren't these variables just entered into the factor analysis in the first place, yielding pattern coefficients and correlations with the factors directly? There could be several reasons why one might not do this. The additional scores might only have become available after the original factor analysis was carried out. Or the additional variables might have been excluded from the factor analysis to avoid distorting it or biasing it in some way; for example, some variables might have been excluded because of artifactually high correlations with included variables, or because they were external reference variables which were desired for help in interpreting the factors, but which one did not want influencing the factor analysis itself. Or one might have an extremely large number of variables available, only a subset of which could feasibly be used for a factor analysis, but all of whose relationships with the factors would be of interest. In any of these situations, an extension analysis could be the answer.

Higher Order Factors

One of the products of an analysis into oblique factors is the matrix **F** of correlations among the factors. This is an intercorrelation matrix, and intercorrelation matrices can be factored. Such a factor analysis of the intercorrelations among factors is called a *second-order* factor analysis.

If this factor analysis is also oblique, there will be a matrix of intercorrelations among the second-order factors, which can in turn be factored. This would be called a *third-order* factor analysis. If the third-order factor analysis is oblique . . . . And so on.

In principle, this process could go on indefinitely, provided one started with enough variables, but in practice second-order factor analyses are fairly uncommon, third-order factor analyses are decidedly rare, and fourth-order factor analyses are practically nonexistent. However, the general idea of a hierarchical arrangement of factors is reasonably straightforward. One might, for example, imagine factoring a variety of arithmetic items to form scales for addition, multiplication, etc., with these in turn components of a numerical ability factor, and this as a subcomponent of general intelligence.

Because second- and third-order factor analyses are just factor analyses of correlation matrices, they can be carried out by the same methods used for first-order analyses, with the same issues involved: estimation of communalities, number of factors, orthogonal or oblique rotation, and so on. (A decision at any stage for orthogonal rotation terminates the sequence.)

Factor methods involving statistical tests, such as maximum likelihood, should probably be avoided for exploratory higher order analyses, because the statistical rationales based on sample size are derived for the case of first-order correlations or covariances and would be of doubtful applicability to the factor intercorrelation matrices involved in higher order analyses. However, standard model-fitting methods, as described in earlier chapters, can be used to fit models involving first- and higher-order factors simultaneously to data in a confirmatory factor analysis.

Direct expression of higher order factors

It may be useful in interpreting higher order factors to express directly their relationship to the original variables (Cattell & White, see Cattell, 1978). The path diagram of Fig. 6.1 illustrates the situation. The pattern coefficients of second-order factor A would be *b, c,* and *d* for the first-order factors C, D, and E. For the original variables G, H, I, J, and K, they would be *bg, bh, ci, cj + dk,* and *dl,* respectively.

Table 6-8 shows the three pattern matrices involved. P_{01} and P_{12} are the pattern matrices obtained in the first- and second-order factor analyses. As you should verify, the third matrix P_{02} can be obtained from these by the matrix multiplication $P_{01}P_{12}$. Thus, multiplication of the two factor pattern matrices will yield the factor pattern matrix directly relating second-order factors to the original variables. For a third-order analysis, $P_{01}P_{12}P_{23}$ would yield the factor pattern P_{03} relating the third-order factors to the original variables. The extension to still higher orders is straightforward.

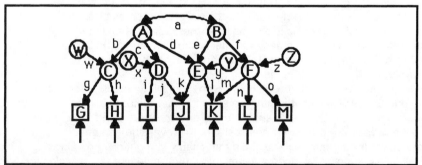

Fig. 6.1 Path diagram representing a higher-order factor analysis. C, D, E, F = first-order factors; A, B = second-order factors; G, H, I, J, K, L, M = observed variables; W, X, Y, Z = residuals from second order analysis.

Table 6-8 Factor patterns of Fig. 6.1: (a) variables related to first-order factors; (b) first-order factors related to second-order factors; (c) variables related directly to second-order factors

P_{01}					P_{12}			P_{02}		
	C	D	E	F		A	B		A	B
G	g	-	-	-	C	b	-	G	bg	-
H	h	-	-	-	D	c	-	H	bh	-
I	-	i	-	-	E	d	e	I	ci	-
J	-	j	k	-	F	-	f	J	cj+dk	ek
K	-	-	l	m				K	dl	el+fm
L	-	-	-	n				L	-	fn
M	-	-	-	o				M	-	fo

Note: Dash indicates zero path. Subscripts 2, 1, 0 refer to 2nd-order factors, 1st-order factors, and variables.

Schmid-Leiman transformation

Another approach to relating higher-order factors directly to the observed variables is that due to Schmid and Leiman (1957). This representation is illustrated in Fig. 6.2 for the same case as that of Fig. 6.1.

The strategy followed is a hierarchical one: The higher order factors are allowed to account for as much of the correlation among the observed variables

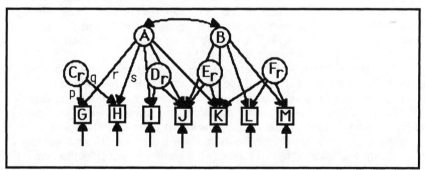

Fig. 6.2 Path diagram of higher-order factor analysis with first-order factors residualized. A, B = second-order factors of original analysis; C_r, D_r, E_r, F_r = residualized first-order factors of original analysis; G to M = variables.

as they can, and the lower order factors are reduced to residual factors uncorrelated with the higher order factors. If the correlation among the lower-order factors is explained entirely by the higher-order factors, as is the case in the example, the residual factors will be uncorrelated with each other as well. Although the relative amount of influence attributed to the lower order factors is decreased by this transformation, they may gain in clarity of interpretation, for each now represents the independent contribution of the factor in question. If, say, A represented a broad influence in the personality domain such as extraversion, and C, D, and E represented such component traits as sociability, impulsivity, risk taking, and the like, this procedure would allow extraversion to account for as much as possible of the intercorrelation among observable extraverted behaviors (G, H, I, J, K), and the residualized C_r, D_r, and E_r would represent effects specific to impulsivity, risk-taking, and so on. One might argue in particular cases whether this model better represents the underlying causal influences than does the original representation of Fig. 6.1, but when it does, the Schmid-Leiman transformation will be useful.

Basically, the procedure is as follows: The pattern matrix for the highest order (in this case the second) is obtained as for the Cattell-White transformation of the preceding section, by $P_{01}P_{12}$, based on the original first- and second-order analyses. Then, the next-lower order factors (here, the first-order factors) are residualized by scaling down their original pattern coefficients by the multiplication $P_{01}U_1$, where U_1 is a diagonal matrix of the square roots of the uniquenesses from the higher order analysis.

The reader may find this process easier to understand if it is looked at in path terms. The key step is to realize that the residualized factors C_r, D_r, etc. of Fig. 6.2 are the direct equivalents of the second-order residuals W, X, etc. in Fig. 6.1. The square roots of the uniquenesses, u, used in the rescaling are just the values of the paths w, x, etc. in Fig. 6.1, and the paths p, q, etc. in Fig. 6.2 are equivalent to the compound paths wg and wh in Fig. 6.1. In the Schmid-Leiman transformation we break the causation of, say, variable G into two independent paths (plus a residual). These two paths are labeled p and r in Fig. 6.2, and they correspond to wg and bg in Fig. 6.1. W is of course a causal source independent of A, by its definition as a residual.

Fig. 6.3 and Table 6-9 illustrate the procedure numerically with a simple example. (This particular example is too small actually to have yielded a determinate solution in an exploratory second-order analysis, but will suffice to illustrate the Schmid-Leiman procedure.) Fig. 6.3(a) is the original two-level path model, whereas diagram (b) is the alternative Schmid-Leiman representation, after B and C have been transformed to uncorrelated residual factors. Diagrams (a) and (b) imply exactly the same correlation matrix and communalities: for example, r_{DE} is .6 x .8 = .48 on the left, and .36 x .48 + .48 x .64 = .48 on the right. The communality of D is $.6^2$ = .36 on the left, and $.36^2$ + $.48^2$ = .36 on the right.

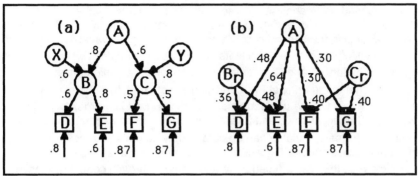

Fig. 6.3 (a) A simple two-level factor model, and (b) the same model after a Schmid-Leiman transformation. B_r and C_r are residualized versions of B and C.

Table 6-9 Matrices for Schmid-Leiman example of Fig. 6.3

R	D	E	F	G	h^2		F	B	C	h^2	u^2	u
D	1.000	.480	.144	.144	.36		B	1.00	.48	.64	.36	.60
E		1.000	.192	.192	.64		C		1.00	.36	.64	.80
F			1.000	.250	.25							
G				1.000	.25							

P_{01}	B	C		P_{12}	A		P_{02}	A		P_{01}	B_r	C_r	h^2
D	.60	.00		B	.80		D	.48		D	.36	.00	.36
E	.80	.00		C	.60		E	.64		E	.48	.00	.64
F	.00	.50					F	.30		F	.00	.40	.25
G	.00	.50					G	.30		G	.00	.40	.25

Note: P_{01} and P_{12} presumed to be obtained in a first- and second-order factor analysis of correlation matrix **R**, with the second-order analysis based on factor correlation matrix **F** from the first-order analysis. P_{02} obtained as $P_{01}P_{12}$, the Cattell-White formula. The P_{01} matrix on the right for the Schmid-Leiman residualized factors B_r and C_r is obtained as $P_{01}U_1$, where U_1 is a diagonal matrix of u, the square roots of the uniquenesses of B and C, based on the second-order analysis (upper right).

Table 6-9 shows the correlation matrix **R** among the observed variables, the correlation matrix **F** among the first-order factors that is the basis of the second-order analysis, and (left, below) the pattern matrices P_{01} and P_{12} of the first- and second-order analyses (these matrices contain the paths at the first and second levels of Fig. 6.3(a)). At the bottom center of the table is the pattern matrix P_{02} relating the second-order factor A to the original variables (obtained via the Cattell-White formula), and to its right the pattern matrix P_{01} for the residualized factors B_r and C_r after the Schmid-Leiman transformation. These are proportional to the original P_{01} coefficients (bottom, left). The rescaling is by the square roots of the uniquenesses u of the original first-order factors (top right). Note that because C_r and B_r are independent of each other and of A, the communality for each variable can be obtained by summing the squares of the coefficients across rows of P_{02} and P_{01} (lower right in the table).

Note also that the reduced correlation matrix R_r (with communalities in the diagonal) can be obtained by adding together two independent components: $P_{02}P_{02}{}'$ and $P_{01}P_{01}{}'$, representing, respectively, the contribution of the general factor A and the group factors B_r and C_r.

Finally, the reader should note the complete equivalence of the matrix results and the path results: i.e., in this simple case the values in Fig. 6.3(b) can be obtained virtually by inspection from Fig. 6.3(a), as the products of the two levels of paths. The picture is not quite so simple if the higher-order factors don't completely explain the intercorrelations of the lower-order factors and there are correlated residuals to be taken into account, but the principle still holds.

Hierarchical trait theories have long been popular, especially with British writers, since Spearman's successors first introduced a layer of group factors between *g* and the specifics. Higher order factor analysis in general, and the Schmid-Leiman transformation in particular, represent convenient ways of formalizing theories of this character.

Nonlinear Factor Analysis

Ordinary factor analysis, like the other path models that have been discussed in the earlier chapters of this book, assumes linear relationships between the latent variables--the factors--and the observed, measured variables. What if the relationships in some real-world case are not linear?

If they are nonlinear but monotonic--i.e., the two change together in a constant direction, though not necessarily in equivalent amounts--an ordinary linear approach will often yield a decent first approximation. But suppose the relationship is nonmonotonic, say, an inverted-U function of the kind that may hold between motivation and complex performance, where increasing levels of motivation up to a point improve performance and thereafter detract from it. What then?

The issue has been addressed by R. P. McDonald (1962, 1967), who notes that if one does an ordinary factor analysis of the correlations among variables related to a latent variable by a curvilinear function, one will tend to obtain two factors. But how can one distinguish the two factors obtained in this case from the two factors obtained when there are two latent variables and ordinary linear relationships?

McDonald's suggestion: Obtain scores for individual subjects on the two factors (actually, for technical reasons he prefers to use principal component rather than factor scores). Plot these scores on a scatter diagram. If the two sets of obtained component scores really reflect a single underlying variable curvilinearly related to the observed measurements, the plotted points should tend to fall along a curved line representing the relationship.

Let us consider an example. Suppose that we have several observed variables Y that are related to a latent variable X by equations of the general form:

$$Y = aX + bX^2 + c .$$

(Recognize the similarity to the case discussed earlier of nonlinear relationships among latent variables--there, however, the nonlinearities were in the structural model, and the measurement model was assumed to be linear; here we are considering a nonlinear measurement model.)

The preceding equation specifies a curvilinear relationship between X and Y. For example, suppose that $a = 1$, $b = -1$, $c = 15$, and X varies from -3 to +4 in integer steps. Fig. 6.4 shows the resulting curve. The linear correlation between X and Y is zero, but there is a perfect nonlinear relationship.

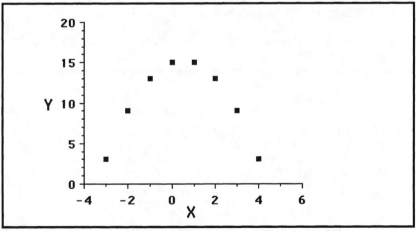

Fig. 6.4 Graph of curvilinear relationship ($a = 1$, $b = -1$, $c = 15$).

Table 6-10 Equations to produce scores on tests Y1 to Y5 from given values of latent variable X and specific variables C1 to C5

$$Y1 = X + 2X^2 - C1$$
$$Y2 = 4X - X^2 + 2C2$$
$$Y3 = -X - 3X^2 + C3$$
$$Y4 = -2X + .5X^2 - 2C4$$
$$Y5 = -3X + X^2 + C5$$

Table 6-10 shows a hypothetical example of five tests, Y1 to Y5, each of which is related to the underlying variable X by a quadratic equation of the type mentioned; the tests differ, however, in the relative strength and sign of the linear and quadratic components, and in the contribution of the unique component *c*.

For illustrative purposes, 100 simulated subjects were assigned scores on these five tests, by drawing for each subject six random integers in the range ±5, one representing X and one each of the five C's, and inserting them in the formulas for the five Y's. These scores were then intercorrelated and two factors extracted by a standard factor analysis program (SPSS FACTOR), using 1s in the diagonal to yield principal components. The correlation matrix, the pattern coefficients, and the eigenvalues are given in Table 6-11. Notice that by the Kaiser-Guttman rule this is a very clear two-factor structure. Figure 6.5 shows a scatterplot of the scores on component 2 plotted against component 1.

Table 6-11 Principal components analysis of the intercorrelations of five hypothetical tests on 100 subjects

	Correlations					Factor pattern		
	Y1	Y2	Y3	Y4	Y5	C1	C2	h^2
Y1	1.00	-.20	-.98	.17	.47	.75	-.65	.99
Y2		1.00	.23	-.55	-.82	-.74	-.53	.83
Y3			1.00	-.19	-.50	-.77	.63	.99
Y4				1.00	.61	.64	.51	.68
Y5					1.00	.90	.28	.89

Eigenvalues: 2.92, 1.45, .49, .13, .02

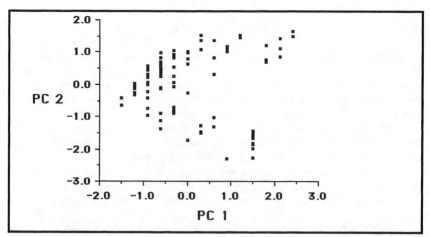

Fig. 6.5 Scatterplot of first two principal component scores from factor analysis of Table 6-11.

The curvilinear trend of the points in Fig. 6.5 is evident. The orientation of the parabolic curve on the graph is somewhat arbitrary, since it depends on just how the two factors emerge, and this will vary with the particular constitution of the tests. McDonald discusses methods of rotating the configuration to a standard orientation, and fitting a parabola to the data, but we need not pursue these matters here.

McDonald also discusses more complex possible cases. For example, a three-factor solution might reflect three ordinary linear latent variables, or one linear and one quadratic relationship, or two linear variables and their product, or first, second, and third powers of a single variable. Although such cases can in principle be handled by the present approach, in practice the discrimination among these alternatives would often place considerable demands on the quality and quantity of available data.

Fortunately for the simplicity of life, the variables that social and behavioral scientists measure are most often linearly or at least monotonically related to the underlying latent variables, so that linear methods will normally serve at least as a first approximation. But not always--so if you are working in a domain in which you suspect that nonmonotonic relationships might be present, it would probably not be a bad idea to calculate some principal component scores and do a little plotting. One caution: This method will work better with variables of fairly high communality. With variables of low communality, the amount of scatter of scores due to specificity and error is likely to make it difficult to distinguish any systematic trends in the data. If a latent variable is really only very weakly related to observed variables, establishing the exact form of that relationship may not be easy.

Chapter 6 Notes

Analytic rotation methods. Browne (2001) gives a thorough review of the history of such methods, both orthogonal and oblique. He also provides via his website (http://quantrm2.psy.ohio-state.edu/browne/) a comprehensive program for exploratory factor analysis (CEFA). Rozeboom (1992) discusses strategies for finding alternative good rotational solutions.

Orthomax. Browne (2001) discusses an even more general class of analytic rotation criteria, the Crawford-Ferguson family, which covers oblique rotation as well, and reduces to orthomax in the orthogonal case.

Additional oblique rotation methods. Among those that have been proposed are Geomin (Yates, 1987), Promaj (Trendafilov, 1994), Promin (Lorenzo-Seva, 1999), and Simplimax (Kiers, 1994). Several are variants of Promax.

Rotation criteria variants. Some computer packages calculate these criteria in forms that are slightly different from but equivalent to those given in this book.

Rotation in multiple groups. McArdle and Cattell (1994) discuss the simultaneous rotation of factor solutions in several different groups.

Bootstrap. Evaluating the stability of rotated factor solutions by means of bootstrap procedures is discussed by Lambert et al. (1991). Chan et al. (1999) use the bootstrap to assess consistency of factors across groups when rotated to maximum similarity by a Procrustes procedure.

Standard errors. Calculating the standard errors of rotated factor loadings in exploratory factor analysis is discussed by Cudeck and O'Dell (1994). They conclude that the matter is complex, and that rules of thumb of the form "interpret all loadings whose absolute value exceeds .30" are often grossly inaccurate. (Note that bootstrapping--see above--is sometimes a possibility.)

Factor scores. For a discussion of alternative approaches, see Saris et al. (1978), ten Berge and Knol (1985), and Bentler and Yuan (1997). The matter of factor score indeterminacy is discussed at length in an issue of *Multivariate Behavioral Research* (Vol. 31, No. 4, 1996). For a discussion of indeterminacy in SEM models generally, see McDonald and Bolt (1998).

Cross-validation. MacCallum et al. (1994) discuss various strategies of partial cross-validation for factor analysis and other SEM models--an example might be cross-validating factor loadings but not factor covariances.

Factor analyses of ipsative measures. The special problems involved in factor analyzing so-called "ipsative" measures, such as rankings or Q-sorts, are discussed by Dunlap and Cornwell (1994).

Higher-order factor analysis. Undheim and Gustafsson (1987), Harlow and Newcomb (1990), Benson and Bandelos (1992), Bickley et al. (1995), and Keith (1997) provide examples. Rindskopf and Rose (1988) discuss some of the issues arising in a confirmatory factor analysis approach to higher-order analyses. Gustafsson and Balke (1993) describe a slightly different model, which they call the *nested factor model*. It is obtained by the direct fitting of a model of the form of that in Fig. 6.3(b).

Nonlinear factor analysis. A paper by Etezadi-Amoli and McDonald (1983) describes a "second generation" version. See Lingoes and Guttman (1967) for an approach to a "nonmetric factor analysis."

Chapter 6 Exercises

1. Using as a target matrix the Varimax solution of problem 9 in Chapter 5 (page 186) raised to the 4th power, carry out the Procrustes matrix calculations. Obtain **P** and **F** for this Promax solution and compare to the oblique solutions in that problem.

2. Extend the analysis of Table 6-7 (page 200) to incorporate a third new variable, whose correlations with variables C through H are .00, -.20, .00, .80, .50 and .00, respectively.

3. Take the oblique factor solution below, and carry out a second-order factor analysis; i.e., extract a single principal factor from the **F** matrix. Report P_{12}.

$$
\mathbf{P} \quad
\begin{array}{rrr}
.01 & .01 & .58 \\
.01 & -.00 & .50 \\
.01 & .65 & .33 \\
.74 & .02 & .01 \\
.02 & .81 & -.06 \\
.75 & -.02 & -.01 \\
\end{array}
$$

$$
\mathbf{F} \quad
\begin{array}{rrr}
1.00 & .41 & .49 \\
 & 1.00 & .94 \\
 & & 1.00 \\
\end{array}
$$

4. Relate the second-order factor in the preceding problem directly to the original first-order variables.

5. Subject the analysis of problems 3 and 4 to a Schmid-Leiman transformation.

6. Apply a Varimax rotation to the factor pattern of Table 6-11. How would you interpret the resulting rotated factors in terms of the equations in Table 6-10?

7. Repeat the analysis of Thurstone's box problem (previous chapter), using a different method of factor extraction and a different oblique rotation procedure. Compare your results with those obtained in Chapter 5.

Chapter Seven:
Issues in the Application of Latent Variable Models

In this chapter we expand our horizons with regard to latent variable analysis and its application. We begin with a discussion of exploratory model modification and the implications of alternative models, and we end with a couple of critiques of the causal modeling enterprise. In between, we consider how latent variable analysis might be extended to handle additional kinds of problems, and whether the construction of path diagrams might be mechanized.

Exploratory Modification of a Model

A model is applied to some data. It fits badly. What next?

A sensible strategy in many cases is to try to find out why the model doesn't fit, and change it so that it fits better. One needs to be a bit careful here, because presumably one is not just interested in fitting this particular data set better, but in fitting other data sets well in the future--data sets which involve these same measures in new samples of subjects, or other measures presumed to be relevant to the same underlying constructs, or other situations in which these constructs are involved. In other words, one wants genuine improvement in measurement or theory, not just a procedure for decreasing chi square.

Remember that the chi square after model modifications based on information from the present data set no longer has the same statistical meaning as chi square from the initial test of a model, because of possible capitalization on chance features of the data in making the changes. The smaller the sample, the greater this risk, because in a small sample, chance will have more effect on the correlations or covariances, and so there is a greater likelihood that some model changes will be made to accommodate features of this particular data set which will simply not be there in the next one.

Keeping in mind, then, that we will need to discount the apparent merits of a revised model--the more so, the smaller the sample and the more extensive the data-influenced revisions--how do we go about accomplishing these modifications in the first place? There is no one prescription that will fit every case, but there are strategies that may be helpful.

Divide and conquer

A first step that is nearly always worth considering is to ascertain to what extent the lack of fit resides in the measurement and in the structural parts of the model. This is straightforward to do. One simply fits to the data a confirmatory factor analysis model in which the latent variables are allowed to be completely intercorrelated, and the paths from them to the observed variables are as specified in the measurement part of the original model. To the extent that this model fits badly, we know that the misfit is in the measurement part of the original model, because in allowing all possible correlations among the latent variables, we have a structural submodel that is guaranteed to fit perfectly.

It is also instructive to compare the χ^2 from this confirmatory factor analysis with the χ^2 from the original model fitting. If they do not differ significantly, we know that the structural part of the original model is not creating a substantial additional misfit to that produced by the measurement part.

In this event, should we congratulate ourselves that our structural theory, which is probably what mainly interests us, is correct, even though our measurement is rotten? No. On the face of it, what we have shown is that a theory of the form we propose could account for the relationships among the latent variables, but until we have a satisfactory measurement model, we don't know that the latent variables are in fact the constructs specified by our theory.

Had it turned out in the confirmatory factor analysis that the measurement part of the model fit well, and significantly better than the whole model, we would have localized the problem to the structural model, and we could proceed to tackle that directly. However, if, as usually happens, the initial tests suggest problems in the measurement model or in both, it will normally be desirable to start work with the measurement model, as there is little point in having a theory that works, but not for the variables intended.

Improving a measurement model

Suppose, then, that there are problems in the measurement model. Inspecting the results of the confirmatory factor analysis solution should give clues as to their nature.

There are two main sources of difficulty in measurement models. First, some indicators may fail to reflect the constructs they are supposed to measure. For example, they may have low factor loadings, or factor loadings of the wrong sign. (If they appear to have *large* loadings of the wrong sign, one should check the possibility that something has been inadvertently reversed in scoring.) One way of dealing with a variable which loads poorly is simply to drop it. However, one should always consider the consequences before taking such a step. Are the remaining measures conceptually adequate for defining the latent variable? Suppose there are, say, three indicators reflecting one aspect of the latent variable, and two indicators which reflect some other, essential aspect. Even though the fit of the measurement model would be improved by dropping the latter two, you shouldn't do it if it will produce a shift in the meaning of the latent variable which makes it unsuitable for testing the original theory.

If you have a latent variable which has only two indicators, and there appear to be measurement problems with it--again, think before acting. If one measure is conceptually superior to the other, you might be better off using just it, fixing its path to an estimate of the square root of its reliability. If both measures seem conceptually valid, you might try setting their paths equal. Adding this constraint will increase chi square, but often by very little, and to the extent that it produces a more sensible measurement model it should behave better in cross-validation. Later in this chapter we will discuss circumstances in which one might wish to consider reversing the direction of the arrows between latent and observed variables to deal with measurement model problems.

The second main source of measurement model misfit is that indicators may to some extent reflect constructs other than the one they are intended to measure. If an indicator in fact reflects two constructs, but it is taken as a measure of one and given a zero path from the other, there will be a misfit. The model is now discrepant with reality, because the correlations of this measure with others are reflecting both aspects of it, but the model assumes that only one aspect is present. Again, the choice of whether to omit such an ambiguous measure or to allow paths to it from both latent variables will depend on such considerations as whether one has adequate measures of both without it (drop it) or not (probably keep it, although it may distort relations between the two constructs by bringing in a correlation due to the specific aspects of the measure).

Model-fitting programs such as EQS or LISREL provide diagnostic indicators that can be helpful in deciding which additional paths from latent variables to indicators might improve the fit of the model. These are called Modification Indices in LISREL and Lagrange Multiplier Tests in EQS. What they do for you is tell you roughly how much the χ^2 for the model will be improved by freeing each fixed path present in the model. In the case of a typical confirmatory factor analysis model, the fixed paths are the zero paths between each factor and the variables that are *not* supposed to load on it. If a few of these have large modification indices, they should be examined as possible cases of measures loading on multiple factors, and suitable remedies considered. As both the LISREL and the EQS manuals emphasize, one should not just free paths blindly. This will reduce χ^2s, but it can also produce nonsensical models. Furthermore, freeing certain paths can have major effects on the modification indices of others, so that one should be cautious about introducing wholesale changes at a given step. EQS has a multivariate version of the Lagrange test that can help here.

There are other possibilities that may be considered in tackling an ailing measurement model. (1) Consider the introduction of one or more method factors, to account for covariation among measures which is due to shared methods rather than the latent variables of the theory--see the discussion of multitrait-multimethod matrices in Chapter 3. The contribution of method variance to the correlations among measures in the social and behavioral sciences is often considerable. One review estimated that method variance accounts for about 25% and trait variance about 40% of the total for personality and aptitude measures, with the remainder error variance. For attitude measures, method variance played an even larger role--about 40% method variance and 30% content variance. (2) Allow correlated residuals between pairs of measures that share some specific basis of covariation over and above their participation in common factors. Modification indices can give clues to possible candidates for this treatment, as can large isolated entries in the residual matrix (the difference between the observed and implied correlation matrices). Correlated residuals can be introduced between the indicants of a given latent variable or across latent variables. Again, if they have a rational basis, their chances of standing up in cross-validation are better.

The choice between 1 and 2 above depends largely on how many variables are involved. If a method artifact or shared specific variance affects just two variables, introducing a correlated residual is the simplest way to handle it. If several variables are involved, introducing an additional factor is more efficient, and conceptually more powerful. In between are cases that can be handled either way.

A final possible strategy is to decide that the measurement model is "good enough," despite a substantial χ^2, and go directly on to the structural model. For example, one may determine from the confirmatory factor analysis that each latent variable is well measured by its proposed indicators, and that the only problem is that there are a number of lesser secondary loadings, correlated residuals, and the like, which are clearly nonzero, hence the χ^2, but are small in comparison with the defining loadings. One would then use the χ^2 from the confirmatory factor analysis as a reference from which to examine the effect of changes in the structural part of the model. This strategy may be particularly attractive when working with very large samples, where quite small departures from ideal measurement can lead to large χ^2s. If one is in an exploratory mode anyway, there is clearly no mandate that *all* measurement problems must be resolved completely before *any* structural problems can be addressed.

A variant of this last strategy is to form a composite variable from the indicators of each factor and use that as a single indicator of the latent variable, with its path fixed to the square root of the internal consistency reliability (for a standardized variable) and its residual fixed to the error variance. The merit of this strategy is that the investigation of the structural model is quicker, cheaper, and cleaner, because of the smaller matrix and the elimination of distractions from the measurement model. A possible disadvantage is that the measurement part of the model is frozen, and changes in it can no longer develop in response to changes in the structural part of the model.

Improving the fit of a structural model

Changing a structural model is changing one's theory, and should always be done with that in mind. No simple rules will always apply. One can use the information provided by the fitting program to see whether existing paths are significantly different from zero. If not, one might consider dropping some of them from the model. Or one can look at modification indices to get an idea what the effects on the fit would be if one were to add particular paths, allow covariances, or the like. Or one can inspect residuals to see what aspects of the data are not well accounted for by the model as it stands. Probably one should consider all these sources of information to get ideas about possible changes, but modifications should not be made without careful consideration of their implications for the substantive theory that the model is intended to reflect.

Such a caution is emphasized by a study by MacCallum (1986), who investigated the merits of a simple automatic model-improvement strategy: If a model does not fit, make the single change that most improves its fit. Repeat as necessary until a nonsignificant χ^2 is achieved. Then test for and delete any unnecessary paths. MacCallum took known models, imposed simple specification errors (for example, a path might be omitted or an extra one added), and fit the models to random samples of data from populations in which the true models held. All models had a correctly specified measurement portion--the errors occurred only in the structural model. The model-improvement strategy described above was applied in each case.

The results were moderately complex, but the following examples should give a feel for them. For a sample size of 300 cases and just a single omitted path, only 10 of 20 attempts were successful in reaching the true model. With the same sample size and a more poorly specified model (two paths omitted, one added), the true model was never achieved in 20 tries, although sometimes one or two correct steps toward it were taken. With the latter model and N = 100 there were many problems, such as improper solutions or a failure to reject the initial incorrect model. Only 8 of 20 tries even got as far as making one legitimate change, and in 7 of the 8 it was a wrong one.

In short, such an automatic procedure of structural model modification cannot generally be recommended--and if one tries it with small samples, one must be very brave indeed. In a subsequent study (Silvia & MacCallum, 1988), it was shown that with larger samples (N = 500) and with the use of some relevant prior theoretical knowledge, such searches were more often successful in arriving at a known true model, although by no means always so.

In any case, the outcome of any structural model modification is a new theory. It should hardly be necessary to point out that one needs to *test* that new theory on fresh data before proclaiming its merits to the world--i.e., cross-validation is essential when exploratory modification of a structural model is undertaken. And it is prudent even when changes are confined to the measurement model, particularly when the changes are extensive or the samples are small.

Alternative Models

There is always more than one way to account for a particular set of
interrelationships among variables, and the path modeler should be aware of
this fact. In this section we consider two examples, one involving the direction
of the causal arrows between latent and manifest variables, and one involving
more general issues of equivalence among models.

Are observed variables causes or effects of latent variables?

It is traditional in structural equation modeling--as evidenced in most of the path
diagrams in this book--to have the arrows in the measurement model go from
the latent variable to the observed indicator of it. But this may not always be
sensible.

Consider the path model in Fig. 7.1, from a hypothetical study of life
satisfaction in an elderly population, drawn as a traditional structural modeler
would do it. On the left side we have two latent variables, Health, indexed by
several particular classes of medical problems, and Financial Resources,
indexed by Current Earnings and Retirement Income; these are seen as
contributing to Life Satisfaction on the right, indexed by ratings by Self, Spouse,
and Friend. Let's worry a little about the direction of the causal arrows for the
latent variables on the left side of the diagram. The way the diagram is drawn,
health is a general condition of the individual, which is reflected in the
pathology of various body systems. But one could look at it differently, as in Fig.
7.2, which holds that health is just a summary construct reflecting the degree to

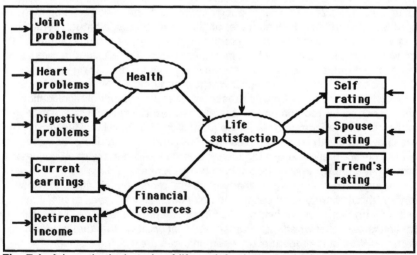

Fig. 7.1 A hypothetical study of life satisfaction: conventional measurement
model.

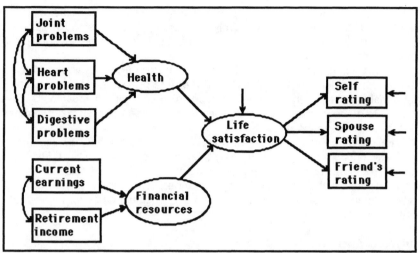

Fig. 7.2 A hypothetical study of life satisfaction: indicators causing latent variables.

which a person has things wrong with various bodily systems.

An important difference is that looking at it as in Fig. 7.1 implies that there will be positive correlations among the indicators, and looking at it as in Fig. 7.2 does not. That is, Fig. 7.1 says that because heart problems and joint problems are both indicators of a general condition called health, their correlation will be the product of the individual paths from that construct; thus if both are good measures of health they will by that fact be substantially correlated. Figure 7.2 makes no such claim. The conditions could be correlated, but they could be independent. In any case, their correlation would not depend on their status as measures of health. Without arguing the merits of either approach in this particular case, it is clear that the approaches are different, and that in constructing a path model one might want to consider both as possibilities.

A more striking instance is presented by the Financial Resources latent variable, because here one would clearly want to have current earnings and retirement income act as sources (Fig. 7.2) rather than as indicants (Fig. 7.1). Fig. 7.1 implies that current earnings will be positively correlated with retirement income, but in a real elderly population the correlation might well be negative, if individuals who have inadequate retirement incomes must depend on income from working. In an ordinary measurement model, two negatively correlated indicators, each with positive paths to the construct (Fig. 7.1) will create problems, but there is no inherent difficulty with having alternative sources of something called Financial Resources (Fig. 7.2), which is in turn an important contributor to something called Life Satisfaction. (The measurement of the latter, by the way, is quite satisfactorily handled by the traditional paradigm in this example: one can think of Life Satisfaction as a condition of the individual which affects the ratings given by the three informants, and one would expect their ratings of it--if valid--to be positively correlated.) In short, sometimes one will want to do it one way, sometimes the other, but both possibilities should be kept in mind.

Constructing models in which causal arrows run from observed to latent variables can be done directly in some SEM programs, but may require a little legerdemain in others. In the latter, one can link the observed variables by fixed 1.0 paths to dummy latent variables. Then paths can be run from these dummy variables to others in the model.

Note that in Fig. 7.2 the latent variables of health and financial resources are shown as completely determined by the specified causes (no residual arrow). This is necessary here in order to achieve an identified solution. In an expanded study, with downstream paths from health and financial resources to additional manifest variables, one could solve for residual paths for these two latent variables as well.

Equivalent structural models

Arrows which might run in either direction are not just a feature of measurement models. As you deal with structural models, you should be aware that often one can make quite radical changes in a model--for example, by reversing the direction of one or more of its causal arrows--and still have a model that fits the data exactly as well as before, but with quite different values for its paths. (Stelzl, 1986, discusses the conditions under which this will happen.) Let us consider the example shown in Table 7-1 and Fig. 7.3.

The six variables D through I represent two measures for each of three latent variables: a mother's verbal aptitude, her child's verbal aptitude, and the amount of reading aloud to the child that the mother has done.

Table 7-1 Correlations among six hypothetical variables (for example of Fig. 7.3), N = 100

	D	E	F	G	H	I
D	1.00	.56	.38	.34	.50	.50
E		1.00	.43	.38	.58	.58
F			1.00	.72	.43	.43
G				1.00	.38	.38
H					1.00	.64
I						1.00

220

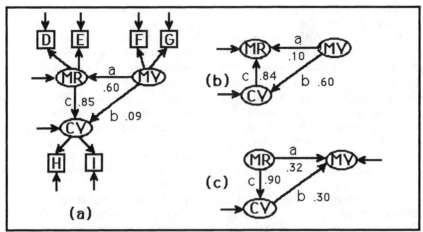

Fig. 7.3 Three alternative models of relations among MV (mother's verbal aptitude), CV (child's verbal aptitude), and MR (mother's reading to child). (Same measurement model throughout.)

On the left in the figure, model (a), is a model whose structural portion assumes that a mother's reading aloud to her child has a causal effect on the development of the child's verbal aptitude. The model also assumes that a mother's verbal aptitude may affect how much she is inclined to read to the child, as well as possibly having a direct effect on the child's verbal aptitude, an effect that might, for example, occur via the genes she has transmitted to her child. If we solve this model for the correlations in Table 7-1, we obtain a very good fit indeed, the χ^2 is .02, based on 7 df. The value of the path from mother's verbal aptitude to her reading to the child (path *a*) is .60, the direct path from her own verbal aptitude to her child's verbal aptitude (path *b*) is .09, and the effect of mother's reading on child's verbal aptitude (path *c*) is .85. Obviously, mother's reading aloud is a key variable in explaining the child's verbal aptitude.

But suppose that we were to entertain a quite different hypothesis, namely, that a mother's reading to a child has no effect whatever on its verbal aptitude; but, on the other hand, that the amount of reading a mother does to her child over the years is affected by how much the child enjoys it, which is in part a function of the child's verbal aptitude. We now have the structural model shown as (b). If we fit that model to the data, we obtain exactly the same good fit, and the same low χ^2. But the values of the paths, and the interpretation of the model, are now quite different. There is a substantial direct determination of child's verbal aptitude by mother's verbal aptitude (*b* = .60). Mother's verbal aptitude has only a very minor effect on how much she reads to the child (*a* = .10). Path *c* remains strong (.84), although now, of course, it represents an entirely different causal effect. A developmental psychologist with hereditarian theoretical preferences might like this second model better, with its direct mother-child transmission, and a psychologist of environmentalist inclinations might fancy the first. The point, however, is that both models are exactly equivalent in their fit to the data. And so, for that matter, are others--including such unlikely models as (c)--which both psychologists might be pained to find has an identical χ^2 of .02, for $a = .32$, $b = .30$, and $c = .90$.

The practical moral: Think about each causal arrow in your path diagram. If there is reasonable doubt about which direction it goes, it might make sense to replace the directed path by a simple correlation or a reversed path and see how much difference this makes for other paths in the model. Sometimes the effects of such a change will be quite localized. If so, the interpretation of other paths may still be secure. If not . . . . Well, surely you would want at least to be aware of this fact when discussing your results.

Not everyone is, apparently. One study examined 53 published examples of SEM analyses. In over 80% of them mathematically equivalent models could be found, often in large numbers, and yet in no paper did the authors explicitly acknowledge or discuss the existence of such potential rivals to their favored model.

Can path diagrams be constructed automatically?

Interesting work by Judea Pearl (e.g., 1998, 2000) of UCLA and by a group of scientists at Carnegie Mellon University (e.g., Spirtes, Richardson, Meek, Scheines, & Glymour, 1998) suggests that the answer to this question is at least "sometimes."

Indeed, Pearl argues that one of the basic requirements of an intelligent system is that it be able to construct models of cause-and-effect relationships in its environment. It can't rely exclusively on built-in knowledge, but has to be able to translate observational information, basically correlational in character, into causal models--i.e., it must construct path diagrams, or their equivalent.

What are the clues that people (or other intelligent systems) use to do this? Consider three events A, B, and C. A is correlated with C, and B with C, but A and B are uncorrelated. When confronted with this situation, people normally give the interpretation (a) in Figure 7.4, not the interpretation (b), which implies exactly the same correlations, and hence is equally consistent with the observations. Why this preference? Pearl says, for at least two reasons. Reason 1: Model (a) is a simpler explanation than model (b)--it has one less arrow. Reason 2: Model (a) will be more stable than model (b) in the face of mild fluctuations. If one of the two paths in (a) changes a bit with time or circumstance, r_{AB} remains zero, but if this happens to any one of the paths in (b), r_{AB} is no longer zero.

Also of great importance in identifying cause is temporal sequence. If we know that C follows A and B in time, our choice of (a) over (b) is even more

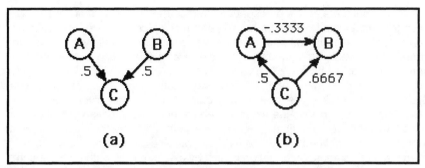

Fig. 7.4 Two alternative causal patterns implying the same correlations.

compelling, whereas if we observe C preceding A and B, we will have to struggle with explanations like (b), invoke additional variables, disbelieve our eyes and wait for more data, or whatever. But Pearl emphasizes that even without temporal information, an intelligent system trying to get along in our world, if it observes A and B correlated with C but not with each other, should pick explanation (a). Presumably, systems that do this are better adapted to survive, and will thus have evolved a preference for parsing their environments according to the criteria of simplicity and stability that underlie the choice of (a) over (b).

IC*

Can one mechanize a search for prospective causal sequences in a welter of correlational data? Several schemes of this sort have been translated into computer programs. I briefly describe one called IC*, the IC standing for "Inductive Causation," and the asterisk meaning that latent (i.e., unobserved) variables are allowed to occur.

The details of this algorithm are beyond our scope here, but roughly speaking it proceeds in three steps:

1. Locate pairs of observed variables which cannot be disconnected by holding other observed variables constant; these are then joined by lines--as yet without arrowheads--i.e., they represent prospective causal arrows, but the direction of causation is not known, and some may not even be causal, but represent correlations produced by unobserved latent variables, which of course weren't controlled.

2. Locate patterns in this network of the sort in Fig. 7.4(a), to begin to assign directions to causes.

3. Add further arrowheads according to additional rules, until no more can be added.

The outcome of this procedure is a diagram that consists of some definitely established causal paths, some others which may either be causal or correlated via a latent common cause, some which are definitely the latter, and some which remain ambiguous: *a* may cause *b*, *b* may cause *a*, or a latent variable may affect both.

We need not dwell on the procedural details, because it seems likely that the algorithms in biological brains involve some form of massively parallel processing, in contrast to the extensive and exhaustive serial searches carried out by the computer algorithms. Nevertheless, the fact that the latter are able to turn purely covariational input into path diagrams, even incomplete ones, is instructive. If temporal information is also available, the algorithms are much faster and more efficient--for example, in step 1 they need only hold constant events prior to the pair under consideration, and in later steps, when causal arrows are found their direction is immediately known: from earlier to later. If one can also rule out latent variables, matters are even further simplified, but from the perspective of this book, that would hardly do.

The work of these modelers also bears on a topic addressed earlier in this chapter: that of equivalent models. The incomplete path diagram generated by the IC* procedure automatically defines a set of equivalent models. Each completely unspecified path can be replaced by a causal path running from *a* to *b*, one running from *b* to *a*, or a two-headed curved arrow connecting the two; each partially specified path admits two options. These variations represent equivalent (and equivocal) interpretations of the given data set.

The idea of finding models empirically, as opposed to generating them *a priori*, is in some ways analogous in spirit to exploratory versus confirmatory factor analysis. In both cases we start with some general ideas about how the world is structured and search a database of relationships among observed variables for structures which meet the criteria. The two differ: IC* is focused on elucidating causal relations among the observed variables, and regards latent variables as more or less a nuisance, whereas exploratory factor analysis focuses on the latent variables, seeking to locate a small number of them and specify their relationships to the observed variables.

Despite this difference in focus, latent variable modelers will continue to watch with interest the developments in this area. It seems unlikely that IC* or its descendants will replace LISREL and its fellows in the hearts of structural equation modelers anytime soon. However, those interested in equivalent models, in model identification, in specification searches, or in the causal status of SEM may find useful ideas here.

Modes of Latent Variable Analysis

In this section we look at a number of different modes in which data can be approached in factor analysis and other latent variable methods.

R, Q, P, O, T, and S techniques of factor analysis

Cattell (1952) has suggested that sets of data to be factor analyzed may be classified along three dimensions; by considering these in pairs he defines what he calls R, Q, P, O, T, and S techniques of factor analysis. The relationships among these are summarized in Table 7-2, which is based on a similar table in Gorsuch (1983, p. 312). The reader interested in more details than are given here, or further references to the literature on this topic, will find Gorsuch a useful source.

In this view, the three basic dimensions of data are tests or measures, persons or objects measured, and situations or occasions of measurement. In the most common form of factor analysis, one factors the relationships among tests or measures that are correlated for a sample of persons based on a single occasion of measurement. Cattell calls this *R technique*. A data matrix for typical R technique analysis is shown at the left in Table 7-3 (next page). Each of the seven tests has been given to a number of persons. A correlation coefficient is calculated for each pair of tests, i.e., between each pair of columns in Table 7-3(a). The resulting 7 x 7 correlation matrix among tests is the basis for the factor analysis.

The data matrix on the right of Table 7-3 is for the complement of R technique, *Q technique*. The form of data matrix is the transpose of that used in R technique--the rows are tests and the columns are people. The intercorrelations, still calculated among all possible pairs of columns and still for

Table 7-2 Relationships among R, Q, P, O, T, and S techniques

	What is factored	Correlation across	Example
One occasion			
R technique	measures	persons	basic personality traits
Q technique	persons	measures	personality typology
One person			
P technique	measures	occasions	individual personality structure
O technique	occasions	measures	individual psychological environment
One measure			
T technique	occasions	persons	anxiety-arousing situations
S technique	persons	occasions	anxious person types

Table 7-3 Data matrices for R and Q techniques

			(a) R technique							(b) Q technique			
	T1	T2	T3	T4	T5	T6	T7			Al	Ben	Carl. . .Zach	
Al	5	1	2	6	3	5	7		T1	5	2	7 . . . 1	
Ben	2	6	7	1	8	5	2		T2	1	6	4 . . . 4	
Carl	7	4	3	6	4	4	8		T3	2	7	3 . . . 5	
:	:	:	:	:	:	:	:		:	:	:	: :	
Zach	1	4	5	2	5	6	4		T7	7	2	8 . . . 4	

data gathered on a single occasion, are correlations among people rather than correlations among tests. They express how much Al is like Ben, or Ben is like Zach, on these tests. In the particular example in Table 7-3(b), Al and Ben are negatively correlated. They are systematically unlike each other--on those tests where Ben has relatively high scores Al scores low, and vice versa. Al and Carl, on the other hand, are positively correlated, agreeing on their high and low tests.

Note that resemblances based on correlations ignore possible differences in means. Al and Carl's correlation reflects the fact that they show the same *pattern* of scores, even though Carl's scores tend to be systematically higher. The correlation between them would not change if we were to add two points to every one of Al's tests, although this would make Al and Carl's scores more alike in absolute terms. Nor would the correlation decrease if we were to add 10 points to each one of Carl's scores, although in some ways this would make Al and Carl very different. For these reasons one might prefer sometimes to use another measure of association than an ordinary Pearson correlation for Q technique--for example, some measure of distances between profiles (see Overall & Klett, 1972, Chapter 8, for a discussion).

One should also be aware that Q technique correlations can be quite sensitive to the scales of the tests over which they are computed. Merely changing the scoring of test 3 in Table 7-3, to give 10 points per item instead of one, although trivial in concept, will in fact drastically affect the correlations--for example, it changes the correlation over the 7 tests between Al and Ben from -.81 to +.92. (Can you see why?) For this reason, it is often desirable to standardize the rows of the data matrix (i.e., express the test scores in standard score form) prior to doing the correlations for a Q-type factor analysis-- particularly if the test scores are in noncomparable units. (This is sometimes referred to as *double-centering* the data matrix, because the correlation itself effectively standardizes by columns.)

R technique seeks the dimensions underlying groupings of tests or measures and might be used, for example, in a study of basic personality traits. Q technique seeks the dimensions underlying clusters of persons and might be used, say, in a study of personality types. In practice, the two approaches might in fact lead to the same underlying latent variables: Either a study of personality scales or of person types might lead one to an introversion-extraversion dimension. Nevertheless, the routes taken and the intermediate products of the analyses would be quite different in the two cases.

The next two techniques, P and O, are also complementary to one another, but they both use just a single subject, tested on repeated occasions.

In *P technique*, shown on the left in Table 7-4, one considers two measures similar if scores on them tend to vary together over occasions in the life of an individual. In the table, measures T1 and Tm appear to go together, as do T2 and T3, with the two sets tending to be negatively related. P technique is best suited for use with measures of states, such as moods or motive arousal, which can be expected to vary from day to day in the life of an individual. Its merit is that it can give a picture of the mood or motive structure of that particular person. Some personality psychologists, who have objected to the usual R-type factor analysis as only yielding a picture of a mythical "average person" (no example of which may actually exist!), should find a P technique approach more congenial.

An illustration of a study using P technique is that of Cattell and Cross (1952), in which multiple measures designed to assess the strengths of a number of motivational states (anxiety, self-confidence, sex drive, fatigue, and the like) were obtained twice daily for a particular individual--a 24-year-old drama student--over a period of 40 days. A factor analysis of the intercorrelations of these measures over the 80 occasions yielded some patterns much like those that had been found in previous R-type researches, but others that appeared to be idiosyncratic to this particular individual--or at any rate, to his life during this period.

O technique, the complement of P technique, has not apparently been much used, although it is an interesting idea. Its correlations (Table 7-4(b)) are based on the similarity of occasions in one person's life, assessed across a multiplicity of measures. It asks which are the occasions that go together in terms of a person's reactions to them--which situations arouse anxiety, which are challenging, which depressing. One might think of this as a way of getting

Table 7-15 Data matrices for P and O techniques

(a) P technique					(b) O technique				
	T1	T2	T3	... Tm		Day1	Day2	Day3	... DayN
Day1	7	1	2	... 8	T1	7	4	2	... 1
Day2	4	2	3	... 5	T2	1	2	6	... 7
Day3	2	6	8	... 3	T3	2	3	8	... 6
:	:	:	:	:	:	:	:	:	:
DayN	1	7	6	... 2	Tm	8	5	3	... 2

at the structure of a person's psychological environment, of the events to which he or she responds in characteristic ways. For the same reasons as in Q technique, preliminary standardization of scores on the measures used will often be desirable in O technique.

The final pair of complementary approaches, *T* and *S techniques*, seem also not to have been much explored. They restrict themselves to a single response measure but assess it across both persons and situations. In T technique one looks at resemblances among situations in their effect on the response measure, and in S technique at resemblances among persons. For example, in a study such as that of Endler, Hunt, and Rosenstein (1962), in which ratings of anxiety were obtained across both persons and situations, one could either factor the different types of situations to study the relationships among anxiety-arousing situations (T technique), or factor the persons to obtain a typology of persons based on the situations that arouse their anxiety (S technique). In either case one might infer latent dimensions such as physical versus social anxiety, or realistic versus imaginary fears.

Three-mode factor analysis

The six types of factor analysis described in the preceding section can be considered to represent different ways of collapsing a three-dimensional rectangular data matrix--see Fig. 7.5. The two horizontal dimensions of the cube are measures, and situations or occasions, the vertical dimension is persons. Any point within the cube represents the score of a particular person on a particular measure on a particular occasion.

If we take a slice off the left front face of the cube (or any slice parallel to it), we have data from a single occasion and hence an R or a Q technique study, depending on whether we choose to run our correlations vertically or horizontally. If we take a slice off the right face, or parallel to it, we have data

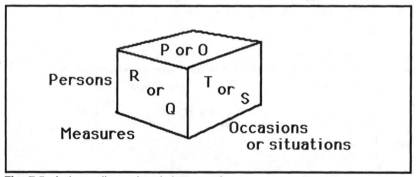

Fig. 7.5 A three-dimensional data matrix.

from a single measure, and hence a T or S technique study. And if we take a slice off the top, or any horizontal slice, we have data from a single person, and P or O technique, depending on whether we calculate our correlations among the measures or the occasions.

But can we do a single, overall analysis of the whole data cube? Yes, we can. The procedure is known as three-mode factor analysis and was developed by Ledyard Tucker (1964). We do not attempt to describe the method at the level of calculational detail, but, roughly, it results in three sets of factors resulting from the analysis of correlations involving measures, persons, and situations, and a *core matrix* that relates the three separate sets of factors.

Tucker presents an analysis of the Endler, Hunt, and Rosenstein anxiety data. The measures were different responses that might be associated with anxiety (e.g., "heart beats faster," "need to urinate frequently"); the situations were such potentially anxiety-arousing situations as making a speech or going on an initial date; the persons were the student subjects doing the ratings. Factors were reported for each of the three modes separately: for example, "heart beats faster" and "get uneasy feeling" went together on a measures factor; "speak before large group" and "job interview" went together on a situations factor; and three person-dimensions emerged among the subjects. The core matrix showed relationships involving all three modes: for example, one of the person types showed distress responses in interpersonal situations, while two other types tended to show exhilaration; the latter two types differed, however, in their responses to situations with inanimate or unknown dangers.

Three-mode analyses in structural equation modeling

Analogous approaches to data in three modes occur in structural equation analysis, although they have not been so formally systematized as in factor analysis. A multitrait-multimethod matrix is three-mode: traits, methods, and persons. And so may be a structural equation analysis of events over time: multiple measures on each of a sample of persons taken on each of several occasions. In each case the simultaneous analysis over the three modes is capable of providing information unattainable from any two modes considered separately.

Many opportunities have yet to be explored for extending such analyses to new kinds of problems. You might want to think about what it might mean to do, say, structural equation analyses of O or S types in your own substantive area of interest. Also, there is no law that says that three modes is the limit. For example, Cattell in one place discusses as many as 10 modes (1966b). Finally, there are many variations possible *within* any single design--for example, instead of achievement test scores on schoolchildren across grades, how about economic indicators on countries across decades? The risk of ever having to say "everything has been done" seems negligible.

Criticisms of Latent Variable Modeling

Any structural modeler who wants to find out what an intelligent and articulate critic can say against this enterprise should certainly read a trenchant critique by D. A. Freedman (1987a). This article, plus a number of responses by structural modelers and others and a reply by Freedman, constitute a whole issue of the *Journal of Educational Statistics.*

Freedman's critique

Freedman is not one to pull punches. In his second paragraph he says: "Indeed, path models are now widely used in the social sciences, to disentangle complex cause-and-effect relationships. Despite their popularity, I do not believe they have in fact created much new understanding of the phenomena they are intended to illuminate. On the whole, they may divert attention from the real issues, by purporting to do what cannot be done--given the limits on our knowledge of the underlying processes" (1987a, p. 101f). And later in his introduction: "At bottom, my critique is pretty simple-minded: Nobody pays much attention to the assumptions, and the technology tends to overwhelm common sense" (p. 102).

A key objection of Freedman's is that structural modelers tend to interpret the results of their model fitting *as if* they had done an experiment, when in fact they have not.

Suppose we fit a path model of the sort shown on the left in Fig. 7.6, and obtain a value of .05 for the path coefficient. What do we conclude? That sending people to school for another year will increase their incomes by 5%? That, roughly, is what structural modelers *do* tend to conclude, if they conclude anything at all, says Freedman, only they usually do it in situations sufficiently

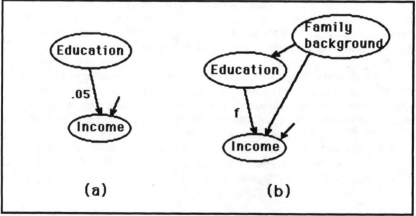

Fig. 7.6 Two models of the relationship between education and income.

more complicated than this to obscure what is going on.

Now if we had actually done the experiment of sending a random sample of people to school for an extra year, fine. But as we have not, our conclusion is vulnerable to anything we have done wrong in our modeling, such as omitting important variables, and this is true *regardless of how well our model fits the data we have.* In the example, Freedman points out that there might be a third variable in this situation, family background, that affects both education and income, and whose inclusion would most likely change the value of the path *f* from education to income (righthand diagram). Very well, says the modeler, "now we've got it: *f* represents the impact of education on income, with family background controlled for."

"Unfortunately," Freedman continues, "it is not so easy. How do we know that it is right this time? How about age, sex, or ability, just for starters? How do we know when the equations will reliably predict the results of interventions-- without doing the experiment?" (p. 104).

Freedman distinguishes between *descriptive models* which simply describe relationships, and *structural models* which purport to give causal explanations. He believes that much of the latent variable modeling literature consists of the former masquerading as the latter. "In my opinion, the confusion between descriptive and structural models pervades the social-science scholarly literature of the past 20 years, and has distorted the research agenda of a generation. In the end, this confusion might easily destroy the idea of scientific right and wrong" (1987b, p. 221).

Freedman goes on: "The modelers I count among my friends are interesting and attractive personalities, and serious scholars. However, on behalf of the models themselves, the core of the enterprise, I can find only two points to make: They may have heuristic value for certain investigators; and some day, there may be a real one."

Freedman is right on the first point--latent variable models can be helpful in describing causal relationships involving measured and unmeasured variables, and that is why we have taken the time and effort to learn about them in this book. In one sense, he is wrong on the second, because there will *never* be a "real one." Causal models are inherently hypothetical; they have a big *If* up front. *If* we assume a model like this, then such-and-such consequences follow. This is a very useful thing to be able to do, because, as all causal modelers know, what follows from our model, at least on the first try, is usually quite discrepant from the real-world data that we are attempting to explain. However, Freedman is quite right to chide modelers who assume that when they eventually arrive at a model that does fit their data, the scientific enterprise is over. Of course not. What they then have (at most) is a theory that can explain these facts. *They do not know that this theory is true*, in the commonsense meaning of this term, until they (or others) have done the experiments or the cross-validitory and confirmatory observational studies necessary to test and support it.

So long as we want to try to describe complex real-life phenomena as they occur in their natural settings, it seems to me that our chief alternatives are the literary essay and the path model. Many as are the merits of literary essays, the path model has one immense advantage from a scientific standpoint. It is much, much easier to demonstrate that its conclusions are incorrect.

But having done this, and having found that our models have problems, then what? Should we retreat to simple models of simple situations, in the hope that eventually we will improve our understanding of the complex phenomenon with which we began? Or should we continue to work with our complex models to try to locate the wrong assumptions that are making them behave badly with respect to the data? Tastes will differ here, but so long as there are those who hold to the second view, there will be structural modelers. Personally, I think that our best hope is that there continue to be both kinds of people; that they both vigorously continue to pursue their respective strategies; and that, at least from time to time, they talk to each other.

Cliff's caveats

In a somewhat friendlier article entitled "Some cautions concerning the application of causal modeling methods," Norman Cliff (1983) gives some gentle warnings and sensible advice to the users of programs such as LISREL: "Initially, these methods seemed to be a great boon to social science research, but there is some danger that they may instead become a disaster, a disaster because they seem to encourage one to suspend his normal critical faculties. Somehow the use of one of these computer procedures lends an air of unchallengeable sanctity to conclusions that would otherwise be subjected to the most intense scrutiny" (p. 116).

I hope that if you have gotten this far in this book you have enough sense of how these models work and do not work, and of some of the vicissitudes to which they are subject, that "unchallengeable sanctity" will not characterize your attitude toward conclusions drawn from their use. But it is worth reminding ourselves briefly of the four principles of elementary scientific inference that Cliff suggests are particularly likely to be violated in the initial flush of enthusiasm of causal modelers:

> The first principle is that the data do not confirm a model, they only fail to disconfirm it, together with the corollary that when the data do not disconfirm a model, there are many other models that are not disconfirmed either. The second principle is that *post hoc* does not imply *propter hoc*. That is, if *a* and *b* are related, and *a* followed *b* in time, it is not necessarily true that *b* caused *a*. The third principle is that just because we name something does not mean that we understand it, or even that we have named it correctly. And the fourth principle is that *ex post facto* explanations are untrustworthy (pp. 116-117).

Let us look at each of these four principles in a little more detail.

The unanalyzed variable

Suppose that a particular model "fits"--i.e., it is not rejected, given the data. That does not mean that other models would not fit equally well, maybe even better. Suppose, for example, there is some variable V that we have overlooked that is related to the variables X, Y, and Z, which we have included in our model. We can run LISREL or EQS forward, backward, or upside down on a model of X, Y, and Z, but it will not tell us that a model with V in it would have fit better. We can only be reasonably sure that if there is such a V and it has causal effects on variables included in our model, our estimates of some of the paths in our model will be wrong. As Cliff puts it: "These programs are not magic. They cannot tell the user about what is not there" (p. 118).

Post hoc is not *propter hoc*

Cliff cites an incautious author who concludes, on the basis of a significant arrow in a path diagram, that "Father's Occupation caused [Child's] Intelligence." Cliff goes on, "It may be that it does, but somehow I doubt it. It seems unlikely that, if ever the causal variables involved in scores on modern 'intelligence' tests are sorted out, one's father's occupation will ever be one of them" (p. 120). Of course, there may be variables *correlated* with father's occupation that *do* play a causal role, but that takes us back to the preceding point.

To make things worse, time of measurement is not always a safe guide to the sequence of events. "Consider the possibility that we measure a child's intelligence in the fifth grade and her father's occupation when she is in the tenth" (p. 120). Should we then put in a causal arrow leading from the earlier to the later event?

The fact that we can name it does not mean we know what it is

Latent variables are only defined by way of their associations with manifest variables. Because we are always to some degree wrong about what our manifest variables mean (there is always some degree of invalidity and unreliability of measurement), Cliff says, ". . . we can only interpret our results very cautiously unless or until we have included enough indicators of a variable in our analysis, and have satisfied not only ourselves but skeptical colleagues and critics that we have done so" (p. 121). Even a "confirmatory" factor analysis does not escape these problems. It just tells us that we have *one* set of parameters that is consistent with the data. "There are typically an infinity of alternative sets of parameters which are equally consistent with the data, many of which would lead to entirely different conclusions concerning the nature of the latent variables" (pp. 122-123).

Ex post facto explanations are untrustworthy

Once a model has been modified to make it fit better to a given data set, one can no longer take the probability values associated with subsequent goodness-of-fit tests at face value. If a model has been adjusted on the basis of its fit or lack of fit to a particular body of data, its statistical status is precarious until it can be tested on a new body of data that did not contribute to the adjustment.

One way to deal with this problem is cross-validation. Split the initial data set in half, play around with model-fitting on one half of the data until you get a model you are happy with, and *then* carry out the statistical test--once--on the unused half of the data. The χ^2 will then be legitimate. This procedure has its disadvantages--for one thing, it requires twice the sample size--but it has the preeminent advantage of not leaving the investigator and his readers with results which "they know are unstable to an unknown degree" (p. 124).

In conclusion

Neither Cliff nor I would wish to discourage you from the use of causal model-fitting methods, which in his view represent "perhaps the most important and influential statistical revolution to have occurred in the social sciences" (1983, p. 115). He concludes, and I can only echo: "programs such as LISREL and its relatives provide completely unprecedented opportunities . . . . With their aid, conclusions can be made which heretofore would have been impossible, but only provided the analysis is approached intelligently, tough-mindedly, and honestly" (p. 125).

Go do it.

Chapter 7 Notes

Improving measurement models. Anderson and Gerbing (1982, 1988) discuss the merits of doing a confirmatory factor analysis to start, and offer much other practical advice; other authors, e.g., Bentler and Bonett (1980) and James et al. (1982), have also advocated localizing misfits to the structural or the measurement parts of the model. Burt (1981), under the label of "interpretational confounding," discusses the relative roles played by the covariance among the indicators of a given latent variable and covariances with the indicators of other latent variables in defining the construct. The smaller the number of indicators per latent variable, the greater tends to be the role of the latter kind of covariation, which may make latent variables hard to interpret. These various issues are further explored in an interchange between Kumar and Dillon (1987a,b) and Anderson et al. (1987). For some arguments against the separation of structural and measurement models in model fitting, see Hayduk (1996); on the other side, for favorable views on the use of factor

234

analysis in the construction of measurement models, see Gerbing and Hamilton (1994, 1996). For a thoughtful discussion and some Monte Carlo results on the choice of indicators for latent variables, see Little et al. (1999).

Modification indices, etc. A review of the status of Modification Indices/Lagrange Multiplier Tests and their opposite numbers, T-Values, z-tests, and Wald Tests, is provided by Satorra (1989).

Trait and method variance. The review mentioned in the text is by Cote and Buckley (1987); it covers some 70 multitrait-multimethod studies.

Improving structural models. Lance et al. (1988) use confirmatory factor analysis for dealing with the measurement model, but for the structural model suggest a different approach in which one examines the model one equation at a time (using ordinary multiple regression methods) rather than all at once. In a Monte Carlo study, they found this strategy to be relatively effective in detecting known misspecifications. Lehmann and Gupta (1989) propose a regression-based approach at both stages, first for the measurement model and then for the structural model. A more radically different approach is taken by Spirtes, Scheines, and Glymour (1990a; Spirtes et al., 1993; Scheines et al., 1998). Their strategy, using a program named TETRAD (Glymour et al., 1988), emphasizes the systematic generation of many possible alternatives to a given model and rapid tests, rather than elaborate model-fitting with a few models. They report Monte Carlo studies in which TETRAD substantially outperformed EQS and LISREL in locating correct models. Not altogether surprisingly, Bentler and Chou (1990) and Jöreskog and Sörbom (1990) express some reservations; Spirtes et al. (1990b) reply. See also Glymour et al. (1988). Marcoulides, Drezner, and Schumacker (1998), and Marcoulides and Drezner (2001, 2003) suggest three other algorithms for specification searches in SEM: tabu search, a genetic algorithm, and a so-called "ant colony" algorithm.

Kaplan (1990) takes a more traditional approach to model modification, but advocates the use of an "expected parameter change" statistic in addition to the usual modification indices. His article is followed by a number of comments from experts in the field (MacCallum, Bentler, Steiger, Bollen, Tanaka, Hayduk), with a reply by Kaplan. See also MacCallum et al. (1992).

Observed variables--causes or effects? The terminology varies: "formative" vs. "reflective" indicators refers to the same distinction as "cause" vs. "effect" indicators. Cohen et al. (1990), Bollen and Lennox (1991), and MacCallum and Browne (1993) provide discussions of causal indicators, and Edwards and Bagozzi (2000) discuss the principles that underlie a choice between the two kinds. Bollen and Ting (2000) provide a statistical test for distinguishing them.

An alternative approach to structural modeling, called Partial Least Squares (PLS), is distinguished by its use of indicators of the causal type. For accounts and applications of PLS, see Wold (1982), Fornell and Bookstein (1982), Dijkstra (1983), Wellhofer (1984), Lohmöller (1988), and Chin and Newsted (1999). A discussion of the relationships between PLS and conventional SEM methods is provided by McDonald (1996).

Equivalent structural models. Lee and Hershberger (1990) give an alternative formulation of Stelzl's rules for equivalence, and distinguish between "equivalence in principle" (models that are equivalent for any data set) and models which are equivalent for a particular data set under consideration, but may not be for others. MacCallum et al. (1993) is the study mentioned in the text that checked 53 published SEM studies for the presence of equivalent models. Hershberger (1994), Hayduk (1996), Williams et al. (1996), and Raykov and Penev (2001) provide additional discussion of the topic.

Can path diagrams be constructed automatically? The account in this chapter is mostly based on Pearl's (2000) book *Causality: Models, reasoning, and inference*, especially Chapter 2, "A theory of inferred causation." The concept of "*d*-separation" is involved in step 1 of IC*; structures like those of Fig. 7.4(a) are called "*v*-structures" or "colliders." Pearl's approach covers discrete states and relations of probability between them, as well as the continuous quantitative variables emphasized here. Interested readers may wish to follow up with the other references cited and Shipley's (2000) *Cause and correlation in biology;* see also Hayduk et al. (2003) on *d*-separation. The TETRAD programs of the Carnegie Mellon group (see Note on improving structural models) are in this tradition. See Glymour (2001) for an account with an emphasis on psychology.

Modes of factor analysis. Cronbach (1984) discusses R, P, Q, etc. techniques. Kroonenberg (1983) provides an extensive annotated bibliography on three-mode factor analysis. See also a review by Snyder (1988). Three-mode longitudinal applications are discussed by Kroonenberg, Lammers, and Stoop (1985). Nesselroade and Ghisletta (2003) discuss O, P, Q, R, S and T techniques and their relationship to several different models of change over time.

Critique and controversy. For other examples of criticisms of the causal modeling enterprise, varying widely along a friendly/hostile dimension, see Martin (1982), Baumrind (1983), Biddle and Marlin (1987), and Breckler (1990); Huba and Bentler (1982) reply to Martin. Steiger (2001) expresses concern at the inadequacies of introductory texts in SEM. He lists a number of issues that users of SEM "should probably be aware of to avoid being a danger to themselves or others" (p. 331), but which he finds neglected or misrepresented in most introductory texts.

Publication. If you are planning to publish a study in this area yourself, you might find Steiger's (1988), Hoyle and Panter's (1995), and Boomsma's (2000) advice and comments useful.

Chapter 7 Exercises

1. For 100 married couples, two measures each of husband's happiness and wife's happiness are obtained, with the correlations shown. Fit path models which assume (a) that husband's happiness affects wife's happiness, but not vice versa; (b) that wife's happiness affects husband's happiness, but not vice versa; (c) that husband's and wife's happiness affect each other equally; and (d) that husband's and wife's happiness are simply correlated. Comment on the results.

	HH1	HH2	WH1	WH2
Husband's Happiness 1	1.00	.65	.35	.30
Husband's Happiness 2		1.00	.30	.35
Wife's Happiness 1			1.00	.60
Wife's Happiness 2				1.00

2. Suppose AC and BC in Fig. 7.4(a), page 223, were each .6 instead of .5. What values would the three paths in (b) need to take in order to make it equivalent to (a)? (Solve by trial and error to two decimal places, or, if you like, do a little algebra to get an exact solution.)

3. Carry out an exploratory Q-technique factor analysis of the data in Table 7-3, using the scores for the 4 persons on all 7 tests. Comment on your results.

4. Suggest an example of T technique that might be relevant to experimental psychology.

5. Is the study of Judd and Milburn (see Chapter 4) a four-mode structural analysis? (Give your reasoning.)

6. Think of an additional caveat that you might offer a beginner in causal modeling.

Appendix A: Simple Matrix Operations

This appendix reviews some basic aspects of matrix algebra, confining itself
to those used in this book and proceeding largely by example rather than by
formal definition and proof.

Matrices

A *matrix* is a rectangular array of numbers. Examples of three matrices, **A**, **B**,
and **D**, are given in Fig. A.1. Matrix **A** has *dimensions* 4 x 3 (the number of *rows*
precedes the number of *columns*). **B** and **D** are *square* 3 x 3 matrices; they can
alternatively be described as being of *order* 3. Matrices **B** and **D** are also
symmetric matrices: Each row of the matrix is identical with the corresponding
column, so that the matrix is symmetrical around the *principal diagonal* that runs
from its upper left to lower right. A symmetric matrix is necessarily square, but a
square matrix is not necessarily symmetric: The first three rows of matrix **A**
would constitute a square, nonsymmetric matrix.

1	4	7	1.00	.32	.64	2	0	0
6	2	5	.32	1.00	.27	0	-3	0
3	3	0	.64	.27	1.00	0	0	-1
4	6	1						
	A			**B**			**D**	

Fig. A.1 Some examples of matrices.

Matrix **B** happens to be a familiar example of a symmetric matrix, a
correlation matrix. A variance-covariance matrix would provide another
example. Matrix **D** is a *diagonal* matrix: all zeroes except for the principal
diagonal.   If the values in the diagonal of **D** were all 1s, it would have a special
name: an *identity* matrix, symbolized **I**. A matrix of all zeroes is called a *null*
matrix.

Matrices are ordinarily designated by bold-face capital letters.

The transpose of a matrix

The *transpose* of a matrix is obtained by interchanging each row with its
corresponding column. Thus, the transpose of matrix **A** in Fig. A.1,
conventionally designated **A´**, is:

1	6	3	4
4	2	3	6
7	5	0	1

in which the first column of **A** becomes the first row of **A´**, and so on. In the case of a symmetric matrix, **A´ = A**, as you can see if you attempt to transpose matrix **B** or **D** in Fig. A.1.

Note that the transpose of a 4 x 3 matrix will have the dimensions 3 x 4 because rows and columns are interchanged. The transpose of a square matrix will be another square matrix of the same order, but it will not be the same matrix unless the original matrix was symmetric.

Vectors and scalars

A single row or column of numbers is called a *vector.* Examples of *column* and *row* vectors are shown in Fig. A.2. The two vectors are of *length* 4 and 3, respectively. Column vectors are designated by lower case bold-face letters-- e.g., vector **a**. Row vectors, as transposes of column vectors, are marked with a prime symbol--e.g., vector **b´**.

---

a: 1   **b´:**   .3   1.0   .5
        2
        4   **c:**   17.3
        3

Fig. A.2 Column and row vectors and a scalar.

Single numbers, of the kind familiar in ordinary arithmetic, are referred to in matrix terminology as *scalars* and are usually designated by lower case roman letters--e.g., scalar c in Fig. A.2.

Addition and subtraction of matrices

Two matrices, which must be of the same dimensions, may be *added* together by adding algebraically the corresponding elements of the two matrices, as shown for the two 3 x 2 matrices **A** and **B** in Fig. A.3. A matrix may be *subtracted* from another by reversing the signs of its elements and then adding, as in ordinary algebra. Examples are shown at the right in Fig. A.3.

---

1 2	0 1	1 3	1 1	-1 -1
4 6	0 -1	4 5	4 7	-4 -7
5 -2	3 -1	8 -3	2 -1	-2 1
A	**B**	**A+B**	**A−B**	**B−A**

Fig. A.3 Matrix addition and subtraction.

Two column vectors of the same length, or two row vectors of the same length, may be added or subtracted in the same way. (As, of course, may two scalars.)

Multiplication of vectors and matrices

A row vector and a column vector of the same length may be multiplied by obtaining the sum of the products of their corresponding elements, as illustrated in Fig. A.4 for **a´b**. Note that this is a multiplication in the order *row* vector times *column* vector. In matrix arithmetic the order of matrices or vectors in a

$$
\begin{array}{llll}
\textbf{a´}: 1\ \ 0\ \ 2\ \ 3 & \textbf{b}: & 1 & 1 \times 1 = 1 \\
& & 2 & 0 \times 2 = 0 \\
& & 4 & 2 \times 4 = 8 \\
& & 3 & 3 \times 3 = \underline{9} \\
& & & \textbf{a´b} = 18
\end{array}
$$

Fig. A.4 An example of the vector multiplication **a´b**.

multiplication is *not* the indifferent matter that it is in scalar arithmetic, where ab = ba. The product **ba´** is something entirely different from **a´b** (as we see shortly).

Two matrices may be multiplied by multiplying each of the row vectors of the first matrix in turn times each of the column vectors of the second matrix. Each of these vector multiplications yields a single number that constitutes an element of a row of the product matrix. A step-by-step example is given in Fig. A.5. Notice that the result matrix has as many *rows* as the *first* matrix, and as many *columns* as the *second*, and that for multiplication to be possible, the rows of the first matrix and the columns of the second must be equal in length. Two matrices are said to *conform* for multiplication when this last condition holds--an easy way of checking is to see that the second dimension of the first matrix agrees with the first dimension of the second: that is, a 3 x 5 matrix can be multiplied times a 5 x 2, or a 7 x 2 times a 2 x 3. The middle numbers in the sequence must match; the outer numbers give the dimensions of the result. In the first example, the 5s match and the result will be a 3 x 2 matrix; in the second example, the 2s match and the result will be 7 x 3. In Fig. A.5, the multiplication was of a 3 x 2 times a 2 x 2 matrix; the middle 2s match and the result was 3 x 2. Working through a sample case or two will make it evident to you why these rules hold.

These principles generalize to longer series of matrix multiplications: If **W**, **X**, **Y**, and **Z** are, respectively, of dimensions 4 x 2, 2 x 3, 3 x 7, and 7 x 5, the multiplication **WXYZ** can be carried out and the result will be of dimension 4 x 5. (You can see this by carrying out the steps successively: 4 x 2 times

```
1 3    4 5        1st row of A, 1st col of B     1 x 4 = 4
2 1    2 2                                        3 x 2 = 6
0 2                                                     10
 A      B         1st row of A, 2nd col of B     1 x 5 = 5
                                                 3 x 2 = 6
                                                      11
                  2nd row of A, 1st col of B     2 x 4 = 8
                                                 1 x 2 = 2
                                                      10
                  2nd row of A, 2nd col of B     2 x 5 = 10
                                                 1 x 2 = 2
                                                      12
                  3rd row of A, 1st col of B     0 x 4 = 0
                                                 2 x 2 = 4
                                                       4
                  3rd row of A, 2nd col of B     0 x 5 = 0
                                                 2 x 2 = 4
result AB:  10  11                                     4
            10  12
             4   4
```

Fig. A.5 Step-by-step example of the matrix multiplication **A** times **B**.

2 x 3 is proper and will yield a 4 x 3 matrix; 4 x 3 times 3 x 7 will work and yield a 4 x 7 matrix; and so on.) The rules also hold for vectors, considered as 1 x n or n x 1 matrices. Thus, a 1 x 4 row vector times a 4 x 1 column vector yields a 1 x 1 single number result (as we have seen in Fig. A.4). A 4 x 1 column vector times a 1 x 4 row vector, on the other hand, would produce a 4 x 4 matrix as an answer, and that matrix would be obtained by applying the regular rules of matrix multiplication: taking each row (of length 1) of the column vector and multiplying it successively by each column of the row vector to yield the elements of the rows of the result vector. (You might want to verify that for the two vectors of Fig. A.4, the first two rows of the product **ab´** would be 1 2 4 3 and 0 0 0 0, and the first two rows of **ba´** would be 1 0 2 3 and 2 0 4 6.)

Because the order of matrix multiplication is important, the terms *pre-* and *postmultiplication* are often used to eliminate ambiguity. In the product **AB**, **B** is said to be premultiplied by **A**, or **A** to be postmultiplied by **B**. In the product **a´Ba**, the matrix is pre- and postmultiplied by the vector. (Incidentally, can you see that **B** must be a square matrix, that the result will be a scalar, and why one would seldom run across the alternative product **aBa´**?)

Some special cases of matrix multiplication

The basis of these rules will be self-evident if you work through an example or two.

    1. A matrix pre- or postmultiplied by a null matrix yields a null matrix. (The null matrix acts like a zero in scalar arithmetic.)

    2. A matrix pre or postmultiplied by an identity matrix is unchanged. (The identity matrix acts like a 1 in scalar arithmetic.)

    3. Premultiplying a matrix by a diagonal matrix rescales the rows of the matrix by the corresponding elements of the diagonal matrix; postmultiplying by a diagonal matrix rescales the columns. (Try **AD** or **DB** in Fig. A.1, for example.)

    4. Pre- or postmultiplying a matrix by its transpose can always be done and yields a symmetric matrix.

Multiplying a vector or matrix by a scalar

Multiplying a matrix or vector by a scalar is done by multiplying every element in the matrix or vector by that scalar. In a series of matrix operations, the location of a scalar does not matter, and may be changed at will: **ka´BC** = **a´kBC** = **a´BkC** = **a´BC**k, where k is a scalar. (But of course **ka´BC** doesn't equal **kBa´C** or **ka´CB**--the vectors and matrices cannot in general be reordered.)

The inverse of a matrix

There is no operation of matrix division as such, but a matrix *inverse* is the matrix analogue of a reciprocal of a number in scalar arithmetic, so multiplying by an inverse is the matrix equivalent of dividing.

    The inverse of a matrix **A**, symbolized by **A**$^{-1}$, is a matrix such that **AA**$^{-1}$ or **A**$^{-1}$**A** equals an identity matrix. (Just as k x 1/k = 1.) Only square matrices have inverses, and not all of them do--if a matrix has some rows or columns that are linearly predictable from others, it will have no inverse. A matrix that has no inverse is called *singular*. Matrix inversion is a basic step in solving matrix equations: If **BX** = **A**, and **B** has an inverse, you can solve for **X** by premultiplying both sides of the equation by **B**$^{-1}$, i.e.:

$$\mathbf{BX} = \mathbf{A}$$
$$\mathbf{B}^{-1}\mathbf{BX} = \mathbf{B}^{-1}\mathbf{A}$$
$$\mathbf{IX} = \mathbf{B}^{-1}\mathbf{A}$$
$$\mathbf{X} = \mathbf{B}^{-1}\mathbf{A}$$

    Obtaining the inverse of a matrix tends in general to be a large computational task. Let a computer do it. You can always check to see whether the result it has given you is correct by carrying out the multiplication AA^{-1}, which should equal I within rounding error.

Some useful facts about inverses:

1. The inverse of the transpose of a matrix is the transpose of its inverse: $(A')^{-1} = (A^{-1})'$.

2. Taking the inverse of an inverse yields the original matrix: $(A^{-1})^{-1} = A$.

3. The inverse of a symmetric matrix is also symmetric.

$$
\begin{array}{cccc}
\begin{array}{ccc} 1 & 0 & 0 \\ 0 & 1 & 0 \\ 0 & 0 & 1 \end{array} &
\begin{array}{ccc} 1 & 0 & 0 \\ 0 & 1 & 0 \\ 0 & 0 & 1 \end{array} &
\begin{array}{ccc} 2 & 0 & 0 \\ 0 & 3 & 0 \\ 0 & 0 & -4 \end{array} &
\begin{array}{ccc} 1/2 & 0 & 0 \\ 0 & 1/3 & 0 \\ 0 & 0 & -1/4 \end{array} \\[2mm]
I & I^{-1} & D & D^{-1}
\end{array}
$$

$$
\begin{array}{ccc}
\begin{array}{cc} 4 & 2 \\ 5 & 3 \end{array} &
\dfrac{1}{12-10}\begin{bmatrix} 3 & -2 \\ -5 & 4 \end{bmatrix} = &
\begin{array}{cc} 1.5 & -1.0 \\ -2.5 & 2.0 \end{array} \\[2mm]
A & & A^{-1}
\end{array}
$$

Fig. A.6 Some special cases of matrix inversion.

A few special cases of matrix inversion that do not require extensive computation are illustrated in Fig. A.6. You might want to verify these by showing that $AA^{-1} = I$ in each case.

1. The inverse of an identity matrix is itself.

2. A diagonal matrix can be inverted by replacing each diagonal element by its reciprocal.

3. The inverse of a 2 x 2 matrix, for example:

$$
\begin{array}{cc} a & b \\ c & d \end{array}
$$

may be obtained by interchanging the two diagonal elements a and d, changing the signs of the two off-diagonal elements b and c, and multiplying the result by the scalar $1/(ad - bc)$.

Inverse or transpose of a product

The *transpose* of a product of matrices is equal to the product of the transposes of the matrices, *taken in reverse order.* $(ABCD)' = D'C'B'A'$.

The *inverse* of a product of matrices is equal to the product of the inverses of the matrices, taken in reverse order:

$$(ABCD)^{-1} = D^{-1}C^{-1}B^{-1}A^{-1}$$

Of course, this presupposes that the necessary inverses exist, i.e., that **A, B, C,** and **D** are square, nonsingular matrices (they must also all be of the same order for the multiplication to be possible).

Eigenvalues and eigenvectors of a correlation or covariance matrix

If **C** is an $m \times m$ variance-covariance or correlation matrix, it can be decomposed into a matrix product $\mathbf{VL^2V'}$, where **V** is a square $m \times m$ matrix whose columns are called the *eigenvectors* of matrix **C**, and $\mathbf{L^2}$ is a diagonal matrix of numbers, customarily arranged in descending order of size, called the *eigenvalues* of **C**. **V** and $\mathbf{L^2}$ are so chosen as to have the following additional properties:

$$\mathbf{V'V = I},$$
$$\text{and} \quad \mathbf{Cv = l^2v},$$

where l^2 is any one of the eigenvalues and **v** the corresponding eigenvector. That is, the eigenvectors are mutually *orthogonal* (=uncorrelated), and each has the property that when it postmultiplies the matrix **C** the result is a vector proportional to itself, the coefficient of proportionality being the eigenvalue.

Eigenvalues and eigenvectors are also sometimes known as characteristic roots and characteristic vectors, or latent roots and latent vectors.

The calculation of eigenvalues and eigenvectors, even more than the calculation of inverses, is a task for computers. Again, you can always verify that the results the computer gives you have the properties specified. Fig. A.7 gives eigenvectors and eigenvalues for the correlation matrix of Fig. A.1.

A few useful additional properties of eigenvalues:

1. The sum of the elements of the principal diagonal, called the *trace*, of **C** and $\mathbf{L^2}$ are equal.

2. The product of the eigenvalues of a matrix is called the *determinant* of the matrix. The determinant of matrix **C** is symbolized |C|. A singular matrix, one which has one or more rows or columns linearly predictable from others, has one or more zero eigenvalues and thus a determinant of zero.

3. The number of nonzero eigenvalues of a matrix is called the *rank* of the matrix, which is the number of nonredundant rows or columns it contains.

1.00 .32 .64	1.846 0 0	-.641 .261 .721
.32 1.00 .27	0 .797 0	-.443 -.894 -.070
.64 .27 1.00	0 0 .358	-.627 .364 -.689
C	$\mathbf{L^2}$	**V**

$$\text{tr } \mathbf{L^2} = 3.00 \quad |C| = .526$$

Fig. A.7 Eigenvalues and eigenvectors of a correlation matrix.

Appendix B: Derivation of Matrix Version of Path Equations

In this appendix we show how the McArdle-McDonald matrix equation described in Chapter 2 can be derived from the structural-equation translation of a path diagram.

Figure B.1 repeats the path diagram used in the example, with the structural equations given to the right of the figure.

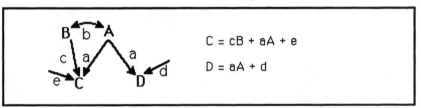

Fig. B.1 Path model for example.

Now we write out these same equations so that each of them has on its right-hand side all the variables in the path diagram. This means putting in a lot of zero coefficients but gets the equations into a convenient form to express as matrices. For completeness, structural equations have been added for A and B, although these are not very exciting because neither has any incoming causal arrows from other variables in the diagram. In each equation, the first four terms indicate causal arrows from other variables (hence the variable itself always gets a zero coefficient). The last term in each expression is the residual. Source variables such as A and B have by definition all of their causes external to the path diagram, so they are treated as "all residual."

$$A = 0A + 0B + 0C + 0D + A$$
$$B = 0A + 0B + 0C + 0D + B$$
$$C = aA + cB + 0C + 0D + e$$
$$D = aA + 0B + 0C + 0D + d$$

Next we write this in matrix form. (You might want to check to assure yourself that the matrix formulation is indeed the equivalent of the equations.)

$$
\begin{matrix} A \\ B \\ C \\ D \end{matrix}
\quad = \quad
\begin{matrix} 0 & 0 & 0 & 0 \\ 0 & 0 & 0 & 0 \\ a & c & 0 & 0 \\ a & 0 & 0 & 0 \end{matrix}
\quad \times \quad
\begin{matrix} A \\ B \\ C \\ D \end{matrix}
\quad + \quad
\begin{matrix} A \\ B \\ e \\ d \end{matrix}
$$

Now let's call these matrices, from left to right, **v**, **A**, **v** (again), and **u**. The matrix equation can then be written:

$$\mathbf{v} = \mathbf{Av} + \mathbf{u} .$$

By simple matrix algebra, we solve for **v**:

$$\mathbf{v} - \mathbf{Av} = \mathbf{u}$$
$$(\mathbf{I} - \mathbf{A})\mathbf{v} = \mathbf{u}$$
$$\mathbf{v} = (\mathbf{I} - \mathbf{A})^{-1}\mathbf{u} \ .$$

If we assume the variables all to be in deviation-score form, the matrix of covariances among all the variables may be obtained as **vv**´ $/n$, or

$$(\mathbf{I} - \mathbf{A})^{-1}\mathbf{uu}´(\mathbf{I} - \mathbf{A})^{-1}´/n \ .$$

Let us call **uu**´$/n$ --which is itself a covariance matrix--**S**. Then:

$$\mathbf{vv}´/n = (\mathbf{I} - \mathbf{A})^{-1} \mathbf{S} (\mathbf{I} - \mathbf{A})^{-1}´.$$

Pre- and postmultiplication by **F** and **F**´ selects the observed variables **C**:

$$\mathbf{C} = \mathbf{F} (\mathbf{I} - \mathbf{A})^{-1} \mathbf{S} (\mathbf{I} - \mathbf{A})^{-1}´ \mathbf{F}´,$$

which is the McArdle-McDonald equation.

Obtaining $(\mathbf{I} - \mathbf{A})^{-1}$

McArdle and McDonald point out that the matrix $(\mathbf{I} - \mathbf{A})^{-1}$ can be obtained for unlooped path diagrams as:

$$\mathbf{I} + \mathbf{A} + \mathbf{AA} + \mathbf{AAA} + \ldots,$$

where the series is carried out until the product terms become zero. If there are no compound paths in the diagram that contain more than one consecutive straight arrow in the same direction, this will occur after the term **A**; with a maximum of two consecutive straight arrows, it will be after **AA**; and so on.

The example of Fig. B.1 contains only single straight arrows in its paths. Thus, **AA** (as you should verify) is a null matrix. Therefore,

$$(\mathbf{I} - \mathbf{A})^{-1} = \mathbf{I} + \mathbf{A} = \begin{array}{cccc} 1 & 0 & 0 & 0 \\ 0 & 1 & 0 & 0 \\ a & c & 1 & 0 \\ a & 0 & 0 & 1 \end{array}$$

as used for the Chapter 2 example.

In Chapter 1, "direct" and "indirect" causal effects were discussed. Note that matrix **A** represents direct effects, and **AA**, **AAA**, etc. indirect effects.

Appendix C: LISREL Matrices and Examples

LISREL makes basic distinctions between independent and dependent variables in addition to latent and observed variables. Thus the latent variables in the structural model are of two kinds: the source latent variables, Ksi, and the downstream latent variables, Eta. The measurement model, that connects the latent to the observed variables, consists of two submodels, referred to as the "X-side" and the "Y-side." The X-side contains the indicators of the source latent variables, the Ksis, and the Y-side contains the indicators of the downstream latent variables, the Etas.

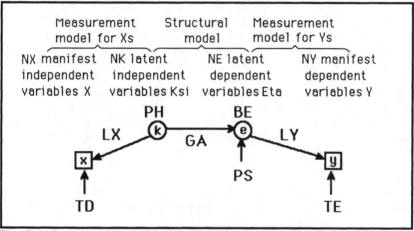

Fig. C.1 Summary of matrix representation in LISREL.

Figure C.1 summarizes the relationships in LISREL. The portions of the diagram to the left and the right constitute the two measurement submodels; the portion in the middle is the structural model. The latent independent variables Ksi (NK of them) constitute the vector **k**. The latent dependent variables Eta are downstream variables; there are NE of them, in **e**. There are NX observed independent variables X, and NY observed dependent variables Y. The Xs and Ys are all treated as downstream variables--fallible observed indexes only imperfectly reflecting the true latent variables lying behind them. The vertical upward arrows in Fig. C.1 represent the residual paths for the three sets of downstream variables--of course, there are none for the Ksis, which are source variables. The two-letter symbols next to the arrows in the diagram represent the eight basic LISREL matrices (not all problems need all of these). The matrices **LX** and **LY** represent the paths from latent to observed variables, and **TD** and **TE** the variance-covariance matrices of residuals (diagonal matrices, if the residuals are assumed to be uncorrelated). These four matrices constitute the measurement model. The dimensions of these matrices follow from the numbers of variables involved: **LX** is NX x NK, **LY** is NY x NE, and **TD** and **TE** are square matrices of order NX and NY, respectively.

In the structural model, **GA** contains paths from Ksis to Etas--from source to downstream latent variables. **PH** represents the variance-covariance matrix of the source variables, and **BE** any paths between downstream latent variables. **GA** is of dimension NE x NK, and **PH** and **BE** are of order NK and NE, respectively. **PS**, the variance-covariance matrix of the residuals of the downstream latent variables, is also a square matrix of order NE.

The input to LISREL sets up the eight matrices with a combination of fixed values (usually 1s and 0s) and unknowns to be solved for. (With SIMPLIS, this occurs automatically.) The multiplication of these matrices yields the implied values of the correlations (or covariances) that are used by the minimization part of the program. The overall matrix formula used by LISREL, with its eight matrices, is considerably more elaborate than the McArdle-McDonald formula, which involves three; we will not need to go into the details.

Table C-1 shows one way of defining input to LISREL for the Chapter 2 example of Fig. 2.5, repeated for convenience here as Fig. C.2. Above the program itself are the three matrices required for this problem, **LX**, **PH**, and **TD**--they are what we are trying to specify, not part of the input itself. The first line of the actual input is a title. The second gives data specifications: number of input variables = 4; number of observations (cases) = 100; the matrix to be analyzed is a correlation matrix (CM would mean covariance matrix). The third line specifies that a correlation matrix is to be read, in free-field format (items separated by any number of spaces). If the matrix were to be in other than lower triangular form, or in a fixed format, this would be specified as well. The correlations follow in lines 4 through 7. The lines from MODEL to START define the matrices and starting values of the model.

As noted in the text, the general philosophy of LISREL is that things are assumed to be in some typical form by default unless otherwise specified. The MODEL line says that there are 4 X-variables and 2 Ksi variables. The "ST" specifies that the **PH** matrix is to be a correlation matrix (symmetrical, with 1s fixed in the diagonal and free values elsewhere). Because nothing is said

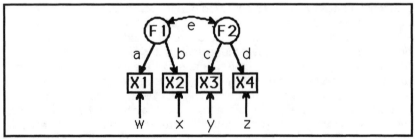

Fig. C.2 Path diagram for first example.

248

Table C-1 The necessary LISREL matrices, and an example of LISREL input for solving the path diagram of Fig. C.2

The matrices

```
   LX            PH          TD
   a  0          1  e        w  0  0  0
   b  0          e  1        0  x  0  0
   0  c                      0  0  y  0
   0  d                      0  0  0  z
```

The input
```
INPUT FOR FIG C.2 PROBLEM
DATA   NI=4   NO=100    MA=KM
KM
 1.00
  .50  1.00
  .10    .10  1.00
  .20    .30    .20  1.00
MODEL   NX=4   NK=2   PH=ST
FREE   LX 1 1   LX 2 1   LX 3 2   LX 4 2
START  .5   ALL
OUTPUT NS
```

about **LX** and **TD**, these matrices are assumed to be in their default forms-- respectively, a rectangular matrix with all values fixed to zero, and a diagonal matrix with all diagonal values free. Nothing more is needed for **TD**. The line beginning FREE specifies exceptions: **LX** locations 1 and 2 of column 1, and 3 and 4 of column 2, are to be free values to be solved for, not the fixed zeros currently specified. The line beginning START sets an initial value of .5 into all free values. The NS in the OUTPUT line tells LISREL to use the starting values we have provided, rather than calculate its own. Because OUTPUT carries no additional specifications, the standard output will be produced and the standard fitting criterion will be used (for LISREL this is maximum likelihood).

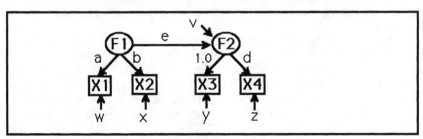

Fig. C.3 Path model for second example.

Table C-2 LISREL matrices and input for Fig. C.3 example

The matrices

LX	LY	PH	GA	PS	TD		TE	
a	1	1	e	v	w	0	y	0
b	d				0	x	0	z

The input
```
INPUT FOR FIG C.3 PROBLEM
```

[lines 2-7 same as for previous example]

```
SELECT
3 4 1 2
MODEL NX=2 NK=1 NY=2 NE=1 PH=ST LX=FR LY=FR
FIX   LY 1 1
START 1.0 LY 1 1
OUTPUT SS   UL
```

Table C-2 shows the input required for the second model, that of Fig. C.3. There are now seven LISREL matrices, as shown above the program. (**BE** is the unused eighth--there can be no arrows between downstream latent variables, since there is only one Eta.) Aside from the title, there are no changes in the first seven lines of the input, through the correlation matrix. The next two lines reorder the input: LISREL requires that dependent variables (the third and the fourth in the correlation matrix as read) precede independent variables (1 and 2). The MODEL line indicates two X and two Y variables, and one Ksi and one Eta. **LX** and **LY** are started as FREE matrices, and then, in the next two lines, the first element of **LY** is fixed and set to 1, to scale the latent variable. **GA, PS, TD**, and **TE** are in their default forms, so no further specification is necessary for them. The UL in the OUTPUT line requests that fitting be done using an ordinary ("unweighted") least squares criterion. SS asks for a standardized solution. This time LISREL is permitted to calculate its own start values.

Many input variations are possible in LISREL. Matrices specifying the model can be given explicitly, if desired; or one can specify matrices to be diagonal, symmetrical, and so on. Lines of the form EQUAL LX 1 1 LX 2 1 can be used to specify that LX 2 1 is constrained to be equal to LX 1 1. Raw data or matrices can be read in from an external file. Various kinds of information can be requested in the output. The LISREL manual may be consulted for details.

Appendix D: Various Goodness-of-Fit Indices

Several examples of typical fit indices will be described briefly. First we consider four sample-based indices: the Bentler-Bonett normed fit index, NFI, a df-adjusted version of it, PNFI, and two corresponding goodness-of-fit indices used by LISREL--GFI and AGFI. Then we examine briefly a philosophically different index, Akaike's information criterion, AIC, and a related index, Cudeck and Browne's estimated cross-validation index, ECVI. After that, we go on to discuss a number of population-based indices. (References may be found in Notes to Chapter 2)

Bentler and Bonett's normed fit index: NFI

Bentler and Bonett (1980) suggest that the goodness of fit of a particular model may be usefully assessed relative to the fit of some baseline "null model." Such a null model would be an arbitrary, highly restricted model--say, that all correlations are zero, or that all correlations are equal, or some such--which would represent a baseline level that any realistic model would be expected to exceed. The index would then represent the point at which the model being evaluated falls on a scale running from this baseline model to perfect fit. The normed fit index may be defined as:

$$NFI = 1 - (F_k/F_b)$$

where the subscripts k and b refer to the model in question and the baseline model, respectively. As you can see, if the fit is excellent (F_k is close to zero) the righthand part of the expression approaches zero, and NFI approaches 1. At the other extreme, if the fit is little better than that of the baseline model (F_k is close to F_b) the righthand part of the expression approaches one, and NFI approaches zero. NFI can logically be negative, if the model tested happens to fit worse than the baseline model, but in practice this is unlikely; if it should happen, it would certainly be a reason not to be proud of the model in question. NFI cannot go above 1.0, which represents a perfect fit. (NFI--and most of the other indices we will consider--can alternatively be defined via χ^2. In this case, χ^2 can simply be substituted for F, because multiplying the numerator and denominator of the ratio on the right by N - 1 does not alter the ratio.)

LISREL's goodness-of-fit index: GFI

The program LISREL provides a similar index, one which compares the fit of a given model to that of no model at all--i.e., to the fit index applied to the original covariance matrix. That is,

$$GFI = 1 - (F_k/F_s)$$

where F_k, as before, refers to the fit of the model in question, and F_s refers to the fit with the observed covariance matrix **S** substituted for **S-C**. For maximum likelihood estimation, F_s may be obtained as $1/2 \, tr \, (SC^{-1})^2$, via the formula given in the section on fit functions in Chapter 2--or, approximately, as $1/2 \, m$, where m is the number of variables in the covariance matrix.

GFI is thus of the same general form as NFI, and like it compares the fit of any particular model to a baseline, but the baseline is different. The GFI deals with explained covariance relative to total covariance rather than comparing the relative lack of fit of two models.

Examples of fit indices may be seen in Table D-1, where various fit criteria are applied to a series of increasingly constrained models. The first two rows of the table correspond to the one-factor model and the two-factor model fit to the four-variable correlation matrix in Fig. 2.8 and Table 2-12 (pages 62-63). The next three rows represent increasing constraints placed upon the one-factor model: that paths a and b are equal, that $a = b$ and $c = d$, and that all four factor loadings are equal. The last row of the table gives a null or baseline model that represents the hypothesis that the four variables are mutually uncorrelated. All fits in the table are based on a maximum likelihood criterion, and treat the correlation matrix as a covariance matrix of standardized variables. The larger sample size from the example, 240, is used throughout.

First, note that that F, χ^2, NFI, and GFI (marked by asterisks in the table) always get worse, or at least no better, as we move down the table. (As we go down, the models involve successively fewer free parameters, as indicated by the increase in degrees of freedom.) NFI goes to zero as we reach the null model, which represents its baseline, but GFI does not, because a model of uncorrelated variables accounts for a reasonable proportion of the covariance matrix in this example. Against GFI's lower baseline, any given level of fit receives a higher score than against NFI's higher baseline. An arbitrary rule of

Table D-1 Comparison of several sample-based criteria of model fit, for models of Fig. 2.8

model	F	χ^2	df	NFI	PNFI	GFI	AGFI	AIC	ECVI
	*	*		*		*			
2-factor	.0063	1.51	1	.977	.163	.997	.969	19.51	.083
1-factor	.0390	9.31	2	.858	.286	.981	.903	25.31	.107
a=b	.0404	9.66	3	.853	.426	.980	.933	23.66	.100
a=b, c=d	.0423	10.11	4	.846	.564	.979	.948	22.11	.094
a=b=c=d	.0423	10.11	5	.846	.705	.979	.958	20.11	.085
null	.2748	65.68	6	.000	.000	.866	.776	73.68	.309

thumb (such as ".90 or better represents a good fit") obviously doesn't mean the same thing in the two cases--only the 2-factor model would meet that criterion for the NFI, but all five models do for the GFI, and even the null model comes close. The superficial similarity of being on a 0 to 1 scale does not make such indices automatically equivalent to one another and it does not justify assuming that a particular value, such as .90, will have the same meaning across indices.

Parsimony adjustments: PNFI and AGFI

A problem that disturbs some users of simple fit indices such as NFI or GFI (or, for that matter, F or χ^2) is that within any nested series of models the fit always improves as the models solve for more free parameters. For example, a perfect fit can always be achieved by fitting one free parameter for each observed variance or covariance, but such a model would be of no scientific interest. What we want is models that fit well, but include relatively few unknown parameters. This has led to a number of proposals for indices that evaluate fit while penalizing the use of more parameters in achieving it. One of these is the parsimonious fit index of James, Mulaik, and Brett (1982), which adjusts NFI by the ratio of degrees of freedom of the observed model to the baseline model.

$$PNFI = (df_k/df_b) \, NFI$$

The 2-factor model in the Table D-1 example, which fits very well according to the NFI, achieves this fit by solving for 9 unknowns (the four factor loadings, the four residuals, and the correlation between the factors), and this lack of parsimony is severely penalized in its low PNFI. Or compare the models in the second and fifth rows of the table. The former solves for all four factor loadings separately, the latter for just the one common value, gaining three degrees of freedom in the process. Yet the latter, in terms of NFI (or F or χ^2) fits nearly as well as the former, and thus shows up much more favorably on PNFI, which gives it credit for achieving this level of fit with fewer unknowns.

LISREL's Adjusted Goodness-of-Fit Index, AGFI, also applies an adjustment based on the ratio of degrees of freedom of the model being fitted and the baseline matrix, but rather than applying it to the GFI as a whole, it applies it only to the righthand portion:

$$AGFI = 1 - (F_k/F_s)(df_s/df_k),$$

where df_s is $m(m + 1)/2$, the number of unduplicated elements in the covariance matrix. Note that the df ratio is inverted because it is being applied to the part that is subtracted from 1. In the Table D-1 example, it is evident that when the fit is good, this part is small, and thus the parsimony adjustment has a much less drastic effect on AGFI than on PNFI. The 2-factor model, although its fit is reduced slightly by the adjustment, still qualifies as the best of the five non-null models, instead of dropping to the worst as with the PNFI. Nevertheless the adjustment for parsimony does make a difference--the highly parsimonious $a = b = c = d$ model does relatively well on the AGFI, coming in a close second to the 2-factor model.

Two other strategies: AIC and ECVI

The last two columns of Table D-1 show two other fit indices that take parsimony into account. The first, Akaike's Information Criterion, AIC, has a rationale derived from information theory. It involves a simple parsimony adjustment, additive rather than multiplicative. The index is given in various forms, but a simple one is:

$$AIC = \chi^2 + 2q,$$

where q is the number of unknown parameters being solved for. AIC is a badness-of-fit indicator, with small values indicating good fits and large values poor ones. A low χ^2 obtained by fitting few parameters (small q) is the ideal. Decreasing χ^2 by solving for more parameters will only be a benefit if χ^2 is decreased by more than 2.0 for each parameter added. In Table D-1 going from the 1-factor to the 2-factor model results in a drop in χ^2 of 7.8 for one added parameter, so AIC decreases. But going from the row 5 to the row 4 model adds one parameter and doesn't decrease χ^2 at all, so AIC increases by 2.0. Note that in this particular example the rank order of the models is the same by AIC as by AGFI--row 1 best, and then rows 5, 4, 3, 2, and 6, respectively. PNFI disagrees sharply on the row 1 model but rank-orders the rest the same.

The last column of Table D-1 contains Browne and Cudeck's Expected Cross-Validation Index, ECVI. It turns out to be closely related to AIC, although developed from a somewhat different perspective. The idea is that models that fit well *and* are simple stand a better chance of fitting well in a new sample than models that are not simple--because models with many parameters will have capitalized on chance more in the fitting process. (An empirical study by Cudeck and Browne supporting this notion is discussed in Chapter 6.) From this idea, Browne and Cudeck derive an index:

$$ECVI = F_k + 2q/(N - m - 2),$$

with q and m referring as before to the number of free parameters solved for and the number of variables in the matrix. The smaller the ECVI, the better the model is expected to cross-validate in a new sample--ECVI is in fact an estimate of the F we would obtain if we compared the implied covariance matrix **C** based on our present solution to the **S** from a new sample drawn from this population. ECVI will be larger than the F obtained in the present sample, because the latter is assumed to have capitalized on chance features of the present sample. The amount of such capitalization--represented by the second term on the right of the expression--will be small for economical models (small q) and large samples (large N).

To see the relationship of ECVI to AIC, imagine both terms on the right of the expression for ECVI to be multiplied by N - 1. Recall that N - 1 times F will yield χ^2 for the first term. For the second term, $(N - 1)/(N - m - 2)$ only slightly exceeds 1.0 for reasonably large N--in the example, this ratio is 1.021. If so, the second term will differ only slightly from $2q$. Thus ECVI will typically rank models in about the same order of merit as AIC, as is the case in Table D-1.

An attractive feature of ECVI is that confidence intervals are available for it. For the .083 in the first row of Table D-1, the 90% confidence interval was computed by the model-fitting program as .000 to .116. Thus we know not only what kind of fit to expect on average in a new sample, but we have some idea of how precise our knowledge is.

Population-based criteria of model fit

As noted earlier, there has been recent interest in fit criteria that try to estimate the part of the lack of fit that is due to the discrepancy between model and reality in the population, as distinct from that arising merely from sampling error. Looked at in another way, the multiplication of a minimum F by N - 1 gives a quantity distributed as chi square when the model fits in the population; when the model does not fit, the distribution of (N - 1)F follows a somewhat different theoretical distribution, called noncentral chi square. This distribution is characterized by a quantity called the noncentrality parameter, which depends on the degree of discrepancy. This noncentrality parameter provides the underlying basis for the population-based criteria of fit that we consider next.

The noncentrality parameter can be estimated by the difference between a given best-fit χ^2 and its degrees of freedom. A rescaled version of the parameter, labeled *d* in Table D-2 (next page), is obtained by dividing χ^2 - df by N-1. It will be convenient for defining the population fit indices.

Population versions of NFI and GFI: RNI and G1

A population-based version of the normed fit index NFI, called the relative noncentrality index RNI by Marsh and the fit index FI by Bentler, can be obtained as

$$RNI = 1 - d_k/d_b ,$$

that is, by replacing the Fs in the sample-based formula by the corresponding *d*s. Although this index will usually fall between 0 and 1, it won't always do so-- a d_k can be negative if a sample χ^2 is less than its corresponding df, and this

Table D-2 Comparison of some population-based criteria of model fit, for the same models as in Table D-1

model	d	df	RNI (FI, CFI)	G1	TLI (NNFI)	CI	RMSEA
2-factor	.0021	1	.992	.999	.949	.999	.046
1-factor	.0306	2	.877	.985	.633	.985	.124
a=b	.0279	3	.888	.986	.777	.986	.096
a=b, c=d	.0256	4	.898	.987	.846	.987	.080
a=b=c=d	.0214	5	.914	.989	.897	.989	.065
null	.2497	6	.000	.889	.000	.883	.204

can happen, especially in small samples, where an unusually small χ^2 might well occur by chance. If so, RNI will exceed 1. Bentler has suggested a modification of RNI that simply changes values greater than 1 to 1, and negative values to zero; he labeled this the Comparative Fit Index, CFI.

A population-based analogue of LISREL's GFI has been proposed by Steiger. He calls it Gamma1, and obtains it via the formula:

$$G1 = m/(m + 2d_k) .$$

It is evident that as d_k approaches zero, G1 will approach 1.0. Its behavior at the opposite end of the scale is less immediately obvious, but it seems unlikely that it would ever approach zero--indeed, one would expect d_k to be in general less than 1/2 m, the approximate value of F_s; this would imply a minimum value of .5 for G1. Values for RNI and G1 for the sequence of models used in Table D-1 are given in Table D-2. Note that because χ^2 and df are both involved in obtaining d, these indices, unlike their two sample-based counterparts, do not necessarily always decrease as one moves down the column. In fact, their order of preference among models in these examples corresponds to that of the parsimony adjusted sample-based indices AGFI, AIC, and ECVI. Note also that RNI and G1 yield relatively higher numerical values than NFI and GFI do, making the choice of any arbitrary threshold of fit, such as .90, even less appealing. (Even the null model is barely below .90 in the case of G1!)

Two other population-based indices: CI and TLI

A different way of placing d on a 0 to 1 scale was suggested by McDonald. He calls it the Centrality Index, CI. It is defined as

$$CI = e^{-1/2\, d_k},$$

where e is the constant 2.71828. . ., the base of natural logarithms. When d_k is zero, the exponent will be zero, and CI will equal 1.0. For large d_k, CI will be small--how small will in part be a function of the number of variables in the matrix. For our example, where $m = 4$, d_k is unlikely to exceed one-half that, or 2, which would imply a minimum CI of about .37. In the examples of Table D-2, it can be seen that CI is quite similar to G1--slightly lower by the bottom of the column, but still with a large value for the so-called "null model."

An interesting index, which historically antedates the others, was introduced in 1973 in a factor analysis context by Tucker and Lewis, and reintroduced in 1980 by Bentler and Bonett under the label of Nonnormed Fit Index, or NNFI. It is usually labeled NNFI in the output of model-fitting programs, but is more often referred to elsewhere as the Tucker-Lewis Index, TLI. It has been defined in several different ways, but the fact that it amounts to a parsimony-adjusted version of the RNI can be most easily seen via the definition:

$$TLI = 1 - (d_k/d_b)(df_b/df_k).$$

That is, the TLI is the RNI with the subtractive part multiplied by a ratio of the degrees of freedom of the baseline and current models. Note that this adjustment is applied to the righthand part, in the spirit of LISREL's AGFI, rather than to the index as a whole, as in the case of the PNFI. Note also that a further parsimony adjustment is being made to an index which already contains an implicit allowance for parsimony, as do all the d-based indices. The advantage of the row 5 model over the row 2 model in Table D-2, which reflects the former's greater parsimony, is considerably larger for the TLI than for CI or G1.

The Tucker-Lewis Index, especially when computed from a small sample, may sometimes exceed 1.0 or be negative--this simply reflects sampling error: a value greater than 1.0 may be interpreted as representing a good fit, and one less than zero a poor one. Some prefer simply to adjust such values to 1.0 and 0, respectively; the resulting index may be called the normed Tucker-Lewis Index, or NTLI. Except at the extremes, TLI and NTLI are identical.

For comparison with the other population-based indices, the RMSEA discussed in Chapter 2 is also included in Table D-2. By either of the standards mentioned in the text, the fit of the 2-factor model in the first row of the table would be considered excellent, and that of the parsimonious 5 df model acceptable. The fits of the 3 df and 4 df models might be judged to be marginal, and the fit of the 2 df and the null models clearly unacceptable.

Appendix E: Phantom Variables

A phantom variable (Rindskopf, 1984b) is an unmeasured latent variable with no residual. Phantom variables can be used to trick model-fitting programs into imposing constraints that are not normally within their repertoire.

For example, if one wishes to specify that the path from A to C in Fig. E.1(a) is equal to the square of the path from A to B, one can do it by inserting the phantom variable P in the lower path, as shown in (b), and setting the three paths labeled x to be equal. Or if one wishes the path AC to be three times the value of path AB, in Fig. E.2(a), one can proceed as in (b), fixing the path from A to P to the value 3 and equating xs.

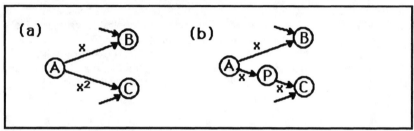

Fig. E.1 Phantom variables example: x^2.

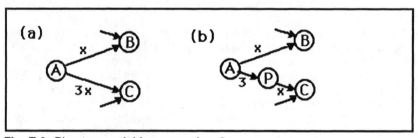

Fig. E.2 Phantom variables example: $3x$.

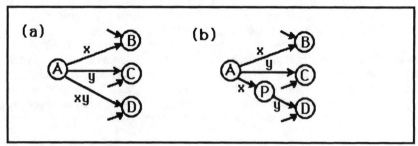

Fig. E.3 Phantom variables example: xy.

If one wants AD to equal the product of paths AB and AC (Fig. E.3(a)), one can proceed as in (b), equating *x*s and *y*s. Or if one wants AD to equal the sum of AB and AC (Fig. E.4(a)), two phantom variables, as shown in (b), will do the trick. A weighted sum of *x* and *y* can be obtained by fixing appropriate values on the paths from A. Many other variations may be achieved, remembering that products are represented by serial paths, and sums by paths in parallel.

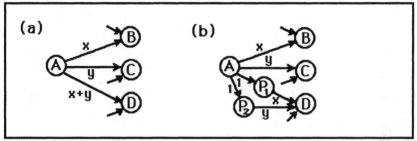

Fig. E.4 Phantom variables example: $x + y$.

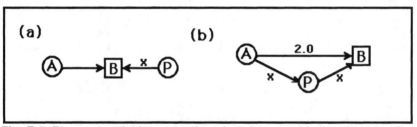

Fig. E.5 Phantom variables examples: keeping a residual variance positive and imposing an inequality constraint.

If one wants to require a residual variance to remain positive, the arrangement shown in Fig. E.5(a) will do it. The variance of the phantom variable is fixed to 1.0, and its contribution to the variance of B is equal to the square of the path coefficient x, and thus must be positive (or zero). Finally, Fig. E.5(b) illustrates the imposition of an inequality constraint using phantom variables. It is desired to make the path from A to B greater than or equal to 2.0. The addition of the phantom variable P and its associated paths will do the trick, since the value of x^2 cannot be negative. If one wishes the path to be *less* than or equal to 2.0, insert a second phantom variable into one of the x paths, with -1.0 on one side and x on the other.

The topic of phantom variables is perhaps not likely to be of lasting importance in SEM. Increasingly, SEM programs include facilities for imposing constraints directly. In the meantime, phantom variables are fun, and can provide ways of escaping the limitations of a particular model-fitting program.

Appendix F: Data Matrix for Thurstone's Box Problem

Box	V1	V2	V3	V4	V5	V6	V7	V8	V9	V10
1	89	50	27	56	34	21	11	8	3	23
2	94	45	38	54	81	34	11	6	4	98
3	69	102	7	103	42	32	11	11	0	99
4	122	96	41	78	61	66	11	11	9	145
5	88	91	92	90	96	82	11	12	11	286
6	182	16	1	96	37	20	14	7	-1	154
7	167	47	30	70	77	36	14	7	7	201
8	169	110	3	118	45	29	14	11	1	60
9	185	87	40	137	77	48	14	10	8	231
10	158	89	104	118	116	94	14	11	11	401
11	137	158	2	149	47	39	14	14	-1	180
12	160	144	41	134	77	85	14	14	8	293
13	164	140	93	143	117	117	15	15	11	492
14	265	36	16	100	43	17	16	7	0	157
15	253	41	37	99	101	26	15	6	7	186
16	229	107	38	143	122	56	17	11	7	351
17	252	74	92	150	138	104	17	11	12	486
18	256	158	4	194	48	43	16	14	0	210
19	249	160	33	226	87	73	17	14	7	432
20	253	165	85	196	151	132	16	13	11	604
21	97	29	18	52	27	28	11	7	0	48
22	91	39	45	57	65	33	11	7	7	124
23	81	80	10	101	28	16	10	12	-1	77
24	83	75	39	83	62	63	12	10	9	148
25	88	108	95	91	96	97	12	12	11	315
26	159	29	7	88	41	16	13	7	1	50
27	166	57	42	86	94	45	14	6	7	223
28	157	90	6	117	47	28	14	10	0	95
29	122	85	35	112	74	63	14	12	7	265
30	171	80	101	114	130	93	14	11	12	393
31	174	163	18	173	39	54	15	14	-1	200
32	158	148	49	158	80	88	14	14	7	383
33	165	142	86	146	101	114	14	14	12	445
34	246	46	13	113	52	4	15	7	-1	107
35	263	38	58	87	110	37	16	6	9	207
36	215	85	41	149	101	65	16	10	6	311
37	231	87	83	144	144	82	17	12	13	483
38	235	176	21	185	48	35	16	14	-2	168
39	252	159	43	199	90	78	16	14	7	418
40	248	157	83	199	139	124	16	14	13	554

Note to Table: Data matrix for 40 boxes on 10 variables, Thurstone's Box Problem example in Chapter 5 (data from Kaiser & Horst, 1975, all scores x 10). The boxes are ordered in the table by increasing X dimension; boxes 21-40 represent a repetition of boxes 1-20, with different errors.

Appendix G: Table of Chi Square

df	P= .99	.90	.70	.50	.30	.10	.05	.01
1	.00	.02	.15	.46	1.07	2.71	3.84	6.64
2	.02	.21	.71	1.39	2.41	4.60	5.99	9.21
3	.12	.58	1.42	2.37	3.66	6.25	7.82	11.34
4	.30	1.06	2.20	3.36	4.88	7.78	9.49	13.28
5	.55	1.61	3.00	4.35	6.06	9.24	11.07	15.09
6	.87	2.20	3.83	5.35	7.23	10.64	12.59	16.81
7	1.24	2.83	4.67	6.35	8.38	12.02	14.07	18.48
8	1.65	3.49	5.53	7.34	9.52	13.36	15.51	20.09
9	2.09	4.17	6.39	8.34	10.66	14.68	16.92	21.67
10	2.56	4.86	7.27	9.34	11.78	15.99	18.31	23.21
11	3.05	5.58	8.15	10.34	12.90	17.28	19.68	24.72
12	3.57	6.30	9.03	11.34	14.01	18.55	21.03	26.22
13	4.11	7.04	9.93	12.34	15.12	19.81	22.36	27.69
14	4.66	7.79	10.82	13.34	16.22	21.06	23.68	29.14
15	5.23	8.55	11.72	14.34	17.32	22.31	25.00	30.58
16	5.81	9.31	12.62	15.34	18.42	23.54	26.30	32.00
17	6.41	10.08	13.53	16.34	19.51	24.77	27.59	33.41
18	7.02	10.86	14.44	17.34	20.60	25.99	28.87	34.80
19	7.63	11.65	15.35	18.34	21.69	27.20	30.14	36.19
20	8.26	12.44	16.27	19.34	22.78	28.41	31.41	37.57
21	8.90	13.24	17.18	20.34	23.86	29.62	32.67	38.93
22	9.54	14.04	18.10	21.34	24.94	30.81	33.92	40.29
23	10.20	14.85	19.02	22.34	26.02	32.01	35.17	41.64
24	10.86	15.66	19.94	23.34	27.10	33.20	36.42	42.98
25	11.52	16.47	20.87	24.34	28.17	34.38	37.65	44.31
26	12.20	17.29	21.79	25.34	29.25	35.56	38.88	45.64
27	12.88	18.11	22.72	26.34	30.32	36.74	40.11	46.96
28	13.56	18.94	23.65	27.34	31.39	37.92	41.34	48.28
29	14.26	19.77	24.58	28.34	32.46	39.09	42.56	49.59
30	14.95	20.60	25.51	29.34	33.53	40.26	43.77	50.89
z	-2.33	-1.28	-.52	.00	.52	1.28	1.64	2.33

Note: Table entries are values of χ^2 exceeded P proportion of the time, for given df. Abridged from Table III, in R. A. Fisher *Statistical Methods for Research Workers* (13th Ed.), Hafner, 1958. Used by permission. For df greater than 30, the quantity $[2\chi^2]^{1/2} - [2df-1]^{1/2}$ may be evaluated as a normal deviate (bottom row).

262

Appendix H: Noncentral Chi Square for Estimating Power

df	Power .50	.60	.70	.80	.90	.99
1	3.84	4.90	6.17	7.85	10.51	18.37
2	4.96	6.22	7.71	9.64	12.66	21.40
3	5.76	7.16	8.79	10.91	14.17	23.52
4	6.42	7.93	9.69	11.94	15.41	25.25
5	6.99	8.59	10.46	12.83	16.47	26.73
6	7.51	9.19	11.15	13.63	17.42	28.05
7	7.97	9.74	11.77	14.35	18.29	29.25
8	8.41	10.24	12.35	15.03	19.09	30.36
9	8.82	10.71	12.90	15.66	19.84	31.40
10	9.20	11.16	13.41	16.25	20.54	32.37
20	12.27	14.72	17.50	20.97	26.14	40.11
30	14.61	17.44	20.62	24.56	30.39	45.95
40	16.57	19.70	23.22	27.55	33.93	50.82
50	18.31	21.71	25.52	30.20	37.07	55.13
60	19.88	23.53	27.60	32.59	39.89	58.99
70	21.32	25.20	29.51	34.78	42.48	62.54
80	22.66	26.75	31.29	36.83	44.89	65.84
90	23.92	29.10	32.95	38.74	47.15	68.93
100	25.12	29.58	34.53	40.55	49.29	71.85

Note: Entries are noncentral χ^2s required for indicated power (top) for given df (side), at .05 significance level. Abridged from Haynam, G. E., Govindarajulu, Z., and Leone, F. C. (1973). "Tables of the cumulative non-central chi-square distribution." In *Selected tables in mathematical statistics* (Vol. 1, pp. 1-42). Providence, RI: American Mathematical Society. Used by permission of the American Mathematical Society

Appendix I: Power of a test of poor fit and sample sizes needed for powers of .80 and .90

df	N 100	N 300	N 500	N needed for power of .80	N needed for power of .90
1	.07	.15	.26	2475	3427
2	.10	.27	.43	1289	1763
3	.13	.36	.56	891	1206
4	.15	.44	.66	690	927
5	.18	.51	.75	569	758
6	.20	.58	.81	487	646
7	.22	.64	.86	428	564
8	.24	.69	.90	384	503
9	.26	.73	.93	349	455
10	.28	.77	.95	320	417
20	.46	.96	~1.00	188	239
30	.61	.99	~1.00	141	177
40	.72	~1.00	~1.00	115	144
50	.81	~1.00	~1.00	99	123
60	.87	~1.00	~1.00	88	109
70	.91	~1.00	~1.00	80	98
80	.94	~1.00	~1.00	73	90
90	.96	~1.00	~1.00	68	83
100	.97	~1.00	~1.00	64	78

Note: Lefthand columns: the power to reject the hypothesis of poor fit (RMSEA $\geq$ .10), given population RMSEA of .05, for indicated sample size (top) and df (side). Assumes .05 significance level. Righthand columns: Ns required for powers of .80 and .90 for this test. Follows method of MacCallum, Browne, and Sugawara (1996).

Answers to Exercises

Chapter 1

1 & 2. Various legitimate diagrams are possible, depending on assumptions made--for examples, those shown:

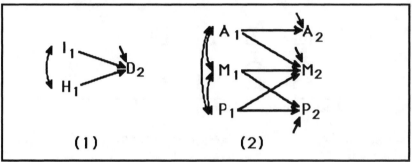

Fig. J.1 Problems 1 & 2--possible answers.

3. An example: Stress (A) leads to anxiety (B), which in turn is reflected in responses to a questionnaire scale (C) and a physiological measure (D). The residual arrows mean that anxiety is also affected by factors other than stress as measured, and that questionnaire scores and the physiological measurement do not reflect anxiety perfectly.

4. Source variables: A, B, W, X, Y, Z. Downstream variables: C, D, E, F, G.

5. That it is completely determined by A and B.

6. $r_{AF} = ae + bf + hcf$; $r_{DG} = cdg + bhdg$; $r_{CE} = ahd$; $r_{EF} = dcf + dhbf + dhae$.

7. $s^2_C = a^2 + i^2$; $s^2_D = b^2 + c^2 + 2bhc$; $s^2_F = e^2 + f^2 + 2eabf + 2eahcf + j^2$.

8. No. There are (4 x 5)/2 = 10 observed covariances, and 12 unknowns--a, b, c, d, e, f, g, h, i, j, k, l. Or, in terms of correlations, there are 6 observed correlations and 8 unknown paths to be solved (excluding residuals).

9. $c_{CD} = a^* s^2_A b^* + a^* c_{AB} c^*$
   $c_{FG} = e^*a^* c_{AB} d^*g^* + f^*b^* c_{AB} d^*g^* + f^*c^* s^2_B d^*g^*$
   $c_{AG} = c_{AB} d^*g^*$
   $s^2_G = g^{*2} s^2_E + l^{*2} s^2_Z$ [or] $g^{*2} k^{*2} s^2_Y + g^{*2} d^{*2} s^2_B + l^{*2} s^2_Z$
   $s^2_D = b^{*2} s^2_A + c^{*2} s^2_B + 2b^*c^* c_{AB}$

10. $D = bA + cB$; $E = dB + kY$; $F = eC + fD + jX$.

11. For example: (additional labeling ok)

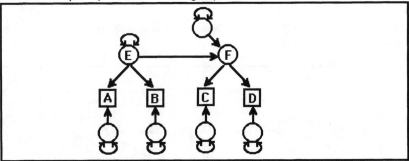

Fig J.2 RAM path diagram, problem 11.

12. $r_{BC} = c + ba = .70$; $r_{CD} = a^2 + cba = .48$; $r_{BD} = ba = .30$.
    $a = .6$; $b = .5$; $c = .4$ [or] $a = -.6$; $b = -.5$; $c = .4$.
    $d = \sqrt{(1 - .36)} = .8$; $e = \sqrt{(1 - .36 - .16 - .24)} = .49$.

13. $ab \times bc/ac = b^2 = .42 \times .14/.12 = .49$; $b = .7$.
    $a = .6$; $c = .2$; [or] $b = -.7$; $a = -.6$; $c = -.2$.

Chapter 2

Note: In this and the next two chapters, suggestions are sometimes given regarding problem setups for path-oriented and for structural equation oriented programs. This should cover most SEM programs that a beginner is likely to be using, including SIMPLIS, EQS, CALIS, AMOS, SEPATH and RAMONA. If you are using Mx, translate your path diagram into the McArdle-McDonald matrices A, S, and F and proceed as in the example in the text.

1. The results for the first complete cycle and for the next three major cycles are:

	a	b	c	r_{AC}	r_{AD}	r_{CD}	criterion
Cycle 1	.5	.5	.5	.25	.25	.25	.035
1a	.501	.5	.5	.2505	.2505	.25	.0348005
1b	.5	.501	.5	.2505	.25	.2505	.0348505
1c	.5	.5	.501	.25	.2505	.2505	.0347505*
Cycle 2	.5	.5	.6	.25	.30	.30	.015
Cycle 3	.6	.5	.6	.30	.36	.30	.0041
Cycle 4	.6	.5	.7	.30	.42	.35	.0004

2. The calculated values, using the equations on p. 14, are a = .5855, b = .5223, and c = .6831. The iterative solution of .6, .5, and .7 at cycle 4 is approaching these, and at this point is accurate to one decimal place.

3. For example:

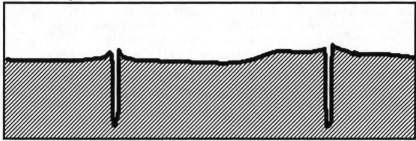

Fig. J.3 A difficult terrain for a simple search program.

4. **A**

	A	B	C	D
A	0	0	0	0
B	a	0	0	0
C	0	b	0	0
D	0	c	0	0

S

	A	B	C	D
A	1	0	0	0
B	0	x^2	0	0
C	0	0	y^2	0
D	0	0	0	z^2

F

	A	B	C	D
A	1	0	0	0
B	0	1	0	0
C	0	0	1	0

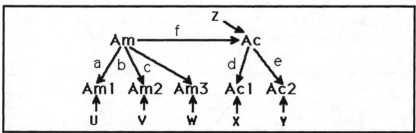

Fig. J.4 Path model for Problem 5.

5. *Hints:* For path-oriented programs, follow the path model above. There will be 4 paths from Am (to Am1, Am2, Am3, and Ac) and 2 paths from Ac (to Ac1 and Ac2), plus residuals. For structural equation oriented programs, there will be 6 structural equations--one for each of the 5 observed variables and one

for Ac, each including a residual term. The problem is like that in Fig. 2.6, but with one more indicator for the source latent variable.

Results: Standardized paths: a = .920, b = .761, c = .652, d = .879, e = .683, f = .356. Residual variances: U = .153, V = .420, W = .575, X = .228, Y = .534, Z = .873. $\chi^2 = 5.80$, 4 df, p > .20. The model is consistent with the data. It implies that a little more than one third (.356) of ambition translates into achievement, when both are expressed in standard-score units.

6. Model 1 ($\chi^2 = 16.21$, 7df) is a significantly poor fit to the data, and a significantly worse fit than any of the other three (χ^2_{diff} 8.09, 2df; 13.71, 3df; 14.93, 6df). None of the others can be rejected (p > .05 for each), but the third fits significantly better than the second (χ^2_{diff} 5.62, 1df).

7.

model	χ^2	unknowns	df	RMSEA
null	25.00	0	10	.123
1.	16.21	3	7	.115
2.	8.12	5	5	.079
3.	2.50	6	4	.000
4.	1.28	9	1	.053

Model 4 in absolute terms is the closest fit ($\chi^2 = 1.28$), but involves many parameters. According to RMSEA, it is an acceptable but not an excellent fit. Model 3 is relatively parsimonious, and an excellent fit by RMSEA, for which the null model and Model 1 are unacceptable and Model 2 marginally acceptable.

8. The implied matrix will consist of .36s within and .18s across factors. $\chi^2 = 5.08$. As a test of a specific hypothesized path (1 df) the power would be 61%; an N of about 77 would be needed for 80% power (7.85/5.08 x 50).

9.

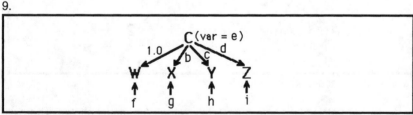

Fig. J.5 Path diagram for problem 9.

Hints: For path input--there are 4 paths, from C to each of W, X, Y, and Z (plus residuals). For structural equation input--there are 4 structural equations, for W, X, Y, and Z. In both, path *a* is fixed in value to 1.0, and there is one variance to solve for, *e*. Don't forget to specify a least squares solution.

    Results: Unstandardized: $a^* = 1.000$, $b^* = 1.120$, $c^* = 1.351$, $d^* = .829$, $e^* = .364$. Standardized: $a = .604$, $b = .676$, $c = .815$, $d = .500$, $e = 1.00$. Residual variances: $f = .636$, $g = .543$ $h = .335$, $I = .749$.

10. $a = 1.0 \times \sqrt{.364}/1 = .603$; $b = 1.120 \times \sqrt{.364}/1 = .676$, etc.

11. 10 observed statistics minus 8 parameters = 2 df. From the Table: Power = .43; N = 1289 needed for power of .80.

Chapter 3

1. *Hints:* Like Fig. 3.5, except with a third observed variable. Path input-- 3 paths (plus residuals). Structural equation input--equations for each of the 3 observed variables. For parallel tests, specify equalities for both paths and residuals, for tau-equivalence, for paths only. (The method of imposing equality varies with the program--some do it by special statement, "constraint," "set," "let," etc., some just by giving variables the same name.)

    Goodness of fit (maximum likelihood solution):

    parallel: $\chi^2 = 10.35$, 4 df, $p < .05$

    tau-equivalent: $\chi^2 = 5.96$, 2 df, $p > .05$

Reject hypothesis that tests are parallel; hypothesis of tau-equivalence cannot be rejected (but with this small sample, this does not mean that it fits very well--in fact the RMSEA of .241 would suggest a poor approximation.)

2. A model with the three paths from F_2 constrained to be equal has a χ^2 of 288.21 for 26 df; thus $\chi^2_{diff} = 62.00$ with 2df; with this huge sample we can conclude that the modest differences are real ones.

3. Within trait across method: .71, .53, .43, .48, .42, .22, .46, .24, .31; median = .43.

    Within method across trait: .37, -.24, -.14, .37, -.15, -.19, .23, -.05, -.12; median absolute value = .19.

    Across method and trait: .35, -.18, -.15, .39, -.27, -.31, .31, -.22, -.10, .17, -.04, -.13, .36, -.15, -.25, .09, -.04, -.11; median absolute value = .175. Suggests reasonable convergent and discriminant validity of traits, and not a great deal of influence of measurement method.

4. *Hints:* Full model: for path input--9 paths from trait factors, 9 from method factors, 9 residuals, 6 factor variances fixed to 1.0, 3 covariances among trait factors; for structural equations--9 equations, each involving 2 factors and a

residual, variances and covariances as above.
Goodness of fit (maximum likelihood solution):

both kinds of factors	$\chi^2 = 14.15$, 15 df, p > .50
trait only:	$\chi^2 = 21.94$, 24 df, p > .50
method only:	$\chi^2 = 232.77$, 27 df p < .001

Trait factors, with or without method factors, fit well. Method factors alone do not yield an acceptable fit. Method factors do not add significantly to the fit of trait factors ($\chi^2_{diff} = 7.79$, 9 df, p > .50).

5.

CZ	r_{XZ}	r_{XY}	$r_{XY \cdot Z}$
[.7	.504	.5184	.3544]
.9	.648	.5184	.1698
1.0	.72	.5184	.0
.5	.36	.5184	.4467
.0	.00	.5184	.5184

Only as CZ approaches 1.0 does $r_{XY \cdot Z}$ become small. With values of .5 or less it is only slightly reduced.

6 & 7.

8. Line 2 solution: $\chi^2 = 18.89$, 28 df. Without z for occupational aspiration: $\chi^2 = 30.62$, 29 df, $\chi^2_{diff} = 11.73$, 1 df, p < .001. Without z for educational aspiration: $\chi^2 = 19.32$, 29 df; $\chi^2_{diff} = .43$, 1 df, p > .50. Residual correlation of the friends' educational aspirations is not statistically significant, but that for occupational aspirations is.

9. Show that inclusion of covariances between the residuals from RPA and REA or ROA, and FPA and FEA or FOA, leads to a significant decrease in χ^2.

10. $V_A = V_X + V_S$ $C_{AC,AD} = hV_{XZ} + hV_{ZS}$
$C_{B,AC} = 0$ $V_Y = c^2V_X + d^2V_Z + 2cdi + eV_{XZ} + V_W$

Chapter 4

1. *Hints:* Path input--5 factors, one with paths to 8 variables, 4 with paths to 2 each (plus 8 residuals). Structural equation input--8 equations, each with the general factor, a specific factor, and a residual. In both cases--12 equalities imposed, 5 factor variances set to 1.0, no factor covariances.
     Result: $\chi^2 = 72.14$, 24 df, p < .001; reject such a model.

2. *Hint:* remove 4 equality constraints.

   Result: $\chi^2 = 65.53$, 20 df. $\chi^2_{diff} = 6.61$, 4 df, $p > .10$. This model does not fit significantly better.

3. With different structural and measurement models (text), $\chi^2 = 24.56$, with 32 df. Requiring the measurement model to be the same yields $\chi^2 = 119.33$ with 56 df; $\chi^2_{diff} = 94.77$, with 24 df, $p < .001$. The same measurement model does not fit in both groups.

4. *Hint:* Four groups, differing only in the fixed genetic correlation, with appropriate within-group equality constraints.

   Result: For the original solution based on correlations, χ^2 is 74.83 with 69 df, $p > .20$. For the hypothesis of parallel tests, χ^2 is 91.59 with 79 df, $p > .15$. So $\chi^2_{diff} = 16.76$, 10 df, $p > .05$. Thus, one would not reject the hypothesis that the three scales are parallel tests of numerical ability. (Under this model, the genetic paths *a* are .665, the residual variances *b* are .561, and the residual covariances are *c* = .209 across tests within persons, *d* = .244 for the same test across persons, and *e* = .150 across both tests and persons.)

5. A single-factor model with factor pattern the same for both sexes, but latent variable mean and variance and residual variances allowed to differ, fits the data quite adequately: $\chi^2 = 9.25$, 10 df, $p > .50$; RMSEA = 0. Allowing the factor patterns to differ between men and women does not significantly improve the fit: $\chi^2 = 4.61$, 7 df; $\chi^2_{diff} = 4.64$, 3 df, $p \approx .20$. (If in the first condition the residuals are also required to be equal, the fit is still satisfactory: $\chi^2 = 15.71$, 14 df, $p > .30$.)

6. The nonlinear model fits a bit better than the original linear model, but still not acceptably ($\chi^2 = 17.30$, 8 df, $p < .03$). The RMSEA of .083 is marginal, and a poor fit in the population cannot be rejected (upper 90% CI = .138). The two models are not nested, so a direct chi-square test of the difference between them cannot be made.

Chapter 5

1. Eigenvalues: 1.6912, .9458, .7866, .5764

Eigenvectors:

-.601	.109	.282	-.740
-.476	.256	-.834	.107
.277	.951	.128	-.037
-.579	.133	.456	.663

Principal Factors:

-.781	.106	.250	-.562
-.620	.249	-.740	.081
.361	.925	.114	-.028
-.753	.129	.404	.503

R_1 .61
.48 .38
-.28 -.22 .13
.59 .47 -.27 .57

R_2 .62
.51 .45
-.18 .01 .99
.60 .50 -.15 .58

R_3 .68
.33 .99
-.16 -.08 1.00
.70 .20 -.11 .75

$R_4 = R$

Successive matrices do improve in fit, but much of this improvement, after R_1, is in fitting the diagonal elements.

2. R_r

.49	.28	-.14	.42
.28	.16	-.08	.24
-.14	-.08	.04	-.12
.42	.24	-.12	.36

Eigenvalues: 1.0500, .0000, .0000, .0000

v_1 .683
.390
-.195
.586

P_1 .700
.400
-.200
.600

PP' reconstructs R_r exactly.

3. SMCs: .962, .800, .962, .791, .842

4. Eigenvalues: 2.867, 1.798, .217, .098, .019. Two factors by either criterion.

5. First factor loadings: .977, .137, .984, .530, .132. $\chi^2 = 243.77$, 10 df, $p < .001$. Reject hypothesis of one common factor.

6. P

.79	.06
.89	-.06
.07	.68
-.08	.61

F

1.00	.57
.57	1.00

S

.82	.51
.85	.45
.45	.72
.26	.56

7.

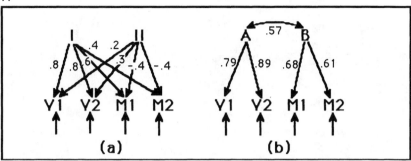

Fig. J.6 Path diagrams for unrotated (a) and rotated (b) factors.

8. Path diagram h²s: .62, .79, .46, .37.
   h²s from $\mathbf{P}_0$ rows: .68, .73, .52, .32.

The two are similar but not identical. The h²s from the path diagram may be either larger or smaller because some of the small omitted paths are positive and some negative, resulting in covariance contributions of both signs.

9. $\mathbf{P}_{varimax}$ .78 .28 $\mathbf{P}_{oblimin}$ .79 .07 $\mathbf{P}_{orthob}$ .78 .07
    .83 .19   .88 -.04   .88 -.05
    .28 .67   .10 .66   .06 .68
    .11 .55   -.05 .59   -.09 .61

   $\mathbf{F}_{varimax}$ 1.00 .00 $\mathbf{F}_{oblimin}$ 1.00 .52 $\mathbf{F}_{orthob}$ 1.00 .56
    .00 1.00   .52 1.00   .56 1.00

Either oblique **P** is similar to the Problem 6 solution. The orthogonal **P** has similar high loadings, but its low loadings are not as close to zero.

10.

Chapter 6

1. $\mathbf{P}_{promax}$ .77 .09   **F** 1.00 .53
    .86 -.02   .53 1.00
    .07 .68
    -.08 .60   Quite similar to other oblique solutions

2. Add a row .17 .55 to **S** and a row -.14 .62 to **P**.

3. P_{12} .56
        .74
        .88

4. $P_{02} = P_{01}P_{12}$.   The coefficients are .52, .45, .78, .44, .56, and .40.

5. **P**
        .52 .01 .01 .28
        .45 .01 -.00 .24
        .78 .01 .44 .16
        .44 .61 .01 .00
        .56 .02 .55 -.03
        .40 .62 -.01 -.00

6. **P**   .13 .98
     -.91 -.09
     -.16 -.98
      .82 .04
      .86 .39

Large coefficients on the first factor correspond to equations that give relatively large weights to X, and on the second, to equations that give relatively large weights to X^2.

7.

Chapter 7

1. *Hint:* A path model for part (a) is shown in Fig. J.7.

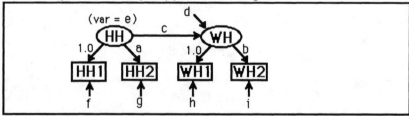

Fig. J.7 Path diagram for problem 1, part (a).

The three are equivalent models. All fits identical ($\chi^2 = 1.78$, 1 df, p > .10), but path values and residual variances change in the structural model.

2. AC = .6, BC = .94, AB = -.56. (Exact solution: BC = .9375 and AB = -.5625; possible equations BC = AC/(1 - AC^2), AB = -BC x AC.)

3. **P** .778 Al   Eigenvalues: 3.12, .67, .15, .06
        -.999 Ben   (factor solution--principal factors
         .943 Carl   with iteration for communalities,
        -.643 Zach   starting from SMCs)

The data are fairly well described by a single factor, on which Carl and Al are alike and opposite to Ben and Zach.

4. For example, one might obtain a measure of motor skill for a sample of persons under a number of different conditions, and intercorrelate and factor the conditions to study the major dimensions of their influence on motor skill.

5. Conceivably, but it is perhaps better described as a three-mode analysis carried out in two groups (college and noncollege). The three modes are persons, occasions ('72, '74, '76), and attitudes (toward busing, criminals, jobs).

6.

References

Akaike, H. (1987). Factor analysis and AIC. *Psychometrika, 52*, 317-332.

Allison, P. D. (2000). Multiple imputation for missing data: A cautionary tale. *Sociological Methods & Research, 28*, 301-309.

Allison, P. D. (2002). *Missing data.* Thousand Oaks, CA: Sage.

Alwin, D. F. (1988). Measurement and the interpretation of effects in structural equation models. In J. S. Long (Ed.), *Common problems/proper solutions: Avoiding errors in quantitative research* (pp. 15-45). Thousand Oaks, CA: Sage.

Anderson, J. C., & Gerbing, D. W. (1982). Some methods for respecifying measurement models to obtain unidimensional construct measurement. *Journal of Marketing Research, 19*, 453-460.

Anderson, J. C., & Gerbing, D. W. (1984). The effect of sampling error on convergence, improper solutions, and goodness-of-fit indices for maximum likelihood confirmatory factor analysis. *Psychometrika, 49*, 155-173.

Anderson, J. C., & Gerbing, D. W. (1988). Structural equation modeling in practice: A review and recommended two-step approach. *Psychological Bulletin, 103*, 411-423.

Anderson, J. C., Gerbing, D. W., & Hunter, J. E. (1987). On the assessment of unidimensional measurement: Internal and external consistency, and overall consistency criteria. *Journal of Marketing Research, 24*, 432-437.

Anderson, R. D. (1996). An evaluation of the Satorra-Bentler distributional misspecification correction applied to the McDonald fit index. *Structural Equation Modeling, 3*, 203-227.

Arbuckle, J. L. (1996). Full information estimation in the presence of incomplete data. In G. A. Marcoulides & R. E. Schumacker (Eds.), *Advanced structural equation modeling: Issues and techniques* (pp. 243-277). Mahwah, NJ: Lawrence Erlbaum Associates.

Arbuckle, J. L., & Wothke, W. (1999). *Amos 4.0 user's guide.* Chicago: SPSS Inc.

Arminger, G., Clogg, C.C., & Sobel, M. E. (Eds.) (1995). *Handbook of statistical modeling for the social and behavioral sciences.* New York: Plenum.

Asher, H. B. (1983). *Causal modeling* (2nd ed.). Beverly Hills, CA: Sage.

Austin, J. T., & Calderón, R. F. (1996). Theoretical and technical contributions to structural equation modeling: An updated annotated bibliography. *Structural Equation Modeling, 3*, 105-175.

Babakus, E., Ferguson, C. E., Jr., & Jöreskog, K. G. (1987). The sensitivity of confirmatory maximum likelihood factor analysis to violations of measurement scale and distributional assumptions. *Journal of Marketing Research, 24*, 222-228.

Bagozzi, R. P., & Yi, Y. (1989). On the use of structural equation models in experimental designs. *Journal of Marketing Research, 26*, 271-284.

Bagozzi, R. P., & Yi, Y. (1990). Assessing method variance in multitrait-multimethod matrices: The case of self-reported affect and perceptions at work. *Journal of Applied Psychology, 75,* 547-560.

Baker, R. L., Mednick, B., & Brock, W. (1984). An application of causal modeling techniques to prospective longitudinal data bases. In S. A. Mednick, M. Harway & K. M. Finello (Eds.), *Handbook of longitudinal research. Vol. I: Birth and childhood cohorts* (pp.106-132). New York: Praeger.

Bandalos, D. L. (1993). Factors influencing cross-validation of confirmatory factor analysis models. *Multivariate Behavioral Research, 28,* 351-374.

Bartholomew, D. J. (1987). *Latent variable models and factor analysis.* New York: Oxford University Press.

Bartholomew, D. J. (2002). Old and new approaches to latent variable modeling. In G. A. Marcoulides & I. Moustaki (Eds.), *Latent variable and latent structure models* (pp.1-13). Mahwah, NJ: Lawrence Erlbaum Associates.

Baumrind, D. (1983). Specious causal attributions in the social sciences: The reformulated stepping-stone theory of heroin use as exemplar. *Journal of Personality and Social Psychology, 45,* 1289-1298.

Bekker, P. A., Merckens, A., & Wansbeek, T. J. (1994). *Identification, equivalent models, and computer algebra.* San Diego, CA: Academic Press.

Benson, J., & Bandalos, D. L. (1992). Second-order confirmatory factor analysis of the *Reactions to Tests* scale with cross-validation. *Multivariate Behavioral Research, 27,* 459-487.

Benson, J., & Fleishman, J. A. (1994). The robustness of maximum likelihood and distribution-free estimators to non-normality in confirmatory factor analysis. *Quality & Quantity, 28,* 117-136.

Bentler, P. M. (1980). Multivariate analysis with latent variables: Causal modeling. *Annual Review of Psychology, 31,* 419-456.

Bentler, P. M. (1986). Structural modeling and *Psychometrika:* An historical perspective on growth and achievements. *Psychometrika, 51,* 35-51.

Bentler, P. M. (1990). Comparative fit indexes in structural models. *Psychological Bulletin, 107,* 238-246.

Bentler, P. M. (1995). *EQS structural equations program manual.* Encino CA: Multivariate Software.

Bentler, P. M., & Bonett, D. G. (1980). Significance tests and goodness of fit in the analysis of covariance structures. *Psychological Bulletin, 88,* 588-606.

Bentler, P. M., & Chou, C.-P. (1990). Model search with TETRAD II and EQS. *Sociological Methods & Research, 19,* 67-79.

Bentler, P. M., & Dudgeon, P. (1996). Covariance structure analysis: Statistical practice, theory, and directions. *Annual Review of Psychology, 47,* 563-592.

Bentler, P. M., & Huba, G. J. (1979). Simple minitheories of love. *Journal of Personality and Social Psychology, 37,* 124-130.

Bentler, P. M., & Lee, S.-Y. (1979). A statistical development of three-mode factor analysis. *British Journal of Mathematical and Statistical Psychology, 32,* 87-104.

Bentler, P. M., & McClain, J. (1976). A multitrait-multimethod analysis of reflection-impulsivity. *Child Development, 47,* 218-226.

Bentler, P. M., & Weeks, D. G. (1980). Linear structural equations with latent variables. *Psychometrika, 45,* 289-308.

Bentler, P. M., & Weeks, D. G. (1985). Some comments on structural equation models. *British Journal of Mathematical and Statistical Psychology, 38,* 120-121.

Bentler, P. M., & Woodward, J. A. (1978). A head start reevaluation: Positive effects are not yet demonstrable. *Evaluation Quarterly, 2,* 493-510.

Bentler, P. M., & Yuan, K.-H. (1997). Optimal conditionally unbiased equivariant factor score estimators. In M. Berkane (Ed.), *Latent variable modeling and applications to causality* (pp. 259-281). New York: Springer-Verlag.

Bentler, P. M., & Yuan, K.-H. (1998). Tests for linear trend in the smallest eigenvalues of the correlation matrix. *Psychometrika, 63,* 131-144.

Berkane, M. (Ed.) (1997). *Latent variable modeling and applications to causality.* New York: Springer-Verlag.

Berkane, M., & Bentler, P. M. (1987). Distribution of kurtoses, with estimates and tests of homogeneity of kurtosis. *Statistics and Probability Letters, 5,* 201-207.

Bickley, P. G., Keith, T. Z., & Wolfle, L. M. (1995). The three-stratum theory of cognitive abilities: Test of the structure of intelligence across the life span. *Intelligence, 20,* 309-328.

Biddle, B. J., & Marlin, M. M. (1987). Causality, confirmation, credulity, and structural equation modeling. *Child Development, 58,* 4-17.

Bielby, W. T. (1986). Arbitrary metrics in multiple-indicator models of latent variables. *Sociological Methods & Research, 15,* 3-23.

Blom, P. & Christoffersson, A. (2001). Estimation of nonlinear structural equation models using empirical characteristic functions. In R. Cudeck, S. du Toit, & D. Sörbom (Eds.), *Structural equation modeling: Present and future. A Festschrift in honor of Karl Jöreskog* (pp. 443-460). Lincolnwood IL: Scientific Software International.

Bollen, K. A. (1987). Outliers and improper solutions: A confirmatory factor analysis example. *Sociological Methods & Research, 15,* 375-384.

Bollen, K. A. (1989a). A new incremental fit index for general structural equation models. *Sociological Methods & Research, 17,* 303-316.

Bollen, K. A. (1989b). *Structural equations with latent variables.* New York: Wiley.

Bollen, K. A. (1995). Structural equation models that are nonlinear in latent variables: A least-squares estimator. In P. Marsden (Ed.), *Sociological Methodology 1995* (pp. 223-251). Oxford: Blackwell.

Bollen, K. A. (2001). Two-stage least squares and latent variable models: Simultaneous estimation and robustness to misspecifications. In R. Cudeck, S. du Toit, & D. Sörbom (Eds.), *Structural equation modeling: Present and future. A Festschrift in honor of Karl Jöreskog* (pp. 119-138). Lincolnwood IL: Scientific Software International.

Bollen, K. A. (2002). Latent variables in psychology and the social sciences. *Annual Review of Psychology, 53*, 605-634.

Bollen, K. A., & Jöreskog, K. G. (1985). Uniqueness does not imply identification. *Sociological Methods & Research, 14*, 155-163.

Bollen, K., & Lennox, R. (1991). Conventional wisdom on measurement: A structural equation perspective. *Psychological Bulletin, 110*, 305-314.

Bollen, K. A., & Liang, J. (1988). Some properties of Hoelter's CN. *Sociological Methods & Research, 16*, 492-503.

Bollen, K. A., & Long, J. S. (Eds.) (1993). *Testing structural equation models.* Thousand Oaks, CA: Sage.

Bollen, K. A., & Stine, R. A. (1993). Bootstrapping goodness-of-fit measures in structural equation models. In K. A. Bollen & J. S. Long (Eds.), *Testing structural equation models* (pp. 111-135). Thousand Oaks, CA: Sage.

Bollen, K. A., & Ting, K.-F. (2000). A tetrad test for causal indicators. *Psychological Methods, 5*, 3-22.

Boomsma, A. (1982). The robustness of LISREL against small sample sizes in factor analysis models. In K. G. Jöreskog & H. Wold (Eds.), *Systems under indirect observation* (Part I, pp. 149-174). Amsterdam: North-Holland.

Boomsma, A. (1985). Nonconvergence, improper solutions, and starting values in LISREL maximum likelihood estimation. *Psychometrika, 50*, 229-242.

Boomsma, A. (2000). Reporting analyses of covariance structures. *Structural Equation Modeling, 7*, 461-483.

Boomsma, A., & Hoogland, J. J. (2001). The robustness of LISREL modeling revisited. In R. Cudeck, S. du Toit, & D. Sörbom (Eds.), *Structural equation modeling: Present and future. A Festschrift in honor of Karl Jöreskog* (pp. 139-168). Lincolnwood IL: Scientific Software International.

Boomsma, D. I., Martin, N. G., & Neale, M. C. (Eds.) (1989). Genetic analysis of twin and family data: Structural modeling using LISREL. *Behavior Genetics, 19*, 3-161.

Bouchard, T.J., Jr., & Loehlin, J. C. (2001). Genes, evolution, and personality. *Behavior Genetics, 31*, 243-273.

Bozdogan, H. (1987). Model selection and Akaike's Information Criterion (AIC): The general theory and its analytical extensions. *Psychometrika, 52*, 345-370.

Bracht, G. H., & Hopkins, K. D. (1972). Stability of educational achievement. In G. H. Bracht, K. D. Hopkins, & J. C. Stanley (Eds.), *Perspectives in educational and psychological measurement* (pp. 254-258). Englewood Cliffs, NJ: Prentice-Hall.

Breckler, S. J. (1990). Applications of covariance structure modeling in psychology: Cause for concern? *Psychological Bulletin, 107*, 260-273.

Breivik, E., & Olsson, U. H. (2001). Adding variables to improve fit: The effect of model size on fit assessment in LISREL. In R. Cudeck, S. du Toit, & D. Sörbom (Eds.), *Structural equation modeling: Present and future. A Festschrift in honor of Karl Jöreskog* (pp. 169-194). Lincolnwood IL: Scientific Software International.

Brito, C., & Pearl, J. (2002). A new identification condition for recursive models with correlated errors. *Structural Equation Modeling, 9*, 459-474.

Brown, R. L. (1994). Efficacy of the indirect approach for estimating structural equation models with missing data: A comparison of five methods. *Structural Equation Modeling, 1*, 287-316.

Browne, M. W. (1984). Asymptotically distribution-free methods for the analysis of covariance structures. *British Journal of Mathematical and Statistical Psychology, 37*, 62-83.

Browne, M. W. (1987). Robustness of statistical inference in factor analysis and related models. *Psychometrika, 74*, 375-384.

Browne, M. W. (2001). An overview of analytic rotation in exploratory factor analysis. *Multivariate Behavioral Research, 36*, 111-150.

Browne, M. W., & Arminger, G. (1995). Specification and estimation of mean- and covariance-structure models. In G. Arminger, C. C. Clogg, & M. E. Sobel (Eds.), *Handbook of statistical modeling for the social and behavioral sciences* (pp. 185-249). New York: Plenum.

Browne, M. W., & Cudeck, R. (1993). Alternative ways of assessing model fit. In K. A. Bollen & J. S. Long (Eds.), *Testing structural equation models* (pp. 136-162). Thousand Oaks, CA: Sage.

Browne, M. W., & du Toit, S. H. C. (1991). Models for learning data. In L. M. Collins & J. L. Horn (Eds.), *Best methods for the analysis of change* (pp. 47-68). Washington DC: American Psychological Association.

Browne, M. W., & du Toit, S. H. C. (1992). Automated fitting of nonstandard models. *Multivariate Behavioral Research, 27*, 269-300.

Browne, M. W., MacCallum, R. C., Kim, C.-T., Andersen, B. L., & Glaser, R. (2002). When fit indices and residuals are incompatible. *Psychological Methods, 7*, 403-421.

Bryk, A. S., & Raudenbush, S. W. (1992). *Hierarchical linear models: Applications and data analysis.* Thousand Oaks, CA: Sage.

Bullock, H. E., Harlow, L. L., & Mulaik, S. A. (1994). Causation issues in structural equation modeling research. *Structural Equation Modeling, 1*, 253-267.

Burt, R. S. (1981). A note on interpretational confounding of unobserved variables in structural equation models. In P. V. Marsden (Ed.), *Linear models in social research* (pp. 299-318). Beverly Hills, CA: Sage.

Busemeyer, J. R., & Jones, L. E. (1983). Analysis of multiplicative combination rules when the causal variables are measured with error. *Psychological Bulletin, 93*, 549-562.

Byrne, B. M. (1994). *Structural equation modeling with EQS and EQS/Windows.* Thousand Oaks, CA: Sage.

Byrne, B. M. (1998). *Structural equation modeling with LISREL, PRELIS, and SIMPLIS: Basic concepts, applications, and programming.* Mahwah, NJ: Lawrence Erlbaum Associates.

Byrne, B. M. (2001). *Structural equation modeling with AMOS: Basic concepts, applications, and programming.* Mahwah, NJ: Lawrence Erlbaum Associates.

Byrne, B. M., & Goffin, R. D. (1993). Modeling MTMM data from additive and multiplicative covariance structures: An audit of construct validity concordance. *Multivariate Behavioral Research, 28*, 67-96.

Campbell, D. T., & Fiske, D. W. (1959). Convergent and discriminant validation by the multitrait-multimethod matrix. *Psychological Bulletin, 56*, 81-105.

Cattell, R. B. (1952). The three basic factor-analytic research designs--their interrelations and derivatives. *Psychological Bulletin, 49*, 499-520.

Cattell, R. B. (1966a). The scree test for the number of factors. *Multivariate Behavioral Research, 1*, 245-276.

Cattell, R. B. (1966b). The data box: Its ordering of total resources in terms of possible relational systems. In R. B. Cattell (Ed.), *Handbook of multivariate experimental psychology* (pp. 67-128). Chicago: Rand McNally.

Cattell, R. B. (1978). *The scientific use of factor analysis.* New York: Plenum.

Cattell, R. B., & Cross, K. P. (1952). Comparison of ergic and self-sentiment structures found in dynamic traits by R- and P-techniques. *Journal of Personality, 21*, 250-271.

Cattell, R. B., & Jaspers, J. (1967). A general plasmode (No. 30-10-5-2) for factor analytic exercises and research. *Multivariate Behavioral Research Monographs, 67-3*, 1-211.

Cattell, R. B., & Muerle, J. L. (1960). The "maxplane" program for factor rotation to oblique simple structure. *Educational and Psychological Measurement, 20*, 569-590.

Cattell, R. B., & Sullivan, W. (1962). The scientific nature of factors: A demonstration by cups of coffee. *Behavioral Science, 7*, 184-193.

Chan, W., Ho, R. M., Leung, K., Chan, D. K.-S., & Yung, Y.-F. (1999). An alternative method for evaluating congruence coefficients with Procrustes rotation: A bootstrap procedure. *Psychological Methods, 4*, 378-402.

Cheong, J., MacKinnon, D. P., & Khoo, S. T. (2003). Investigation of mediational processes using parallel process latent growth curve modeling. *Structural Equation Modeling, 10*, 238-262.

Cheung, G. W., & Rensvold, R. B. (2002). Evaluating goodness-of-fit indexes for testing measurement invariance. *Structural Equation Modeling, 9*, 233-255.

Chin, W. W., & Newsted, P. R. (1999). Structural equation modeling analysis with small samples using partial least squares. In R. H. Hoyle (Ed.) *Statistical strategies for small sample research* (pp. 307-341). Thousand Oaks, CA: Sage.

Chou, C.-P., & Bentler, P. M. (1995). Estimates and tests in structural equation modeling. In R. H. Hoyle (Ed.), *Structural equation modeling: Concepts, issues, and applications* (pp. 37-55). Thousand Oaks, CA: Sage.

Chou, C.-P., Bentler, P. M., & Satorra, A. (1991). Scaled test statistics and robust standard errors for non-normal data in covariance structure analysis: A Monte Carlo study. *British Journal of Mathematical and Statistical Psychology, 44,* 347-357.

Cliff, N. (1983). Some cautions concerning the application of causal modeling methods. *Multivariate Behavioral Research, 18,* 115-126.

Clogg, C. C. (1995). Latent class models. In G. Arminger, C. C. Clogg, & M. E. Sobel (Eds.), *Handbook of statistical modeling for the social and behavioral sciences* (pp. 311-359). New York: Plenum.

Coan, R. W. (1959). A comparison of oblique and orthogonal factor solutions. *Journal of Experimental Education, 27,* 151-166.

Cohen, J. (1977). *Statistical power analysis for the behavioral sciences* (rev. ed.). New York: Academic Press.

Cohen, P., Cohen, J., Teresi, J., Marchi, M., & Velez, C. N. (1990). Problems in the measurement of latent variables in structural equations causal models. *Applied Psychological Measurement, 14,* 183-196.

Cole, D. A., Maxwell, S. E., Arvey, R., & Salas, E. (1993). Multivariate group comparisons of variable systems: MANOVA and structural equation modeling. *Psychological Bulletin, 114,* 174-184.

Collins, L. M., & Horn, J. L. (Eds.) (1991). *Best methods for the analysis of change.* Washington DC: American Psychological Association.

Collins, L. M., & Sayer, A. G. (Eds.) (2001). *New methods for the analysis of change.* Washington DC: American Psychological Association.

Connell, J. P., & Tanaka, J. S. (Eds.) (1987). Special section on structural equation modeling. *Child Development, 58,* 1-175.

Coovert, M. D., Craiger, J. P., & Teachout, M. S. (1997). Effectiveness of the direct product versus confirmatory factor model for reflecting the structure of multimethod-multirater job performance data. *Journal of Applied Psychology, 82,* 271-280.

Corten, I. W., Saris, W. E., Coenders, G., van der Velde, W., Aalberts, C. E., & Kornelis, C. (2002). Fit of different models for multitrait-multimethod experiments. *Structural Equation Modeling, 9,* 213-232.

Cote, J. A., & Buckley, M. R. (1987). Estimating trait, method, and error variance: Generalizing across 70 construct validation studies. *Journal of Marketing Research, 24,* 315-318.

Cronbach, L. J. (1984). A research worker's treasure chest. *Multivariate Behavioral Research, 19,* 223-240.

Cudeck, R. (1988). Multiplicative models and MTMM matrices. *Journal of Educational Statistics, 13*, 131-147.

Cudeck, R. (1989). Analysis of correlation matrices using covariance structure models. *Psychological Bulletin, 105*, 317-327.

Cudeck, R. (2000). Exploratory factor analysis. In H. E. A. Tinsley & S. D. Brown (Eds.), *Handbook of applied multivariate statistics and mathematical modeling* (pp. 265-296). San Diego CA: Academic Press.

Cudeck, R., & Browne, M. W. (1983). Cross-validation of covariance structures. *Multivariate Behavioral Research, 18*, 147-167.

Cudeck, R., & Henly, S. J. (1991). Model selection in covariance structures analysis and the "problem" of sample size: A clarification. *Psychological Bulletin, 109*, 512-519.

Cudeck, R., du Toit, S. & Sörbom, D. (Eds.), *Structural equation modeling: Present and future. A Festschrift in honor of Karl Jöreskog.* Lincolnwood IL: Scientific Software International.

Cudeck, R., & O'Dell, L. L. (1994). Applications of standard error estimates in unrestricted factor analysis: Significance tests for factor loadings and correlations. *Psychological Bulletin, 115*, 475-487.

Curran, P. J., Bollen, K. A., Paxton, P., Kirby, J., & Chen, F. (2002). The noncentral chi-square distribution in misspecified structural equation models: Finite sample results from a Monte Carlo simulation. *Multivariate Behavioral Research, 37*, 1-36.

Cuttance, P., & Ecob, R. (Eds.) (1987). *Structural modeling by example.* Cambridge: Cambridge University Press.

de Leeuw, J., Keller, W. J., & Wansbeek, T. (Eds.) (1983). Interfaces between econometrics and psychometrics. *Journal of Econometrics, 22*, 1-243.

DeFries, J. C., Johnson, R. C., Kuse, A. R., McClearn, G. E., Polovina, J., Vandenberg, S. G., & Wilson, J. R. (1979). Familial resemblance for specific cognitive abilities. *Behavior Genetics, 9*, 23-43.

Dijkstra, T. (1983). Some comments on maximum likelihood and partial least squares methods. *Journal of Econometrics, 22*, 67-90.

Ding, L., Velicer, W. F., & Harlow, L. L. (1995). Effects of estimation methods, number of indicators per factor, and improper solutions on structural equation modeling fit indices. *Structural Equation Modeling, 2*, 119-144.

Dolan, C. V. (1992). *Biometric decomposition of phenotypic means in human samples.* Unpublished doctoral dissertation, University of Amsterdam.

Dolan, C. V., & Molenaar, P. C. M. (1994). Testing specific hypotheses concerning latent group differences in multi-group covariance structure analysis with structured means. *Multivariate Behavioral Research, 29*, 203-222.

du Toit, S. H. C., & Browne, M. W. (2001). The covariance structure of a vector ARMA time series. In R. Cudeck, S. du Toit, & D. Sörbom (Eds.), *Structural equation modeling: Present and future. A Festschrift in honor of Karl Jöreskog* (pp. 279-314). Lincolnwood IL: Scientific Software International.

du Toit, S. H. C., & Cudeck, R. (2001). The analysis of nonlinear random coefficient regression models with LISREL using constraints. In R. Cudeck, S. du Toit, & D. Sörbom (Eds.), *Structural equation modeling: Present and future. A Festschrift in honor of Karl Jöreskog* (pp. 259-278). Lincolnwood IL: Scientific Software International.

Duncan, O. D. (1966). Path analysis: Sociological examples. *American Journal of Sociology, 72*, 1-16.

Duncan, O. D. (1975). *Introduction to structural equation models.* New York: Academic Press.

Duncan, O. D., Haller, A. O., & Portes, A. (1968). Peer influences on aspirations: A reinterpretation. *American Journal of Sociology, 74*, 119-137.

Duncan, S. C., & Duncan, T. E. (1994). Modeling incomplete longitudinal substance use data using latent variable growth curve methodology. *Multivariate Behavioral Research, 29*, 313-338.

Duncan, T. E., Duncan, S. C., Strycker, L. A., Li, F., & Alpert, A. (1999). *An introduction to latent variable growth curve modeling: Concepts, issues, and applications.* Mahwah, NJ: Lawrence Erlbaum Associates.

Dunlap, W. P., & Cornwell, J. M. (1994). Factor analysis of ipsative measures. *Multivariate Behavioral Research, 29*, 115-126.

Dwyer, J. H. (1983). *Statistical models for the social and behavioral sciences.* New York: Oxford University Press.

Edwards, J. R., & Bagozzi, R. P. (2000). On the nature and direction of relationships between constructs and measures. *Psychological Methods, 5*, 155-174.

Enders, C. K. (2001). A primer on maximum likelihood algorithms available for use with missing data. *Structural Equation Modeling, 8*, 128-141.

Enders, C. K., & Bandalos, D. L. (2001). The relative performance of full information maximum likelihood estimation for missing data in structural equation models. *Structural Equation Modeling, 8*, 430-457.

Endler, N. S., Hunt, J. M., & Rosenstein, A. J. (1962). An S-R inventory of anxiousness. *Psychological Monographs, 76,* (Whole No. 536).

Etezadi-Amoli, J., & McDonald, R. P. (1983). A second generation nonlinear factor analysis. *Psychometrika, 48*, 315-342.

Everitt, B. S. (1984). *An introduction to latent variable models.* London: Chapman and Hall.

Fabrigar, L. R., Wegener, D. T., MacCallum, R. C., & Strahan, E. J. (1999). Evaluating the use of exploratory factor analysis in psychological research. *Psychological Methods, 4*, 272-299.

Fan, X., Thompson, B., & Wang, L. (1999). Effects of sample size, estimation methods, and model specification on structural equation modeling fit indexes. *Structural Equation Modeling, 6*, 56-83.

Finch, J. F., West, S. G., & MacKinnon, D. P. (1997). Effects of sample size and nonnormality on the estimation of mediated effects in latent variable models. *Structural Equation Modeling, 4,* 87-107.

Finkel, D., Pedersen, N. L., Reynolds, C. A., Berg, S., de Faire, U., & Svartengren, M. (2003). Genetic and environmental influences on decline in biobehavioral markers of aging. *Behavior Genetics, 33,* 107-123.

Fisher, R. A. (1958). *Statistical Methods for Research Workers* (13th Ed.). Darien CT: Hafner.

Fitzgerald, F. S. (1982). The rich boy. In *The diamond as big as the Ritz and other stories.* Harmondsworth, UK: Penguin.

Fornell, C., & Bookstein, F. L. (1982). Two structural equation models: LISREL and PLS applied to consumer exit-voice theory. *Journal of Marketing Research, 19,* 440-452.

Fouladi, R. T. (2000). Performance of modified test statistics in covariance and correlation structure analysis under conditions of multivariate nonnormality. *Structural Equation Modeling, 7,* 356-410.

Fox, J. (1980). Effect analysis in structural equation models: Extensions and simplified methods of computation. *Sociological Methods & Research, 9,* 3-28.

Fox, J. (1985). Effect analysis in structural equation models II: Calculation of specific indirect effects. *Sociological Methods & Research, 14,* 81-95.

Fraser, C., & McDonald, R. P. (1988). COSAN: Covariance structure analysis. *Multivariate Behavioral Research, 23,* 263-265.

Freedman, D. A. (1987a). As others see us: A case study in path analysis. *Journal of Educational Statistics, 12,* 101-128.

Freedman, D. A. (1987b). A rejoinder on models, metaphors, and fables. *Journal of Educational Statistics, 12,* 206-223.

Gerbing, D. W., & Anderson, J. C. (1985). The effects of sampling error and model characteristics on parameter estimation for maximum likelihood confirmatory factor analysis. *Multivariate Behavioral Research, 20,* 255-271.

Gerbing, D. W., & Anderson, J. C. (1993). Monte Carlo evaluations of goodness-of-fit indices for structural equation models. In K. A. Bollen & J. S. Long (Eds.),*Testing structural equation models* (pp. 40-65). Thousand Oaks, CA: Sage.

Gerbing, D. W., & Hamilton, J. G. (1994). The surprising viability of a simple alternate estimation procedure for construction of large-scale structural equation measurement models. *Structural Equation Modeling, 1,* 103-115.

Gerbing, D. W., & Hamilton, J. G. (1996). Viability of exploratory factor analysis as a precursor to confirmatory factor analysis. *Structural Equation Modeling, 3,* 62-72.

Glymour, C. (2001). *The mind's arrows: Bayes nets and graphical causal models in psychology.* Cambridge, MA: MIT Press.

Glymour, C., Scheines, R., Spirtes, P., & Kelly, K. (1988). TETRAD: Discovering causal structure. *Multivariate Behavioral Research, 23,* 279-280.

Goffin, R. D. (1993). A comparison of two new indices for the assessment of fit of structural equation models. *Multivariate Behavioral Research, 28,* 205-214.

Goffin, R. D., & Jackson, D. N. (1992). Analysis of multitrait-multirater performance appraisal data: Composite direct product method versus confirmatory factor analysis. *Multivariate Behavioral Research, 27,* 363-385.

Gold, M. S. & Bentler, P. M. (2000). Treatments of missing data: A Monte Carlo comparison of RBHDI, iterative stochastic regression imputation, and Expectation-Maximization. *Structural Equation Modeling, 7,* 319-355.

Gold, M. S., Bentler, P. M., & Kim, K. H. (2003). A comparison of maximum-likelihood and asymptotically distribution-free methods of treating incomplete nonnormal data. *Structural Equation Modeling, 10,* 47-79.

Goldberger, A. S. (1971). Econometrics and psychometrics. *Psychometrika, 36,* 83-107.

Goldstein, H. (1995). *Multilevel statistical models* (2nd. ed.). London: E. Arnold.

Gorsuch, R. L. (1983). *Factor analysis* (2nd ed.). Hillsdale, NJ: Lawrence Erlbaum Associates.

Gottman, J. M. (Ed.) (1995). *The analysis of change.* Mahwah, NJ: Lawrence Erlbaum Associates.

Graham, J. W., & Hofer, S. M. (2000). Multiple imputation in multivariate research. In T. D. Little, K. U. Schnabel, & J Baumert (Eds.), *Modeling longitudinal and multilevel data: Practical issues, applied approaches, and specific examples* (pp. 201-218). Mahwah, NJ: Lawrence Erlbaum Associates.

Gustafsson, J.-E., & Balke, G. (1993). General and specific abilities as predictors of school achievement. *Multivariate Behavioral Research, 28,* 407-434.

Guttman, L. (1954). A new approach to factor analysis: The radex. In P. F. Lazarsfeld (Ed.), *Mathematical thinking in the social sciences* (pp. 258-348). Glencoe, IL: The Free Press.

Hägglund, G. (2001). Milestones in the history of factor analysis. In R. Cudeck, S. du Toit, & D. Sörbom (Eds.), *Structural equation modeling: Present and future. A Festschrift in honor of Karl Jöreskog* (pp. 11-38). Lincolnwood IL: Scientific Software International.

Haller, A. O., & Butterworth, C. E. (1960). Peer influences on levels of occupational and educational aspiration. *Social Forces, 38,* 289-295.

Hancock, G. R. (1997). Structural equation modeling methods for hypothesis testing of latent variable means. *Measurement and Evaluation in Counseling and Development, 30,* 91-105.

Hancock, G. R., & Freeman, M. J. (2001). Power and sample size for the root mean square error of approximation test of not close fit in structural equation modeling. *Educational and Psychological Measurement, 61*, 741-758.

Harkness, J. A., Van de Vijver, F. J. R., & Mohler, P. Ph. (Eds.) (2003). *Cross-cultural survey methods*. Hoboken, NJ: Wiley.

Harlow, L. L., & Newcomb, M. D. (1990). Towards a general hierarchical model of meaning and satisfaction in life. *Multivariate Behavioral Research, 25*, 387-405.

Harman, H. H. (1976). *Modern factor analysis* (3rd ed., rev.). Chicago: University of Chicago Press.

Harris, C. W. (1962). Some Rao-Guttman relationships. *Psychometrika, 27*, 247-263.

Harris, C. W., & Kaiser, H. F. (1964). Oblique factor analytic solutions by orthogonal transformations. *Psychometrika, 29*, 347-362.

Hayduk, L. A. (1987). *Structural equation modeling with LISREL: Essentials and advances*. Baltimore: Johns Hopkins University Press.

Hayduk, L. A. (1996). *LISREL issues, debates, and strategies*. Baltimore: Johns Hopkins University Press.

Hayduk, L. A., & Glaser, D. N. (2000). Jiving the four-step, waltzing around factor analysis, and other serious fun. *Structural Equation Modeling, 7*, 1-35.

Hayduk, L., et al. (2003). Pearl's d-separation: One more step into causal thinking. *Stuctural Equation Modeling, 10*, 289-311.

Haynam, G. E., Govindarajulu, Z., & Leone, F. C. (1973). Tables of the cumulative non-central chi-square distribution. In *Selected tables in mathematical statistics* (Vol. 1, pp. 1-42). Providence, RI: American Mathematical Society.

Heck, R. H. (2001). Multilevel modeling with SEM. In G. A. Marcoulides & R. E. Schumacker (Eds.), *New developments and techniques in structural equation modeling* (pp. 89-127). Mahwah, NJ: Lawrence Erlbaum Associates.

Heiman, N., Stallings, M. C., Hofer, S. M., & Hewitt, J. K. (2003). Investigating age differences in the genetic and environmental structure of the Tridimensional Personality Questionnaire in later adulthood. *Behavior Genetics, 33*, 171-180.

Heise, D. R. (1975). *Causal analysis*. New York: Wiley.

Hendrickson, A. E., & White, P. O. (1964). Promax: A quick method for rotation to oblique simple structure. *British Journal of Mathematical and Statistical Psychology, 17*, 65-70.

Hershberger, S. L. (1994). The specification of equivalent models before the collection of data. In A. von Eye & C. C. Clogg (Eds.), *Latent variables analysis: Applications for developmental research* (pp. 68-105). Thousand Oaks, CA: Sage.

References

Hinman, S., & Bolton, B. (1979). *Factor analytic studies 1971-1975.* Troy, NY: Whitston Publishing.

Holahan, C. J., & Moos, R. H. (1991). Life stressors, personal and social resources, and depression: A 4-year structural model. *Journal of Abnormal Psychology, 100,* 31-38.

Homer, P. M., & Kahle, L. R. (1988). A structural equation test of the value-attitude-behavior hierarchy. *Journal of Personality and Social Psychology, 54,* 638-646.

Hoogland, J. J., & Boomsma, A. (1998). Robustness studies in covariance structure modeling: An overview and a meta-analysis. *Sociological Methods & Research, 26,* 329-367.

Horn, J. L. (1965). A rationale and test for the number of factors in factor analysis. *Psychometrika, 30,* 179-185.

Howell, R. D. (1996). Structural equation modeling in a Windows environment. *Journal of Marketing Research, 33,* 377-381.

Hox, J. J. (1995). Amos, EQS, and LISREL for Windows: A comparative review. *Structural Equation Modeling, 2,* 79-91.

Hox, J. J. (2002). *Multilevel analysis: Techniques and applications.* Mahwah, NJ: Lawrence Erlbaum Associates.

Hoyle, R. H. (Ed.) (1995). *Structural equation modeling: Concepts, issues, and applications.* Thousand Oaks, CA: Sage.

Hoyle, R. H., & Kenny, D. A. (1999). Sample size, reliability, and tests of statistical mediation. In R. H. Hoyle (Ed.) *Statistical strategies for small sample research* (pp. 195-222). Thousand Oaks, CA: Sage.

Hoyle, R. H., & Panter, A. T. (1995). Writing about structural equation models. In R. H. Hoyle (Ed.), *Structural equation modeling: Concepts, issues, and applications* (pp. 158-176). Thousand Oaks, CA: Sage.

Hu, L., & Bentler, P. M. (1995). Evaluating model fit. In R. H. Hoyle (Ed.), *Structural equation modeling: Concepts, issues, and applications* (pp. 76-99). Thousand Oaks, CA: Sage.

Hu, L., & Bentler, P. M. (1998). Fit indices in covariance structure modeling: Sensitivity to underparameterized model misspecification. *Psychological Methods, 3,* 424-453.

Hu, L., & Bentler, P. M. (1999). Cutoff criteria for fit indexes in covariance structure analysis: Conventional criteria versus new alternatives. *Structural Equation Modeling, 6,* 1-55.

Hu, L., Bentler, P. M., & Kano, Y. (1992). Can test statistics in covariance structure analysis be trusted? *Psychological Bulletin, 112,* 351-362.

Huba, G. J., & Bentler, P. M. (1982). On the usefulness of latent variable causal modeling in testing theories of naturally occurring events (including adolescent drug use): A rejoinder to Martin. *Journal of Personality and Social Psychology, 43,* 604-611.

Huba, G. J., & Harlow, L. L. (1983). Comparison of maximum likelihood, generalized least squares, ordinary least squares, and asymptotically distribution free parameter estimates in drug abuse latent variable causal models. *Journal of Drug Education, 13*, 387-404.

Huba, G. J., & Harlow, L. L. (1987). Robust structural equation models: Implications for developmental psychology. *Child Development, 58*, 147-166.

Humphreys, L. G., & Montanelli, R. G., Jr. (1975). An investigation of the parallel analysis criterion for determining the number of common factors. *Multivariate Behavioral Research, 10*, 193-205.

Hunter, J. E., Gerbing, D. W., & Boster, F. J. (1982). Machiavellian beliefs and personality: Construct invalidity of the Machiavellianism dimension. *Journal of Personality and Social Psychology, 43*, 1293-1305.

Hurley, J. R., & Cattell, R. B. (1962). The Procrustes program: Producing direct rotation to test a hypothesized factor structure. *Behavioral Science, 7*, 258-262.

Jaccard, J., & Wan, C. K. (1995). Measurement error in the analysis of interaction effects between continuous predictors using multiple regression: Multiple indicator and structural equation approaches. *Psychological Bulletin, 117*, 348-357.

James, L. R., & Singh, B. K. (1978). An introduction to the logic, assumptions, and basic analytic procedures of two-stage least squares. *Psychological Bulletin, 85*, 1104-1122.

James, L. R., Mulaik, S. A., & Brett, J. M. (1982). *Causal analysis: Assumptions, models, and data.* Beverly Hills: Sage.

Jennrich, R. I., & Sampson, P. F. (1966). Rotation for simple loadings. *Psychometrika, 31*, 313-323.

Jöreskog, K. G. (1998). Interaction and nonlinear modeling: Issues and approaches. In R. E. Schumacker & G. A. Marcoulides (Eds.), *Interaction and nonlinear effects in structural equation modeling* (pp. 239-250). Mahwah, NJ: Lawrence Erlbaum Associates.

Jöreskog, K. G., & Lawley, D. N. (1968). New methods in maximum likelihood factor analysis. *British Journal of Mathematical and Statistical Psychology, 21*, 85-96.

Jöreskog, K. G., & Sörbom, D. (1979). *Advances in factor analysis and structural equation models.* Cambridge, MA: Abt Books.

Jöreskog, K. G., & Sörbom, D. (1990). Model search with TETRAD II and LISREL. *Sociological Methods & Research, 19*, 93-106.

Jöreskog, K. G., & Sörbom, D. (1993). *LISREL 8: Structural equation modeling with the SIMPLIS command language.* Mahwah, NJ: Lawrence Erlbaum Associates.

Jöreskog, K. G., & Yang, F. (1996). Nonlinear structural equation models: The Kenny-Judd model with interaction effects. In G. A. Marcoulides & R. E. Schumacker (Eds.), *Advanced structural equation modeling: Issues and techniques* (pp. 57-88). Mahwah, NJ: Lawrence Erlbaum Associates.

Judd, C. M., & Kenny, D. A. (1981). Process analysis: Estimating mediation in treatment evaluations. *Evaluation Review, 5,* 602-619.

Judd, C. M., & Milburn, M. A. (1980). The structure of attitude systems in the general public: Comparisons of a structural equation model. *American Sociological Review, 45,* 627-643.

Kaiser, H. F. (1990). On initial approximations for communalities. *Psychological Reports, 67,* 1216.

Kaiser, H. F. (1958). The varimax criterion for analytic rotation in factor analysis. *Psychometrika, 23,* 187-200.

Kaiser, H. F., & Caffrey, J. (1965). Alpha factor analysis. *Psychometrika, 30,* 1-14.

Kaiser, H. F., & Horst, P. (1975). A score matrix for Thurstone's box problem. *Multivariate Behavioral Research, 10,* 17-25.

Kaiser, H. F., & Madow, W. G. (1974, March). *The KD method for the transformation problem in exploratory factor analysis.* Paper presented to the Psychometric Society, Palo Alto, CA.

Kano, Y. (1997). Software. *Behaviormetrika, 24,* 85-125.

Kano, Y. (2001). Structural equation modeling for experimental data. In R. Cudeck, S. du Toit, & D. Sörbom (Eds.), *Structural equation modeling: Present and future. A Festschrift in honor of Karl Jöreskog* (pp. 381-402). Lincolnwood IL: Scientific Software International.

Kaplan, D. (1990). Evaluating and modifying covariance structure models: A review and recommendation. *Multivariate Behavioral Research, 25,* 137-155.

Kaplan, D. (1995). Statistical power in structural equation modeling. In R. H. Hoyle (Ed.), *Structural equation modeling: Concepts, issues, and applications* (pp. 100-117). Thousand Oaks, CA: Sage.

Kaplan, D. (2000). *Structural equation modeling: Foundations and extensions.* Thousand Oaks, CA: Sage.

Kaplan, D., & Elliott, P. R. (1997). A model-based approach to validating education indicators using multilevel structural equation modeling. *Journal of Educational and Behavioral Statistics, 22,* 323-347.

Kaplan, D., Harik, P., & Hotchkiss, L. (2001). Cross-sectional estimation of dynamic structural equation models in disequilibrium. In R. Cudeck, S. du Toit, & D. Sörbom (Eds.), *Structural equation modeling: Present and future. A Festschrift in honor of Karl Jöreskog* (pp. 315-339). Lincolnwood IL: Scientific Software International.

Kaplan, D., & Wenger, R. N. (1993). Asymptotic independence and separability in covariance structure models: Implications for specification error, power, and model modification. *Multivariate Behavioral Research, 28,* 467-482.

Keith, T. Z. (1997). Using confirmatory factor analysis to aid in understanding the constructs measured by intelligence tests. In D. P. Flanagan, J. L. Genschaft, & P. L. Harrison (Eds.), *Contemporary intellectual assessment: Theories, tests, and issues* (pp. 373-402). New York: Guilford.

Kenny, D. A. (1979). *Correlation and causality.* New York: Wiley.

Kenny, D. A., & Judd, C. M. (1984). Estimating the nonlinear and interactive effects of latent variables. *Psychological Bulletin, 96,* 201-210.

Kiers, H. A. L. (1994). Simplimax: Oblique rotation to an optimal target with simple structure. *Psychometrika, 59,* 567-579.

Kiiveri, H., & Speed, T. P. (1982). Structural analysis of multivariate data: A review. In S. Leinhardt (Ed.), *Sociological methodology 1982* (pp. 209-289). San Francisco, Jossey-Bass.

Kim, J.-O., & Ferree, G. D., Jr. (1981). Standardization in causal analysis. *Sociological Methods & Research, 10,* 187-210.

Kim, K. H., & Bentler, P. M. (2002). Tests of homogeneity of means and covariance matrices for multivariate incomplete data. *Psychometrika, 67,* 609-624.

Kline, R. B. (1998a). *Principles and practice of structural equation modeling.* New York: Guilford.

Kline, R. B. (1998b). Software programs for structural equation modeling: Amos, EQS, and LISREL. *Journal of Psychoeducational Assessment, 16,* 343-364.

Kroonenberg, P. M. (1983). Annotated bibliography of three-mode factor analysis. *British Journal of Mathematical and Statistical Psychology, 36,* 81-113.

Kroonenberg, P. M., Lammers, C. J., & Stoop, I. (1985). Three-mode principal components analysis of multivariate longitudinal organizational data. *Sociological Methods & Research, 14,* 99-136.

Kühnel, S. M. (1988). Testing MANOVA designs with LISREL. *Sociological Methods & Research, 16,* 504-523.

Kumar, A., & Dillon, W. R. (1987a). The interaction of measurement and structure in simultaneous equation models with unobservable variables. *Journal of Marketing Research, 24,* 98-105.

Kumar, A., & Dillon, W. R. (1987b). Some further remarks on measurement-structure interaction and the unidimensionality of constructs. *Journal of Marketing Research, 24,* 438-444.

La Du, T. J., & Tanaka, J. S. (1989). Influence of sample size, estimation method, and model specification on goodness-of-fit assessments in structural equation models. *Journal of Applied Psychology, 74,* 625-635.

La Du, T. J., & Tanaka, J. S. (1995). Incremental fit index changes for nested structural equation models. *Multivariate Behavioral Research, 30,* 289-316.

Lambert, Z. V., Wildt, A. R., & Durand, R. M. (1991). Approximating confidence intervals for factor loadings. *Multivariate Behavioral Research, 26*, 421-434.

Lance, C. E., Cornwell, J. M., & Mulaik, S. A. (1988). Limited information parameter estimates for latent or mixed manifest and latent variable models. *Multivariate Behavioral Research, 23*, 171-187.

Laplante, B., Sabourin, S., Cournoyer, J. W., & Wright, J. (1998). Estimating nonlinear effects using a structured means intercept approach. In R. E. Schumacker & G. A. Marcoulides (Eds.), *Interaction and nonlinear effects in structural equation modeling* (pp. 183-202). Mahwah, NJ: Lawrence Erlbaum Associates.

Lautenschlager, G. J. (1989). A comparison of alternatives to conducting Monte Carlo analyses for determining parallel analysis criteria. *Multivariate Behavioral Research, 24*, 365-395.

Lawley, D. N., & Maxwell, A. E. (1971). *Factor analysis as a statistical method* (2nd ed.). London: Butterworths.

Lawrence, F. R., & Hancock, G. R. (1998). Assessing change over time using latent growth modeling. *Measurement and Evaluation in Counseling and Development, 30*, 211-224.

Lawrence, F. R., & Hancock, G. R. (1999). Conditions affecting integrity of a factor solution under varying degrees of overextraction. *Educational and Psychological Measurement, 59*, 549-579.

Lazarsfeld, P. F. (1950). The logical and mathematical foundation of latent structure analysis. In S. A. Stouffer, L. Guttman, E. A. Suchman, P. F. Lazarsfeld, S. A. Star, & J. A. Clausen, *Measurement and prediction* (pp. 362-412). Princeton, NJ: Princeton University Press.

Lazarsfeld, P. F., & Henry, N. W. (1968). *Latent structure analysis.* New York: Houghton Mifflin.

Lee, S., & Hershberger, S. (1990). A simple rule for generating equivalent models in covariance structure modeling. *Multivariate Behavioral Research, 25*, 313-334.

Lee, S.-Y., & Zhu, H.-T. (2000). Statistical analysis of nonlinear structural equation models with continuous and polytomous data. *British Journal of Mathematical and Statistical Psychology, 53*, 209-232.

Lee, S.-Y., & Zhu, H.-T. (2002). Maximum likelihood estimation of nonlinear structural equation models. *Psychometrika, 67*, 189-210.

Lehmann, D. R., & Gupta, S. (1989). PACM: A two-stage procedure for analyzing structural models. *Applied Psychological Measurement, 13*, 301-321.

Li, C.-C. (1975). *Path analysis: A primer.* Pacific Grove, CA: Boxwood Press.

Li, F., Duncan, T. E., & Acock, A. (2000). Modeling interaction effects in latent growth curve models. *Structural Equation Modeling, 7*, 497-533.

Lingoes, J. C., & Guttman, L. (1967). Nonmetric factor analysis: A rank reducing alternative to linear factor analysis. *Multivariate Behavioral Research, 2*, 485-505.

Little, R. J. A., & Rubin, D. B. (1987). *Statistical analysis with missing data.* New York: Wiley.

Little, R. J. A., & Schenker, N. (1995). Missing data. In G. Arminger, C. C. Clogg, & M. E. Sobel (Eds.), *Handbook of statistical modeling for the social and behavioral sciences* (pp. 39-75). New York: Plenum.

Little, T. D. (1997). Means and covariance structures (MACS) analyses of cross-cultural data: Practical and theoretical issues. *Multivariate Behavioral Research, 32*, 53-76.

Little, T. D., Lindenberger, U., & Nesselroade, J. R. (1999). On selecting indicators for multivariate measurement and modeling with latent variables: When "good" indicators are bad and "bad" indicators are good. *Psychological Methods, 4*, 192-211.

Loehlin, J. C. (1992). *Genes and environment in personality development.* Newbury Park, CA: Sage.

Loehlin, J. C., & Vandenberg, S. G. (1968). Genetic and environmental components in the covariation of cognitive abilities: An additive model. In S. G. Vandenberg (Ed.), *Progress in human behavior genetics* (pp. 261-278). Baltimore: Johns Hopkins Press.

Loehlin, J. C., Willerman, L., & Horn, J. M. (1985). Personality resemblances in adoptive families when the children are late-adolescent or adult. *Journal of Personality and Social Psychology, 48*, 376-392.

Lohmöller, J.-B. (1988). The PLS program system: Latent variables path analysis with partial least squares estimation. *Multivariate Behavioral Research, 23*, 125-127.

Long, J. S. (1983a). *Confirmatory factor analysis: A preface to LISREL.* Beverly Hills, CA: Sage.

Long, J. S. (1983b). *Covariance structure models: An introduction to LISREL.* Beverly Hills, CA: Sage.

Long, J. S. (Ed.). (1988). *Common problems/proper solutions: Avoiding errors in quantitative research.* Thousand Oaks, CA: Sage.

Lorenzo-Seva, U. (1999). Promin: A method for oblique factor rotation. *Multivariate Behavioral Research, 34*, 347-365.

Lubke, G. H., & Dolan, C. V. (2003). Can unequal residual variances across groups mask differences in residual means in the common factor model? *Stuctural Equation Modeling, 10*, 175-192.

MacCallum, R. (1983). A comparison of factor analysis programs in SPSS, BMDP, and SAS. *Psychometrika, 48*, 223-231.

MacCallum, R. (1986). Specification searches in covariance structure modeling. *Psychological Bulletin, 100*, 107-120.

MacCallum, R. C. (1995). Model specification: Procedures, strategies, and related issues. In R. H. Hoyle (Ed.), *Structural equation modeling: Concepts, issues, and applications* (pp. 16-36). Thousand Oaks, CA: Sage.

MacCallum, R. C., & Browne, M. W. (1993). The use of causal indicators in covariance structure models: Some practical issues. *Psychological Bulletin, 114*, 533-541.

MacCallum, R. C., Browne, M. W., & Sugawara, H. M. (1996). Power analysis and determination of sample size for covariance structure modeling. *Psychological Methods, 1*, 130-149.

MacCallum, R. C., & Hong, S. (1997). Power analysis in covariance structure modeling using GFI and AGFI. *Multivariate Behavioral Research, 32*, 193-210.

MacCallum, R. C., Roznowski, M., Mar, C. M., & Reith, J. V. (1994). Alternative strategies for cross-validation of covariance structure models. *Multivariate Behavioral Research, 29*, 1-32.

MacCallum, R. C., Roznowski, M., & Necowitz, L. B. (1992). Model modifications in covariance structure analysis: The problem of capitalization on chance. *Psychological Bulletin, 111*, 490-504.

MacCallum, R. C., & Tucker, L. R. (1991). Representing sources of error in the common-factor model: Implications for theory and practice. *Psychological Bulletin, 109*, 502-511.

MacCallum, R. C., Wegener, D. T., Uchino, B. N., & Fabrigar, L. R. (1993). The problem of equivalent models in applications of covariance structure analysis. *Psychological Bulletin, 114*, 185-199.

MacCallum, R. C., Widaman, K. F., Preacher, K. J., & Hong, S. (2001). Sample size in factor analysis: The role of model error. *Multivariate Behavioral Research, 36*, 611-637.

MacCallum, R. C., Widaman, K. F., Zhang, S., & Hong, S. (1999). Sample size in factor analysis. *Psychological Methods, 4*, 84-99.

Maiti, S. S., & Mukherjee, B. N. (1990). A note on the distributional properties of the Jöreskog-Sörbom fit indices. *Psychometrika, 55*, 721-726.

Marcoulides, G. A., & Drezner, Z. (2001). Specification searches in structural equation modeling with a genetic algorithm. In G. A. Marcoulides & R. E. Schumacker (Eds.), *New developments and techniques in structural equation modeling* (pp. 247-268). Mahwah, NJ: Lawrence Erlbaum Associates.

Marcoulides, G. A., & Drezner, Z. (2003). Model specification searches using ant colony optimization algorithms. *Structural Equation Modeling, 10*, 154-164.

Marcoulides, G. A., Drezner, Z., & Schumacker, R. E. (1998). Model specification searches in structural equation modeling using Tabu search. *Structural Equation Modeling, 5*, 365-376.

Marcoulides, G. A., & Moustaki, I. (Eds.) (2002). *Latent variable and latent structure models*. Mahwah, NJ: Lawrence Erlbaum Associates.

Marcoulides, G. A., & Schumacker, R. E. (Eds.) (1996). *Advanced structural equation modeling: Issues and techniques*. Mahwah, NJ: Lawrence Erlbaum Associates.

Marcoulides, G. A., & Schumacker, R. E. (Eds.) (2001). *New developments and techniques in structural equation modeling.* Mahwah, NJ: Lawrence Erlbaum Associates.

Marsden, P. V. (Ed.) (1981). *Linear models in social research.* Beverly Hills, CA: Sage.

Marsh, H. W. (1998). Pairwise deletion for missing data in structural equation models: Nonpositive definite matrices, parameter estimates, goodness of fit, and adjusted sample sizes. *Structural Equation Modeling, 5*, 22-36.

Marsh, H. W., Balla, J. R., & Hau, K.-T. (1996). An evaluation of incremental fit indices: A clarification of mathematical and empirical properties. In G. A. Marcoulides & R. E. Schumacker (Eds.), *Advanced structural equation modeling: Issues and techniques* (pp. 315-353). Mahwah, NJ: Lawrence Erlbaum Associates.

Marsh, H. W., Balla, J. R., & McDonald, R. P. (1988). Goodness-of-fit indexes in confirmatory factor analysis: The effect of sample size. *Psychological Bulletin, 103*, 391-410.

Marsh, H. W., & Byrne, B. M. (1993). Confirmatory factor analysis of multitrait-multimethod self-concept data: Between-group and within-group invariance constraints. *Multivariate Behavioral Research, 28*, 313-349.

Marsh, H. W., & Grayson, D. (1995). Latent variable models of multitrait-multimethod data. In R. H. Hoyle (Ed.), *Structural equation modeling: Concepts, issues, and applications* (pp. 177-198). Thousand Oaks, CA: Sage.

Marsh, H. W., & Hocevar, D. (1983). Confirmatory factor analysis of multitrait-multimethod matrices. *Journal of Educational Measurement, 20*, 231-248.

Martin, J. A. (1982). Application of structural modeling with latent variables to adolescent drug use: A reply to Huba, Wingard and Bentler. *Journal of Personality and Social Psychology, 43*, 598-603.

Maruyama, G., & McGarvey, B. (1980). Evaluating causal models: An application of maximum-likelihood analysis of structural equations. *Psychological Bulletin, 87*, 502-512.

Maruyama, G. M. (1998). *Basics of structural equation modeling.* Thousand Oaks, CA: Sage.

Mason, W. M., House, J. S., & Martin, S. S. (1985). On the dimensions of political alienation in America. In N. Tuma (Ed.), *Sociological methodology 1985* (pp. 111-151). San Francisco: Jossey-Bass.

Maxwell, A. E. (1977). *Multivariate analysis in behavioural research.* New York: Wiley.

McAleer, M. (1995). The significance of testing empirical non-nested models. *Journal of Econometrics, 67*, 149-171.

McArdle, J. J. (1980). Causal modeling applied to psychonomic systems simulation. *Behavior Research Methods and Instrumentation, 12*, 193-209.

McArdle, J. J. (1986). Latent variable growth within behavior genetic models. *Behavior Genetics, 16,* 163-200.

McArdle, J. J. (1996). Current directions in structural factor analysis. *Current Directions in Psychological Science, 5,* 11-18.

McArdle, J. J. (2001). A latent difference score approach to longitudinal dynamic structural analysis. In R. Cudeck, S. du Toit, & D. Sörbom (Eds.), *Structural equation modeling: Present and future. A Festschrift in honor of Karl Jöreskog* (pp. 341-380). Lincolnwood IL: Scientific Software International.

McArdle, J. J., & Boker, S. M. (1990). *RAMpath: Path diagram software.* Denver: Data Transforms Inc.

McArdle, J. J., & Cattell, R. B. (1994). Structural equation models of factorial invariance in parallel proportional profiles and oblique confactor problems. *Multivariate Behavioral Research, 29,* 63-113.

McArdle, J. J., & Hamagami, F. (1996). Multilevel models from a multiple group structural equation perspective. In G. A. Marcoulides & R. E. Schumacker (Eds.), *Advanced structural equation modeling: Issues and techniques* (pp. 89-124). Mahwah, NJ: Lawrence Erlbaum Associates.

McArdle, J. J., & Hamagami, F. (2003). Structural equation models for evaluating dynamic concepts within longitudinal twin analyses. *Behavior Genetics, 33,* 137-159.

McArdle, J. J., & McDonald, R. P. (1984). Some algebraic properties of the Reticular Action Model for moment structures. *British Journal of Mathematical and Statistical Psychology, 37,* 234-251.

McDonald, R. P. (1985). *Factor analysis and related methods.* Hillsdale, NJ: Lawrence Erlbaum Associates.

McDonald, R. P. (1989). An index of goodness-of-fit based on noncentrality. *Journal of Classification, 6,* 97-103.

McDonald, R. P. (1962). A general approach to nonlinear factor analysis. *Psychometrika, 27,* 397-415.

McDonald, R. P. (1967). Nonlinear factor analysis. *Psychometric Monographs,* No. 15.

McDonald, R. P. (1978). A simple comprehensive model for the analysis of covariance structures. *British Journal of Mathematical and Statistical Psychology, 31,* 59-72.

McDonald, R. P. (1996). Path analysis with composite variables. *Multivariate Behavioral Research, 31,* 239-270.

McDonald, R. P., & Bolt, D. M. (1998). The determinacy of variables in structural equation models. *Multivariate Behavioral Research, 33,* 385-401.

McDonald, R. P., & Marsh, H. W. (1990). Choosing a multivariate model: Noncentrality and goodness of fit. *Psychological Bulletin, 107,* 247-255.

McDonald, R. P., & Mulaik, S. A. (1979). Determinacy of common factors: A nontechnical review. *Psychological Bulletin, 86,* 297-306.

McGue, M., & Christensen, K. (2003). The heritability of depression symptoms in elderly Danish twins: Occasion-specific versus general effects. *Behavior Genetics, 33*, 83-93.

McIntosh, A. R., & Gonzalez-Lima, F. (1991). Structural modeling of functional neural pathways mapped with 2-deoxyglucose: Effects of acoustic startle habituation on the auditory system. *Brain Research, 547*, 295-302.

McIver, J. P., Carmines, E. G., & Zeller, R. A. (1980). Multiple indicators. Appendix in R. A. Zeller & E. G. Carmines, *Measurement in the social sciences* (pp. 162-185). Cambridge: Cambridge University Press.

McNemar, Q. (1969). *Psychological statistics* (4th ed.) New York: Wiley.

Mehta, P. D., & West, S. G. (2000). Putting the individual back into individual growth curves. *Psychological Methods, 5*, 23-43.

Meredith, W. (1991). Latent variable models for studying differences and change. In L. M. Collins & J. L. Horn (Eds.), *Best methods for the analysis of change* (pp. 149-163). Washington DC: American Psychological Association.

Meredith, W. (1993). Measurement invariance, factor analysis and factorial invariance. *Psychometrika, 58*, 525-543.

Meredith, W., & Tisak, J. (1990). Latent curve analysis. *Psychometrika, 55*, 107-122.

Millsap, R. E. (1998). Group differences in regression intercepts: Implications for factorial invariance. *Multivariate Behavioral Research, 33*, 403-424.

Millsap, R. E. (2001). When trivial constraints are not trivial: The choice of uniqueness constraints in confirmatory factor analysis. *Structural Equation Modeling, 8*, 1-17.

Molenaar, P. C. M., Huizenga, H. M., & Nesselroade, J. R. (2003). The relationship between the structure of interindividual and intraindividual variability: A theoretical and empirical vindication of developmental systems theory. In U. M. Staudinger & U. Lindenberger (Eds.), *Understanding human development: Dialogues with lifespan psychology* (pp. 339-360). Boston: Kluwer.

Molenaar, P. C. M., & von Eye, A. (1994). On the arbitrary nature of latent variables. In A. von Eye & C. C. Clogg (Eds.), *Latent variables analysis: Applications for developmental research* (pp. 226-242). Thousand Oaks, CA: Sage.

Morrison, D. F. (1976). *Multivariate statistical methods* (2nd ed.). New York: McGraw-Hill.

Moulder, B. C., & Algina, J. (2002). Comparison of methods for estimating and testing latent variable interactions. *Structural Equation Modeling, 9*, 1-19.

Mueller, R. O. (1996). *Basic principles of structural equation modeling: An introduction to LISREL and EQS*. New York: Springer-Verlag.

Mulaik, S. A. (1972). *The foundations of factor analysis*. New York: McGraw-Hill.

Mulaik, S. A. (1986). Factor analysis and *Psychometrika*: Major developments. *Psychometrika, 51*, 23-33.

Mulaik, S. A. (1987). Toward a conception of causality applicable to experimentation and causal modeling. *Child Development, 58*, 18-32.

Mulaik, S. A., James, L. R., Van Alstine, J., Bennett, N., Lind, S., & Stilwell, C. D. (1989). Evaluation of goodness-of-fit indices for structural equation models. *Psychological Bulletin, 105*, 430-445.

Muthén, B. (1984). A general structural equation model with dichotomous, ordered categorical, and continuous latent variable indicators. *Psychometrika, 49*, 115-132.

Muthén, B. O. (1989a). Latent variable modeling in heterogeneous populations. *Psychometrika, 54*, 557-585.

Muthén, B. O. (1989b). Factor structure in groups selected on observed scores. *British Journal of Mathematical and Statistical Psychology, 42*, 81-90.

Muthén, B. O. (1993). Goodness of fit with categorical and other nonnormal variables. In K. A. Bollen & J. S. Long (Eds.),*Testing structural equation models* (pp. 205-234). Thousand Oaks, CA: Sage.

Muthén, B. (1997). Latent variable growth modeling with multilevel data. In M. Berkane (Ed.), *Latent variable modeling and applications to causality* (pp. 149-161). New York: Springer-Verlag.

Muthén, B., & Jöreskog, K. G. (1983). Selectivity problems in quasi-experimental studies. *Evaluation Review, 7*, 139-174.

Muthén, B., & Kaplan, D. (1985). A comparison of some methodologies for the factor analysis of non-normal Likert variables. *British Journal of Mathematical and Statistical Psychology, 38*, 171-189.

Muthén, B., & Speckart, G. (1985). Latent variable probit ANCOVA: Treatment effects in the California Civil Addict Programme. *British Journal of Mathematical and Statistical Psychology, 38*, 161-170.

Muthén, L. K., & Muthén, B. O. (2002). How to use a Monte Carlo study to decide on sample size and determine power. *Structural Equation Modeling, 9*, 599-620.

Neale, M. C. (1995). *Mx: Statistical modeling* (3rd. ed.). Box 980126 MCV, Richmond VA 23298.

Neale, M. C. (1998). Modeling interaction and nonlinear effects with Mx: A general approach. In R. E. Schumacker & G. A. Marcoulides, (Eds.), *Interaction and nonlinear effects in structural equation modeling* (pp. 43-61). Mahwah, NJ: Lawrence Erlbaum Associates.

Neale, M. C., & Cardon, L.R. (1992). *Methodology for genetic studies of twins and families*. Dordrecht: Kluwer.

Neale, M. C., & McArdle, J. J. (2000). Structured latent growth curves for twin data. *Twin Research, 3*, 165-177.

Nesselroade, J. R. (2002). Elaborating the differential in differential psychology. *Multivariate Behavioral Research, 37*, 543-561.

Nesselroade, J. R., & Baltes, P. B. (1984). From traditional factor analysis to structural-causal modeling in developmental research. In V. Sarris & A. Parducci (Eds.), *Perspectives in psychological experimentation: Toward the year 2000* (pp. 267-287). Hillsdale, NJ: Lawrence Erlbaum Associates.

Nesselroade, J. R., & Ghisletta, P. (2003). Structuring and measuring change over the life span. In U. M. Staudinger & U. Lindenberger (Eds.), *Understanding human development: Dialogues with lifespan psychology* (pp. 317-337). Boston: Kluwer.

Neuhaus, J. O., & Wrigley, C. (1954). The quartimax method: An analytic approach to orthogonal simple structure. *British Journal of Statistical Psychology, 7,* 81-91.

Nevitt, J., & Hancock, G. R. (2000). Improving the root mean square error of approximation for nonnormal conditions in structural equation modeling. *Journal of Experimental Education, 68,* 251-268.

Nevitt, J., & Hancock, G. R. (2001). Performance of bootstrapping approaches to model test statistics and parameter standard error estimation in structural equation modeling. *Structural Equation Modeling, 8,* 353-377.

Newcomb, M. D., & Bentler, P. M. (1983). Dimensions of subjective female orgasmic responsiveness. *Journal of Personality and Social Psychology, 44,* 862-873.

O'Brien, R. M., & Reilly, T. (1995). Equality in constraints and metric-setting measurement models. *Structural Equation Modeling, 2,* 1-12.

Oczkowski, E. (2002). Discriminating between measurement scales using nonnested tests and 2SLS: Monte Carlo evidence. *Structural Equation Modeling, 9,* 103-125.

Olsson, U. H., Foss, T., Troye, S. V., & Howell, R. D. (2000). The performance of ML, GLS, and WLS estimation in structural equation modeling under conditions of misspecification and nonnormality. *Structural Equation Modeling, 7,* 557-595.

Olsson, U. H., Troye, S. V., & Howell, R. D. (1999). Theoretic fit and empirical fit: The performance of maximum likelihood versus generalized least squares estimation in structural equation models. *Multivariate Behavioral Research, 34,* 31-58.

Overall, J. E., & Klett, C. J. (1972). *Applied multivariate analysis.* New York: McGraw-Hill.

Pearl, J. (1998). Graphs, causality, and structural equation models. *Sociological Methods & Research, 27,* 226-284.

Pearl, J. (2000). *Causality: Models, reasoning, and inference.* Cambridge: Cambridge University Press.

Ping, R. A., Jr. (1996). Latent variable interaction and quadratic effect estimation: A two-step technique using structural equation analysis. *Psychological Bulletin, 119,* 166-175.

Powell, D. A., & Schafer, W. D. (2001). The robustness of the likelihood ratio chi-square test for structural equation models: A meta-analysis. *Journal of Educational and Behavioral Statistics, 26,* 105-132.

Pugesek, B. H., Tomer, A., & von Eye, A. (2003). *Structural equation modeling: Applications in ecological and evolutionary biology.* Cambridge: Cambridge University Press.

Rahe, R. H., Hervig, L., & Rosenman, R. H. (1978). Heritability of Type A behavior. *Psychosomatic Medicine, 40,* 478-486.

Rao, C. R. (1955). Estimation and tests of significance in factor analysis. *Psychometrika, 20,* 93-111.

Raykov, T. (2000). On the large-sample bias, variance, and mean squared error of the conventional noncentrality parameter estimator of covariance structure models. *Structural Equation Modeling, 7,* 431-441.

Raykov, T. (2001). Approximate confidence interval for difference in fit of structural equation models. *Structural Equation Modeling, 8,* 458-469.

Raykov, T., & Marcoulides, G. A. (2000). *A first course in structural equation modeling.* Mahwah, NJ: Lawrence Erlbaum Associates.

Raykov, T., & Penev, S. (2001). The problem of equivalent structural equation models: An individual residual perspective. In G. A. Marcoulides & R. E. Schumacker (Eds.), *New developments and techniques in structural equation modeling* (pp. 297-321). Mahwah, NJ: Lawrence Erlbaum Associates.

Reichardt, C. S., & Coleman, S. C. (1995). The criteria for convergent and discriminant validity in a multitrait-multimethod matrix. *Multivariate Behavioral Research, 30,* 513-538.

Reise, S. P., & Duan, N. (Eds.) (2003). *Multilevel modeling: Methodological advances, issues, and applications.* Mahwah, NJ: Lawrence Erlbaum Associates.

Reise, S. P., Widaman, K. F., & Pugh, R. H. (1993). Confirmatory factor analysis and item response theory: Two approaches for exploring measurement invariance. *Psychological Bulletin, 114,* 552-566.

Rigdon, E. E. (1994). SEMNET: Structural equation modeling discussion network. *Structural Equation Modeling 1,* 190-192.

Rigdon, E. E. (1995). A necessary and sufficient identification rule for structural models estimated in practice. *Multivariate Behavioral Research, 30,* 359-383.

Rigdon, E. E. (1996). CFI versus RMSEA: A comparison of two fit indexes for structural equation modeling. *Structural Equation Modeling, 3,* 369-379.

Rigdon, E. E., Schumacker, R. E., & Wothke, W. (1998). A comparative review of interaction and nonlinear modeling. In R. E. Schumacker & G. A. Marcoulides (Eds.), *Interaction and nonlinear effects in structural equation modeling* (pp. 1-16). Mahwah, NJ: Lawrence Erlbaum Associates.

Rindskopf, D. (1984a). Stuctural equation models: Empirical identification, Heywood cases, and related problems. *Sociological Methods & Research, 13*, 109-119.

Rindskopf, D. (1984b). Using phantom and imaginary latent variables to parameterize constraints in linear structural models. *Psychometrika, 49*, 37-47.

Rindskopf, D., & Rose, T. (1988). Some theory and applications of confirmatory second-order factor analysis. *Multivariate Behavioral Research, 23*, 51-67.

Rivera, P., & Satorra, A. (2002). Analyzing group differences: A comparison of SEM approaches. In G. A. Marcoulides & I. Moustaki (Eds.), *Latent variable and latent structure models* (pp. 85-104). Mahwah, NJ: Lawrence Erlbaum Associates.

Rovine, M. J. (1994). Latent variables models and missing data analysis. In A. von Eye & C. C. Clogg (Eds.), *Latent variables analysis: Applications for developmental research* (pp. 181-225). Thousand Oaks, CA: Sage.

Rozeboom, W. W. (1978). Estimation of cross-validated multiple correlation: A clarification. *Psychological Bulletin, 85*, 1348-1351.

Rozeboom, W. W. (1992). The glory of suboptimal factor rotation: Why local minima in analytic optimization of simple structure are more blessing than curse. *Multivariate Behavioral Research, 27*, 585-599.

Rust, R. T., Lee, C., & Valente, E., Jr. (1995). Comparing covariance structure models: A general methodology. *International Journal of Research in Marketing, 12*, 279-291.

Saris, W. E. & Aalberts, C. (2003). Different explanations for correlated disturbance terms in MTMM studies. *Structural Equation Modeling, 10*, 193-213.

Saris, W. E., de Pijper, M., & Mulder, J. (1978). Optimal procedures for estimating factor scores. *Sociological Methods & Research, 7*, 85-106.

Saris, W. E., & Satorra, A. (1993). Power evaluations in structural equation models. In K. A. Bollen & J. S. Long (Eds.), *Testing structural equation models* (pp. 181-204). Thousand Oaks, CA: Sage.

Saris, W. E., & Stronkhorst, L. H. (1984). *Causal modelling in nonexperimental research.* Amsterdam: Sociometric Research Foundation.

SAS Institute. (1990). *SAS/STAT user's guide* (Version 6, 4th ed.). Cary, NC: SAS Institute.

Satorra, A. (1989). Alternative test criteria in covariance structure analysis: A unified approach. *Psychometrika, 54*, 131-151.

Satorra, A. (1990). Robustness issues in structural equation modeling: A review of recent developments. *Quality & Quantity, 24*, 367-386.

Satorra, A. (2001). Goodness of fit testing of structural equation models with multiple group data and nonnormality. In R. Cudeck, S. du Toit, & D. Sörbom (Eds.), *Structural equation modeling: Present and future. A Festschrift in honor of Karl Jöreskog* (pp. 231-256). Lincolnwood IL: Scientific Software International.

Satorra, A., & Saris, W. E. (1985). Power of the likelihood ratio test in covariance structure analysis. *Psychometrika, 50*, 83-90.

Schafer, J. L. (1997). *Analysis of incomplete multivariate data*. London: Chapman & Hall.

Scheines, R., Spirtes, P., Glymour, C., Meek, C., & Richardson, T. (1998). The TETRAD Project: Constraint based aids to causal model specification. *Multivariate Behavioral Research, 33*, 65-117. [Comments by J. Pearl, J. Woodward, P. K. Wood, K.-F. Ting, and reply by the authors, pp. 119-180.]

Schermelleh-Engel, K., Klein, A., & Moosbrugger, H. (1998). Estimating nonlinear effects using a latent moderated structural equations approach. In R. E. Schumacker & G. A. Marcoulides (Eds.), *Interaction and nonlinear effects in structural equation modeling* (pp. 203-238). Mahwah, NJ: Lawrence Erlbaum Associates.

Schmid, J., & Leiman, J. M. (1957). The development of hierarchical factor solutions. *Psychometrika, 22*, 53-61.

Schmitt, N., & Stults, D. M. (1986). Methodology review: Analysis of multitrait-multimethod matrices. *Applied Psychological Measurement, 10*, 1-22.

Schoenberg, R., & Richtand, C. (1984). Application of the EM method: A study of maximum likelihood estimation of multiple indicator and factor analysis models. *Sociological Methods & Research, 13*, 127-150.

Schumacker, R. E. (2002). Latent variable interaction modeling. *Structural Equation Modeling, 9*, 40-54.

Schumacker, R. E., & Lomax, R. G. (1996). *A beginner's guide to structural equation modeling*. Mahwah, NJ: Lawrence Erlbaum Associates.

Schumacker, R. E., & Marcoulides, G. A. (Eds.) (1998). *Interaction and nonlinear effects in structural equation modeling*. Mahwah, NJ: Lawrence Erlbaum Associates.

Schweizer, K. (1992). A correlation-based decision-rule for determining the number of clusters and its efficiency in uni- and multi-level data. *Multivariate Behavioral Research, 27*, 77-94.

Seidel, G., & Eicheler, C. (1990). Identification structure of linear structural models. *Quality & Quantity, 24*, 345-365.

Sharma, S., Durvasula, S., & Dillon, W. R. (1989). Some results on the behavior of alternate covariance structure estimation procedures in the presence of non-normal data. *Journal of Marketing Research, 26*, 214-221.

Shipley, B. (2000). *Cause and correlation in biology: A user's guide to path analysis, structural equations and causal inference*. Cambridge: Cambridge University Press.

Shrout, P. E., & Bolger, N. (2002). Mediation in experimental and nonexperimental studies: New procedures and recommendations. *Psychological Methods, 7*, 422-445.

Silvia, E. S. M., & MacCallum, R. C. (1988). Some factors affecting the success of specification searches in covariance structure modeling. *Multivariate Behavioral Research, 23*, 297-326.

Snyder, C. W., Jr. (1988). Multimode factor analysis. In J. R. Nesselroade & R. B. Cattell (Eds.), *Handbook of multivariate experimental psychology* (2nd ed., pp. 289-316). New York: Plenum.

Sobel, M. E. (1988). Direct and indirect effects in linear structural equation models. In J. S. Long (Ed.), *Common problems/proper solutions: Avoiding errors in quantitative research* (pp. 46-64). Thousand Oaks, CA: Sage.

Sobel, M. E. (1995). Causal inference in the social and behavioral sciences. In G. Arminger, C. C. Clogg, & M. E. Sobel (Eds.), *Handbook of statistical modeling for the social and behavioral sciences* (pp. 1-38). New York: Plenum.

Sörbom, D. (1974). A general method for studying differences in factor means and factor structure between groups. *British Journal of Mathematical and Statistical Psychology, 27,* 229-239.

Spearman, C. (1904). "General intelligence," objectively determined and measured. *American Journal of Psychology, 15*, 201-292.

Spirtes, P., Glymour, C., & Scheines, R. (1993). *Causation, prediction, and search.* New York: Springer-Verlag.

Spirtes, P., Richardson, T., Meek, C., Scheines, R., & Glymour, C. (1998). Using path diagrams as a structural equation modeling tool. *Sociological Methods & Research, 27*, 182-225.

Spirtes, P., Scheines, R., & Glymour, C. (1990a). Simulation studies of the reliability of computer-aided model specification using the TETRAD II, EQS, and LISREL programs. *Sociological Methods & Research, 19*, 3-66.

Spirtes, P., Scheines, R., & Glymour, C. (1990b). Reply to comments. *Sociological Methods & Research, 19*, 107-121.

SPSS Inc. (1990). *SPSS reference guide.* Chicago: SPSS Inc.

Steenkamp, J.-B. E. M., & Baumgartner, H. (1998). Assessing measurement invariance in cross-national consumer research. *Journal of Consumer Research, 25*, 78-90.

Steiger, J. H. (1988). Aspects of person-machine communication in structural modeling of correlations and covariances. *Multivariate Behavioral Research, 23*, 281-290.

Steiger, J. H. (1989). *EzPATH: Causal modeling.* Evanston, IL: SYSTAT Inc.

Steiger, J. H. (1990). Structural model evaluation and modification: An interval estimation approach. *Multivariate Behavioral Research, 25*, 173-180.

Steiger, J. H. (1998). A note on multiple sample extensions of the RMSEA fit index. *Structural Equation Modeling, 5*, 411-419.

Steiger, J. H. (2000). Point estimation, hypothesis testing, and interval estimation using the RMSEA: Some comments and a reply to Hayduk and Glaser. *Structural Equation Modeling, 7*, 149-162.

Steiger, J. H. (2001). Driving fast in reverse: The relationship between software development, theory, and education in structural equation modeling. *Journal of the American Statistical Association, 96*, 331-338.

Stelzl, I. (1986). Changing a causal hypothesis without changing the fit: Some rules for generating equivalent path models. *Multivariate Behavioral Research, 21*, 309-331.

Steyer, R., & Schmitt, M. J. (1990). Latent state-trait models in attitude research. *Quality & Quantity, 24*, 427-445.

Stine, R. (1989). An introduction to bootstrap methods: Examples and ideas. *Sociological Methods and Research, 18*, 243-291.

Stoolmiller, M. (1994). Antisocial behavior, delinquent peer association, and unsupervised wandering for boys: Growth and change from childhood to early adolescence. *Multivariate Behavioral Research, 29*, 263-288.

Stoolmiller, M. (1995). Using latent growth curve models to study developmental processes. In J. M. Gottman (Ed.), *The analysis of change* (pp. 103-138). Mahwah, NJ: Lawrence Erlbaum Associates.

Stoolmiller, M., & Bank, L. (1995). Autoregressive effects in structural equation models: We see some problems. In J. M. Gottman (Ed.), *The analysis of change* (pp. 261-276). Mahwah, NJ: Lawrence Erlbaum Associates.

Sugawara, H. M., & MacCallum, R. C. (1993). Effect of estimation method on incremetal fit indexes for covariance structure models. *Applied Psychological Measurement, 17*, 365-377.

Tanaka, J. S. (1987). "How big is big enough?": Sample size and goodness of fit in structural equation models with latent variables. *Child Development, 58*, 134-146.

Tanaka, J. S. (1993). Multifaceted conceptions of fit in structural equation models. In K. A. Bollen & J. S. Long (Eds.), *Testing structural equation models* (pp. 10-39). Thousand Oaks, CA: Sage.

Tanaka, J. S., & Huba, G. J. (1985). A fit index for covariance structure models under arbitrary GLS estimation. *British Journal of Mathematical and Statistical Psychology, 38*, 197-201.

Tanaka, J. S., & Huba, G. J. (1987). Assessing the stability of depression in college students. *Multivariate Behavioral Research, 22*, 5-19.

Tanaka, J. S., & Huba, G. J. (1989). A general coefficient of determination for covariance structure models under arbitrary GLS estimation. *British Journal of Mathematical and Statistical Psychology, 42*, 233-239.

Tanguma, J. (2001). Effects of sample size on the distribution of selected fit indices: A graphical approach. *Educational and Psychological Measurement, 61*, 759-776.

ten Berge, J. M. F., & Knol, D. L. (1985). Scale construction on the basis of components analysis: A comparison of three strategies. *Multivariate Behavioral Research, 20*, 45-55.

Tesser, A., & Paulhus, D. L. (1976). Toward a causal model of love. *Journal of Personality and Social Psychology, 34*, 1095-1105.

References

Thurstone, L. L. (1947). *Multiple-factor analysis.* Chicago, University of Chicago Press.

Tisak, J., & Tisak, M. S. (2000). Permanency and ephemerality of psychological measures with application to organizational commitment. *Psychological Methods, 5*, 175-198.

Trendafilov, N. T. (1994). A simple method for Procrustean rotation in factor analysis using majorization theory. *Multivariate Behavioral Research, 29*, 385-408.

Tucker, L. R. (1964). The extension of factor analysis to three-dimensional matrices. In N. Frederiksen & H. Gulliksen (Eds.), *Contributions to mathematical psychology* (pp. 109-127). New York: Holt, Rinehart and Winston.

Tucker, L. R., & Lewis, C. (1973). A reliability coefficient for maximum likelihood factor analysis. *Psychometrika, 38*, 1-10.

Tukey, J. W. (1954). Causation, regression and path analysis. In O. Kempthorne, T. A. Bancroft, J. W. Gowen & J. L. Lush (Eds.), *Statistics and mathematics in biology* (pp. 35-66). Ames, IA: Iowa State College Press.

Turner, N. E. (1998). The effect of common variance and structure pattern on random data eigenvalues: Implications for the accuracy of parallel analysis. *Educational and Psychological Measurement, 58*, 541-568.

Undheim, J. O., & Gustafsson, J.-E. (1987). The hierarchical organization of cognitive abilities: Restoring general intelligence through the use of linear structural relations (LISREL). *Multivariate Behavioral Research, 22*, 149-171.

van der Linden, W. J., & Hambleton, R. K. (Eds.) (1997). *Handbook of modern item response theory.* New York: Springer-Verlag.

Vandenberg, S. G. (1962). The Hereditary Abilities Study: Hereditary components in a psychological test battery. *American Journal of Human Genetics, 14*, 220-237.

Velicer, W. F. (1976). Determining the number of components from the matrix of partial correlations. *Psychometrika, 41*, 321-327.

Verhees, J., & Wansbeek, T. J. (1990). A multimode direct product model for covariance structure analysis. *British Journal of Mathematical and Statistical Psychology, 43*, 231-240.

von Eye, A., & Clogg, C. C. (Eds.) (1994). *Latent variables analysis: Applications for developmental research.* Thousand Oaks, CA: Sage.

von Eye, A., & Fuller, B. E. (2003). A comparison of the SEM software packages Amos, EQS, and LISREL. In B. H. Pugesek, A. Tomer, & A. von Eye (Eds.), *Structural equation modeling: Applications in ecological and evolutionary biology* (pp. 355-391). Cambridge: Cambridge University Press.

Waller, N. G. (1993). Seven confirmatory factor analysis programs: EQS, EzPATH, LINCS, LISCOMP, LISREL 7, SIMPLIS, and CALIS. *Applied Psychological Measurement, 17*, 73-100.

Walters, R. G., & MacKenzie, S. B. (1988). A structural equations analysis of the impact of price promotions on store performance. *Journal of Marketing Research, 25,* 51-63.

Wang, L., Fan, X., & Willson, V. L. (1996). Effects of nonnormal data on parameter estimates and fit indices for a model with latent and manifest variables: An empirical study. *Structural Equation Modeling, 3,* 228-247.

Wellhofer, E. S. (1984). To "educate their volition to dance in their chains": Enfranchisement and realignment in Britain, 1885-1950. *Comparative Political Studies, 17,* 3-33, 351-372.

Wen, Z., Marsh, H. W., & Hau, K.-T. (2002). Interaction effects in growth modeling: A full model. *Structural Equation Modeling, 9,* 20-39.

Weng, L.-J., & Cheng, C.-P. (1997). Why might relative fit indices differ between estimators? *Structural Equation Modeling, 4,* 121-128.

Werts, C. E., & Linn, R. L. (1970). Path analysis: Psychological examples. *Psychological Bulletin, 74,* 193-212.

Werts, C. E., Linn, R. L., & Jöreskog, K. G. (1977). A simplex model for analyzing academic growth. *Educational and Psychological Measurement, 37,* 745-756.

West, S. G., Finch, J. F., & Curran, P. J. (1995). Structural equation models with nonnormal variables: Problems and remedies. In R. H. Hoyle (Ed.), *Structural equation modeling: Concepts, issues, and applications* (pp. 56-75). Thousand Oaks, CA: Sage.

Widaman, K. F. (1985). Hierarchically nested covariance structure models for multitrait-multimethod data. *Applied Psychological Measurement, 9,* 1-26.

Widaman, K. F. (1993). Common factor analysis versus principal component analysis: Differential bias in representing model parameters? *Multivariate Behavioral Research, 28,* 263-311.

Widaman, K. F., & Thompson, J. S. (2003). On specifying the null model for incremental fit indices in structural equation modeling. *Psychological Methods, 8,* 16-37.

Wiggins, R. D., & Sacker, A. (2002). Strategies for handling missing data in SEM: A user's perspective. In G. A. Marcoulides & I. Moustaki (Eds.), *Latent variable and latent structure models* (pp. 105-120). Mahwah, NJ: Lawrence Erlbaum Associates.

Willett, J. B., & Sayer, A. G. (1994). Using covariance structure analysis to detect correlates and predictors of individual change over time. *Psychological Bulletin, 116,* 363-381.

Willett, J. B., & Sayer, A. G. (1996). Cross-domain analyses of change over time: Combining growth modeling and covariance structure analysis. In G. A. Marcoulides & R. E. Schumacker (Eds.), *Advanced structural equation modeling: Issues and techniques* (pp. 125-157). Mahwah, NJ: Lawrence Erlbaum Associates.

Williams, L. J., Bozdogan, H., & Aiman-Smith, L. (1996). Inference problems with equivalent models. In G. A. Marcoulides & R. E. Schumacker (Eds.), *Advanced structural equation modeling: Issues and techniques* (pp. 279-314). Mahwah, NJ: Lawrence Erlbaum Associates.

Williams, L. J., & Holahan, P. J. (1994). Parsimony-based fit indices for multiple-indicator models: Do they work? *Structural Equation Modeling, 1,* 161-189.

Williams, R., & Thomson, E. (1986). Normalization issues in latent variable modeling. *Sociological Methods & Research, 15,* 24-43.

Windle, M., Barnes, G. M., & Welte, J. (1989). Causal models of adolescent substance use: An examination of gender differences using distribution-free estimators. *Journal of Personality and Social Psychology, 56,* 132-142.

Wold, H. (1982). Soft modeling: The basic design and some extensions. In K. G. Jöreskog & H. Wold (Eds.), *Systems under indirect observation* (Part II, pp. 1-54). Amsterdam: North-Holland.

Wolfle, L. (2003). The introduction of path analysis to the social sciences, and some emergent themes: An annotated bibliography. *Structural Equation Modeling, 10,* 1-34.

Wood, J. M., Tataryn, D. J., & Gorsuch, R. L. (1996). Effects of under- and overextraction on principal axis factor analysis with varimax rotation. *Psychological Methods, 1,* 354-365.

Wothke, W. (1996). Models for multitrait-multimethod matrix analysis. In G. A. Marcoulides & R. E. Schumacker (Eds.), *Advanced structural equation modeling: Issues and techniques* (pp. 7-56). Mahwah, NJ: Lawrence Erlbaum Associates.

Wothke, W. (2000). Longitudinal and multi-group modeling with missing data. In T. D. Little, K. U. Schnabel, & J. Baumert (Eds.), *Modeling longitudinal and multilevel data: Practical issues, applied approaches, and specific examples* (pp. 219-240). Mahwah, NJ: Lawrence Erlbaum Associates.

Wothke, W., & Browne, M. W. (1990). The direct product model for the MTMM matrix parameterized as a second order factor analysis model. *Psychometrika, 55,* 255-262.

Wright, S. (1920). The relative importance of heredity and environment in determining the piebald pattern of guinea-pigs. *Proceedings of the National Academy of Sciences, 6,* 320-332.

Wright, S. (1960). Path coefficients and path regressions: Alternative or complementary concepts? *Biometrics, 16,* 189-202.

Yang-Wallentin, F. (2001). Comparisons of the ML and TSLS estimators for the Kenny-Judd model. In R. Cudeck, S. du Toit, & D. Sörbom (Eds.), *Structural equation modeling: Present and future. A Festschrift in honor of Karl Jöreskog* (pp. 425-442). Lincolnwood IL: Scientific Software International.

Yates, A. (1987). *Multivariate exploratory data analysis: A perspective on exploratory factor analysis.* Albany, NY: State University of New York Press.

Yuan, K.-H., & Bentler, P. M. (1997). Mean and covariance structure analysis: Theoretical and practical improvements. *Journal of the American Statistical Association, 92,* 767-774.

Yuan, K.-H., & Bentler, P. M. (1998). Normal theory based test statistics in structural equation modeling. *British Journal of Mathematical and Statistical Psychology, 51,* 289-309.

Yuan, K.-H., & Bentler, P. M. (2000a). On equivariance and invariance of standard errors in three exploratory factor models. *Psychometrika, 65,* 121-133.

Yuan, K.-H., & Bentler, P. M. (2000b). Three likelihood-based methods for mean and covariance structure analysis with nonnormal missing data. *Sociological Methodology, 30,* 165-200.

Yuan, K.-H., & Bentler, P. M. (2001a). Unified approach to multigroup structural equation modeling with nonstandard samples. In G. A. Marcoulides & R. E. Schumacker (Eds.), *New developments and techniques in structural equation modeling* (pp. 35-56). Mahwah, NJ: Lawrence Erlbaum Associates.

Yuan, K.-H., & Bentler, P. M. (2001b). Effect of outliers on estimation and tests in covariance structure analysis. *British Journal of Mathematical and Statistical Psychology, 54,* 161-175.

Yuan, K.-H., Chan, W., & Bentler, P. M. (2000). Robust transformation with applications to structural equation modeling. *British Journal of Mathematical and Statistical Psychology, 53,* 31-50.

Yung, Y.-F., & Bentler, P. M. (1994). Bootstrap-corrected ADF test statistics in covariance structure analysis. *British Journal of Mathematical and Statistical Psychology, 47,* 63-84.

Yung, Y.-F., & Bentler, P. M. (1996). Bootstrapping techniques in analysis of mean and covariance structures. In G. A. Marcoulides & R. E. Schumacker (Eds.), *Advanced structural equation modeling: Issues and techniques* (pp. 195-226). Mahwah, NJ: Lawrence Erlbaum Associates.

Zwick, W. R., & Velicer, W. F. (1986). Comparison of five rules for determining the number of components to retain. *Psychological Bulletin, 99,* 432-442.

Index

Orthomax factor rotation program 183, 193, 210.
outliers 59-60, 82.
overdetermined path diagram 14-15, 31. *See also* identification.

P technique 225, 227-228, 236.
pairwise deletion 76.
parallel analysis 168, 184.
parallel tests 13, 95-98.
parsimonious normed fit index. *See* PNFI.
partial correlation 102-103. *See also* path coefficient.
partial least squares. *See* PLS.
path analysis 1, 8-16; and structural equation analysis 23-24, 245-246; standardized and unstandardized 24-28, 31; with manifest and latent variables 13-14, 28-29.
path coefficient 12-14, 18-21; unstandardized 24-28.
path diagram 2-16; and factor models 17-22, 153, 159; and structural equations 23-24, 245-246; matrix representation of 40-44, 245-246.
pattern, factor. *See* factor pattern.
Pearl, Judea. *See* automatic construction of path diagrams.
phantom variables 114, 258-259.
PLS 235.
PNFI (parsimonious normed fit index) goodness-of-fit index 251-254.
police, study of attitudes toward 92-95.

poor fit, test of 69; power 73, 83, 264; examples 94, 97, 123, 126, 134, 141.
population-based fit indices 67-69, 255-257.
power to reject model 61, 70-73, 83, 263-264.
PRELIS program 51.
principal components 29, 31; in nonlinear factor analysis 207-210; programs 182.
principal factors 155-160, 163, 170, 175; in box problem 178-179; programs 182.
Procrustes factor rotation program 183, 194-195.
Promaj factor rotation program 210.
Promax factor rotation program 171, 183, 194-195, 210.
Promin factor rotation program 210.
psychometric applications of model fitting 95-102. *See also* reliability.
publication in SEM 236.

Q technique 225-226, 228, 236.
Quartimax factor rotation program 171-174, 183.
Quartimin variant of Oblimin 174-175.

R technique 225-228, 236.
RAM (reticular action model) 16, 51, 81.
RAMONA model-fitting program 44, 51, 80.
raw score path rules 26-28, 43-44.
reciprocal paths 7, 90, 106-111.
recursive and nonrecursive 31. *See* looped path models.
reduced correlation matrix 155-159. *See also* communality.